DATE DUE

# THE NONPROFIT ALMANAC

## 2008

Kennard T. Wing,
Thomas H. Pollak, and
Amy Blackwood

Foreword by
Elizabeth T. Boris

THE URBAN INSTITUTE PRESS
Washington, D.C.

**THE URBAN INSTITUTE PRESS**
2100 M Street, N.W.
Washington, D.C. 20037

Library of Congress Cataloging-in-Publication Data

The nonprofit almanac 2008 / Kennard T. Wing . . . [et al.].
    p. cm.
 Includes bibliographical references and index.
 ISBN 978-0-87766-736-0
 1. Nonprofit organizations—United States—Statistics. I. Wing,
Kennard T.
 HD2769.2.U6N64 2008
 361.70973'090511—dc22

                                            2008001347


Printed in the United States of America

12 11 10 09 08          1 2 3 4 5

**THE URBAN INSTITUTE** is a nonprofit, nonpartisan policy research and educational organization established in Washington, D.C., in 1968. Its staff investigates the social, economic, and governance problems confronting the nation and evaluates the public and private means to alleviate them. The Institute disseminates its research findings through publications, its web site, the media, seminars, and forums.

Through work that ranges from broad conceptual studies to administrative and technical assistance, Institute researchers contribute to the stock of knowledge available to guide decisionmaking in the public interest.

Conclusions or opinions expressed in Institute publications are those of the authors and do not necessarily reflect the views of officers or trustees of the Institute, advisory groups, or any organizations that provide financial support to the Institute.

# Contents

List of Figures     viii

List of Tables     x

Foreword     xv

1    The Nonprofit Sector and Its Place in the National Economy     1

2    Wage and Employment Trends     27

3    Trends in Private Giving and Volunteering     69

4    Financial Trends     115

5    The Size, Scope, and Finances of Public Charities     139

Glossary     237

Sources     245

About the Authors     247

Index     249

# Figures

**1.1**  Nonprofit Organizations' Share of U.S. Gross Domestic Product, 2006    9

**1.2**  Nonprofit Organizations' Share of Wage and Salary Accruals in the U.S. Economy, 2006    10

**1.3**  Wage and Salary Accruals by Economic Sector, 1948–2006 (percent)    11

**1.4**  Wages and Salaries of Nonprofit Institutions Serving Households Compared with Government Wages and Salaries, 1948–2006 (percent)    11

**1.5**  Revenue of Nonprofit Institutions Serving Households, 1992–2005 ($ billions)    17

**1.6**  Nonprofit Employees and Nonprofit Employment as a Percentage of U.S. Nonfarm Employment, 1998–2005    21

**2.1**  Distribution of Nonprofit Wages by Industry, 2005 (percent)    32

**2.2**  Average Annual Nonprofit Compensation per Employee by Industry, 2005 ($ thousands)    33

**2.3**  Annual Growth Rate in Total Nonprofit Wages and Employment by Industry, 1998–2005 (percent)    34

**2.4**  Annual Growth Rate in Average Annual Nonprofit Compensation per Employee by Industry, 1998–2005 (percent)    35

**3.1**  Private Giving Compared with National Income, 1965–2006 (percent)    73

**3.2**  Private Contributions in Current Dollars and as a Percentage of Nonprofit Outlays, 1992–2005    73

**3.3**  Distribution of Private Contributions by Recipient Area, 2006 (percent)    76

**3.4**  Private Giving by Living Individuals and Foundations, 1965–2006 (percent)    79

**3.5**  Per Capita Individual Charitable Contributions, 1965–2006    82

**3.6**  Distribution of Total Estimated Household Giving, 2002 (percent)    83

**3.7**  Number and Value of Charitable Bequests by Year Filed, 1987–2005    89

**3.8**  Cash and Noncash Charitable Contributions, 1985–2005 (percent)    94

**3.9**  Volunteers by Their Main Organization, 2002–2006 (percent)    98

**3.10**  Distribution of Average Volunteer Time by Activity, 2006 (percent)    100

**3.11**  Volunteers by Activity, 2006 (percent)    101

**3.12**  Number of Foundations and Amount of Grants Made by Year, 1994–2005    104

**3.13**  Distribution of Foundations by Number, Assets, and Grants, 2005 (percent)    106

**4.1**  Revenue of Nonprofit Institutions Serving Households, 1992–2006 ($ billions)    116

**4.2**  Sources of Revenue for Nonprofit Institutions Serving Households, 2006 (percent)    116

**4.3**  Revenue for Nonprofit Institutions Serving Households by Source, 1992–2006 ($ billions)    117

**4.4**  Types of Revenue for Nonprofit Institutions Serving Households, 1992–2006 (percent)    118

**4.5**  Transfer Receipts for Nonprofit Organizations Serving Households by Source, 1992–2006 ($ billions)    119

**4.6**  Transfer Receipts for Nonprofit Institutions Serving Households by Source, 1992–2006 (percent)    119

**4.7**  Asset Income for Nonprofit Institutions Serving Households by Source, 2006 (percent)    120

**4.8**  Asset Income for Nonprofit Institutions Serving Households by Source, 1992–2006 ($ billions)    120

**4.9**  Uses of Funds by Nonprofit Institutions Serving Households, 2006 (percent)    121

**4.10**  Outlays from Nonprofit Institutions Serving Households by Use, 1992–2006 ($ billions)    122

**4.11**  Outlays from Nonprofit Institutions Serving Households by Use, 1992–2006 (percent)    122

**4.12**  Consumption Expenditures for Nonprofit Institutions Serving Households by Subsector, 2006 (percent)    123

**4.13**  Consumption Expenditures for Nonprofit Institutions Serving Households by Subsector, 1992–2006 (percent)    124

**4.14**  Consumption Expenditures for Nonprofit Subsectors, 1992–2006 ($ billions)    124

**4.15**  Transfer Payments from Nonprofit Institutions Serving Households by Recipient, 2006 (percent)    125

**4.16**  Transfer Payments from Nonprofit Institutions Serving Households by Recipient, 1992–2006 ($ billions)    126

**4.17**  Transfer Payments from Nonprofit Institutions Serving Households by Recipient, 1992–2006 (percent)    126

**5.1**  Number and Expenses of Reporting Public Charities, 2005    142

**5.2**  Sources of Revenue for Reporting Public Charities, 2005 (percent)    145

**5.3**  Sources of Revenue for Reporting Public Charities, Excluding Hospitals and Higher Education, 2005 (percent)    145

**5.4**  Sources of Revenue for Arts, Culture, and Humanities Reporting Public Charities, 2005 (percent)    169

**5.5**  Number, Assets, Revenues, and Expenses of Arts, Culture, and Humanities Public Charities, 2005    170

**5.6**  Sources of Revenue for Education Reporting Public Charities, 2005 (percent)    173

**5.7**  Number, Assets, Revenues, and Expenses of Education Public Charities, 2005    174

**5.8**  Sources of Revenue for Environment and Animals Reporting Public Charities, 2005 (percent)    177

**5.9**    Number, Assets, Revenues, and Expenses of Environment
and Animals Public Charities, 2005    178

**5.10**   Sources of Revenue for Health Reporting Public Charities, 2005
(percent)    181

**5.11**   Number, Assets, Revenues, and Expenses of Health Public Charities,
2005    182

**5.12**   Sources of Revenue for Human Service Reporting Public Charities,
2005 (percent)    186

**5.13**   Number, Assets, Revenues, and Expenses of Human Service
Public Charities, 2005    187

**5.14**   Sources of Revenue for International and Foreign Affairs Reporting
Public Charities, 2005 (percent)    192

**5.15**   Sources of Revenue for Other Reporting Public Charities, 2005
(percent)    196

**5.16**   Number, Assets, Revenues, and Expenses for Other Public Charities,
2005    197

## Tables

**1.1**    Types of Tax-Exempt Organizations and Number, Expenses, and Assets
by Type, 2005    2

**1.2**    Organizations, Expenses, and Assets in the Nonprofit Sector, 2005    4

**1.3**    Scope of the Nonprofit Sector as Classified by the North American
Industry Classification System, 2005    6

**1.4**    Gross Value Added to the U.S. Economy by Sector, 1929–2006 ($ billions)    12

**1.5**    Wage and Salary Accruals by Economic Sector, 1948–2006 ($ billions)    15

**1.6**    Estimated Wages for Nonprofits Serving Business, 1990–2006 ($ billions)    19

**1.7**    Nonprofit Wages and the Wage Value of Volunteer Work, 2003–2006    20

**1.8**    U.S. Employment in the Nonprofit Sector, 1998–2005    20

**2.1**    Nonprofit Wages by Industry, 1998–2005 ($ millions)    28

**2.2**    Nonprofit Employment by Industry, 1998–2005    30

**2.3**    Average Annual Compensation per Nonprofit Employee by Industry,
1998–2004 ($)    31

**2.4**    Nonprofit Wages Covered by Unemployment Insurance, for Industries
Whose Tax Status Is Identified in the Economic Census, 1990–2006
($ millions)    36

**2.5**    Nonprofit Wages Reported to the U.S. Census Bureau or Covered by
Unemployment Insurance, in Select Industries with Many Employees
Exempt from Unemployment Insurance, 1990–2005 ($ millions)    37

**2.6**    Wages Reported to the Internal Revenue Service for Two-Digit Industries
Whose Tax Status Is Not Identified in the Economic Census, 1998–2005
($ millions)    38

**2.7** Nonprofit Employees Covered by Unemployment Insurance, for Industries Whose Tax Status Is Identified in the Economic Census, 1990–2006    39

**2.8** Nonprofit Employees Reported to the Census Bureau or Covered by Unemployment Insurance, in Select Industries with Many Employees Exempt from Unemployment Insurance, 1990–2005    40

**2.9** Estimated Employment for Two-Digit Industries Whose Tax Status Is Not Identified in the Economic Census, 1998–2005    41

**2.10** Nonprofit Wages Covered by Unemployment Insurance, Six-Digit Industries Whose Tax Status Is Identified in the Economic Census, 1990–1997 ($ millions)    42

**2.11** Nonprofit Wages Covered by Unemployment Insurance, Six-Digit Industries Whose Tax Status Is Identified in the Economic Census, 1998–2006 ($ millions)    45

**2.12** Nonprofit Employment Covered by Unemployment Insurance, Six-Digit Industries Whose Tax Status Is Identified in the Economic Census, 1990–1997    50

**2.13** Nonprofit Employment Covered by Unemployment Insurance, Six-Digit Industries Whose Tax Status Is Identified in the Economic Census, 1998–2006    54

**2.14** Alternative Estimate of Nonprofit Employees, 2004 (thousands)    59

**2.15** National Taxonomy of Exempt Entities Core Codes Comprising NAICS Industries Whose Reported Wages Were Aggregated from Internal Revenue Service Data    60

**3.1** Private Contributions to Nonprofit Organizations by National Income and Nonprofit Outlays, 1965–2006    71

**3.2** Distribution of Private Contributions to Nonprofit Organizations by Type of Nonprofit, 1966–2006    74

**3.3** Private Contributions to Nonprofit Organizations by Source, 1965–2006    77

**3.4** Per Capita Contributions and Individual Contributions to Nonprofit Organizations, 1965–2006    80

**3.5** Household Charitable Giving by Recipient Organization, 2002    82

**3.6** Household Charitable Giving by Income Range and Itemizer Status, 2002    84

**3.7** Household Charitable Giving by Income and by Age, Marital Status, and Race/Ethnicity, 2002    85

**3.8** Estate Tax Returns and Charitable Bequests, Selected Years, 1987–2005    88

**3.9** Estimates of Individual Charitable Contributions by Tax-Itemization Status, 1985–2005    90

**3.10** Distribution of Itemizers' Cash and Noncash Charitable Contributions, 1985–2005    93

**3.11** Average Charitable Deduction for All Tax Returns and for Itemizers with Charitable Deductions, 1985–2005    95

**3.12** Charitable Contributions from Itemizers with Adjusted Gross Income
of $1 Million or More, 1993–2005                                                96

**3.13** Number, Hours, and Dollar Value of Volunteers, 2002–2006             97

**3.14** Volunteers by Main Type of Organization, 2002–2006 (percent)         97

**3.15** Volunteers by Demographic Group, 2002–2006 (percent)                 99

**3.16** Distribution of Average Annual Volunteer Hours by Activity, 2003–2006   100

**3.17** Volunteers by Activity, 2003–2006 (percent)                          101

**3.18** Number, Hours, and Dollar Value of Volunteers, 1965–2003,
Selected Years                                                                 102

**3.19** Grants Made, Gifts Received, and Assets Held by Foundations,
1975–2005                                                                      103

**3.20** Number of Foundations, Grants Made, Gifts Received, and Assets
by Type of Foundation, 2000–2005                                              105

**3.21** Grants by Foundation Assets, 2002–2004                               107

**3.22** Number of Larger Foundations Created by Year, through 2004           108

**3.23** Number and Value of Grants Made by Foundations, by Major
Categories, 2001–2005                                                          109

**4.1** Revenues for Nonprofit Institutions Serving Households ($ billions)    127

**4.2** Outlays from Nonprofit Institutions Serving Households ($ billions)    128

**4.3** NAICS Industries Included in Bureau of Economic Analysis
Consumption Categories                                                         129

**4.4** Cumulative Percentage Change of Public Charity Revenues as Measured
in Constant Dollars, 1992–2005                                                 131

**4.5** Annual Percentage Change of Public Charity Revenues as Measured
in Constant Dollars, 1992–2005                                                 132

**5.1** Size and Financial Scope of the Nonprofit Sector, 1995–2005           140

**5.2** Registration and Filing Requirements for 501(c)(3) Organizations      141

**5.3** Reporting Public Charities by Founding Date, 2005 (percent)           143

**5.4** Reporting Public Charities by Subsector, 2005                         144

**5.5** Revenues and Expenses for Reporting Public Charities, 2005            146

**5.6** Change in the Number of Reporting Public Charities by Category,
1995, 2000, and 2005                                                           149

**5.7** Change in Total Revenue for Reporting Public Charities by Category,
1995, 2000, and 2005                                                           153

**5.8** Change in Public Support for Reporting Public Charities by Category,
1995, 2000, and 2005                                                           156

**5.9** Change in Total Expenses for Reporting Public Charities by Category,
1995, 2000, and 2005                                                           159

**5.10** Change in Total Assets for Reporting Public Charities by Category,
1995, 2000, and 2005                                                           162

**5.11** Change in Net Assets for Reporting Public Charities by Category,
1995, 2000, and 2005                                                           164

**5.12** Revenues and Expenses for Reporting Public Charities in Arts, Culture, and Humanities, 2005          167

**5.13** Revenues and Expenses for Reporting Public Charities in Education, 2005          171

**5.14** Revenues and Expenses for Reporting Public Charities in the Environment and Animals, 2005          175

**5.15** Revenues and Expenses for Reporting Public Charities in Health, 2005          179

**5.16** Revenues and Expenses for Reporting Public Charities in Human Service, 2005          183

**5.17** Revenues and Expenses for Reporting Public Charities in International and Foreign Affairs, 2005          189

**5.18** Revenues and Expenses for Reporting Public Charities in Other Categories, 2005          193

**5.19** Number, Revenue, Expenses, and Assets of Reporting Public Charities by State, 2005          198

**5.20** Change in the Number of Reporting Public Charities by State, 1995, 2000, and 2005          202

**5.21** The 10 States with the Highest Growth in Number of Reporting Public Charities, 1995–2005          204

**5.22** Change in Total Revenue for Reporting Public Charities by State, 1995, 2000, and 2005          205

**5.23** The 10 States with the Highest Growth in Total Revenue Reported by Public Charities, 1995–2005          208

**5.24** Change in Public Support for Reporting Public Charities by State, 1995, 2000, and 2005          209

**5.25** The 10 States with the Highest Growth in Public Support Reported by Public Charities, 1995–2005          212

**5.26** Change in Total Expenses for Reporting Public Charities by State, 1995, 2000, and 2005          213

**5.27** The 10 States with the Highest Growth in Expenses Reported by Public Charities, 1995–2005          216

**5.28** Change in Total Assets for Reporting Public Charities by State, 1995, 2000, and 2005          217

**5.29** The 10 States with the Highest Growth in Assets Reported by Public Charities, 1995–2005          220

**5.30** Change in Net Assets for Reporting Public Charities by State, 1995, 2000, and 2005          221

**5.31** The 10 States with the Highest Growth in Net Assets Reported by Public Charities, 1995–2005          224

# Foreword

The nonprofit sector continues to grow faster than business or government. A small, but significant part of the U.S. economy, this collection of organizations is on the leading edge of service provision and knowledge generation—the new economy model. Private higher education and medical research and treatment institutions enjoy worldwide acclaim, and myriad nonprofit civic, human services, arts, environmental, and advocacy agencies are motivating forces in our dynamic and pluralist nation—a closely watched and widely emulated model of civil society.

As the sector grows in size and financial clout, policymakers and the public need information to assess the impact of nonprofits and ensure their accountability. Nonprofit leaders and boards of directors require information to understand their organizations' economic and service niches as they plan for the future. With this edition of the *Nonprofit Almanac*, we unveil a new generation of data that will make this fluid and changing sector more transparent and easier to assess.

Nonprofits are known for providing services and receiving donations and grants. But they are also major employers that often contract with governments and charge fees to cover the provision of human services, health care, education, and other services. Indeed, nonprofits pay more wages than the wholesale, retail, transportation, or information industries. The sector contributed products and services that added $666 billion to America's gross domestic product in 2006. They also draw on voluntary labor and donations that produce both public benefits and personal fulfillment.

Variety typifies this sector. Huge professionally managed universities, hospitals, and development agencies and small volunteer-run soup kitchens, choruses, and mentoring groups are all part of the nonprofit sector. Some rely more on fees and contracts; others, more on donations. Yet, many nonprofits are small and have few, if any, staff.

It is this mix of varying finances, public-service activities, and private benefits that gives the nonprofit sector its special character and makes it difficult to characterize or explain in strictly economic terms. Since nonprofits are largely tax exempt and more than half—public charities and private foundations—are eligible to receive tax-deductible donations, congressional scrutiny and demands for accountability and transparency are inevitable. Yet, the government does not allocate adequate resources for oversight or collect the data on nonprofits that it routinely does on other economic sectors. Incremental improvements are under way, however, and recent changes in government data sources benefit this volume, which builds on and goes beyond earlier editions.

Further improvements in nonprofit data sources also bode well for transparency and accountability. The required annual information returns, IRS Forms 990, can now be filed electronically. (See software developed by the National Center for Charitable Statistics at http://efile.form990.org.) The advent of electronically prepared Forms 990 will dramatically improve the quality, completeness, and timeliness of both state and federal nonprofit financial reports. Yet, since electronic filing is not yet universal, the full promise of better data still awaits.

Unfortunately, data on nonprofit employment are currently difficult to compile. States control researchers' access, and some do not permit their data to be used in national estimates. While researchers have worked around these roadblocks, we must have better access to data on nonprofit employment and wages.

Another problem in compiling data is built into the North American Industry Classification System, which replaced the Standard Industrial Classification System. It lacks a designation for nonprofit organizations, which means that researchers must estimate the number of nonprofits in many categories.

Despite the caveats, this edition of the *Nonprofit Almanac* portrays a sector that is more robust than ever and shows its growing significance to the American economy. As the number of organizations and their financial impact increases, the sector must be better understood so that its goals stay closely tied to the public's needs and its resources are harnessed creatively and efficiently.

**Elizabeth T. Boris**
*Director*
Center on Nonprofits and Philanthropy
The Urban Institute

# 1

# The Nonprofit Sector and Its Place in the National Economy

What is the nonprofit sector? Ask a dozen experts, you'll get at least two dozen answers. Also referred to as the charitable, voluntary, tax-exempt, independent, third, or philanthropic sector, the sector's many names suggest the variety of definitions used in the past.

Sometimes different definitions of the nonprofit sector result from different purposes. For example, the Internal Revenue Service (IRS) is primarily concerned with collecting tax revenue, so for it, the sector's most important characteristic is exemption from corporate income tax. According to the Internal Revenue Code, more than 30 different types of legal entities are exempt from such taxes (see this chapter's appendix). They are listed in table 1.1, along with the number of each type registered as of 2005. Including all of these 1.4 million registered organizations results in a fairly broad view of the nonprofit sector, but not the broadest.

However, religious congregations and other nonprofits with less than $5,000 in annual revenue are not required to register with the IRS, so many nonprofits are missing from IRS registration lists. In addition to churches, small voluntary associations such as parent-teacher associations, neighborhood associations, and community theaters are underrepresented. On the other hand, some inactive and defunct organizations remain on the registry.

For donors, the most important consideration might be whether their donations are tax deductible. With a few minor exceptions, that is true only for donations made to public charities and private foundations, the two types of organizations exempt under section 501(c)(3). Although charities are the most common nonprofit, limiting the definition to charities results in a relatively small nonprofit sector. Past editions of this almanac have defined the independent sector as all 501(c)(3) organizations, including all religious organizations and congregations, as well as all 501(c)(4) organizations. The 501(c)(4) organizations are termed "social welfare" organizations in the IRS code and include a disparate collection of organizations, including health

*1*

Shelton State Libraries
Shelton State Community College

**Table 1.1.** Types of Tax-Exempt Organizations and Number, Expenses, and Assets by Type, 2005

| Section of 1986 IRS code | Description of organization | Entities registered with the IRS | Entities reporting to the IRS | Expenses of reporting entities ($ millions) | Assets of reporting entities ($ millions) |
|---|---|---|---|---|---|
| 501(c)(1) | Corporations organized under act of Congress | 100 | 4 | 8 | 146 |
| 501(c)(2) | Title-holding corporations for exempt organizations | 5,850 | 2,783 | 1,220 | 13,177 |
| 501(c)(3) | Religious, charitable, and similar organizations | 984,386 | 400,709 | 1,099,799 | 2,436,067 |
| 501(c)(4) | Civic leagues and social welfare organizations | 116,890 | 24,327 | 44,067 | 66,766 |
| 501(c)(5) | Labor, agricultural, and horticultural organizations | 56,819 | 20,591 | 18,844 | 26,143 |
| 501(c)(6) | Business leagues, chambers of commerce, real estate boards, and trade boards | 71,878 | 30,798 | 29,872 | 54,954 |
| 501(c)(7) | Social and recreational clubs | 56,369 | 16,567 | 10,466 | 20,608 |
| 501(c)(8) | Fraternal beneficiary societies and associations | 63,318 | 7,077 | 12,919 | 91,088 |
| 501(c)(9) | Voluntary employee-beneficiary associations | 10,088 | 6,887 | 126,975 | 143,134 |
| 501(c)(10) | Domestic fraternal societies and associations | 20,944 | 2,822 | 541 | 2,710 |
| 501(c)(11) | Teachers' retirement fund associations | 14 | 7 | 157 | 1,228 |
| 501(c)(12) | Benevolent life insurance associations, mutual ditch or irrigation companies, mutual or cooperative telephone companies, etc. | 5,901 | 3,540 | 34,807 | 81,722 |
| 501(c)(13) | Cemetery companies | 9,808 | 2,221 | 790 | 8,255 |
| 501(c)(14) | State-chartered credit unions and mutual reserve funds | 3,565 | 1,304 | 14,366 | 289,040 |
| 501(c)(15) | Mutual insurance companies or associations | 1,646 | 558 | 2 | 2,807 |
| 501(c)(16) | Cooperative organizations to finance crop operations | 16 | 12 | 22 | 344 |
| 501(c)(17) | Supplemental unemployment benefit trusts | 300 | 115 | 325 | 287 |
| 501(c)(18) | Employee-funded pension trusts created before June 25, 1959 | 1 | 1 | 146 | 1,701 |
| 501(c)(19) | War veterans organizations | 35,113 | 6,576 | 1,103 | 2,451 |
| 501(c)(20) | Legal service organizations | 9 | 5 | 2 | 2 |
| 501(c)(21) | Black lung benefits trusts | 28 | 0 | 0 | 0 |
| 501(c)(22) | Withdrawal liability payment funds | 0 | 0 | 0 | 0 |
| 501(c)(23) | Veterans organizations created before 1880 | 2 | 2 | 228 | 2,680 |
| 501(c)(24) | Trusts described in section 4049 of the Employment Retirement Security Act of 1974 | 1 | 0 | 0 | 0 |
| 501(c)(25) | Title-holding corporations or trusts with multiple parents | 1,133 | 931 | 913 | 27,856 |

*(continued)*

**Table 1.1.** Types of Tax-Exempt Organizations and Number, Expenses, and Assets by Type, 2005 *(continued)*

| Section of 1986 IRS code | Description of organization | Entities registered with the IRS | Entities reporting to the IRS | Expenses of reporting entities ($ millions) | Assets of reporting entities ($ millions) |
|---|---|---|---|---|---|
| 501(c)(26) | State-sponsored organizations providing health coverage for high-risk individuals | 10 | 8 | 269 | 103 |
| 501(c)(27) | State-sponsored workers' compensation reinsurance organizations | 12 | 4 | 1,231 | 6,056 |
| 501(d) | Religious and apostolic organizations | 160 | 0 | 0 | 0 |
| 501(e) | Cooperative hospital service organizations | 18 | 11 | 449 | 571 |
| 501(f) | Cooperative service organizations of operating educational organizations | 1 | 0 | 0 | 0 |
| Other | Organizations not classified above, including charitable risk pools | 4,105 | 163 | 424 | 475 |
| | Total | 1,448,485 | 528,023 | 1,401,454 | 3,291,886 |

*Sources:* Urban Institute, National Center for Charitable Statistics, Core Files (2005) and IRS Business Master Files (2006).
*Notes:* Not all Internal Revenue Code Section 501(c)(3) organizations are included because certain organizations, such as churches (and their integrated auxiliaries or subordinate units) and conventions or associations of churches, need not apply for recognition of tax exemption unless they specifically request a ruling. Private foundations are included among 501(c)(3) organizations.

maintenance organizations and medical plans, civic leagues, many advocacy organizations, and a range of others.

Our primary task in this chapter is not to define the sector one way or another, but to present empirical estimates of its size in relation to the rest of the national economy. Since we must depend on data collected by others, we also depend on whatever definitions of the sector they have used. Different definitions of the sector will be incorporated in estimates based on data from different sources. To the degree possible, we will describe what is included and excluded by each data source. To communicate those distinctions, we will briefly survey the nonprofit landscape.

## The Nonprofit Landscape

Table 1.1 begins to suggest the great variety of organizations within the nonprofit sector. Another way to look at the nonprofit sector is to look at its work. There are two major ways to classify nonprofit activity. The first is the National Taxonomy of Exempt Entities (NTEE), designed specifically to group tax-exempt entities by similarity of purpose, activity, type, and major function. The 26 major categories of the NTEE are shown in table 1.2, along with the number of entities that filed with the IRS in each cat-

**Table 1.2.** Organizations, Expenses, and Assets in the Nonprofit Sector, 2005

| Nonprofit category | Organizations reporting to the IRS | % of organizations reporting to the IRS | Reported expenses ($ millions) | % of total expenses | Reported assets ($ millions) | % of total assets |
|---|---|---|---|---|---|---|
| Arts, culture, and humanities | 43,392 | 8.22 | 26,632 | 1.90 | 94,722 | 2.88 |
| Education | 78,074 | 14.79 | 165,339 | 11.80 | 611,567 | 18.58 |
| Environmental quality, protection, and beautification | 10,382 | 1.97 | 9,487 | 0.68 | 31,840 | 0.97 |
| Animal related | 7,381 | 1.40 | 4,576 | 0.33 | 12,466 | 0.38 |
| Health | 26,904 | 5.10 | 637,067 | 45.46 | 787,570 | 23.92 |
| Mental health, crisis intervention | 9,421 | 1.78 | 23,500 | 1.68 | 19,203 | 0.58 |
| Diseases, disorders, medical disciplines | 12,636 | 2.39 | 18,820 | 1.34 | 22,849 | 0.69 |
| Medical research | 1,798 | 0.34 | 7,098 | 0.51 | 33,107 | 1.01 |
| Crime, legal related | 9,307 | 1.76 | 7,591 | 0.54 | 8,301 | 0.25 |
| Employment, job related | 17,124 | 3.24 | 28,947 | 2.07 | 33,404 | 1.01 |
| Food, agriculture, and nutrition | 6,620 | 1.25 | 7,710 | 0.55 | 7,115 | 0.22 |
| Housing, shelter | 20,146 | 3.82 | 18,579 | 1.33 | 62,820 | 1.91 |
| Public safety | 9,495 | 1.80 | 2,403 | 0.17 | 6,843 | 0.21 |
| Recreation, sports, leisure, athletics | 42,753 | 8.10 | 24,561 | 1.75 | 39,673 | 1.21 |
| Youth development | 7,254 | 1.37 | 5,756 | 0.41 | 12,956 | 0.39 |
| Human services— multipurpose and other | 38,795 | 7.35 | 91,540 | 6.53 | 135,402 | 4.11 |
| International, foreign affairs, national security | 5,732 | 1.09 | 20,843 | 1.49 | 19,630 | 0.60 |
| Civil rights, social action, advocacy | 2,779 | 0.53 | 3,098 | 0.22 | 3,434 | 0.10 |
| Community improvement, capacity building | 45,433 | 8.60 | 29,757 | 2.12 | 91,124 | 2.77 |
| Philanthropy, voluntarism, and grantmaking foundations | 72,825 | 13.79 | 54,842 | 3.91 | 493,945 | 15.00 |
| Science and technology research institutes, services | 3,281 | 0.62 | 12,284 | 0.88 | 14,860 | 0.45 |
| Social science research institutes, services | 926 | 0.18 | 1,520 | 0.11 | 3,129 | 0.10 |
| Other public and societal benefit | 17,803 | 3.37 | 31,866 | 2.27 | 391,442 | 11.89 |

*(continued)*

**Table 1.2.** Organizations, Expenses, and Assets in the Nonprofit Sector, 2005 *(continued)*

| Nonprofit category | Organizations reporting to the IRS | % of organizations reporting to the IRS | Reported expenses ($ millions) | % of total expenses | Reported assets ($ millions) | % of total assets |
|---|---|---|---|---|---|---|
| Religion related, spiritual development | 2,160 | 0.41 | 2,006 | 0.14 | 14,408 | 0.44 |
| Mutual/membership benefit organizations | 34,316 | 6.50 | 165,318 | 11.80 | 339,668 | 10.32 |
| Unknown | 1,286 | 0.24 | 313 | 0.02 | 409 | 0.01 |
| Total | 528,023 | 100.00 | 1,401,454 | 100.00 | 3,291,886 | 100.00 |

*Source:* Urban Institute, National Center for Charitable Statistics, Core Files (2005) and IRS Business Master Files (2006).
*Notes:* Only organizations required to file annually with the IRS (organizations that receive at least $25,000 in gross receipts annually) are included in these figures. Expenses include both operating expenses and grants or transfer payments made to individuals and other organizations.

egory in 2005 and the total expenses they reported. Each category's share of reported expenses is also shown, giving some indication of the relative size of the different categories. Health makes up the largest share of reported expenses with 45.5 percent of the total.

The other major way of classifying nonprofit activity is to use the same industry breakout used in the for-profit sector: the North American Industry Classification System (NAICS). Table 1.3 arrays the nonprofit sector according to this classification scheme. The first column shows the numerical NAICS code assigned to the industry, while the second column is the industry description. The third column shows 2005 estimated nonprofit wages in each industry (not including any imputation for unreported wages). To give some indication of relative size, the fourth column shows how this total annual payroll of nonprofits was divided by NAICS industry in 2005. Again we see the large share represented by hospitals and universities, and that the rest of nonprofits are spread across a wide range of industries.

# The Nonprofit Sector in Comparison with Other Sectors

The federal government agency responsible for measuring the size of the U.S. economy is the Bureau of Economic Analysis of the Department of Commerce (BEA). The BEA divides the economy into four sectors: government, business, households, and nonprofit institutions serving households (NPISHs). In BEA estimates, nonprofits that serve business are included in the business sector. The BEA offers no explicit definition of NPISHs or nonprofits serving business, but portions of NAICS code 813, Membership

**Table 1.3.** Scope of the Nonprofit Sector as Classified by the North American Industry Classification System, 2005

| NAICS code | Industry | Estimated nonprofit wages ($ millions) | % of nonprofit wages |
|---|---|---:|---:|
| 11 | Agriculture, forestry, fishing, and hunting | 282.3 | 0.1 |
| 22 | Utilities | 517.0 | 0.1 |
| 48 | Transportation and warehousing | 72.4 | 0.0 |
| 51 | Information | 2,299.8 | 0.5 |
| 52 | Finance and insurance | 6,349.9 | 1.4 |
| 53 | Real estate and rental and leasing | 114.6 | 0.0 |
| 54 | Professional, scientific, and technical services | 10,937.3 | 2.3 |
| 56 | Administrative and waste management services | 603.7 | 0.1 |
| 611110 | Elementary and secondary schools | 20,715.0 | 4.4 |
| 611210 | Junior colleges | 455.8 | 0.1 |
| 611310 | Colleges, universities, and professional schools | 42,916.3 | 9.1 |
| 611410 | Business and secretarial schools | 45.7 | 0.0 |
| 611420 | Computer training | 29.4 | 0.0 |
| 611430 | Professional and management development training | 462.4 | 0.1 |
| 611511 | Cosmetology and barber schools | 17.5 | 0.0 |
| 611512 | Flight training | 9.7 | 0.0 |
| 611513 | Apprenticeship training | 344.1 | 0.1 |
| 611519 | Other technical and trade schools | 380.1 | 0.1 |
| 611610 | Fine arts schools | 361.9 | 0.1 |
| 611620 | Sports and recreation instruction | 158.9 | 0.0 |
| 611630 | Language schools | 63.2 | 0.0 |
| 611691 | Exam preparation and tutoring | 239.2 | 0.1 |
| 611692 | Automobile driving schools | 22.7 | 0.0 |
| 611699 | All other miscellaneous schools and instruction | 498.7 | 0.1 |
| 611710 | Educational support services | 1,225.9 | 0.3 |
| 621410 | Family planning centers | 473.2 | 0.1 |
| 621420 | Outpatient mental health and substance abuse centers | 4,099.5 | 0.9 |
| 621491 | HMO medical centers | 3,231.5 | 0.7 |
| 621492 | Kidney dialysis centers | 382.0 | 0.1 |
| 621493 | Freestanding ambulatory surgical and emergency centers | 551.8 | 0.1 |

*(continued)*

**Table 1.3.** Scope of the Nonprofit Sector as Classified by the North American Industry Classification System, 2005 *(continued)*

| NAICS code | Industry | Estimated nonprofit wages ($ millions) | % of nonprofit wages |
|---|---|---|---|
| 621498 | All other outpatient care centers | 2,717.8 | 0.6 |
| 621610 | Home health care services | 6,824.8 | 1.5 |
| 621910 | Ambulance services | 819.5 | 0.2 |
| 621991 | Blood and organ banks | 1,767.1 | 0.4 |
| 621999 | All other miscellaneous ambulatory health care services | 121.9 | 0.0 |
| 622110 | General medical and surgical hospitals | 160,706.7 | 34.2 |
| 622210 | Psychiatric and substance abuse hospitals | 1,742.8 | 0.4 |
| 622310 | Specialty (except psychiatric and substance abuse) hospitals | 4,498.2 | 1.0 |
| 623110 | Nursing care facilities | 11,111.8 | 2.4 |
| 623210 | Residential mental retardation facilities | 5,200.9 | 1.1 |
| 623220 | Residential mental health and substance abuse facilities | 3,097.2 | 0.7 |
| 623311 | Continuing care retirement communities | 4,856.3 | 1.0 |
| 623312 | Homes for the elderly | 1,347.2 | 0.3 |
| 623990 | Other residential care facilities | 3,635.5 | 0.8 |
| 624110 | Child and youth services | 3,566.6 | 0.8 |
| 624120 | Services for the elderly and persons with disabilities | 6,443.5 | 1.4 |
| 624190 | Other individual and family services | 7,410.4 | 1.6 |
| 624210 | Community food services | 572.3 | 0.1 |
| 624221 | Temporary shelters | 1,246.2 | 0.3 |
| 624229 | Other community housing services | 661.2 | 0.1 |
| 624230 | Emergency and other relief services | 915.2 | 0.2 |
| 624310 | Vocational rehabilitation services | 5,566.6 | 1.2 |
| 624410 | Child day care services | 5,580.4 | 1.2 |
| 711110 | Theater companies and dinner theaters | 990.1 | 0.2 |
| 711120 | Dance companies | 243.9 | 0.1 |
| 711130 | Musical groups and artists | 988.4 | 0.2 |
| 711190 | Other performing arts companies | 13.4 | 0.0 |
| 711310 | Promoters of performing arts, sports, and similar events with facilities | 638.8 | 0.1 |
| 711320 | Promoters of performing arts, sports, and similar events without facilities | 198.7 | 0.0 |
| 712110 | Museums | 1,894.9 | 0.4 |

*(continued)*

**Table 1.3.** Scope of the Nonprofit Sector as Classified by the North American Industry Classification System, 2005 *(continued)*

| NAICS code | Industry | Estimated nonprofit wages ($ millions) | % of nonprofit wages |
|---|---|---:|---:|
| 712120 | Historical sites | 300.3 | 0.1 |
| 712130 | Zoos and botanical gardens | 662.0 | 0.1 |
| 712190 | Nature parks and other similar institutions | 91.0 | 0.0 |
| 713910 | Golf courses and country clubs | 2,966.5 | 0.6 |
| 713940 | Fitness and recreational sports centers | 1,828.5 | 0.4 |
| 713990 | All other amusement and recreation industries | 369.4 | 0.1 |
| 72 | Accommodation and food services | 271.5 | 0.1 |
| 813110 | Religious organizations | 27,230.6 | 5.8 |
| 813211 | Grantmaking foundations | 2,036.4 | 0.4 |
| 813212 | Voluntary health organizations | 1,491.0 | 0.3 |
| 813219 | Other grantmaking and giving services | 1,471.1 | 0.3 |
| 813311 | Human rights organizations | 1,334.4 | 0.3 |
| 813312 | Environment, conservation, and wildlife organizations | 1,179.4 | 0.3 |
| 813319 | Other social advocacy organizations | 2,671.2 | 0.6 |
| 813410 | Civic and social organizations | 6,297.6 | 1.3 |
| 813910 | Business associations | 6,464.9 | 1.4 |
| 813920 | Professional organizations | 4,157.4 | 0.9 |
| 813930 | Labor unions and similar labor organizations | 3,968.1 | 0.8 |
| 813940 | Political organizations | 254.6 | 0.1 |
| 813990 | Other similar organizations (except business, professional, labor, and political organizations) | 2,675.8 | 0.6 |
| | Industry subtotal | 410,961.5 | 87.5 |
| | Imputation for unreported wages | 32,758.5 | 7.0 |
| | Nonprofit wages, unknown industries | 25,935.0 | 5.5 |
| | Total | 469,655.0 | 100.0 |

*Source:* Authors' estimates, largely based on the tax-exempt share of wages from U.S. Census Bureau, Economic Census (2002); private wages from U.S. Department of Labor, Bureau of Labor Statistics, Quarterly Census of Employment and Wages (2005); and wages from Urban Institute, National Center for Charitable Statistics, IRS Statistics of Income Form 990 Sample Files and Form 990-EZ Sample Files (2006), with error corrections and missing-data interpolations performed by the authors.
*Notes:* These figures only include actual wages paid. They do not take into account volunteer labor.

**Figure 1.1.** Nonprofit Organizations' Share of U.S. Gross Domestic Product, 2006

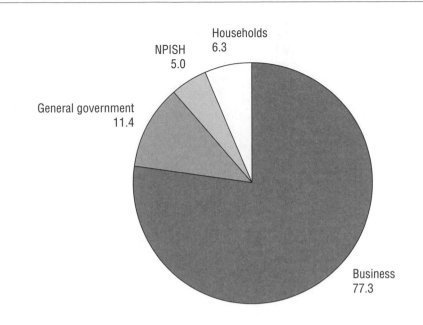

*Source:* Authors' calculations based on U.S. Department of Commerce, Bureau of Economic Analysis, National Income and Product Accounts, table 1.3.5 (2007).
NPISH = nonprofit institutions serving households
*Note:* See table 1.4, this volume, for source data.

Associations and Organizations, and NAICS code 5417, Scientific Research and Development Services, include nonprofits serving business.[1] In any case, the BEA's estimates of NPISHs are the best data available for comparing the different sectors' economic contributions.

According to the BEA, NPISHs contributed $666.1 billion to the gross domestic product (GDP) in 2006, which was 5.0 percent of GDP. Figure 1.1 shows the relative size of the four sectors defined by the BEA. Note that the BEA classifies government enterprises as part of the business sector, rather than the government sector.

BEA economists admit their estimates for the economic product of nonprofits are among the softest in their entire National Income and Product Accounts calculations. First, a price cannot be placed on the output of most nonprofit organizations. Thus, the economic contribution of nonprofits is measured not by the value of what they produce, but by the cost of the resources they consume. Second, except for employee wages and salaries, data on the costs of the resources nonprofits consume are sketchy. Thus, a sounder comparison of the relative size of the different sectors is the amount of wages and salaries paid by each. Figure 1.2 shows this comparison for 2006. According to this

---

1. Personal correspondence with BEA staff, spring 2006.

**Figure 1.2.** Nonprofit Organizations' Share of Wage and Salary Accruals in the U.S. Economy, 2006

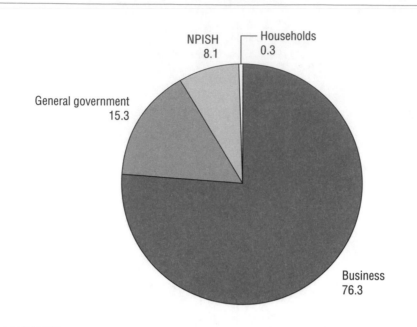

NPISH 8.1
Households 0.3
General government 15.3
Business 76.3

*Source:* Authors' calculations based on U.S. Department of Commerce, Bureau of Economic Analysis, National Income and Product Accounts, table 1.13 (2007).
NPISH = nonprofit institutions serving households
*Note:* See table 1.5, this volume, for source data.

measure, both the government sector and the nonprofit sector account for greater shares of the economy: the government sector rises to 15.3 percent and the NPISH, to 8.1 percent. (The big loser is households, whose economic product as measured primarily consists of the rental value of owner-occupied housing.)

In 2006, NPISHs paid $489.4 billion in wages and salaries. This was just over half the amount paid to government employees, or 53 cents for each dollar paid to government employees. (The percentage drops to 48 percent if government enterprises are included with government.)

Figure 1.3 shows how the share of the national wage bill by sector has been changing over time. From just after World War II to about 1975, the business share of wages dropped steadily while that of government and NPISHs grew. Since then, the business share has fluctuated around its 1975 level and the government share has been dropping, while that of NPISHs continues to expand slowly but steadily.

Figure 1.4 shows a particularly dramatic illustration of the increasing role of the nonprofit sector in our economy: NPISH wages as a percent of general government wages. From a low of 15 percent during the Korean War, NPISH wages have risen in recent years to 53 percent of general government wages, although the rate of increase appears to have moderated in recent years. The share is similar, but somewhat smaller, if government enterprises are included as part of the government sector.

**Figure 1.3.** Wage and Salary Accruals by Economic Sector, 1948–2006 (percent)

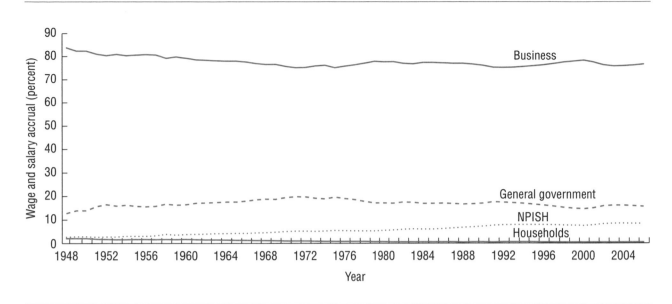

*Source:* Authors' calculations based on U.S. Department of Commerce, Bureau of Economic Analysis, National Income and Product Accounts, table 1.13 (2007).
NPISH = nonprofit institutions serving households
*Note:* See table 1.5, this volume, for source data.

**Figure 1.4.** Wages and Salaries of Nonprofit Institutions Serving Households Compared with Government Wages and Salaries, 1948–2006 (percent)

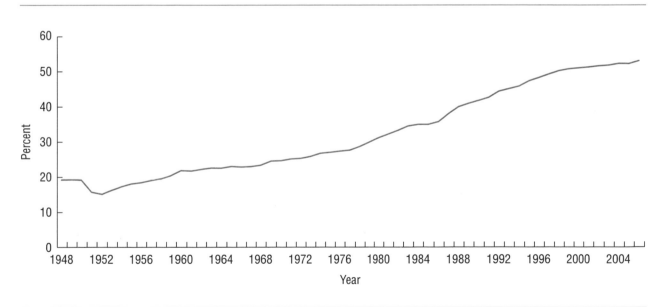

*Source:* Authors' calculations based on U.S. Department of Commerce, Bureau of Economic Analysis, National Income and Product Accounts, table 1.13 (2007).
*Note:* See table 1.5, this volume, for source data.

**Table 1.4.** Gross Value Added to the U.S. Economy by Sector, 1929–2006 ($ billions)

| Year | GDP | Business | Households | NPISH | General government |
|------|-----|----------|------------|-------|--------------------|
| 1929 | 103.6 | 89.6 | 7.4 | 1.5 | 5.2 |
| 1930 | 91.2 | 77.5 | 6.9 | 1.5 | 5.4 |
| 1931 | 76.5 | 63.5 | 6.1 | 1.4 | 5.5 |
| 1932 | 58.7 | 47.1 | 5.1 | 1.3 | 5.2 |
| 1933 | 56.4 | 45.2 | 4.5 | 1.2 | 5.5 |
| 1934 | 66.0 | 53.9 | 4.4 | 1.2 | 6.5 |
| 1935 | 73.3 | 60.7 | 4.4 | 1.3 | 6.9 |
| 1936 | 83.8 | 69.5 | 4.6 | 1.3 | 8.3 |
| 1937 | 91.9 | 77.5 | 5.0 | 1.4 | 8.1 |
| 1938 | 86.1 | 70.9 | 5.0 | 1.5 | 8.8 |
| 1939 | 92.2 | 76.7 | 5.1 | 1.5 | 8.9 |
| 1940 | 101.4 | 85.5 | 5.3 | 1.6 | 9.1 |
| 1941 | 126.7 | 108.2 | 5.6 | 1.6 | 11.2 |
| 1942 | 161.9 | 135.3 | 6.4 | 1.8 | 18.4 |
| 1943 | 198.6 | 158.1 | 7.0 | 2.0 | 31.6 |
| 1944 | 219.8 | 169.0 | 7.8 | 2.2 | 40.8 |
| 1945 | 223.1 | 167.1 | 8.4 | 2.4 | 45.2 |
| 1946 | 222.3 | 177.9 | 8.7 | 2.8 | 32.9 |
| 1947 | 244.2 | 203.3 | 9.6 | 3.4 | 27.9 |
| 1948 | 269.2 | 227.6 | 10.5 | 3.9 | 27.3 |
| 1949 | 267.3 | 223.3 | 11.4 | 4.2 | 28.4 |
| 1950 | 293.8 | 247.7 | 12.8 | 4.6 | 28.7 |
| 1951 | 339.3 | 283.9 | 14.4 | 5.1 | 35.8 |
| 1952 | 358.3 | 296.2 | 16.2 | 5.5 | 40.5 |
| 1953 | 379.4 | 313.0 | 18.1 | 6.1 | 42.2 |
| 1954 | 380.4 | 310.6 | 19.8 | 6.6 | 43.5 |
| 1955 | 414.8 | 340.0 | 21.8 | 7.1 | 45.8 |
| 1956 | 437.5 | 356.8 | 23.7 | 7.8 | 49.2 |
| 1957 | 461.1 | 374.5 | 25.5 | 8.6 | 52.5 |
| 1958 | 467.2 | 374.4 | 27.6 | 9.4 | 55.8 |
| 1959 | 506.6 | 408.2 | 29.8 | 10.3 | 58.3 |
| 1960 | 526.4 | 420.4 | 32.3 | 11.7 | 62.0 |

*(continued)*

**Table 1.4.** Gross Value Added to the U.S. Economy by Sector, 1929–2006 ($ billions)
*(continued)*

| Year | GDP | Business | Households | NPISH | General government |
|------|------|----------|------------|-------|--------------------|
| 1961 | 544.7 | 432.0 | 34.3 | 12.4 | 66.0 |
| 1962 | 585.6 | 464.5 | 36.7 | 13.6 | 70.7 |
| 1963 | 617.7 | 488.7 | 38.8 | 14.8 | 75.5 |
| 1964 | 663.6 | 525.6 | 40.8 | 16.1 | 81.1 |
| 1965 | 719.1 | 571.4 | 43.3 | 17.7 | 86.7 |
| 1966 | 787.8 | 625.1 | 45.9 | 19.9 | 96.9 |
| 1967 | 832.6 | 654.5 | 48.8 | 22.1 | 107.2 |
| 1968 | 910.0 | 714.5 | 51.6 | 25.0 | 119.0 |
| 1969 | 984.6 | 770.3 | 55.6 | 28.7 | 130.0 |
| 1970 | 1,038.5 | 803.6 | 59.4 | 32.0 | 143.6 |
| 1971 | 1,127.1 | 869.9 | 65.1 | 35.7 | 156.4 |
| 1972 | 1,238.3 | 959.0 | 70.3 | 39.5 | 169.4 |
| 1973 | 1,382.7 | 1,079.4 | 76.0 | 44.0 | 183.3 |
| 1974 | 1,500.0 | 1,166.9 | 82.5 | 49.2 | 201.4 |
| 1975 | 1,638.3 | 1,268.5 | 90.3 | 55.1 | 224.5 |
| 1976 | 1,825.3 | 1,423.7 | 98.1 | 60.0 | 243.5 |
| 1977 | 2,030.9 | 1,593.5 | 107.3 | 65.6 | 264.6 |
| 1978 | 2,294.7 | 1,813.4 | 120.4 | 73.4 | 287.5 |
| 1979 | 2,563.3 | 2,032.9 | 135.0 | 82.5 | 313.0 |
| 1980 | 2,789.5 | 2,191.1 | 155.5 | 94.4 | 348.6 |
| 1981 | 3,128.4 | 2,459.4 | 176.8 | 106.9 | 385.3 |
| 1982 | 3,255.0 | 2,520.7 | 195.7 | 119.6 | 419.0 |
| 1983 | 3,536.7 | 2,747.2 | 211.7 | 132.4 | 445.4 |
| 1984 | 3,933.2 | 3,071.8 | 230.2 | 146.0 | 485.2 |
| 1985 | 4,220.3 | 3,290.8 | 249.6 | 156.4 | 523.5 |
| 1986 | 4,462.8 | 3,468.8 | 267.4 | 170.6 | 556.1 |
| 1987 | 4,739.5 | 3,669.9 | 287.6 | 190.8 | 591.2 |
| 1988 | 5,103.8 | 3,948.6 | 312.8 | 212.4 | 630.1 |
| 1989 | 5,484.4 | 4,243.2 | 337.0 | 232.6 | 671.5 |
| 1990 | 5,803.1 | 4,462.6 | 362.9 | 256.0 | 721.6 |
| 1991 | 5,995.9 | 4,569.3 | 383.4 | 277.3 | 765.9 |

*(continued)*

**Table 1.4.** Gross Value Added to the U.S. Economy by Sector, 1929–2006 ($ billions) *(continued)*

| Year | GDP | Business | Households | NPISH | General government |
|------|-----|----------|-----------|-------|--------------------|
| 1992 | 6,337.7 | 4,840.4 | 397.2 | 300.7 | 799.4 |
| 1993 | 6,657.4 | 5,096.2 | 413.7 | 318.3 | 829.3 |
| 1994 | 7,072.2 | 5,444.0 | 439.5 | 331.7 | 857.0 |
| 1995 | 7,397.7 | 5,700.6 | 463.3 | 352.1 | 881.6 |
| 1996 | 7,816.9 | 6,056.7 | 484.7 | 367.5 | 908.0 |
| 1997 | 8,304.3 | 6,471.9 | 509.6 | 386.2 | 936.7 |
| 1998 | 8,747.0 | 6,827.1 | 538.0 | 411.7 | 970.3 |
| 1999 | 9,268.4 | 7,243.4 | 576.4 | 435.9 | 1,012.7 |
| 2000 | 9,817.0 | 7,666.7 | 615.6 | 465.1 | 1,069.6 |
| 2001 | 10,128.0 | 7,841.2 | 662.0 | 498.4 | 1,126.4 |
| 2002 | 10,469.6 | 8,040.5 | 687.7 | 539.6 | 1,201.8 |
| 2003 | 10,960.8 | 8,411.5 | 699.9 | 569.3 | 1,280.1 |
| 2004 | 11,685.9 | 8,987.5 | 744.9 | 605.1 | 1,348.4 |
| 2005 | 12,433.9 | 9,603.2 | 773.3 | 631.4 | 1,425.9 |
| 2006 | 13,194.7 | 10,192.8 | 834.2 | 666.1 | 1,501.5 |

*Source:* U.S. Department of Commerce, Bureau of Economic Analysis, National Income and Product Accounts, table 1.3.5 (2007).
GDP = gross domestic product
NPISH = nonprofit institutions serving households
*Notes:* Value added by the business sector equals the gross domestic product excluding the gross value added by households, nonprofit institutions serving households, and general government. Government enterprises are classified as part of the business sector, as are nonprofits serving business. Value added by the nonprofit sector equals the compensation of employees of nonprofit institutions serving households, the rental value of nonresidential fixed assets owned and used by nonprofit institutions serving households, and rental income from tenant-occupied housing owned by nonprofit institutions serving households. Value added by the general government equals compensation of general government employees plus general government consumption of fixed capital.

# Revenues and Outlays of Nonprofit Institutions Serving Households

Although the GDP and wage estimates presented above are the best available data for comparing the nonprofit sector to the other sectors of the economy, they are not the best measures for appreciating the size of the nonprofit sector. The GDP estimates are net of nonprofits' purchases of other sectors' products, and wages represent only about half of total nonprofit expenditures. Fortunately, the BEA also estimates NPISH revenues and outlays. These are presented in this section.

**Table 1.5.** Wage and Salary Accruals by Economic Sector, 1948–2006 ($ billions)

| Year | Business | Households | NPISH | General government | Total | Government enterprises |
|------|----------|------------|-------|--------------------|-------|------------------------|
| 1948 | 113.2 | 2.4 | 3.2 | 16.8 | 135.6 | 2.2 |
| 1949 | 110.5 | 2.4 | 3.5 | 18.3 | 134.7 | 2.5 |
| 1950 | 120.8 | 2.6 | 3.8 | 20.0 | 147.2 | 2.6 |
| 1951 | 138.4 | 2.6 | 4.1 | 26.3 | 171.4 | 2.9 |
| 1952 | 148.6 | 2.6 | 4.5 | 30.0 | 185.7 | 3.4 |
| 1953 | 160.4 | 2.7 | 5.0 | 30.9 | 199.0 | 3.4 |
| 1954 | 158.0 | 2.6 | 5.4 | 31.4 | 197.4 | 3.5 |
| 1955 | 170.4 | 3.0 | 5.9 | 32.9 | 212.2 | 3.7 |
| 1956 | 184.5 | 3.2 | 6.4 | 35.0 | 229.1 | 3.8 |
| 1957 | 192.7 | 3.3 | 7.0 | 37.0 | 240.0 | 4.0 |
| 1958 | 190.5 | 3.5 | 7.7 | 39.7 | 241.4 | 4.4 |
| 1959 | 206.5 | 3.5 | 8.4 | 41.4 | 259.8 | 4.7 |
| 1960 | 215.6 | 3.8 | 9.6 | 44.1 | 273.1 | 5.1 |
| 1961 | 219.6 | 3.7 | 10.2 | 47.2 | 280.7 | 5.3 |
| 1962 | 233.8 | 3.8 | 11.2 | 50.7 | 299.5 | 5.7 |
| 1963 | 245.1 | 3.8 | 12.1 | 53.9 | 314.9 | 6.1 |
| 1964 | 262.5 | 3.9 | 13.1 | 58.4 | 337.9 | 6.5 |
| 1965 | 282.6 | 3.9 | 14.4 | 62.9 | 363.8 | 7.1 |
| 1966 | 309.5 | 4.0 | 16.1 | 70.7 | 400.3 | 7.7 |
| 1967 | 328.8 | 4.1 | 17.9 | 78.3 | 429.1 | 8.2 |
| 1968 | 359.9 | 4.3 | 20.3 | 87.4 | 471.9 | 9.3 |
| 1969 | 395.1 | 4.4 | 23.3 | 95.4 | 518.2 | 10.2 |
| 1970 | 415.7 | 4.4 | 25.9 | 105.5 | 551.5 | 11.7 |
| 1971 | 437.2 | 4.5 | 28.6 | 114.3 | 584.6 | 12.5 |
| 1972 | 478.6 | 4.6 | 31.3 | 124.3 | 638.8 | 13.5 |
| 1973 | 535.6 | 4.7 | 34.5 | 133.9 | 708.7 | 14.9 |
| 1974 | 585.7 | 4.5 | 38.3 | 143.7 | 772.2 | 16.8 |
| 1975 | 610.1 | 4.6 | 42.5 | 157.7 | 814.9 | 18.5 |
| 1976 | 679.2 | 5.3 | 46.1 | 169.1 | 899.7 | 19.8 |
| 1977 | 756.6 | 5.8 | 50.1 | 181.7 | 994.2 | 20.9 |
| 1978 | 861.3 | 6.4 | 56.4 | 197.1 | 1,121.2 | 22.9 |
| 1979 | 974.2 | 6.3 | 63.3 | 212.1 | 1,255.9 | 25.0 |

*(continued)*

**Table 1.5.** Wage and Salary Accruals by Economic Sector, 1948–2006 ($ billions)
*(continued)*

| Year | Business | Households | NPISH | General government | Total | Government enterprises |
|------|----------|------------|-------|--------------------|-------|------------------------|
| 1980 | 1,066.1 | 6.0 | 72.4 | 233.2 | 1,377.7 | 28.2 |
| 1981 | 1,175.9 | 6.0 | 81.7 | 254.2 | 1,517.8 | 31.7 |
| 1982 | 1,222.2 | 6.1 | 91.1 | 274.4 | 1,593.8 | 33.1 |
| 1983 | 1,289.5 | 6.2 | 99.6 | 289.5 | 1,684.8 | 35.3 |
| 1984 | 1,430.1 | 7.1 | 108.0 | 310.0 | 1,855.2 | 38.1 |
| 1985 | 1,539.3 | 7.2 | 116.1 | 333.0 | 1,995.6 | 40.8 |
| 1986 | 1,628.1 | 7.6 | 126.4 | 354.5 | 2,116.6 | 42.4 |
| 1987 | 1,743.6 | 7.6 | 143.2 | 377.7 | 2,272.1 | 44.9 |
| 1988 | 1,881.8 | 8.1 | 160.8 | 403.1 | 2,453.8 | 48.2 |
| 1989 | 1,983.9 | 8.7 | 175.3 | 429.7 | 2,597.6 | 50.5 |
| 1990 | 2,091.0 | 9.2 | 193.0 | 463.2 | 2,756.4 | 54.6 |
| 1991 | 2,118.8 | 8.9 | 208.3 | 489.8 | 2,825.8 | 57.0 |
| 1992 | 2,222.8 | 9.9 | 225.5 | 509.3 | 2,967.5 | 59.9 |
| 1993 | 2,319.1 | 10.4 | 236.8 | 526.2 | 3,092.5 | 60.5 |
| 1994 | 2,451.4 | 10.8 | 248.4 | 543.1 | 3,253.7 | 63.1 |
| 1995 | 2,602.8 | 11.6 | 264.8 | 560.7 | 3,439.9 | 64.8 |
| 1996 | 2,760.0 | 11.7 | 278.2 | 577.5 | 3,627.4 | 66.9 |
| 1997 | 2,974.1 | 11.7 | 294.4 | 598.9 | 3,879.1 | 69.2 |
| 1998 | 3,234.7 | 13.6 | 313.5 | 625.5 | 4,187.3 | 71.8 |
| 1999 | 3,477.5 | 12.4 | 331.6 | 655.1 | 4,476.6 | 74.3 |
| 2000 | 3,771.3 | 13.2 | 354.1 | 695.2 | 4,833.8 | 79.6 |
| 2001 | 3,826.1 | 12.5 | 375.2 | 734.1 | 4,947.9 | 81.8 |
| 2002 | 3,791.3 | 12.3 | 401.8 | 781.0 | 4,986.4 | 84.9 |
| 2003 | 3,878.6 | 13.6 | 423.1 | 818.1 | 5,133.4 | 86.3 |
| 2004 | 4,074.4 | 14.5 | 444.5 | 852.2 | 5,385.6 | 90.9 |
| 2005 | 4,314.1 | 14.6 | 462.5 | 888.1 | 5,679.3 | 92.8 |
| 2006 | 4,602.9 | 15.2 | 489.4 | 924.7 | 6,032.2 | 96.0 |

*Source:* U.S. Department of Commerce, Bureau of Economic Analysis, National Income and Product Accounts, table 1.13 (2007).
NPISH = nonprofit institutions serving households
*Notes:* Government enterprises are shown for information only; these are included in the totals for business. Wage and salary accruals for nonprofits serving business are also included in business. Business includes domestic business only and excludes wages and salary accruals for the rest of the world, which are not available separately. The business total is the sum of the BEA's wage and salary accruals for corporate business and noncorporate business.

**Figure 1.5.** Revenue of Nonprofit Institutions Serving Households, 1992–2005 ($ billions)

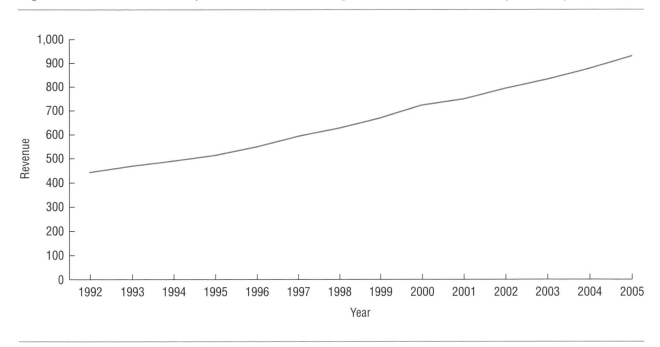

*Source:* Authors' calculations based on U.S. Department of Commerce, Bureau of Economic Analysis, National Income and Product Accounts, table 2.9 (2006).
*Note:* See table 4.1, this volume, for source data.

According to the BEA, NPISHs had $930.0 billion in revenue in 2005. This is 49 percent larger than the 2005 estimate of gross value added to GDP by the sector. Figure 1.5 shows the trend in NPISH revenue from 1992 to 2005. In current dollars, the sector more than doubled over this 13-year period. Since nonprofits generally either spend the money they receive or give it to others, nonprofit outlays show a trend similar to revenue. According to the BEA, in 2005, NPISHs spent $840.5 billion and gave away another $74.7 billion for total outlays of $915.2 billion—a margin of revenue over outlays of just 1.6 percent. Chapter 4 provides additional detail on NPISH revenues and outlays based on the BEA numbers. Chapter 5 provides a detailed look at the revenues of public charities reporting to the IRS. IRS-based revenue numbers are significantly larger than BEA numbers. A detailed explanation is beyond the scope of this chapter, but major sources of the difference include the following:

■ The BEA excludes activities of nonprofit institutions serving business, unrelated sales, secondary sales, and sales to business, government, and the rest of the world.
■ The BEA appears to treat nonprofits that are part of government hospitals and schools as part of government instead of the nonprofit sector, and treats scholarships and fellowships as reductions in revenue rather than expenses.

■ The BEA excludes grants and allocations made by nonprofit institutions that indirectly support households through the support of other nonprofit institutions, and their payments to affiliates.

■ The BEA excludes capital gains and losses.

## Addressing the Limitations of the Estimates

Without question, the BEA estimates presented in this chapter are the best numbers for estimating the size of the nonprofit sector and comparing it to the other sectors. Nevertheless, in an ideal world, they would be supplemented in two ways:

1. The BEA estimates include only NPISHs. Analogous data for nonprofits serving business would be useful, so that we could add them and see the nonprofit sector as a whole.

2. The BEA estimates include only market transactions. The nonprofit sector benefits from significant, valuable volunteer work. Because the BEA values the nonprofit sector's output by the costs of its inputs, unpaid work receives no value in their numbers.

As noted above, the BEA does not define nonprofits serving business in enough detail for us to simply add up the components. Thus, we needed to develop a definition. Based on our analysis, we chose to include 100 percent of business associations and 10 percent of the nonprofit portion of physical, engineering, and biological research services.

Table 1.6 shows the figures making up our estimate. Based on our assumptions, wages for nonprofits serving business were $7.6 billion in 2006. This was just 1.5 percent of total nonprofit wages.

We also wanted to include the value of volunteer time in our estimate of the nonprofit sector's size. Estimates of the wage-equivalent value of volunteer time appear in chapter 3 in table 3.13.

Table 1.7 compares the values of nonprofit wages and volunteer work. In 2006, the wage value of volunteer time was $215.6 billion. This was 43.3 percent of the estimated total wages paid by nonprofits. In total, nonprofit wages plus the wage value of volunteer time was $712.6 billion in 2006.

## Nonprofit Employment

Detailed nonprofit employment estimates by industry are developed in chapter 2. Here we report on overall totals and trends.

In 2005, we estimate paid employment in the nonprofit sector was 12.9 million. From 1998 to 2005, nonprofit employment grew an estimated 16.0 percent, or at a compound

**Table 1.6.** Estimated Wages for Nonprofits Serving Business, 1990–2006 ($ billions)

| Year | Nonprofit physical, engineering, and biological research services[a] | Nonprofit physical, engineering, and biological research services × 10%[b] | Business associations[c] | Nonprofits serving business[b] | NPISH[d] | Total |
|------|------|------|------|------|------|------|
| 1990 | 5.8 | 0.6 | 3.0 | 3.6 | 193.0 | 196.6 |
| 1991 | 6.0 | 0.6 | 3.2 | 3.8 | 208.3 | 212.1 |
| 1992 | 6.1 | 0.6 | 3.4 | 4.0 | 225.5 | 229.5 |
| 1993 | 6.4 | 0.6 | 3.5 | 4.2 | 236.8 | 241.0 |
| 1994 | 6.6 | 0.7 | 3.7 | 4.3 | 248.4 | 252.7 |
| 1995 | 7.0 | 0.7 | 3.9 | 4.6 | 264.8 | 269.4 |
| 1996 | 7.1 | 0.7 | 4.1 | 4.8 | 278.2 | 283.0 |
| 1997 | 7.8 | 0.8 | 4.3 | 5.1 | 294.4 | 299.5 |
| 1998 | 7.7 | 0.8 | 4.6 | 5.4 | 313.5 | 318.9 |
| 1999 | 7.4 | 0.7 | 4.9 | 5.6 | 331.6 | 337.2 |
| 2000 | 7.4 | 0.7 | 5.1 | 5.9 | 354.1 | 360.0 |
| 2001 | 6.4 | 0.6 | 5.5 | 6.1 | 375.2 | 381.3 |
| 2002 | 5.3 | 0.5 | 5.6 | 6.2 | 401.8 | 408.0 |
| 2003 | 5.6 | 0.6 | 5.8 | 6.4 | 423.1 | 429.5 |
| 2004 | 6.1 | 0.6 | 6.1 | 6.7 | 444.5 | 451.2 |
| 2005 | 6.9 | 0.7 | 6.5 | 7.2 | 462.5 | 469.7 |
| 2006 | 7.5 | 0.8 | 6.9 | 7.6 | 489.4 | 497.0 |

*Sources:*
a. Authors' estimates based on private wages from the U.S. Department of Labor, Bureau of Labor Statistics, Quarterly Census of Employment and Wages (1990–2006); U.S. Census Bureau, Economic Census (1997, 2002).
b. Wages for nonprofits serving business are estimated to be the sum of 10 percent of estimated nonprofit wages in physical, engineering, and biological research services and all wages for business associations. The total is the sum of nonprofits serving business and NPISHs.
c. U.S. Department of Labor, Bureau of Labor Statistics, Quarterly Census of Employment and Wages (1990–2006); U.S. Census Bureau, Economic Census (1997, 2002).
d. U.S. Department of Commerce, Bureau of Economic Analysis, National Income and Product Accounts, table 1.13 (2007).
NPISH = nonprofit institutions serving households

annual growth rate of 2.2 percent. During this period, nonprofit employment grew faster than employment in the overall U.S. economy. U.S. nonfarm employment other than nonprofits grew just 5.2 percent from 1998 to 2005, or just 0.7 percent compound annual growth. That means nonprofit employment grew more than three times faster than the rest of the economy from 1998 to 2005. As a result, nonprofit employment grew from 8.8 percent of nonfarm employment in 1998 to 9.7 percent in 2005 (see table 1.8 and figure 1.6).

**Table 1.7.** Nonprofit Wages and the Wage Value of Volunteer Work, 2003–2006

|  | 2003 | 2004 | 2005 | 2006 |
| --- | --- | --- | --- | --- |
| Wage value of volunteering ($ billions)[a] | 193.9 | 215.4 | 217.7 | 215.6 |
| Nonprofit wages ($ billions)[b] | 429.5 | 451.2 | 469.7 | 497.0 |
| Total ($ billions) | 623.4 | 666.5 | 687.4 | 712.6 |
| Wage value of volunteers (% of nonprofit wages) | 45.2 | 47.8 | 46.3 | 43.3 |

*Sources:*
a. Authors' calculations based on U.S. Department of Labor, Bureau of Labor Statistics, American Time Use Survey (2006); Current Employment Statistics (2006); and Current Population Survey, Volunteer Supplement (2006).
b. Authors' estimates based on U.S. Census Bureau, Economic Census (2002); U.S. Department of Commerce, Bureau of Economic Analysis, National Income and Product Accounts, table 1.13 (2007); private wages from U.S. Department of Labor, Bureau of Labor Statistics, Quarterly Census of Employment and Wages (2003–2006).
*Notes:* See table 3.13, this volume, for the authors' calculations for the wage value of volunteering; see table 1.6 for authors' calculations of nonprofit wages.

# Conclusion

The nonprofit sector is incredibly diverse, although hospitals and universities make up a significant portion in dollar terms. How big is it? Nonprofits account for 5 percent of GDP, over 8 percent of the economy's wages, and about 10 percent of employment. Nonprofit wages and employment have both been growing as a share of the total economy, with nonprofit employment growing three times faster than the rest

**Table 1.8.** U.S. Employment in the Nonprofit Sector, 1998–2005

|  | 1998 | 1999 | 2000 | 2001 | 2002 | 2003 | 2004 | 2005 |
| --- | --- | --- | --- | --- | --- | --- | --- | --- |
| Nonprofit employees (thousands)[a] | 11,101 | 11,375 | 11,648 | 11,962 | 12,348 | 12,579 | 12,773 | 12,922 |
| Nonfarm employees (thousands)[b] | 125,930 | 128,993 | 131,785 | 131,826 | 130,341 | 129,999 | 131,435 | 133,703 |
| Nonprofit employees in workforce (%) | 8.8 | 8.8 | 8.8 | 9.1 | 9.5 | 9.7 | 9.7 | 9.7 |

*Sources:*
a. Authors' estimates based on sources from the U.S. Census Bureau, Bureau of Labor Statistics, and Internal Revenue Service, as detailed in the chapter 2 appendix.
b. U.S. Department of Labor, Bureau of Labor Statistics, Current Employment Statistics (1998–2004).
*Note:* See table 2.2., this volume, for authors' estimate of nonprofit employment.

**Figure 1.6.** Nonprofit Employees and Nonprofit Employment as a Percentage of U.S. Nonfarm Employment, 1998–2005

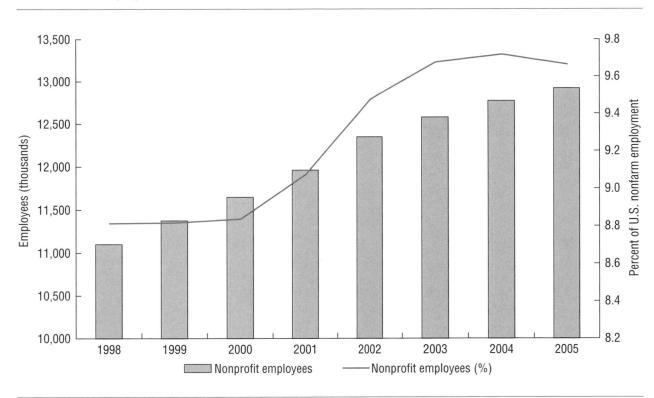

*Source:* Nonprofit employment from authors' estimates, based on sources from the U.S. Census Bureau, Bureau of Labor Statistics, and Internal Revenue Service, as detailed in the chapter 2 appendix. Nonfarm employment from U.S. Department of Labor, Bureau of Labor Statistics, Current Employment Statistics (1998–2004).
*Note:* See table 1.8, this volume, for source data.

of the economy in recent years. In addition to paid employment, nonprofits benefit from significant volunteer work, equivalent in value to almost half the wages the sector pays. Although its economic size is probably the least important aspect of the sector, it is clearly a significant and growing part of the national economy.

# Types of Tax-Exempt Organizations by IRS Code

### 501(c)(1)  Corporations organized under act of Congress

Most of the organizations in this small category are federal credit unions.

### 501(c)(2)  Title-holding corporations for exempt organizations

Such corporations hold titles to another exempt organization's property or to investments generating income for a single exempt organization. At least 3 of the largest 10 title-holding corporations hold investments for the General Electric Pension Trust; another holds investments for the Florida State Board of Administration.

### 501(c)(3)  Religious, charitable, and similar organizations

This category includes organizations (public charities and private foundations) serving broad public purposes that are charitable, educational, religious, scientific, or literary, or that test for public safety. It is by far the largest category of exempt organizations. Among the largest organizations are many hospitals and higher education institutions.

### 501(c)(4)  Civic leagues and social welfare organizations

Seven of ten of the largest organizations by gross receipts are in the health care field and include dental plans and HMOs. However, the smaller organizations are far more diverse and range from service-oriented clubs like Kiwanis International and the Gig Harbor Peninsula Firefighters Association to advocacy-oriented organizations such as the National Organization to Insure a Sound-Controlled Environment, which provides "advocacy and education on aviation noise."

### 501(c)(5)  Labor, agricultural, and horticultural organizations

Most of the largest organizations (ranked by gross receipts or total assets) are labor unions "providing services to working and retired members, or collective bargaining to improve jobs and promote fairness and equality on the job and in society." Examples are the United Steelworkers of America, the International Ladies' Garment Workers' Union, and the American Federation of Teachers. Smaller organizations include many labor unions, as well as some agricultural organizations such as the Mississippi Farm Bureau Federation and the New Mexico Dry Onion Commission, which engages in research and development of to improve onion varieties.

## 501(c)(6)  Business leagues

Included are "business leagues [such as trade associations and professional associations], chambers of commerce, real estate boards, boards of trade, and professional football leagues." Services in many such organizations include protection of professionals' interests, detection and prevention of compensation insolvencies, support of informed professional decisionmaking, and communication with the profession. Examples include the Association of National Advertisers, the Nebraska Telecommunications Association, and the National Association of Securities Dealers.

## 501(c)(7)  Social and recreational clubs

Social and recreational clubs are those "created for pleasure, recreation, or other similar purpose." Many of the largest social clubs by gross receipts and total assets are university-based honor societies, fraternities and sororities, and athletic clubs. Smaller organizations include many regional sports or recreation clubs, including golf clubs, ski clubs, motorcycle clubs, yacht clubs, country clubs, regional wine and food societies, fraternities, and sororities.

## 501(c)(8)  Fraternal beneficiary societies and associations

Such fraternal organizations operate under the lodge system and pay life, sick, accident, or other benefits. The largest four, all multibillion-dollar organizations providing insurance and other services, are Thrivent Financial for Lutherans, the Knights of Columbus, Woodmen of the World (which calls itself the "largest fraternal benefit society with open membership"), and Modern Woodmen of America. The latter states, "members are joined by three common bonds: family financial security, positive family life and service to community."

## 501(c)(9)  Voluntary employee-beneficiary associations

These are organizations created to pay life, sick, accident, and similar benefits to members, their dependents, or other beneficiaries. Members have a common employer, membership in a labor union, or another employment-related common bond. Examples are the General Motors Welfare Trust, the National Benefit Fund for Hospital and Human Service Employees, and the General Electric Company Insurance Plan Trust.

## 501(c)(10)  Domestic fraternal societies and associations

These organizations operate under the lodge system for "religious, charitable, scientific, literary, educational, and fraternal purposes." Most of the largest organizations (by gross receipts and total assets) are regional branches of the Freemasons and the related Royal Order of the Jesters. Smaller organizations include many lodges associated with the Fraternal Order of the Eagles.

## 501(c)(11)  Teachers' retirement fund associations

Only eight organizations reported assets or income. This category also includes teachers' annuity and aid associations.

## 501(c)(12)    Benevolent life insurance associations

This category includes "benevolent life insurance associations, mutual ditch or irrigation companies, [and] mutual or cooperative telephone companies" that are usually "organized and operated on a mutual or cooperative basis." All of the largest organizations, ranked by gross receipts or total assets, are in the electric power and transmission industry and are associations that supply power to member cooperatives or provide other similar services.

## 501(c)(13)    Cemetery companies

These are cemeteries or corporations chartered to operate "solely for the purpose of the disposal of human bodies by burial or cremation."

## 501(c)(14)    State-chartered credit unions and mutual reserve funds

Prevalent are regional credit unions, such as Credit Unions Chartered in the State of Wisconsin and Credit Unions Chartered in Colorado and Ohio. The credit unions do not have capital stock and are "organized and operated under state law for mutual purposes and without profit."

## 501(c)(15)    Mutual insurance companies or associations

The largest organizations by gross receipts and total assets are in the business of insurance, marshaling financial activities, assets, and estate administration. Included are insurance companies in receivership or in liquidation.

## 501(c)(16)    Cooperative organizations to finance crop operations

Many organizations (about 50 percent) are livestock credit associations or corporations, which provide funds to members for the purchase of cattle or for similar purposes in the cattle-breeding industry.

## 501(c)(17)    Supplemental unemployment benefit trusts

501(c)(17) organizations, along with 501(c)(4) and 501(c)(9) organizations, are types of employee associations. Their primary purpose is "providing for payment of supplemental unemployment benefits."

## 501(c)(18)    Employee-funded pension trusts created before June 25, 1959

Only one organization reported assets or income in this category—the Inter-Local Pension Fund of the Graphics Communication International Union.

## 501(c)(19)    War veterans organizations

Qualified are "posts or organizations of past or present members of the Armed Forces of the United States." Examples are posts or auxiliaries of the American Legion, Veterans of Foreign Wars, the Air Force Association, and the Marines Memorial Association.

## 501(c)(20)    Legal service organizations

The IRS describes such an entity as "an organization or trust created in the U.S. for the exclusive function of forming a part of a qualified group legal services plan or plans." It "cannot be exempt under section 501(c)(20) after June 30, 1992. However, it may qualify for exemption under section 501(c)(9)."

## 501(c)(21)   Black lung benefits trusts

These organizations are established to satisfy claims under the Black Lung Act. No organizations report assets or income. Only 28 organizations are currently registered with the IRS.

## 501(c)(22)   Withdrawal liability payment funds

No organizations are currently registered with the IRS.

## 501(c)(23)   Veterans associations created before 1880

The only two organizations that reported assets and income are the Navy Mutual Aid Association and the Army and Air Force Mutual Aid Association.

## 501(c)(24)   Trusts described in section 4049 of the Employee Retirement Income Security Act of 1974

No organizations report assets or income. Only one organization, Spring Prairie Hutterian Brethren Inc., is registered as a 501(c)(24) entity.

## 501(c)(25)   Title-holding corporations or trusts with multiple parents

This type of title-holding organization is either a corporation or a trust, "organized for the exclusive purpose of acquiring, holding title to, and collecting income from real property, and turning over the entire amount less expenses to member organizations exempt from income tax." Examples involve "qualified pensions, profit-sharing, or stock bonus plans, governmental plans, governments and their agencies and instrumentalities, and charitable organizations."

## 501(c)(26)   State-sponsored organizations providing health coverage for high-risk individuals

Nine organizations reported assets or income. The Alaska association, for example, "provides health insurance to Alaska residents who are denied health insurance in the private market because of a medical condition."

## 501(c)(27)   State-sponsored workers' compensation reinsurance organizations

These reimburse member employers for losses under workers' compensation acts. Four organizations report assets or income. For example, the Minnesota Workers' Compensation Assigned Risk Plan is "the source of workers' compensation and employers' liability coverage for Minnesota employers who have been unable to secure other coverage through the voluntary market."

## 501(d)   Religious and apostolic organizations

None of the organizations in this category file Forms 990. Many of the organizations in this small category are Hutterian Brethren communities (closely related to the Amish and Mennonite faiths).

## 501(e)   Cooperative hospital service organizations

This small category comprises organizations such as Hospital Central Services of Chicago and Katahdin Shared Services in rural Maine, which provide their member hospitals with shared equipment, group purchasing, and other services.

**501(f)    Cooperative service organizations of operating educational organizations**
Only one of these organizations was registered with the IRS in 2005 and was not
required to file Form 990. The general purpose of these types of organizations is to
provide investment services for educational organizations.

*Sources:* U.S. Department of the Treasury, Internal Revenue Service, Internal Revenue Code (2004); Urban
Institute, National Center for Charitable Statistics, IRS Business Master Files (2006).

# 2

# Wage and Employment Trends

The primary purpose of this chapter is to provide wage and employment estimates for the various industries or subsectors that comprise the nonprofit sector. Unlike the estimates reported in the other chapters of this book, nonprofit wages and employment data by industry are not currently collected on a comprehensive, annual basis by any government agency. The numbers presented here are the authors' estimates and thus subject to revision as better data and methods become available.

Table 2.1 shows nonprofit wages by industry. Industries not listed, such as construction and manufacturing, contain no nonprofits according to the data sources we used. Unlike the industry estimates reported in table 1.3, the wages in this table include an imputation for unreported wage income. In attempting to tie our estimates back to the BEA wage numbers reported in chapter 1, we find that our industry estimates undervalue wages to some degree, accounting for 94.4 percent of NPISH wages in 2005. The exact causes of this underestimate are unknown, but the results are not surprising given the multiple data sources synthesized to prepare these estimates. From 1998 to 2005, we estimate total nonprofit wages, including nonprofits serving business, increased from $318.9 billion to $469.7 billion, a 47 percent increase or 5.7 percent compound annual growth rate.

Table 2.2 shows nonprofit employment—the number of employees—by industry. According to our estimates, total nonprofit employment increased from 11.1 million in 1998 to 12.9 million in 2005, a 16 percent increase or 2.2 percent compound annual growth rate. Finally, table 2.3 shows annual average compensation per employee by nonprofit industry. Across all industries, we estimate average annual compensation per employee increased from $25,592 in 1998 to $34,339 in 2005. This is a 34 percent increase or compound annual growth rate of 4.3 percent.

Figure 2.1 shows the distribution of nonprofit wages by industry. Health care and social assistance organizations (NAICS 62) account for over half of the sector's wages. Other services (NAICS 81), which contains membership, advocacy, and grantmaking organizations, accounts for 17.8 percent, while educational services (NAICS 61) is third

**Table 2.1.** Nonprofit Wages by Industry, 1998–2005 ($ millions)

| NAICS code | Industry | Wages | | | | | | | |
|---|---|---|---|---|---|---|---|---|---|
| | | 1998 | 1999 | 2000 | 2001 | 2002 | 2003 | 2004 | 2005 |
| 11 | Agriculture, forestry, fishing, and hunting | 274 | 288 | 288 | 333 | 360 | 338 | 333 | 366 |
| 22 | Utilities | 231 | 267 | 307 | 366 | 404 | 420 | 441 | 520 |
| 48–49 | Transportation and warehousing | 46 | 51 | 59 | 59 | 64 | 74 | 75 | 80 |
| 51 | Information | 1,572 | 1,742 | 1,815 | 1,999 | 2,031 | 2,072 | 2,168 | 2,318 |
| 52 | Finance and insurance | 3,983 | 4,285 | 4,433 | 4,661 | 5,232 | 5,401 | 5,780 | 6,637 |
| 53 | Real estate and rental and leasing | 89 | 84 | 90 | 97 | 100 | 99 | 106 | 119 |
| 54 | Professional, scientific, and technical services | 6,333 | 6,525 | 7,551 | 7,989 | 9,440 | 9,740 | 10,173 | 11,599 |
| 56 | Administrative and waste management services | 604 | 647 | 567 | 580 | 618 | 655 | 610 | 605 |
| 61 | Educational services | 45,121 | 48,015 | 51,761 | 55,575 | 60,698 | 64,148 | 67,983 | 72,117 |
| 62 | Health care and social assistance | 164,139 | 173,064 | 184,628 | 198,893 | 213,727 | 230,505 | 243,974 | 257,861 |
| 71 | Arts, entertainment, and recreation | 7,736 | 8,362 | 9,209 | 10,356 | 10,714 | 11,345 | 11,996 | 12,400 |
| 72 | Accommodation and food services | 168 | 193 | 210 | 234 | 256 | 270 | 285 | 296 |

| | | | | | | | | |
|---|---|---|---|---|---|---|---|---|
| 81 | Other services, except government | 53,793 | 57,005 | 60,972 | 64,933 | 70,504 | 73,828 | 77,137 | 78,801 |
| | Industry subtotal | 284,088 | 300,530 | 321,889 | 346,076 | 374,150 | 398,895 | 421,061 | 443,720 |
| | Less nonprofits serving business | 5,378 | 5,628 | 5,888 | 6,106 | 6,159 | 6,404 | 6,722 | 7,155 |
| | Equals NPISH portion of industry subtotal | 278,710 | 294,902 | 316,001 | 339,971 | 367,992 | 392,491 | 414,340 | 436,565 |
| | Plus unknown industry wages | 34,790 | 36,698 | 38,099 | 35,229 | 33,808 | 30,609 | 30,160 | 25,935 |
| | BEA NPISH wages | 313,500 | 331,600 | 354,100 | 375,200 | 401,800 | 423,100 | 444,500 | 462,500 |
| | Total nonprofit wages | 318,878 | 337,228 | 359,988 | 381,306 | 407,959 | 429,504 | 451,222 | 469,655 |

*Source:* Authors' estimates based on U.S. Census Bureau, Economic Census (2002); U.S. Department of Commerce, Bureau of Economic Analysis, National Income and Product Accounts (2007); U.S. Department of Labor, Bureau of Labor Statistics, Quarterly Census of Employment and Wages (1998–2007); and Urban Institute, National Center for Charitable Statistics, Core Files (1998–2006) and IRS Statistics of Income Form 990 and 990-EZ Sample Files (1998–2006).

BEA = U.S. Department of Commerce, Bureau of Economic Analysis

NPISH = nonprofit institutions serving households

*Notes:* Industries are listed as classified by the North American Industry Classification System. The industry subtotal is the sum of the industry-by-industry estimates in the rows above it. Because those estimates include nonprofits serving business but the BEA NPISH estimates do not, we subtract our estimated wages for nonprofits serving business from the industry subtotal, yielding the NPISH portion of our industry subtotal. The difference between that estimate and the BEA NPISH estimate is the wages of nonprofits whose industry classification is unknown. The total nonprofit wages are the BEA NPISH number plus our estimate for nonprofits serving business. Please see the chapter appendix for a detailed description of the authors' methodology.

**Table 2.2.** Nonprofit Employment by Industry, 1998–2005

| NAICS code | Industry | Employees | | | | | | | |
|---|---|---|---|---|---|---|---|---|---|
| | | 1998 | 1999 | 2000 | 2001 | 2002 | 2003 | 2004 | 2005 |
| 11 | Agriculture, forestry, fishing, and hunting | 11,900 | 11,920 | 11,258 | 12,283 | 12,986 | 12,387 | 11,321 | 12,211 |
| 22 | Utilities | 4,131 | 4,587 | 4,850 | 5,557 | 5,980 | 6,185 | 6,107 | 6,875 |
| 48–49 | Transportation and warehousing | 1,272 | 1,368 | 1,507 | 1,487 | 1,585 | 1,783 | 1,731 | 1,833 |
| 51 | Information[a] | 32,354 | 31,837 | 31,126 | 34,684 | 36,045 | 35,772 | 35,319 | 36,602 |
| 52 | Finance and insurance | 72,829 | 74,655 | 70,222 | 70,526 | 80,269 | 79,507 | 80,171 | 86,548 |
| 53 | Real estate and rental and leasing | 2,986 | 2,731 | 2,732 | 2,831 | 2,838 | 2,707 | 2,722 | 2,910 |
| 54 | Professional, scientific, and technical services[a] | 119,255 | 116,928 | 122,689 | 128,217 | 151,150 | 152,644 | 152,656 | 167,560 |
| 56 | Administrative and waste management services | 25,311 | 26,192 | 24,428 | 23,552 | 24,274 | 24,630 | 23,035 | 21,476 |
| 61 | Educational services | 1,972,039 | 2,042,691 | 2,099,986 | 2,143,728 | 2,229,313 | 2,276,988 | 2,346,295 | 2,335,466 |
| 62 | Health care and social assistance | 5,941,902 | 6,060,531 | 6,168,100 | 6,362,231 | 6,555,309 | 6,726,335 | 6,847,509 | 6,999,312 |
| 71 | Arts, entertainment, and recreation | 403,242 | 415,481 | 437,971 | 452,120 | 460,296 | 466,288 | 477,099 | 481,755 |
| 72 | Accommodation and food services | 12,730 | 14,106 | 14,487 | 15,829 | 16,948 | 17,379 | 17,647 | 17,902 |
| 81 | Other services, except government | 2,500,681 | 2,572,398 | 2,658,507 | 2,708,783 | 2,770,701 | 2,776,604 | 2,771,528 | 2,751,202 |
| | Total | 11,100,632 | 11,375,425 | 11,647,863 | 11,961,828 | 12,347,694 | 12,579,209 | 12,773,140 | 12,921,652 |

*Source:* Authors' estimates based on U.S. Census Bureau, Economic Census (2002); U.S. Department of Commerce, Bureau of Economic Analysis, National Income and Product Accounts (2007); U.S. Department of Labor, Bureau of Labor Statistics, Quarterly Census of Employment and Wages (1998–2007); and Urban Institute, National Center for Charitable Statistics, Core Files (1998–2006) and IRS Statistics of Income Form 990 and 990-EZ Sample Files (1998–2006).

*Notes:* Industries are listed as classified by the North American Industry Classification System. Please see the chapter appendix for a detailed description of the authors' methodology.

a. An alternative estimate of 2004 nonprofit employment is shown in table 2.14. The two estimates are not compatible for industries 51 and 54. Possible sources of the difference are explored in the chapter appendix. Readers focused on those two industries should use caution in drawing conclusions based on employment estimates.

**Table 2.3.** Average Annual Compensation per Nonprofit Employee by Industry, 1998–2004 ($)

| NAICS code | Industry | Average Annual Compensation per Nonprofit Employee | | | | | | | |
|---|---|---|---|---|---|---|---|---|---|
| | | 1998 | 1999 | 2000 | 2001 | 2002 | 2003 | 2004 | 2005 |
| 11 | Agriculture, forestry, fishing and hunting | 23,038 | 24,195 | 25,557 | 27,129 | 27,725 | 27,321 | 29,394 | 29,997 |
| 22 | Utilities | 55,799 | 58,184 | 63,362 | 65,951 | 67,539 | 67,912 | 72,180 | 75,580 |
| 48–49 | Transportation and warehousing | 35,839 | 37,163 | 38,853 | 39,912 | 40,659 | 41,451 | 43,042 | 43,670 |
| 51 | Information[a] | 48,593 | 54,720 | 58,320 | 57,624 | 56,346 | 57,926 | 61,372 | 63,336 |
| 52 | Finance and insurance | 54,689 | 57,402 | 63,124 | 66,094 | 65,184 | 67,934 | 72,097 | 76,685 |
| 53 | Real estate and rental and leasing | 29,641 | 30,755 | 33,013 | 34,295 | 35,390 | 36,584 | 38,924 | 41,050 |
| 54 | Professional, scientific, and technical services[a] | 53,109 | 55,808 | 61,546 | 62,306 | 62,458 | 63,810 | 66,642 | 69,224 |
| 56 | Administrative and waste management services | 23,877 | 24,709 | 23,219 | 24,626 | 25,462 | 26,585 | 26,499 | 28,194 |
| 61 | Educational services | 22,881 | 23,506 | 24,648 | 25,925 | 27,227 | 28,172 | 28,975 | 30,879 |
| 62 | Health care and social assistance | 27,624 | 28,556 | 29,933 | 31,262 | 32,604 | 34,269 | 35,630 | 36,841 |
| 71 | Arts, entertainment, and recreation | 19,183 | 20,127 | 21,026 | 22,906 | 23,277 | 24,330 | 25,144 | 25,740 |
| 72 | Accommodation and food services | 13,202 | 13,704 | 14,470 | 14,813 | 15,093 | 15,531 | 16,164 | 16,540 |
| 81 | Other services, except government | 21,511 | 22,160 | 22,935 | 23,971 | 25,446 | 26,589 | 27,832 | 28,642 |
| | Total | 25,592 | 26,419 | 27,635 | 28,932 | 30,301 | 31,711 | 32,965 | 34,339 |

*Source:* Authors' estimates based on U.S. Census Bureau, Economic Census (2002); U.S. Department of Commerce, Bureau of Economic Analysis, National Income and Product Accounts (2007); U.S. Department of Labor, Bureau of Labor Statistics, Quarterly Census of Employment and Wages (1998–2007); and Urban Institute, National Center for Charitable Statistics, Core Files (1998–2006) and IRS Statistics of Income Form 990 and 990-EZ Sample Files (1998–2006).

*Notes:* Industries are listed as classified by the North American Industry Classification System. The estimates here were calculated by dividing the values in table 2.1 by the corresponding values in table 2.2. Please see the chapter appendix for a detailed description of the authors' methodology.

a. If table 2.2 has significantly underestimated employment in industries 51 and 54, average compensation here is overestimated.

**Figure 2.1.** Distribution of Nonprofit Wages by Industry, 2005 (percent)

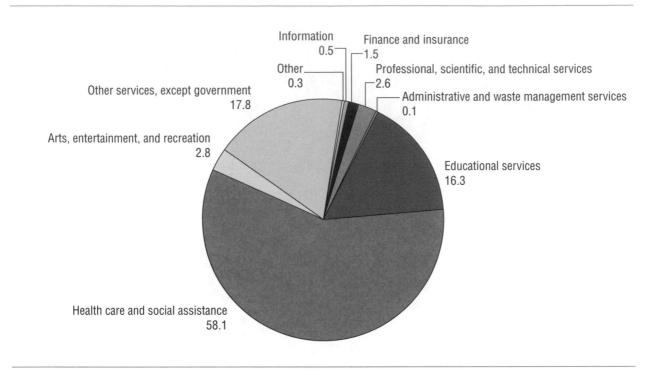

*Source:* Authors' estimates based on U.S. Census Bureau, Economic Census (2002); U.S. Department of Commerce, Bureau of Economic Analysis, National Income and Product Accounts (2006); U.S. Department of Labor, Bureau of Labor Statistics, Quarterly Census of Employment and Wages (2006); and Urban Institute, National Center for Charitable Statistics, Core Files (2006) and IRS Statistics of Income Form 990 and 990-EZ Sample Files (2006).

largest at 16.3 percent. Arts, entertainment, and recreation (NAICS 71) is a distant fourth at 2.8 percent of wages.

Figure 2.2 shows the average annual compensation per employee by nonprofit industry. Utilities (NAICS 22), and finance and insurance (NAICS 52) have the highest average compensation. Average compensation in information (NAICS 51) and professional, scientific, and technical services (NAICS 54) is also higher than the other industries. Accommodation and food services (NAICS 72) has the lowest annual average compensation. This is not surprising because it includes camps, which hire many seasonal employees. The next lowest compensation is in arts, entertainment, and recreation (NAICS 71).

To give a sense of the growth of nonprofits in different industries, figure 2.3 shows the compound annual growth rates in wages and employment from 1998 to 2005. Growth has been faster than average in utilities (NAICS 22), professional, scientific, and technical services (NAICS 54), accommodation and food services (NAICS 72), and transportation and warehousing (NAICS 48). Two industries, real estate and rental and leasing (NAICS 53) and administrative and waste management services (NAICS 56), have been shrinking in employment, although wages continue to grow in current dollars. Wages have grown just under 7 percent per year—and employment, 2.4 percent— in two larger nonprofit industries: health care and social assistance (NAICS 62) and educational services (NAICS 61).

**Figure 2.2.** Average Annual Nonprofit Compensation per Employee by Industry, 2005 ($ thousands)

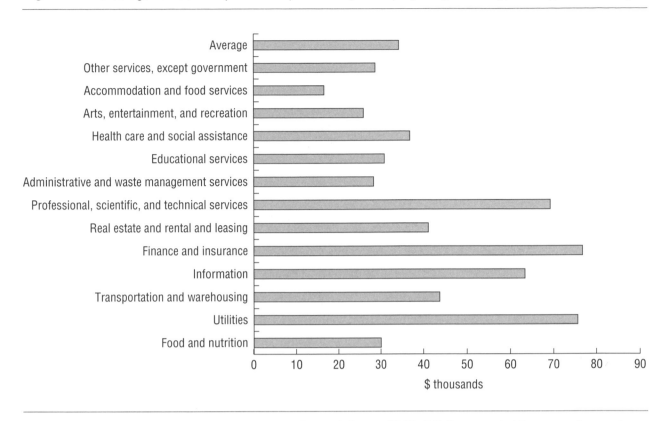

*Source:* Authors' estimates based on U.S. Census Bureau, Economic Census (2002); U.S. Department of Commerce, Bureau of Economic Analysis, National Income and Product Accounts (2006); U.S. Department of Labor, Bureau of Labor Statistics, Quarterly Census of Employment and Wages (2006); and Urban Institute, National Center for Charitable Statistics, Core Files (2006) and IRS Statistics of Income Form 990 and 990-EZ Sample Files (2006).

Finally, figure 2.4 shows the compound annual growth rate in average annual compensation per employee by industry. Compensation in most industries has been increasing about 4 percent per year. Transportation and warehousing (NAICS 48), administrative and waste management services (NAICS 56), and accommodation and food services (NAICS 72) have been somewhat below that. The fastest growth has been in finance and insurance (NAICS 52), and real estate and rental and leasing (NAICS 53).

# Conclusion

Nonprofit employment, and nonprofit wages and employment by industry, remain the biggest missing pieces in our data picture of the nonprofit sector. This chapter presents our best attempt to fill that gap. To our knowledge, this chapter, including the supplementary tables that follow, contains the most detailed and comprehensive estimates of nonprofit wages and employment by industry ever published. We hope it serves as the basis for further comparative analysis among industries within the nonprofit sector and between for-profits and nonprofits in the same industry.

**Figure 2.3.** Annual Growth Rate in Total Nonprofit Wages and Employment by Industry, 1998–2005 (percent)

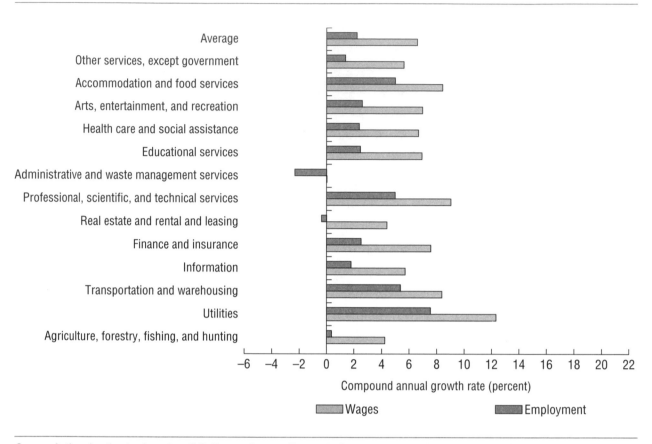

*Source:* Authors' estimates based on U.S. Census Bureau, Economic Census (2002); U.S. Department of Commerce, Bureau of Economic Analysis, National Income and Product Accounts (1998–2007); U.S. Department of Labor, Bureau of Labor Statistics, Quarterly Census of Employment and Wages (1998–2006) and IRS Statistics of Income Form 990 and 990-EZ Sample Files. (1998–2006).

We estimate that the nonprofit sector had 12.9 million paid employees in 2005, and that paid employment grew at an average rate of 2.2 percent per year from 1998 to 2005. Growth rates in employment and wages vary greatly by industry, ranging from a 12.3 percent average annual growth in wages for utilities (NAICS 22) to a 2.3 percent yearly reduction in employment for administrative and waste management services (NAICS 56). Average annual compensation per nonprofit employee also varies widely by industry, and growth in average individual compensation lags significantly in a few industries.

## Supplementary Tables

This section contains additional estimates of wages and employment for nonprofits by industry. These will allow researchers to see the detailed estimates that underlie those presented in tables 2.1 and 2.2—in some cases, in significantly greater detail. Readers

**Figure 2.4.** Annual Growth Rate in Average Annual Nonprofit Compensation per Employee by Industry, 1998–2005 (percent)

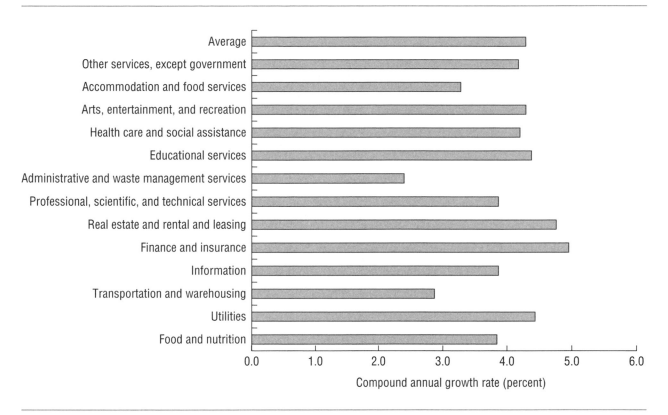

*Source:* Authors' estimates based on U.S. Census Bureau, Economic Census (2002); U.S. Department of Commerce, Bureau of Economic Analysis, National Income and Product Accounts (1998–2007); U.S. Department of Labor, Bureau of Labor Statistics, Quarterly Census of Employment and Wages (1998–2006); and Urban Institute, National Center for Charitable Statistics, Core Files (1998–2006) and IRS Statistics of Income Form 990 and 990-EZ Sample Files (1998–2006).

who wish to know how the data in these tables were combined and modified to yield the estimates in tables 2.1 and 2.2 should refer to the appendix for this chapter. The supplementary tables include the following:

- Table 2.4 depicts wages of nonprofit employees covered by unemployment insurance in NAICS 61, 62, 71, and 81. For most industries, this is the same as total reported wages.

- Since many nonprofit employees in educational institutions and religious organizations are not covered by unemployment insurance, table 2.5 compares covered wages with total reported wages for those industries.

- For industries not covered in table 2.4, table 2.6 shows the wages reported to the IRS. Two-digit industries missing from both table 2.4 and table 2.6 reported no wages to the IRS. This table includes all reporting nonprofits, not just public charities.

- Tables 2.7, 2.8, and 2.9 are analogous to tables 2.4, 2.5, and 2.6, but for employment rather than wages.

**Table 2.4.** Nonprofit Wages Covered by Unemployment Insurance, for Industries Whose Tax Status Is Identified in the Economic Census, 1990–2006 ($ millions)

| NAICS code | 61 | 62 | 71 | 81 | |
|---|---|---|---|---|---|
| Industry | Educational services | Health care and social assistance | Arts, entertainment, and recreation | Other services, except government | Total |
| 1990 | 23,430 | 97,407 | 5,705 | 16,949 | 143,491 |
| 1991 | 25,168 | 106,716 | 5,779 | 17,646 | 155,309 |
| 1992 | 26,785 | 117,053 | 5,658 | 18,790 | 168,286 |
| 1993 | 28,327 | 123,052 | 5,686 | 19,534 | 176,598 |
| 1994 | 29,917 | 129,369 | 5,926 | 20,705 | 185,916 |
| 1995 | 31,714 | 136,297 | 6,202 | 21,802 | 196,014 |
| 1996 | 33,668 | 143,072 | 6,657 | 23,003 | 206,400 |
| 1997 | 36,147 | 151,053 | 6,928 | 24,571 | 218,699 |
| 1998 | 39,310 | 160,643 | 7,585 | 25,501 | 233,039 |
| 1999 | 41,653 | 167,775 | 8,143 | 27,207 | 244,778 |
| 2000 | 44,681 | 177,193 | 8,898 | 29,511 | 260,283 |
| 2001 | 48,395 | 191,572 | 9,481 | 31,888 | 281,337 |
| 2002 | 51,994 | 206,375 | 9,780 | 33,806 | 301,955 |
| 2003 | 56,080 | 221,644 | 10,291 | 35,012 | 323,027 |
| 2004 | 59,644 | 236,148 | 10,774 | 36,578 | 343,144 |
| 2005 | 63,077 | 249,148 | 11,186 | 37,916 | 361,327 |
| 2006 | 67,429 | 266,145 | 11,940 | 40,085 | 385,600 |

*Source:* Authors' estimates based on private wages from U.S. Department of Labor, Bureau of Labor Statistics, Quarterly Census of Employment and Wages (1991–2007) and the tax-exempt share of wages from U.S. Census Bureau, Economic Census (1997, 2002).
*Notes:* Industries are listed as classified by the North American Industry Classification System. Industry 54 (professional, scientific, and technical services) is also included in the Economic Census, however, we believe these data are flawed.

- Tables 2.10 and 2.11 provide wages covered by unemployment insurance at the six-digit NAICS level for industries making up NAICS 61, 62, 71, and 81, for two different time periods.
- Tables 2.12 and 2.13 provide employment covered by unemployment insurance at the six-digit NAICS level for industries making up NAICS 61, 62, 71, and 81, for two different time periods.

**Table 2.5.** Nonprofit Wages Reported to the U.S. Census Bureau or Covered by Unemployment Insurance, in Select Industries with Many Employees Exempt from Unemployment Insurance, 1990–2005 ($ millions)

| NAICS code | 611110 Elementary and secondary schools | | 611210 Junior colleges | | 611310 Colleges, universities, and professional schools | | 611210 + 611310 | | 813110 Religious organizations | |
|---|---|---|---|---|---|---|---|---|---|---|
| Wages | Reported | Covered | Reported | Covered | Reported | Covered | Reported | Covered | Reported | Covered |
| 1990 | 6,575.0 | 5,479.1 | — | 182.1 | — | 16,775.5 | 18,177.0 | 16,957.6 | 10,077.4 | 1,297.7 |
| 1991 | 7,174.1 | 6,028.1 | — | 230.5 | — | 17,871.9 | 19,673.8 | 18,102.4 | 11,000.7 | 1,317.1 |
| 1992 | 8,335.9 | 6,299.9 | — | 242.4 | — | 19,144.6 | 21,351.1 | 19,387.0 | 11,947.6 | 1,410.6 |
| 1993 | 8,659.8 | 6,739.4 | — | 249.8 | — | 20,192.7 | 23,195.3 | 20,442.5 | 12,806.4 | 1,486.7 |
| 1994 | 9,362.8 | 7,214.6 | — | 257.9 | — | 21,244.2 | 24,330.8 | 21,502.1 | 13,636.1 | 1,576.7 |
| 1995 | 10,232.9 | 7,836.2 | — | 267.5 | — | 22,330.0 | 25,504.4 | 22,597.5 | 15,341.4 | 1,693.3 |
| 1996 | 11,086.2 | 8,485.0 | — | 287.1 | — | 23,431.2 | 26,587.2 | 23,718.3 | 16,266.5 | 1,839.8 |
| 1997 | 11,988.7 | 9,313.7 | — | 303.8 | — | 24,898.6 | 28,174.2 | 25,202.5 | 17,529.7 | 2,281.9 |
| 1998 | 12,974.0 | 9,999.8 | 560.0 | 304.7 | 29,043.8 | 27,215.0 | 29,603.8 | 27,519.8 | 18,853.5 | 2,261.3 |
| 1999 | 14,279.3 | 10,949.4 | 547.9 | 293.2 | 30,888.5 | 28,267.8 | 31,436.4 | 28,561.0 | 20,390.6 | 2,506.7 |
| 2000 | 15,458.6 | 11,997.2 | 543.0 | 294.2 | 32,713.7 | 30,014.0 | 33,256.7 | 30,308.2 | 22,089.5 | 2,793.3 |
| 2001 | 16,952.2 | 13,172.4 | 523.1 | 281.3 | 34,823.8 | 32,215.8 | 35,347.0 | 32,497.2 | 23,294.6 | 3,048.3 |
| 2002 | 18,892.4 | 14,376.5 | 511.9 | 256.3 | 37,188.0 | 34,350.0 | 37,699.9 | 34,606.3 | 24,843.7 | 3,311.1 |
| 2003 | 19,760.3 | 15,463.7 | 551.0 | 271.0 | 38,772.3 | 37,104.6 | 39,323.3 | 37,375.6 | 25,756.0 | 3,554.1 |
| 2004 | 20,592.6 | 16,516.0 | 613.5 | 294.1 | 41,033.0 | 39,333.7 | 41,646.5 | 39,627.8 | 26,380.7 | 3,739.7 |
| 2005 | 20,715.0 | 17,553.2 | 455.8 | 314.7 | 42,916.3 | 41,349.7 | 43,372.0 | 41,664.4 | 27,230.6 | 3,914.0 |

*Source:* Reported wages are authors' estimates based on multiplying tax-exempt shares by national total private wages from the U.S. Census Bureau, County Business Patterns (1991–2006). Covered wages are authors' estimates based on multiplying tax-exempt shares by private wages from the U.S. Department of Labor, Bureau of Labor Statistics, Quarterly Census of Employment and Wages (1991–2006). Tax-exempt shares for 611210 and 611310 are employment shares from U.S. Department of Education, National Center for Education Statistics, Integrated Postsecondary Education Data System (2006). Tax-exempt shares for 611110 and 813110 are assumed to be 100 percent.

*Notes:* Industries are listed as classified by the North American Industry Classification System. The column labeled "NAICS 611210 + 611310" is the sum of the two columns to its left, except for 1990–1997 reported wages, when the more detailed breakout was not available.

— = data not available

**Table 2.6.** Wages Reported to the Internal Revenue Service for Two-Digit Industries Whose Tax Status Is Not Identified in the Economic Census, 1998–2005 ($ millions)

| NAICS code | Industry | 1998 | 1999 | 2000 | 2001 | 2002 | 2003 | 2004 | 2005 |
|---|---|---|---|---|---|---|---|---|---|
| 11 | Agriculture, forestry, fishing, and hunting | 213.5 | 221.3 | 218.7 | 248.0 | 271.3 | 264.7 | 252.9 | 282.3 |
| 22 | Utilities | 235.2 | 270.2 | 305.9 | 364.3 | 402.9 | 424.6 | 442.2 | 517.0 |
| 48–49 | Transportation and warehousing | 41.3 | 46.0 | 52.9 | 53.8 | 58.4 | 66.7 | 67.2 | 72.4 |
| 51 | Information | 1,604.3 | 1,753.3 | 1,823.5 | 1,987.0 | 2,022.3 | 2,074.8 | 2,144.6 | 2,299.8 |
| 52 | Finance and insurance | 3,777.8 | 4,097.1 | 4,223.4 | 4,491.6 | 5,037.8 | 5,164.4 | 5,622.3 | 6,349.9 |
| 53 | Real estate and rental and leasing | 86.3 | 81.8 | 86.9 | 93.1 | 96.3 | 94.9 | 101.5 | 114.6 |
| 54 | Professional, scientific, and technical services | 6,038.6 | 6,538.9 | 7,127.5 | 7,533.4 | 8,868.4 | 9,139.9 | 9,548.1 | 10,937.3 |
| 56 | Administrative and waste management services | 530.5 | 569.0 | 563.0 | 575.7 | 613.5 | 641.8 | 627.3 | 603.7 |
| 72 | Accommodation and food services | 156.2 | 180.5 | 193.8 | 216.4 | 236.4 | 247.3 | 259.5 | 271.5 |

*Source:* Urban Institute, National Center for Charitable Statistics, IRS Statistics of Income Form 990 and 990-EZ Sample Files (1998–2006).
*Notes:* Industries are listed as classified by the North American Industry Classification System. Error corrections and missing-data interpolations were performed by the authors. Please see the chapter appendix for a detailed description of the authors' methodology.

**Table 2.7.** Nonprofit Employees Covered by Unemployment Insurance, for Industries Whose Tax Status Is Identified in the Economic Census, 1990–2006

| NAICS code | 61 | 62 | 71 | 81 | |
|---|---|---|---|---|---|
| Industry | Educational services | Health care and social assistance | Arts, entertainment, and recreation | Other services, except government | Total |
| 1990 | 1,096,456 | 4,743,144 | 467,990 | 1,044,464 | 7,352,055 |
| 1991 | 1,103,775 | 4,914,286 | 447,666 | 1,022,204 | 7,487,931 |
| 1992 | 1,112,223 | 5,099,150 | 398,349 | 1,040,952 | 7,650,674 |
| 1993 | 1,128,628 | 5,258,231 | 377,885 | 1,055,754 | 7,820,498 |
| 1994 | 1,128,628 | 5,258,231 | 377,885 | 1,055,754 | 7,820,498 |
| 1995 | 1,188,070 | 5,511,127 | 380,543 | 1,105,635 | 8,185,374 |
| 1996 | 1,231,017 | 5,650,303 | 382,535 | 1,127,386 | 8,391,242 |
| 1997 | 1,275,924 | 5,785,640 | 388,798 | 1,152,111 | 8,602,474 |
| 1998 | 1,331,349 | 5,941,902 | 403,242 | 1,167,192 | 8,843,685 |
| 1999 | 1,374,691 | 6,060,531 | 415,481 | 1,199,868 | 9,050,571 |
| 2000 | 1,420,498 | 6,168,100 | 437,971 | 1,240,964 | 9,267,532 |
| 2001 | 1,474,205 | 6,362,231 | 452,120 | 1,272,986 | 9,561,542 |
| 2002 | 1,526,325 | 6,555,309 | 460,296 | 1,298,571 | 9,840,501 |
| 2003 | 1,580,147 | 6,726,335 | 466,288 | 1,294,493 | 10,067,264 |
| 2004 | 1,625,358 | 6,847,509 | 477,099 | 1,297,155 | 10,247,121 |
| 2005 | 1,669,368 | 6,999,312 | 481,755 | 1,296,363 | 10,446,798 |
| 2006 | 1,718,602 | 7,166,380 | 491,288 | 1,312,405 | 10,688,675 |

*Source:* Authors' estimates largely based on private employment from U.S. Department of Labor, Bureau of Labor Statistics, Quarterly Census of Employment and Wages (1991–2007), and the tax-exempt share of employment from U.S. Census Bureau, Economic Census (1997, 2002).

*Notes:* Industries are listed as classified by the North American Industry Classification System. Industry 54 (professional, scientific, and technical services) is also included in the Economic Census; however, we believe these data are flawed.

- Table 2.14 compares the authors' estimate of employment in all nonprofits with an alternative estimate of employment in public charities only.
- Finally, entities reporting to the IRS are classified according to the NTEE, rather than the NAICS. Table 2.15 shows the NTEE categories comprising each two-digit NAICS industry, as shown in tables 2.6 and 2.9.

**Table 2.8.** Nonprofit Employees Reported to the Census Bureau or Covered by Unemployment Insurance, in Select Industries with Many Employees Exempt from Unemployment Insurance, 1990–2005

| NAICS code | 611110 | | 611210 | | 611310 | | 611210 + 611310 | | 813110 | |
| Industry | Elementary and secondary schools | | Junior colleges | | Colleges, universities, and professional schools | | | | Religious organizations | |
| Employees | Reported | Covered | Reported | Covered | Reported | Covered | Reported | Covered | Reported | Covered |
|---|---|---|---|---|---|---|---|---|---|---|
| 1990 | 451,326 | 329,116 | — | 9,484 | — | 703,830 | 1,023,410 | 713,313 | 1,096,313 | 100,138 |
| 1991 | 469,642 | 336,959 | — | 11,295 | — | 703,183 | 1,061,539 | 714,478 | 1,143,374 | 98,731 |
| 1992 | 524,697 | 341,525 | — | 11,229 | — | 706,590 | 1,108,542 | 717,819 | 1,196,396 | 103,009 |
| 1993 | 538,905 | 356,556 | — | 11,293 | — | 706,009 | 1,152,942 | 717,302 | 1,244,083 | 105,878 |
| 1994 | 563,322 | 356,556 | — | 11,293 | — | 706,009 | 1,167,809 | 717,302 | 1,265,938 | 105,878 |
| 1995 | 588,744 | 389,257 | — | 11,138 | — | 728,292 | 1,182,774 | 739,430 | 1,315,906 | 114,076 |
| 1996 | 609,190 | 405,399 | — | 11,270 | — | 750,446 | 1,190,760 | 761,716 | 1,380,975 | 119,772 |
| 1997 | 639,562 | 424,711 | — | 11,666 | — | 771,413 | 1,224,713 | 783,080 | 1,436,546 | 130,366 |
| 1998 | 659,421 | 444,761 | 22,584 | 11,260 | 1,215,115 | 800,408 | 1,237,698 | 811,668 | 1,469,386 | 135,897 |
| 1999 | 694,749 | 468,747 | 21,013 | 10,213 | 1,242,825 | 811,627 | 1,263,838 | 821,840 | 1,517,882 | 145,352 |
| 2000 | 724,354 | 491,787 | 20,467 | 9,574 | 1,259,745 | 823,716 | 1,280,212 | 833,291 | 1,569,353 | 151,810 |
| 2001 | 747,611 | 513,820 | 18,910 | 9,051 | 1,270,559 | 844,685 | 1,289,468 | 853,736 | 1,595,009 | 159,212 |
| 2002 | 793,638 | 536,094 | 18,304 | 7,836 | 1,300,282 | 865,305 | 1,318,586 | 873,141 | 1,638,915 | 166,785 |
| 2003 | 804,249 | 555,470 | 18,093 | 7,970 | 1,330,471 | 892,532 | 1,348,564 | 900,503 | 1,654,780 | 172,669 |
| 2004 | 808,572 | 570,964 | 18,511 | 8,494 | 1,387,502 | 914,190 | 1,406,013 | 922,684 | 1,649,492 | 175,119 |
| 2005 | 780,883 | 590,152 | 16,314 | 8,879 | 1,397,839 | 929,907 | 1,414,153 | 938,786 | 1,631,943 | 177,104 |

*Sources:* Reported employees are authors' estimates based on multiplying tax-exempt shares by national total private employment from the U.S. Census Bureau, County Business Patterns (1991–2007). Covered employees are authors' estimates based on multiplying tax-exempt shares by private employment from the U.S. Department of Labor, Bureau of Labor Statistics, Quarterly Census of Employment and Wages (1991–2006). Tax-exempt shares for 611210 and 611310 are employment shares from U.S. Department of Education, National Center for Education Statistics, Integrated Postsecondary Education Data System (2006). Tax-exempt shares for 611110 and 813110 are assumed to be 100 percent.
*Notes:* Industries are listed as classified by the North American Industry Classification System. The column labeled "NAICS 611210 + 611310" is the sum of the two columns to its left, except for 1990–1997 reported wages, when the more detailed breakout was not available.
— = data not available

**Table 2.9.** Estimated Employment for Two-Digit Industries Whose Tax Status Is Not Identified in the Economic Census, 1998–2005

| NAICS code | Industry | 1998 | 1999 | 2000 | 2001 | 2002 | 2003 | 2004 | 2005 |
|---|---|---|---|---|---|---|---|---|---|
| 11 | Agriculture, forestry, fishing, and hunting | 11,900 | 11,920 | 11,258 | 12,283 | 12,986 | 12,387 | 11,321 | 12,211 |
| 22 | Utilities | 4,131 | 4,587 | 4,850 | 5,557 | 5,980 | 6,185 | 6,107 | 6,875 |
| 48–49 | Transportation and warehousing | 1,272 | 1,368 | 1,507 | 1,487 | 1,585 | 1,783 | 1,731 | 1,833 |
| 51 | Information | 32,354 | 31,837 | 31,126 | 34,684 | 36,045 | 35,772 | 35,319 | 36,602 |
| 52 | Finance and insurance | 72,829 | 74,655 | 70,222 | 70,526 | 80,269 | 79,507 | 80,171 | 86,548 |
| 53 | Real estate and rental and leasing | 2,986 | 2,731 | 2,732 | 2,831 | 2,838 | 2,707 | 2,722 | 2,910 |
| 54 | Professional, scientific, and technical services | 119,255 | 116,928 | 122,689 | 128,217 | 151,150 | 152,644 | 152,656 | 167,560 |
| 56 | Administrative and waste management services | 25,311 | 26,192 | 24,428 | 23,552 | 24,274 | 24,630 | 23,035 | 21,476 |
| 72 | Accommodation and food services | 12,730 | 14,106 | 14,487 | 15,829 | 16,948 | 17,379 | 17,647 | 17,902 |

*Source:* Authors' estimates based on multiplying the tax-exempt wage share by private employment. Tax-exempt wages by industry are from Urban Institute, National Center for Charitable Statistics, IRS Statistics of Income Form 990 and 990-EZ Sample Files (1998–2006). Private wages and private employment by industry are from U.S. Department of Labor, Bureau of Labor Statistics, Quarterly Census of Employment and Wages (1998–2006).
*Notes:* Industries are listed as classified by the North American Industry Classification System. Limitations of the method of estimating employment are discussed in the appendix for chapter 2.

**Table 2.10.** Nonprofit Wages Covered by Unemployment Insurance, Six-Digit Industries Whose Tax Status Is Identified in the Economic Census, 1990–1997 ($ millions)

| NAICS code | Industry | 1990 | 1991 | 1992 | 1993 | 1994 | 1995 | 1996 | 1997 |
|---|---|---|---|---|---|---|---|---|---|
| 541110 | Offices of lawyers | 607.9 | 621.3 | 663.9 | 677.2 | 694.7 | 713.1 | 743.7 | 791.7 |
| 611110 | Elementary and secondary schools | 5,479.1 | 6,028.1 | 6,299.9 | 6,739.4 | 7,214.6 | 7,836.2 | 8,485.0 | 9,313.7 |
| 611210 | Junior colleges | 182.1 | 230.5 | 242.4 | 249.8 | 257.9 | 267.5 | 287.1 | 303.8 |
| 611310 | Colleges, universities, and professional schools | 16,775.5 | 17,871.9 | 19,144.6 | 20,192.7 | 21,244.2 | 22,330.0 | 23,431.2 | 24,898.6 |
| 611410 | Business and secretarial schools | 25.2 | 21.7 | 20.2 | 18.0 | 17.3 | 16.9 | 16.4 | 16.4 |
| 611420 | Computer training | 2.1 | 2.3 | 2.8 | 3.1 | 3.8 | 5.0 | 6.1 | 7.6 |
| 611430 | Professional and management development training | 112.5 | 118.7 | 137.3 | 143.3 | 154.7 | 168.8 | 201.5 | 221.5 |
| 611511 | Cosmetology and barber schools | 6.2 | 6.3 | 6.0 | 5.9 | 5.5 | 5.3 | 5.2 | 4.8 |
| 611512 | Flight training | 7.4 | 7.1 | 6.6 | 6.1 | 6.5 | 6.6 | 6.6 | 7.5 |
| 611513 | Apprenticeship training | 174.2 | 157.4 | 140.5 | 127.0 | 121.8 | 120.2 | 125.9 | 136.6 |
| 611519 | Other technical and trade schools | 118.7 | 131.8 | 139.9 | 148.6 | 150.6 | 160.4 | 180.5 | 208.3 |
| 611610 | Fine arts schools | 119.3 | 120.3 | 127.5 | 134.2 | 150.1 | 162.5 | 182.0 | 187.1 |
| 611620 | Sports and recreation instruction | 26.6 | 27.9 | 31.2 | 35.7 | 39.7 | 43.4 | 48.8 | 49.9 |
| 611630 | Language schools | 19.6 | 22.2 | 25.5 | 27.3 | 29.6 | 31.6 | 36.2 | 40.1 |
| 611691 | Exam preparation and tutoring | 21.8 | 22.7 | 25.1 | 27.5 | 29.9 | 32.8 | 37.9 | 43.8 |
| 611692 | Automobile driving schools | 5.6 | 5.5 | 5.6 | 5.8 | 6.2 | 6.6 | 6.9 | 7.4 |
| 611699 | All other miscellaneous schools and instruction | 86.3 | 95.0 | 100.4 | 114.4 | 125.0 | 133.8 | 152.6 | 176.0 |
| 611710 | Educational support services | 267.6 | 298.1 | 329.5 | 348.0 | 359.6 | 386.4 | 458.4 | 524.2 |
| 621410 | Family planning centers | 233.3 | 264.5 | 326.4 | 359.0 | 384.1 | 408.2 | 425.6 | 449.6 |
| 621420 | Outpatient mental health and substance abuse centers | 1,323.1 | 1,433.7 | 1,563.7 | 1,729.6 | 1,918.0 | 2,087.7 | 2,252.0 | 2,428.0 |
| 621491 | HMO medical centers | 2,259.0 | 2,359.2 | 2,450.9 | 2,418.4 | 2,570.1 | 2,738.2 | 2,828.8 | 2,716.7 |
| 621492 | Kidney dialysis centers | 87.6 | 104.4 | 124.1 | 140.6 | 153.6 | 172.8 | 193.3 | 223.8 |
| 621493 | Freestanding ambulatory surgical and emergency centers | 223.9 | 305.1 | 337.6 | 338.3 | 359.6 | 399.5 | 410.2 | 413.3 |
| 621498 | All other outpatient care centers | 795.4 | 759.6 | 909.3 | 1,004.3 | 1,134.4 | 1,182.4 | 1,238.6 | 1,300.3 |
| 621610 | Home health care services | 1,571.1 | 2,017.0 | 2,531.0 | 3,036.5 | 3,505.5 | 4,048.8 | 4,387.2 | 4,659.6 |

| Code | Industry | | | | | | | | |
|---|---|---|---|---|---|---|---|---|---|
| 621910 | Ambulance services | 133.0 | 150.6 | 164.6 | 177.2 | 199.2 | 224.1 | 260.3 | 291.0 |
| 621991 | Blood and organ banks | 506.0 | 561.5 | 621.1 | 703.4 | 777.3 | 825.7 | 840.3 | 892.3 |
| 621999 | All other miscellaneous ambulatory health care services | 25.2 | 27.7 | 31.7 | 34.7 | 41.7 | 42.8 | 52.1 | 58.9 |
| 622110 | General medical and surgical hospitals | 66,593.5 | 72,642.9 | 79,336.9 | 82,521.6 | 85,654.6 | 89,020.9 | 92,771.0 | 97,613.1 |
| 622210 | Psychiatric and substance abuse hospitals | 1,092.2 | 1,168.0 | 1,199.6 | 1,153.4 | 1,139.2 | 1,133.4 | 1,089.3 | 1,094.1 |
| 622310 | Specialty (except psychiatric and substance abuse) hospitals | 1,775.6 | 1,987.7 | 2,242.8 | 2,406.1 | 2,479.1 | 2,627.8 | 2,848.7 | 3,048.4 |
| 623110 | Nursing care facilities | 4,213.8 | 4,678.5 | 5,192.0 | 5,562.5 | 6,007.1 | 6,500.0 | 6,923.7 | 7,311.3 |
| 623210 | Residential mental retardation facilities | 1,869.1 | 2,120.3 | 2,302.8 | 2,399.0 | 2,533.1 | 2,750.8 | 2,930.6 | 3,161.9 |
| 623220 | Residential mental health and substance abuse facilities | 1,003.6 | 1,113.8 | 1,173.1 | 1,255.5 | 1,332.3 | 1,464.0 | 1,558.0 | 1,692.6 |
| 623311 | Continuing care retirement communities | 1,728.8 | 1,936.6 | 2,055.7 | 2,165.7 | 2,249.1 | 2,366.8 | 2,526.0 | 2,635.7 |
| 623312 | Homes for the elderly | 554.5 | 617.8 | 677.6 | 722.5 | 778.0 | 829.2 | 978.0 | 1,034.8 |
| 623990 | Other residential care facilities | 1,221.7 | 1,344.8 | 1,511.8 | 1,636.3 | 1,751.1 | 1,960.5 | 2,129.6 | 2,324.1 |
| 624110 | Child and youth services | 976.4 | 1,077.9 | 1,221.0 | 1,336.7 | 1,490.1 | 1,651.7 | 1,811.9 | 2,018.7 |
| 624120 | Services for the elderly and persons with disabilities | 2,085.3 | 2,270.2 | 2,554.6 | 2,712.7 | 2,907.9 | 3,028.3 | 3,161.4 | 3,332.5 |
| 624190 | Other individual and family services | 1,992.6 | 2,180.7 | 2,405.7 | 2,653.1 | 2,892.1 | 3,203.4 | 3,453.0 | 3,732.4 |
| 624210 | Community food services | 269.6 | 346.8 | 380.4 | 398.7 | 424.1 | 426.4 | 415.0 | 391.5 |
| 624221 | Temporary shelters | 268.5 | 318.7 | 389.5 | 418.2 | 474.0 | 532.6 | 557.1 | 608.2 |
| 624229 | Other community housing services | 127.4 | 152.5 | 167.1 | 190.9 | 229.3 | 257.0 | 273.5 | 304.2 |
| 624230 | Emergency and other relief services | 534.3 | 491.1 | 505.5 | 477.4 | 476.1 | 499.0 | 513.2 | 522.6 |
| 624310 | Vocational rehabilitation services | 2,405.5 | 2,548.6 | 2,731.3 | 2,935.8 | 3,109.8 | 3,290.1 | 3,428.4 | 3,704.7 |
| 624410 | Child day care services | 1,537.3 | 1,736.4 | 1,945.5 | 2,163.8 | 2,398.3 | 2,624.5 | 2,814.7 | 3,088.2 |
| 711110 | Theater companies and dinner theaters | 1,792.9 | 1,703.2 | 1,302.6 | 1,066.0 | 991.4 | 907.5 | 856.5 | 794.2 |
| 711120 | Dance companies | 132.0 | 141.0 | 147.9 | 157.1 | 160.7 | 181.2 | 183.3 | 182.7 |
| 711130 | Musical groups and artists | 415.4 | 430.1 | 465.1 | 495.1 | 494.2 | 528.5 | 555.6 | 602.3 |
| 711190 | Other performing arts companies | 3.4 | 3.7 | 3.6 | 4.2 | 5.9 | 6.9 | 6.5 | 7.3 |
| 711310 | Promoters of performing arts, sports, and similar events with facilities | 275.3 | 256.5 | 224.2 | 249.3 | 277.3 | 321.2 | 350.2 | 346.5 |

*(continued)*

**Table 2.10.** Nonprofit Wages Covered by Unemployment Insurance, Six-Digit Industries Whose Tax Status Is Identified in the Economic Census, 1990–1997 ($ millions) *(continued)*

| NAICS code | Industry | 1990 | 1991 | 1992 | 1993 | 1994 | 1995 | 1996 | 1997 |
|---|---|---|---|---|---|---|---|---|---|
| 711320 | Promoters of performing arts, sports, and similar events without facilities | 44.4 | 38.4 | 43.0 | 44.4 | 48.8 | 56.6 | 60.4 | 62.4 |
| 712110 | Museums | 717.9 | 745.7 | 799.4 | 847.4 | 900.2 | 946.4 | 1,143.1 | 1,121.4 |
| 712120 | Historical sites | 127.3 | 132.3 | 133.9 | 135.0 | 168.2 | 169.9 | 192.4 | 199.6 |
| 712130 | Zoos and botanical gardens | 220.9 | 228.4 | 271.5 | 294.2 | 304.1 | 328.2 | 351.5 | 382.3 |
| 712190 | Nature parks and other similar institutions | 28.4 | 28.7 | 29.2 | 33.7 | 38.1 | 44.1 | 45.6 | 49.5 |
| 713910 | Golf courses and country clubs | 999.6 | 1,096.3 | 1,191.9 | 1,261.7 | 1,368.9 | 1,471.1 | 1,573.5 | 1,718.0 |
| 713940 | Fitness and recreational sports centers | 817.6 | 836.2 | 893.5 | 930.2 | 979.9 | 1,042.0 | 1,123.5 | 1,229.8 |
| 713990 | All other amusement and recreation industries | 129.8 | 139.0 | 152.5 | 167.5 | 188.0 | 198.6 | 215.1 | 232.5 |
| 813110 | Religious organizations | 1,297.7 | 1,317.1 | 1,410.6 | 1,486.7 | 1,576.7 | 1,693.3 | 1,839.8 | 2,281.9 |
| 813211 | Grantmaking foundations | 594.6 | 640.3 | 702.9 | 781.1 | 824.9 | 905.5 | 991.2 | 1,077.9 |
| 813212 | Voluntary health organizations | 579.7 | 552.8 | 588.2 | 621.8 | 773.1 | 833.4 | 884.3 | 912.4 |
| 813219 | Other grantmaking and giving services | 737.0 | 761.1 | 836.3 | 857.6 | 896.2 | 944.4 | 1,001.4 | 1,096.3 |
| 813311 | Human rights organizations | 523.5 | 556.5 | 601.8 | 628.3 | 662.3 | 699.6 | 746.2 | 782.6 |
| 813312 | Environment, conservation, and wildlife organizations | 388.7 | 353.5 | 366.5 | 371.0 | 390.7 | 423.9 | 446.7 | 486.1 |
| 813319 | Other social advocacy organizations | 872.4 | 883.7 | 963.6 | 1,037.9 | 1,129.3 | 1,230.9 | 1,295.1 | 1,400.7 |
| 813410 | Civic and social organizations | 3,630.6 | 3,823.6 | 4,034.7 | 4,206.4 | 4,490.5 | 4,719.2 | 4,831.2 | 5,047.5 |
| 813910 | Business associations | 3,004.9 | 3,174.8 | 3,374.5 | 3,526.6 | 3,686.4 | 3,900.3 | 4,096.2 | 4,307.3 |
| 813920 | Professional organizations | 1,596.8 | 1,694.1 | 1,808.3 | 1,918.2 | 2,030.6 | 2,149.9 | 2,309.6 | 2,475.2 |
| 813930 | Labor unions and similar labor organizations | 2,367.3 | 2,488.2 | 2,570.1 | 2,603.6 | 2,657.1 | 2,733.0 | 2,851.3 | 2,987.9 |
| 813940 | Political organizations | 143.9 | 100.8 | 163.5 | 120.7 | 194.0 | 140.0 | 217.4 | 143.7 |
| 813990 | Other similar organizations (except business, professional, labor, and political organizations) | 1,212.2 | 1,299.4 | 1,368.9 | 1,373.6 | 1,393.1 | 1,428.4 | 1,492.1 | 1,571.6 |

*Source:* Authors' estimates based on private wages from U.S. Department of Labor, Bureau of Labor Statistics, Quarterly Census of Employment and Wages (1991–1996) and the tax-exempt share of wages from U.S. Census Bureau, Economic Census (1997, 2002).

*Notes:* Industries are listed as classified by the North American Industry Classification System. Industries 541710 (physical, engineering, and biological research services) and 541720 (research and development in the social sciences and humanities) are also included in the Economic Census; however, we believe these data are flawed.

**Table 2.11.** Nonprofit Wages Covered by Unemployment Insurance, Six-Digit Industries Whose Tax Status Is Identified in the Economic Census, 1998–2006 ($ millions)

| NAICS code | Industry | 1998 | 1999 | 2000 | 2001 | 2002 | 2003 | 2004 | 2005 | 2006 |
|---|---|---|---|---|---|---|---|---|---|---|
| 541110 | Offices of lawyers | 848.7 | 892.6 | 968.0 | 1,029.6 | 1,056.5 | 1,106.9 | 1,164.8 | 1,213.2 | 1,277.0 |
| 611110 | Elementary and secondary schools | 9,999.8 | 10,949.4 | 11,997.2 | 13,172.4 | 14,376.5 | 15,463.7 | 16,516.0 | 17,553.2 | 18,865.1 |
| 611210 | Junior colleges | 304.7 | 293.2 | 294.2 | 281.3 | 256.3 | 271.0 | 294.1 | 314.7 | 317.1 |
| 611310 | Colleges, universities, and professional schools | 27,215.0 | 28,267.8 | 30,014.0 | 32,215.8 | 34,350.0 | 37,104.6 | 39,333.7 | 41,349.7 | 43,942.3 |
| 611410 | Business and secretarial schools | 20.0 | 24.6 | 30.3 | 36.4 | 43.3 | 42.7 | 46.1 | 45.7 | 42.9 |
| 611420 | Computer training | 13.4 | 20.8 | 30.2 | 34.0 | 32.4 | 28.3 | 28.2 | 29.4 | 29.0 |
| 611430 | Professional and management development training | 265.3 | 293.0 | 346.8 | 366.0 | 371.3 | 403.3 | 421.3 | 462.4 | 514.9 |
| 611511 | Cosmetology and barber schools | 5.9 | 7.1 | 8.7 | 10.9 | 13.8 | 14.5 | 16.3 | 17.5 | 19.3 |
| 611512 | Flight training | 8.9 | 9.9 | 11.0 | 11.2 | 9.9 | 9.2 | 9.0 | 9.7 | 10.2 |
| 611513 | Apprenticeship training | 149.9 | 174.6 | 200.1 | 228.3 | 269.1 | 289.5 | 319.9 | 344.1 | 372.8 |
| 611519 | Other technical and trade schools | 238.7 | 256.5 | 273.6 | 308.9 | 336.4 | 363.7 | 361.0 | 380.1 | 401.6 |
| 611610 | Fine arts schools | 202.6 | 230.3 | 256.9 | 291.0 | 323.7 | 333.0 | 340.6 | 361.9 | 391.4 |
| 611620 | Sports and recreation instruction | 58.1 | 67.9 | 82.3 | 99.5 | 121.0 | 130.6 | 146.8 | 158.9 | 174.0 |
| 611630 | Language schools | 46.9 | 52.7 | 59.2 | 66.3 | 65.2 | 67.1 | 68.5 | 63.2 | 65.2 |
| 611691 | Exam preparation and tutoring | 64.3 | 87.3 | 123.2 | 153.6 | 175.5 | 191.5 | 210.9 | 239.2 | 262.5 |

*(continued)*

**Table 2.11.** Nonprofit Wages Covered by Unemployment Insurance, Six-Digit Industries Whose Tax Status Is Identified in the Economic Census, 1998–2006 ($ millions) *(continued)*

| NAICS code | Industry | 1998 | 1999 | 2000 | 2001 | 2002 | 2003 | 2004 | 2005 | 2006 |
|---|---|---|---|---|---|---|---|---|---|---|
| 611692 | Automobile driving schools | 9.5 | 11.4 | 14.8 | 18.5 | 21.8 | 21.2 | 22.0 | 22.7 | 24.9 |
| 611699 | All other miscellaneous schools and instruction | 199.6 | 247.6 | 299.1 | 366.4 | 413.4 | 436.8 | 437.2 | 498.7 | 571.8 |
| 611710 | Educational support services | 507.7 | 658.8 | 639.2 | 734.4 | 814.3 | 909.4 | 1,072.5 | 1,225.9 | 1,424.1 |
| 621410 | Family planning centers | 457.6 | 459.6 | 472.4 | 494.6 | 523.0 | 506.9 | 499.8 | 473.2 | 602.7 |
| 621420 | Outpatient mental health and substance abuse centers | 2,627.7 | 2,706.6 | 2,882.9 | 3,104.7 | 3,338.4 | 3,563.5 | 3,808.3 | 4,099.5 | 4,309.2 |
| 621491 | HMO medical centers | 2,581.5 | 2,394.9 | 2,280.9 | 2,304.0 | 2,340.5 | 2,636.4 | 2,924.7 | 3,231.5 | 3,636.7 |
| 621492 | Kidney dialysis centers | 243.2 | 245.7 | 263.6 | 292.2 | 308.4 | 326.3 | 355.5 | 382.0 | 434.8 |
| 621493 | Freestanding ambulatory surgical and emergency centers | 398.8 | 376.5 | 402.0 | 420.3 | 444.7 | 476.7 | 515.0 | 551.8 | 626.4 |
| 621498 | All other outpatient care centers | 1,425.0 | 1,472.0 | 1,565.5 | 1,711.2 | 1,752.9 | 2,001.1 | 2,235.0 | 2,717.8 | 2,969.1 |
| 621610 | Home health care services | 4,445.1 | 4,078.2 | 4,246.3 | 4,520.9 | 5,060.2 | 5,565.4 | 6,217.1 | 6,824.8 | 7,593.2 |
| 621910 | Ambulance services | 342.9 | 388.8 | 454.0 | 528.3 | 615.6 | 681.5 | 743.0 | 819.5 | 888.5 |
| 621991 | Blood and organ banks | 996.3 | 1,049.6 | 1,163.1 | 1,324.8 | 1,486.0 | 1,630.8 | 1,686.5 | 1,767.1 | 1,909.1 |
| 621999 | All other miscellaneous ambulatory health care services | 70.2 | 73.5 | 86.3 | 96.5 | 109.5 | 110.7 | 114.1 | 121.9 | 134.8 |
| 622110 | General medical and surgical hospitals | 103,905.7 | 108,306.1 | 113,633.2 | 122,564.8 | 132,413.3 | 142,833.7 | 152,593.3 | 160,706.7 | 171,038.5 |
| 622210 | Psychiatric and substance abuse hospitals | 1,161.1 | 1,218.4 | 1,238.8 | 1,367.4 | 1,492.1 | 1,581.4 | 1,682.4 | 1,742.8 | 1,857.4 |

| | | | | | | | | | | |
|---|---|---|---|---|---|---|---|---|---|---|
| 622310 | Specialty (except psychiatric and substance abuse) hospitals | 3,180.3 | 3,147.4 | 3,155.9 | 3,356.1 | 3,558.4 | 3,989.1 | 4,172.2 | 4,498.2 | 4,896.1 |
| 623110 | Nursing care facilities | 7,835.5 | 8,154.4 | 8,692.6 | 9,402.5 | 10,064.8 | 10,378.8 | 10,808.0 | 11,111.8 | 11,671.3 |
| 623210 | Residential mental retardation facilities | 3,427.2 | 3,753.1 | 4,114.9 | 4,506.9 | 4,797.6 | 4,921.4 | 5,081.5 | 5,200.9 | 5,459.5 |
| 623220 | Residential mental health and substance abuse facilities | 1,886.3 | 2,049.7 | 2,235.6 | 2,459.9 | 2,625.5 | 2,800.2 | 2,936.5 | 3,097.2 | 3,339.3 |
| 623311 | Continuing care retirement communities | 2,734.7 | 2,770.8 | 2,971.7 | 3,173.0 | 3,484.1 | 4,028.7 | 4,465.4 | 4,856.3 | 5,302.5 |
| 623312 | Homes for the elderly | 1,084.6 | 1,133.7 | 1,202.2 | 1,218.0 | 1,205.3 | 1,244.4 | 1,285.8 | 1,347.2 | 1,413.8 |
| 623990 | Other residential care facilities | 2,533.9 | 2,786.5 | 3,030.4 | 3,273.3 | 3,411.6 | 3,490.2 | 3,603.4 | 3,635.5 | 3,745.5 |
| 624110 | Child and youth services | 2,182.1 | 2,412.0 | 2,679.4 | 3,001.2 | 3,169.9 | 3,376.6 | 3,473.1 | 3,566.6 | 3,835.1 |
| 624120 | Services for the elderly and persons with disabilities | 3,546.0 | 3,919.2 | 4,016.1 | 4,323.3 | 4,722.8 | 5,298.7 | 5,839.7 | 6,443.5 | 7,231.7 |
| 624190 | Other individual and family services | 4,112.3 | 4,545.4 | 5,102.1 | 5,760.3 | 6,270.7 | 6,597.7 | 6,955.2 | 7,410.4 | 7,972.7 |
| 624210 | Community food services | 431.1 | 460.9 | 513.7 | 565.6 | 546.3 | 559.8 | 567.2 | 572.3 | 589.0 |
| 624221 | Temporary shelters | 696.8 | 776.1 | 853.5 | 959.9 | 1,064.5 | 1,127.0 | 1,188.6 | 1,246.2 | 1,310.0 |
| 624229 | Other community housing services | 343.8 | 387.2 | 431.4 | 456.0 | 529.3 | 582.5 | 614.6 | 661.2 | 727.7 |
| 624230 | Emergency and other relief services | 571.4 | 631.3 | 696.2 | 770.7 | 851.0 | 835.5 | 912.4 | 915.2 | 963.4 |
| 624310 | Vocational rehabilitation services | 3,996.2 | 4,305.9 | 4,636.8 | 5,009.1 | 5,255.2 | 5,367.6 | 5,542.5 | 5,566.6 | 5,773.1 |
| 624410 | Child day care services | 3,425.9 | 3,771.8 | 4,171.4 | 4,606.9 | 4,933.2 | 5,131.7 | 5,326.9 | 5,580.4 | 5,914.1 |
| 711110 | Theater companies and dinner theaters | 808.2 | 795.5 | 874.8 | 926.3 | 954.4 | 962.2 | 1,002.5 | 990.1 | 1,049.1 |
| 711120 | Dance companies | 195.1 | 184.3 | 199.7 | 211.7 | 216.2 | 227.8 | 241.5 | 243.9 | 259.2 |

*(continued)*

**Table 2.11.** Nonprofit Wages Covered by Unemployment Insurance, Six-Digit Industries Whose Tax Status Is Identified in the Economic Census, 1998–2006 ($ millions) *(continued)*

| NAICS code | Industry | 1998 | 1999 | 2000 | 2001 | 2002 | 2003 | 2004 | 2005 | 2006 |
|---|---|---|---|---|---|---|---|---|---|---|
| 711130 | Musical groups and artists | 646.4 | 729.7 | 839.4 | 881.0 | 866.7 | 1,024.4 | 974.0 | 988.4 | 1,135.5 |
| 711190 | Other performing arts companies | 8.4 | 8.6 | 11.1 | 11.1 | 10.4 | 12.0 | 13.1 | 13.4 | 14.8 |
| 711310 | Promoters of performing arts, sports, and similar events with facilities | 407.8 | 496.4 | 471.5 | 494.1 | 501.5 | 543.3 | 600.6 | 638.8 | 725.4 |
| 711320 | Promoters of performing arts, sports, and similar events without facilities | 78.0 | 100.8 | 144.1 | 176.5 | 207.5 | 183.8 | 180.0 | 198.7 | 198.6 |
| 712110 | Museums | 1,243.2 | 1,350.5 | 1,483.8 | 1,619.4 | 1,677.4 | 1,733.2 | 1,799.4 | 1,894.9 | 2,012.2 |
| 712120 | Historical sites | 205.5 | 234.6 | 268.8 | 285.6 | 273.0 | 278.8 | 298.1 | 300.3 | 313.5 |
| 712130 | Zoos and botanical gardens | 418.9 | 475.8 | 508.0 | 546.9 | 561.1 | 593.4 | 634.0 | 662.0 | 710.2 |
| 712190 | Nature parks and other similar institutions | 55.3 | 61.4 | 70.1 | 80.3 | 86.3 | 92.5 | 89.8 | 91.0 | 91.2 |
| 713910 | Golf courses and country clubs | 1,864.8 | 1,995.4 | 2,176.9 | 2,278.2 | 2,399.2 | 2,575.1 | 2,811.4 | 2,966.5 | 3,132.7 |
| 713940 | Fitness and recreational sports centers | 1,384.4 | 1,425.6 | 1,540.7 | 1,643.5 | 1,684.7 | 1,716.1 | 1,768.8 | 1,828.5 | 1,903.7 |
| 713990 | All other amusement and recreation industries | 268.8 | 284.0 | 308.8 | 326.7 | 341.9 | 348.7 | 361.3 | 369.4 | 394.5 |

| | | | | | | | | | | |
|---|---|---|---|---|---|---|---|---|---|---|
| 813110 | Religious organizations | 2,261.3 | 2,506.7 | 2,793.3 | 3,048.3 | 3,311.1 | 3,554.1 | 3,739.7 | 3,914.0 | 4,169.7 |
| 813211 | Grantmaking foundations | 1,198.6 | 1,330.7 | 1,476.0 | 1,664.9 | 1,852.2 | 1,870.8 | 1,905.5 | 2,036.4 | 2,213.0 |
| 813212 | Voluntary health organizations | 969.4 | 995.2 | 1,101.5 | 1,254.4 | 1,318.2 | 1,395.3 | 1,420.4 | 1,491.0 | 1,591.8 |
| 813219 | Other grantmaking and giving services | 1,053.3 | 1,140.4 | 1,264.0 | 1,389.0 | 1,432.4 | 1,455.8 | 1,451.8 | 1,471.1 | 1,499.4 |
| 813311 | Human rights organizations | 872.5 | 948.9 | 1,018.6 | 1,113.0 | 1,185.3 | 1,240.1 | 1,300.7 | 1,334.4 | 1,404.6 |
| 813312 | Environment, conservation, and wildlife organizations | 528.3 | 587.8 | 658.4 | 732.0 | 821.8 | 952.9 | 1,071.4 | 1,179.4 | 1,265.7 |
| 813319 | Other social advocacy organizations | 1,513.6 | 1,675.4 | 1,891.2 | 2,127.5 | 2,340.1 | 2,405.5 | 2,510.8 | 2,671.2 | 2,806.4 |
| 813410 | Civic and social organizations | 4,781.5 | 5,050.9 | 5,452.9 | 5,846.9 | 6,060.0 | 6,103.3 | 6,162.0 | 6,297.6 | 6,525.7 |
| 813910 | Business associations | 4,612.4 | 4,890.2 | 5,148.7 | 5,468.3 | 5,632.0 | 5,840.2 | 6,110.1 | 6,464.9 | 6,854.7 |
| 813920 | Professional organizations | 2,710.1 | 2,906.4 | 3,163.9 | 3,482.7 | 3,697.6 | 3,841.0 | 4,083.2 | 4,157.4 | 4,349.7 |
| 813930 | Labor unions and similar labor organizations | 3,098.9 | 3,224.6 | 3,397.5 | 3,571.7 | 3,721.2 | 3,854.4 | 3,933.2 | 3,968.1 | 4,121.4 |
| 813940 | Political organizations | 211.9 | 177.6 | 259.4 | 202.3 | 316.6 | 233.3 | 378.0 | 254.6 | 413.6 |
| 813990 | Other similar organizations (except business, professional, labor, and political organizations) | 1,688.8 | 1,772.1 | 1,885.6 | 1,986.9 | 2,118.0 | 2,265.3 | 2,511.2 | 2,675.8 | 2,869.2 |

*Source:* Authors' estimates based on private wages from U.S. Department of Labor, Bureau of Labor Statistics, Quarterly Census of Employment and Wages (1998–2007) and the tax-exempt share of wages from U.S. Census Bureau, Economic Census (1997, 2002).

*Notes:* Industries are listed as classified by the North American Industry Classification System. Industries 541710 (physical, engineering, and biological research services) and 541720 (research and development in the social sciences and humanities) are also included in the Economic Census; however, we believe these data are flawed.

**Table 2.12.** Nonprofit Employment Covered by Unemployment Insurance, Six-Digit Industries Whose Tax Status Is Identified in the Economic Census, 1990–1997

| NAICS code | Industry | 1990 | 1991 | 1992 | 1993 | 1994 | 1995 | 1996 | 1997 |
|---|---|---|---|---|---|---|---|---|---|
| 541110 | Offices of lawyers | 21,966 | 21,648 | 21,771 | 21,962 | 21,962 | 21,946 | 22,070 | 22,482 |
| 611110 | Elementary and secondary schools | 329,116 | 336,959 | 341,525 | 356,556 | 356,556 | 389,257 | 405,399 | 424,711 |
| 611210 | Junior colleges | 9,484 | 11,295 | 11,229 | 11,293 | 11,293 | 11,138 | 11,270 | 11,666 |
| 611310 | Colleges, universities, and professional schools | 703,830 | 703,183 | 706,590 | 706,009 | 706,009 | 728,292 | 750,446 | 771,413 |
| 611410 | Business and secretarial schools | 1,424 | 1,163 | 1,031 | 902 | 902 | 803 | 736 | 738 |
| 611420 | Computer training | 129 | 126 | 140 | 157 | 157 | 226 | 260 | 307 |
| 611430 | Professional and management development training | 5,429 | 5,301 | 5,664 | 6,007 | 6,007 | 6,417 | 6,857 | 7,302 |
| 611511 | Cosmetology and barber schools | 691 | 653 | 578 | 530 | 530 | 460 | 441 | 401 |
| 611512 | Flight training | 441 | 411 | 375 | 347 | 347 | 352 | 336 | 354 |
| 611513 | Apprenticeship training | 9,924 | 8,019 | 6,952 | 6,365 | 6,365 | 5,550 | 5,575 | 5,903 |
| 611519 | Other technical and trade schools | 5,923 | 5,839 | 5,840 | 6,038 | 6,038 | 6,365 | 6,833 | 7,255 |
| 611610 | Fine arts schools | 8,514 | 8,504 | 8,846 | 9,236 | 9,236 | 10,395 | 10,949 | 11,407 |
| 611620 | Sports and recreation instruction | 2,791 | 2,823 | 3,050 | 3,446 | 3,446 | 4,128 | 4,357 | 4,512 |
| 611630 | Language schools | 1,964 | 2,212 | 2,444 | 2,606 | 2,606 | 2,869 | 3,138 | 3,395 |
| 611691 | Exam preparation and tutoring | 1,700 | 1,686 | 1,859 | 2,109 | 2,109 | 2,528 | 2,835 | 3,232 |
| 611692 | Automobile driving schools | 287 | 295 | 309 | 326 | 326 | 360 | 370 | 394 |
| 611699 | All other miscellaneous schools and instruction | 5,216 | 5,550 | 5,677 | 6,115 | 6,115 | 6,897 | 7,565 | 8,195 |
| 611710 | Educational support services | 9,595 | 9,756 | 10,114 | 10,589 | 10,589 | 12,031 | 13,648 | 14,739 |
| 621410 | Family planning centers | 12,426 | 14,170 | 15,925 | 16,636 | 16,636 | 17,839 | 18,183 | 18,647 |

| Code | Industry | | | | | | | | |
|---|---|---|---|---|---|---|---|---|---|
| 621420 | Outpatient mental health and substance abuse centers | 67,942 | 70,394 | 73,697 | 79,869 | 79,869 | 91,778 | 95,639 | 99,845 |
| 621491 | HMO medical centers | 64,728 | 64,325 | 63,579 | 61,342 | 61,342 | 64,050 | 65,014 | 62,768 |
| 621492 | Kidney dialysis centers | 3,905 | 4,348 | 4,716 | 5,153 | 5,153 | 6,067 | 6,656 | 7,478 |
| 621493 | Freestanding ambulatory surgical and emergency centers | 6,064 | 7,914 | 8,536 | 8,549 | 8,549 | 9,889 | 10,143 | 10,026 |
| 621498 | All other outpatient care centers | 33,145 | 29,918 | 33,376 | 35,409 | 35,409 | 38,298 | 39,176 | 39,993 |
| 621610 | Home health care services | 97,775 | 115,149 | 132,902 | 151,272 | 151,272 | 189,312 | 201,104 | 209,433 |
| 621910 | Ambulance services | 10,452 | 11,236 | 11,707 | 12,375 | 12,375 | 14,490 | 16,215 | 17,570 |
| 621991 | Blood and organ banks | 24,607 | 24,587 | 25,891 | 28,543 | 28,543 | 31,268 | 30,950 | 31,341 |
| 621999 | All other miscellaneous ambulatory health care services | 1,087 | 1,123 | 1,168 | 1,257 | 1,257 | 1,476 | 1,655 | 1,819 |
| 622110 | General medical and surgical hospitals | 2,773,154 | 2,848,696 | 2,924,663 | 2,972,007 | 2,972,007 | 2,991,660 | 3,049,298 | 3,103,347 |
| 622210 | Psychiatric and substance abuse hospitals | 45,923 | 46,656 | 45,277 | 43,059 | 43,059 | 39,652 | 37,561 | 36,060 |
| 622310 | Specialty (except psychiatric and substance abuse) hospitals | 64,735 | 68,780 | 73,905 | 76,683 | 76,683 | 79,929 | 84,915 | 89,041 |
| 623110 | Nursing care facilities | 309,098 | 320,558 | 335,935 | 347,769 | 347,769 | 370,478 | 380,673 | 384,409 |
| 623210 | Residential mental retardation facilities | 134,389 | 145,844 | 152,179 | 155,688 | 155,688 | 172,990 | 178,882 | 185,242 |
| 623220 | Residential mental health and substance abuse facilities | 65,079 | 68,688 | 68,441 | 71,624 | 71,624 | 78,304 | 80,551 | 84,517 |
| 623311 | Continuing care retirement communities | 130,789 | 138,843 | 138,398 | 141,377 | 141,377 | 144,261 | 147,885 | 147,151 |
| 623312 | Homes for the elderly | 39,615 | 42,657 | 45,222 | 47,705 | 47,705 | 52,181 | 56,737 | 60,633 |
| 623990 | Other residential care facilities | 77,107 | 80,297 | 87,582 | 92,840 | 92,840 | 106,393 | 111,835 | 117,640 |
| 624110 | Child and youth services | 66,429 | 70,448 | 76,815 | 83,340 | 83,340 | 96,548 | 100,864 | 104,380 |
| 624120 | Services for the elderly and persons with disabilities | 154,189 | 163,889 | 175,504 | 185,678 | 185,678 | 200,822 | 207,651 | 215,974 |
| 624190 | Other individual and family services | 133,295 | 136,903 | 144,449 | 156,107 | 156,107 | 180,086 | 188,013 | 196,671 |

(continued)

**Table 2.12.** Nonprofit Employment Covered by Unemployment Insurance, Six-Digit Industries Whose Tax Status Is Identified in the Economic Census, 1990–1997 *(continued)*

| NAICS code | Industry | 1990 | 1991 | 1992 | 1993 | 1994 | 1995 | 1996 | 1997 |
|---|---|---|---|---|---|---|---|---|---|
| 624210 | Community food services | 21,714 | 25,692 | 26,923 | 27,969 | 27,969 | 28,205 | 27,501 | 25,799 |
| 624221 | Temporary shelters | 19,603 | 22,262 | 26,180 | 27,615 | 27,615 | 32,855 | 33,245 | 35,166 |
| 624229 | Other community housing services | 8,565 | 9,789 | 10,270 | 11,360 | 11,360 | 14,014 | 14,437 | 15,521 |
| 624230 | Emergency and other relief services | 30,906 | 27,212 | 26,690 | 24,760 | 24,760 | 23,181 | 23,120 | 22,904 |
| 624310 | Vocational rehabilitation services | 197,099 | 195,323 | 200,145 | 209,162 | 209,162 | 228,526 | 228,719 | 238,753 |
| 624410 | Child day care services | 149,323 | 158,585 | 169,072 | 183,081 | 183,081 | 206,577 | 213,679 | 223,511 |
| 711110 | Theater companies and dinner theaters | 200,771 | 180,382 | 124,457 | 92,607 | 92,607 | 67,841 | 57,630 | 48,386 |
| 711120 | Dance companies | 4,836 | 5,113 | 5,025 | 5,193 | 5,193 | 5,409 | 5,386 | 5,794 |
| 711130 | Musical groups and artists | 27,906 | 25,846 | 24,990 | 26,236 | 26,236 | 27,435 | 27,164 | 27,374 |
| 711190 | Other performing arts companies | 238 | 285 | 285 | 285 | 285 | 316 | 370 | 406 |
| 711310 | Promoters of performing arts, sports, and similar events with facilities | 13,503 | 12,538 | 11,267 | 11,269 | 11,269 | 13,188 | 14,012 | 14,216 |
| 711320 | Promoters of performing arts, sports, and similar events without facilities | 3,101 | 2,378 | 2,323 | 2,347 | 2,347 | 2,713 | 2,814 | 2,950 |
| 712110 | Museums | 42,981 | 42,400 | 44,292 | 46,007 | 46,007 | 49,190 | 51,443 | 54,370 |
| 712120 | Historical sites | 8,025 | 8,635 | 8,525 | 8,796 | 8,796 | 9,334 | 9,446 | 9,947 |
| 712130 | Zoos and botanical gardens | 13,512 | 13,489 | 15,024 | 15,817 | 15,817 | 16,922 | 17,810 | 19,000 |
| 712190 | Nature parks and other similar institutions | 2,431 | 2,350 | 2,258 | 2,552 | 2,552 | 3,244 | 3,294 | 3,454 |

| NAICS | Industry | | | | | | | | |
|---|---|---|---|---|---|---|---|---|---|
| 713910 | Golf courses and country clubs | 70,534 | 73,994 | 77,309 | 80,575 | 80,575 | 90,074 | 94,238 | 99,710 |
| 713940 | Fitness and recreational sports centers | 68,100 | 67,752 | 69,280 | 71,935 | 71,935 | 78,176 | 81,503 | 85,242 |
| 713990 | All other amusement and recreation industries | 12,053 | 12,503 | 13,311 | 14,265 | 14,265 | 16,701 | 17,423 | 17,950 |
| 813110 | Religious organizations | 100,138 | 98,731 | 103,009 | 105,878 | 105,878 | 114,076 | 119,772 | 130,366 |
| 813211 | Grantmaking foundations | 26,972 | 26,395 | 27,238 | 28,221 | 28,221 | 30,216 | 32,893 | 33,614 |
| 813212 | Voluntary health organizations | 28,476 | 26,542 | 26,961 | 28,236 | 28,236 | 33,791 | 33,960 | 33,467 |
| 813219 | Other grantmaking and giving services | 38,508 | 36,088 | 37,425 | 37,157 | 37,157 | 38,450 | 38,929 | 40,695 |
| 813311 | Human rights organizations | 30,853 | 31,085 | 32,111 | 32,467 | 32,467 | 34,308 | 35,149 | 35,615 |
| 813312 | Environment, conservation, and wildlife organizations | 23,531 | 21,203 | 20,605 | 20,241 | 20,241 | 21,285 | 21,792 | 22,876 |
| 813319 | Other social advocacy organizations | 59,269 | 55,940 | 57,075 | 59,307 | 59,307 | 64,231 | 64,786 | 66,441 |
| 813410 | Civic and social organizations | 348,733 | 336,883 | 342,977 | 353,242 | 353,242 | 371,331 | 374,021 | 382,585 |
| 813910 | Business associations | 108,835 | 108,530 | 110,222 | 110,278 | 110,278 | 113,867 | 115,012 | 115,265 |
| 813920 | Professional organizations | 51,804 | 52,802 | 53,048 | 54,421 | 54,421 | 57,410 | 58,530 | 60,395 |
| 813930 | Labor unions and similar labor organizations | 137,755 | 140,111 | 139,771 | 139,622 | 139,622 | 139,934 | 141,993 | 142,447 |
| 813940 | Political organizations | 7,641 | 4,846 | 7,685 | 5,213 | 5,213 | 5,600 | 8,695 | 5,404 |
| 813990 | Other similar organizations (except business, professional, labor, and political organizations) | 81,949 | 83,048 | 82,825 | 81,471 | 81,471 | 81,136 | 81,854 | 82,941 |

*Source:* Authors' estimates largely based on private employment from U.S. Department of Labor, Bureau of Labor Statistics, Quarterly Census of Employment and Wages (1991–1998), and the tax-exempt share of employment from U.S. Census Bureau, Economic Census (1997, 2002).

*Notes:* Industries are listed as classified by the North American Industry Classification System. Industries 541710 (physical, engineering, and biological research services) and 541720 (research and development in the social sciences and humanities) are also included in the Economic Census; however, we believe these data are flawed.

**Table 2.13.** Nonprofit Employment Covered by Unemployment Insurance, Six-Digit Industries Whose Tax Status Is Identified in the Economic Census, 1998–2006

| NAICS code | Industry | 1998 | 1999 | 2000 | 2001 | 2002 | 2003 | 2004 | 2005 | 2006 |
|---|---|---|---|---|---|---|---|---|---|---|
| 541110 | Offices of lawyers | 23,195 | 23,690 | 24,106 | 24,669 | 25,156 | 25,595 | 25,827 | 25,937 | 25,986 |
| 611110 | Elementary and secondary schools | 444,761 | 468,747 | 491,787 | 513,820 | 536,094 | 555,470 | 570,964 | 590,152 | 607,855 |
| 611210 | Junior colleges | 11,260 | 10,213 | 9,574 | 9,051 | 7,836 | 7,970 | 8,494 | 8,879 | 8,703 |
| 611310 | Colleges, universities, and professional schools | 800,408 | 811,627 | 823,716 | 844,685 | 865,305 | 892,532 | 914,190 | 929,907 | 954,991 |
| 611410 | Business and secretarial schools | 866 | 999 | 1,131 | 1,322 | 1,490 | 1,453 | 1,497 | 1,481 | 1,377 |
| 611420 | Computer training | 482 | 705 | 918 | 980 | 964 | 845 | 806 | 793 | 734 |
| 611430 | Professional and management development training | 8,076 | 8,822 | 10,071 | 10,372 | 10,614 | 10,499 | 9,998 | 10,203 | 10,411 |
| 611511 | Cosmetology and barber schools | 437 | 476 | 535 | 629 | 718 | 727 | 760 | 784 | 820 |
| 611512 | Flight training | 391 | 441 | 489 | 493 | 455 | 406 | 390 | 395 | 385 |
| 611513 | Apprenticeship training | 6,182 | 6,797 | 7,494 | 7,972 | 8,955 | 9,499 | 9,974 | 10,102 | 10,224 |
| 611519 | Other technical and trade schools | 7,922 | 8,503 | 9,330 | 10,105 | 10,746 | 11,188 | 11,627 | 12,234 | 12,392 |
| 611610 | Fine arts schools | 12,312 | 13,449 | 14,632 | 15,914 | 17,174 | 18,006 | 18,541 | 19,241 | 19,869 |
| 611620 | Sports and recreation instruction | 5,098 | 5,827 | 6,729 | 7,947 | 9,410 | 10,161 | 11,073 | 11,819 | 12,494 |
| 611630 | Language schools | 3,856 | 4,321 | 4,680 | 5,193 | 5,139 | 5,288 | 5,184 | 4,947 | 5,045 |
| 611691 | Exam preparation and tutoring | 4,387 | 5,642 | 7,097 | 8,363 | 9,682 | 10,331 | 11,357 | 12,572 | 13,652 |
| 611692 | Automobile driving schools | 556 | 725 | 925 | 1,141 | 1,357 | 1,332 | 1,351 | 1,356 | 1,419 |

| Code | Industry | | | | | | | | | |
|---|---|---|---|---|---|---|---|---|---|---|
| 611699 | All other miscellaneous schools and instruction | 9,023 | 10,445 | 12,377 | 14,579 | 16,611 | 16,950 | 17,292 | 18,780 | 19,927 |
| 611710 | Educational support services | 15,334 | 16,952 | 19,012 | 21,639 | 23,775 | 27,490 | 31,859 | 35,723 | 38,302 |
| 621410 | Family planning centers | 18,573 | 18,435 | 18,371 | 18,386 | 18,475 | 17,168 | 16,571 | 15,535 | 16,415 |
| 621420 | Outpatient mental health and substance abuse centers | 102,474 | 106,203 | 109,127 | 112,214 | 115,740 | 120,577 | 124,045 | 130,380 | 133,030 |
| 621491 | HMO medical centers | 60,457 | 55,581 | 52,409 | 53,055 | 53,268 | 55,562 | 57,853 | 60,516 | 64,489 |
| 621492 | Kidney dialysis centers | 7,660 | 7,671 | 8,115 | 8,512 | 8,640 | 8,993 | 9,288 | 9,570 | 9,972 |
| 621493 | Freestanding ambulatory surgical and emergency centers | 9,989 | 9,282 | 9,350 | 9,313 | 9,626 | 10,118 | 10,874 | 11,607 | 12,735 |
| 621498 | All other outpatient care centers | 42,079 | 42,626 | 44,131 | 45,545 | 46,738 | 50,645 | 53,499 | 60,954 | 64,021 |
| 621610 | Home health care services | 197,168 | 181,675 | 180,117 | 182,336 | 194,771 | 208,592 | 222,160 | 236,136 | 249,983 |
| 621910 | Ambulance services | 19,894 | 21,809 | 24,089 | 26,761 | 29,625 | 31,609 | 32,886 | 34,695 | 36,274 |
| 621991 | Blood and organ banks | 33,475 | 34,283 | 36,489 | 40,195 | 43,217 | 45,022 | 44,498 | 45,496 | 47,163 |
| 621999 | All other miscellaneous ambulatory health care services | 2,071 | 2,200 | 2,522 | 2,795 | 3,139 | 3,100 | 3,052 | 3,122 | 3,278 |
| 622110 | General medical and surgical hospitals | 3,191,034 | 3,254,892 | 3,283,586 | 3,364,327 | 3,451,617 | 3,525,704 | 3,562,781 | 3,605,601 | 3,655,810 |
| 622210 | Psychiatric and substance abuse hospitals | 38,814 | 40,555 | 40,492 | 42,843 | 46,345 | 47,217 | 48,070 | 48,508 | 50,131 |
| 622310 | Specialty (except psychiatric and substance abuse) hospitals | 89,559 | 84,467 | 81,525 | 83,229 | 83,408 | 88,768 | 90,029 | 93,077 | 97,174 |
| 623110 | Nursing care facilities | 390,224 | 388,366 | 391,024 | 401,026 | 410,649 | 410,374 | 412,072 | 412,096 | 412,671 |
| 623210 | Residential mental retardation facilities | 189,557 | 199,429 | 206,112 | 216,175 | 225,300 | 228,459 | 230,406 | 231,588 | 235,373 |

*(continued)*

**Table 2.13.** Nonprofit Employment Covered by Unemployment Insurance, Six-Digit Industries Whose Tax Status Is Identified in the Economic Census, 1998–2006 *(continued)*

| NAICS code | Industry | 1998 | 1999 | 2000 | 2001 | 2002 | 2003 | 2004 | 2005 | 2006 |
|---|---|---|---|---|---|---|---|---|---|---|
| 623220 | Residential mental health and substance abuse facilities | 89,942 | 94,816 | 98,683 | 103,834 | 108,064 | 111,614 | 113,372 | 115,906 | 120,693 |
| 623311 | Continuing care retirement communities | 145,063 | 143,281 | 146,217 | 149,331 | 156,890 | 175,842 | 188,936 | 203,162 | 215,692 |
| 623312 | Homes for the elderly | 62,153 | 63,152 | 64,224 | 63,302 | 62,016 | 62,672 | 63,107 | 64,156 | 65,212 |
| 623990 | Other residential care facilities | 121,905 | 128,973 | 134,302 | 139,843 | 141,715 | 141,102 | 141,476 | 141,798 | 141,206 |
| 624110 | Child and youth services | 109,579 | 116,836 | 124,075 | 133,087 | 133,226 | 137,227 | 137,323 | 138,374 | 142,741 |
| 624120 | Services for the elderly and persons with disabilities | 221,477 | 224,921 | 231,452 | 238,882 | 255,725 | 277,900 | 304,958 | 339,970 | 373,263 |
| 624190 | Other individual and family services | 204,871 | 216,521 | 229,538 | 246,400 | 260,113 | 268,938 | 276,264 | 285,483 | 295,291 |
| 624210 | Community food services | 27,121 | 28,324 | 29,511 | 30,753 | 27,940 | 27,484 | 27,332 | 26,528 | 25,842 |
| 624221 | Temporary shelters | 38,345 | 40,672 | 42,656 | 45,480 | 48,666 | 50,170 | 51,787 | 52,962 | 53,822 |
| 624229 | Other community housing services | 16,530 | 17,685 | 18,663 | 19,002 | 20,925 | 21,526 | 21,053 | 22,097 | 23,333 |
| 624230 | Emergency and other relief services | 23,664 | 24,905 | 25,959 | 27,116 | 27,933 | 26,816 | 27,565 | 26,444 | 26,421 |
| 624310 | Vocational rehabilitation services | 247,782 | 257,504 | 264,297 | 271,434 | 273,857 | 274,380 | 276,267 | 275,794 | 277,582 |
| 624410 | Child day care services | 240,445 | 255,470 | 271,062 | 287,053 | 297,679 | 298,756 | 299,986 | 307,759 | 316,763 |
| 711110 | Theater companies and dinner theaters | 44,044 | 38,278 | 39,837 | 40,461 | 38,762 | 38,264 | 36,773 | 35,619 | 36,240 |
| 711120 | Dance companies | 5,835 | 6,065 | 6,437 | 6,748 | 6,640 | 6,953 | 7,650 | 7,263 | 7,448 |

| Code | Industry | | | | | | | | | |
|---|---|---|---|---|---|---|---|---|---|---|
| 711130 | Musical groups and artists | 28,707 | 29,147 | 30,229 | 29,167 | 28,241 | 26,926 | 26,449 | 25,832 | 25,324 |
| 711190 | Other performing arts companies | 398 | 395 | 355 | 325 | 319 | 382 | 370 | 358 | 382 |
| 711310 | Promoters of performing arts, sports, and similar events with facilities | 13,775 | 13,719 | 14,076 | 14,099 | 14,289 | 15,249 | 16,473 | 16,923 | 18,056 |
| 711320 | Promoters of performing arts, sports, and similar events without facilities | 3,590 | 4,535 | 5,914 | 7,284 | 8,770 | 8,237 | 8,319 | 8,458 | 8,339 |
| 712110 | Museums | 56,872 | 60,041 | 62,820 | 65,620 | 65,806 | 65,808 | 65,935 | 67,196 | 68,786 |
| 712120 | Historical sites | 10,374 | 10,802 | 11,466 | 11,658 | 11,628 | 11,819 | 12,330 | 12,068 | 12,069 |
| 712130 | Zoos and botanical gardens | 20,084 | 21,794 | 22,619 | 22,888 | 22,679 | 22,724 | 23,601 | 24,281 | 25,257 |
| 712190 | Nature parks and other similar institutions | 3,419 | 3,539 | 3,917 | 4,140 | 4,336 | 4,431 | 4,346 | 4,210 | 4,022 |
| 713910 | Golf courses and country clubs | 104,501 | 107,468 | 112,362 | 114,112 | 116,614 | 121,405 | 127,412 | 130,813 | 133,619 |
| 713940 | Fitness and recreational sports centers | 92,136 | 99,469 | 106,758 | 113,596 | 118,901 | 120,637 | 123,703 | 125,106 | 127,701 |
| 713990 | All other amusement and recreation industries | 19,506 | 20,228 | 21,183 | 22,022 | 23,313 | 23,453 | 23,738 | 23,628 | 24,045 |
| 813110 | Religious organizations | 135,897 | 145,352 | 151,810 | 159,212 | 166,785 | 172,669 | 175,119 | 177,104 | 179,417 |
| 813211 | Grantmaking foundations | 35,399 | 37,747 | 39,540 | 42,080 | 44,396 | 41,453 | 40,329 | 41,778 | 42,739 |
| 813212 | Voluntary health organizations | 33,207 | 33,734 | 35,061 | 37,795 | 37,295 | 37,833 | 36,516 | 36,834 | 37,123 |
| 813219 | Other grantmaking and giving services | 38,526 | 40,060 | 41,903 | 43,687 | 43,508 | 42,527 | 40,741 | 39,884 | 39,402 |
| 813311 | Human rights organizations | 37,811 | 40,621 | 40,486 | 41,956 | 43,282 | 43,600 | 43,991 | 42,879 | 44,747 |
| 813312 | Environment, conservation, and wildlife organizations | 23,856 | 25,393 | 26,727 | 27,991 | 30,235 | 33,123 | 35,585 | 37,354 | 39,014 |
| 813319 | Other social advocacy organizations | 69,103 | 73,210 | 78,308 | 83,914 | 85,063 | 83,602 | 84,219 | 85,072 | 84,250 |

(continued)

**Table 2.13.** Nonprofit Employment Covered by Unemployment Insurance, Six-Digit Industries Whose Tax Status Is Identified in the Economic Census, 1998–2006 (continued)

| NAICS code | Industry | 1998 | 1999 | 2000 | 2001 | 2002 | 2003 | 2004 | 2005 | 2006 |
|---|---|---|---|---|---|---|---|---|---|---|
| 813410 | Civic and social organizations | 379,212 | 387,132 | 401,243 | 411,679 | 419,690 | 416,569 | 412,083 | 414,028 | 415,336 |
| 813910 | Business associations | 117,490 | 119,619 | 121,378 | 121,232 | 119,146 | 118,583 | 117,688 | 118,662 | 120,446 |
| 813920 | Professional organizations | 63,178 | 65,881 | 68,051 | 69,707 | 72,333 | 71,708 | 71,123 | 70,571 | 71,198 |
| 813930 | Labor unions and similar labor organizations | 141,582 | 141,659 | 143,340 | 142,221 | 141,300 | 139,149 | 136,507 | 133,036 | 132,629 |
| 813940 | Political organizations | 7,713 | 5,859 | 8,191 | 5,866 | 9,395 | 6,196 | 11,775 | 6,223 | 10,544 |
| 813990 | Other similar organizations (except business, professional, labor, and political organizations) | 84,218 | 83,601 | 84,926 | 85,646 | 86,143 | 87,481 | 91,479 | 92,938 | 95,560 |

Source: Authors' estimates largely based on private employment from U.S. Department of Labor, Bureau of Labor Statistics, Quarterly Census of Employment and Wages (1998–2007), and the tax-exempt share of employment from U.S. Census Bureau, Economic Census (1997, 2002).
Notes: Industries are listed as classified by the North American Industry Classification System. Industries 541710 (physical, engineering, and biological research services) and 541720 (research and development in the social sciences and humanities) are also included in the Economic Census; however, we believe these data are flawed.

**Table 2.14.** Alternative Estimate of Nonprofit Employees, 2004 (thousands)

| NAICS code | Industry | All nonprofits | Public charities only |
|---|---|---|---|
| 11 | Agriculture, forestry, fishing, and hunting | 11 | n.a. |
| 22 | Utilities | 6 | n.a. |
| 48–49 | Transportation and warehousing | 2 | n.a. |
| 51 | Information | 35 | 71 |
| 52 | Finance and insurance | 80 | n.a. |
| 53 | Real estate and rental and leasing | 3 | n.a. |
| 52+53 | | 83 | 76 |
| 54 | Professional, scientific, and technical services | 153 | 250 |
| 56 | Administrative and waste management services | 23 | n.a. |
| 61 | Educational services | 2,346 | 1,373 |
| 62 | Health care and social assistance | 6,848 | 6,518 |
| 71 | Arts, entertainment, and recreation | 477 | 243 |
| 72 | Accommodation and food services | 18 | n.a. |
| 81 | Other services, except government | 2,772 | 695 |
| | Total | 12,773 | 9,385 |

*Sources:* Authors' estimates for all nonprofits from table 2.2 based on U.S. Census Bureau, Economic Census (2002); U.S. Department of Commerce, Bureau of Economic Analysis, National Income and Product Accounts (2007); U.S. Department of Labor, Bureau of Labor Statistics, Quarterly Census of Employment and Wages (2006); and Urban Institute, National Center for Charitable Statistics, Core Files (2006) and IRS Statistics of Income Form 990 and 990-EZ Sample Files (2006). Estimates for public charities from Salamon and Sokolowski (2006).
*Notes:* Industries are listed as classified by the North American Industry Classification System. Clearly, the estimates for industries 51 and 54 are not compatible. Possible sources of the difference are discussed in the appendix for chapter 2.
n.a. = not applicable

**Table 2.15.** National Taxonomy of Exempt Entities Core Codes Comprising NAICS Industries Whose Reported Wages Were Aggregated from Internal Revenue Service Data

11. Agriculture, forestry, fishing, and hunting
    K20. Agricultural programs
    K25. Farmland preservation
    K26. Animal husbandry
    K99. Food, agriculture, and nutrition n.e.c.

22. Utilities
    W80. Public utilities

48, 49. Transportation and warehousing
    W40. Public transportation systems

51. Information
    A27. Community celebrations
    A30. Media and communications
    A31. Film and video
    A32. Television
    A33. Printing and publishing
    A34. Radio
    B70. Libraries
    W50. Telecommunications
    X80. Religious media and communications
    X81. Religious film and video
    X82. Religious television
    X83. Religious printing and publishing
    X84. Religious radio

52. Finance and insurance
    E80. Health (general and financing)
    W60. Financial institutions
    W61. Credit unions
    Y20. Insurance providers
    Y22. Local benevolent life insurance associations, mutual irrigation and telephone companies, and like organizations
    Y23. Mutual insurance companies and associations
    Y30. Pension and retirement funds
    Y33. Teachers' retirement fund associations
    Y34. Employee-funded pension trusts
    Y35. Multiemployer pension plans

53. Real estate and rental and leasing
    S47. Real estate associations

54. Professional, scientific, and technical services
    I20. Crime prevention
    I21. Youth violence prevention
    I30. Correctional facilities

*(continued)*

**Table 2.15.** National Taxonomy of Exempt Entities Core Codes Comprising NAICS Industries Whose Reported Wages Were Aggregated from Internal Revenue Service Data *(continued)*

---

I40. Rehabilitation services for offenders

I43. Inmate support

I44. Prison alternatives

I50. Administration of justice

I60. Law enforcement

I80. Legal services

I83. Public interest law

I99. Crime and legal related n.e.c.

A02, B02, C02, D02, E02, F02, G02, H02, I02, J02, K02, K02, L02, M02, N02, O02, P02, Q02, R02, S02, T02, U02, V02, W02, X02, Y02. Management and technical assistance

S43. Small business development

S50. Nonprofit management

H20. Birth defects and genetic diseases research

H25. Down syndrome research

H30. Cancer research

H32. Breast cancer research

H40. Diseases of specific organs research

H41. Eye diseases, blindness, and vision impairments research

H42. Ear and throat diseases research

H43. Heart and circulatory system diseases and disorders research

H44. Kidney diseases research

H45. Lung diseases research

H48. Brain disorders research

H50. Nerve, muscle, and bone diseases research

H51. Arthritis research

H54. Epilepsy research

H60. Allergy-related diseases research

H61. Asthma research

H70. Digestive diseases and disorders research

H80. Specifically named diseases research

H81. AIDS research

H83. Alzheimer disease research

H84. Autism research

H90. Medical disciplines research

H92. Biomedicine and bioengineering research

H94. Geriatrics research

H96. Neurology and neuroscience research

H98. Pediatrics research

H99. Medical research n.e.c.

H9b. Surgical specialties research

U20. General science

U21. Marine science and oceanography

U30. Physical and earth sciences

U31. Astronomy

*(continued)*

**Table 2.15.** National Taxonomy of Exempt Entities Core Codes Comprising NAICS Industries Whose Reported Wages Were Aggregated from Internal Revenue Service Data *(continued)*

U33. Chemistry and chemical engineering
U34. Mathematics
U36. Geology
U40. Engineering and technology
U41. Computer science
U42. Engineering
U50. Biological and life sciences
U99. Science and technology n.e.c.
A05, B05, C05, D05, E05, F05, G05, H05, I05, J05, K05, L05, M05, N05, O05, P05, Q05, R05, S05, T05, U05, V05, W05, X05, Y05. Research institutes and public policy analysis
A24. Folk arts
Q35. International democracy and civil society development
Q50. International affairs, foreign policy, and globalization
Q51. International economic and trade policy
V20. Social science
V21. Anthropology and sociology
V22. Economics
V23. Behavioral science
V24. Political science
V25. Population studies
V26. Law and jurisprudence
V30. Interdisciplinary research
V31. Black studies
V32. Women's studies
V33. Ethnic studies
V34. Urban studies
V35. International studies
V36. Gerontology
V37. Labor studies
V99. Social science n.e.c.
D40. Veterinary services

56. Administrative and waste management services
J20. Employment preparation and procurement
J99. Employment n.e.c.

72. Accommodation and food services
L40. Temporary housing
N20. Camps

*Source:* Urban Institute, National Center for Charitable Statistics, NCCS NTEE/NAICS/SIC Crosswalk (2000).
NAICS = North American Industry Classification System
n.e.c. = not elsewhere classified

# Technical Notes

T here are no annual published sources of nonprofit wages or employment by industry. What is available is limited.

## Sources of Nonprofit Wages or Employment

The BEA publishes an annual series for total wages for NPISHs in its National Income and Products Accounts table 1.13, National Income by Sector, Legal Form of Organization, and Type of Income. It does not include nonprofits serving business. Although the BEA declines to define that term officially, personal correspondence with BEA analysts in spring 2006 revealed that the category is made up of portions of NAICS code 813, Membership Associations and Organizations, and NAICS code 5417, Scientific Research and Development Services.

Every five years, the U.S. Census Bureau publishes in the Economic Census non-profit wage and employment estimates for five industries: NAICS 54 (professional, scientific, and technical services), 61 (educational services), 62 (health care and social assistance), 71 (arts, entertainment, and recreation), and 81 (other services, except government). Total nonprofit wages in the 2002 census were $219.4 billion. That was just 55 percent of the BEA NPISH wages for the same year, $401.8 billion. The 1997 census reported nonprofit wages of $186.7 billion, which was 63 percent of the BEA estimate of $294.4 billion for the same year. The wages missing from the census are understated by these comparisons because the industries we believe make up nonprofits serving business are included in the smaller census estimates but excluded from the larger BEA estimates.

A major reason the census estimates are so low is that the census excludes some important nonprofit industries: elementary and secondary schools (NAICS 6111), junior colleges (NAICS 6112), colleges and universities (NAICS 6113), labor unions and similar labor organizations (NAICS 81393), political organizations (NAICS 81394), and religious organizations (NAICS 8131). Even after these (and other) differences are taken into consideration, however, census wages in 2002 for the five two-digit NAICS industries where nonprofits are tracked were $28.7 billion less than private wages from the Bureau of Labor Statistics' Quarterly Census of Employment and Wages (QCEW) for the same industries, or about 3 percent of QCEW private wages. This may be because the Economic Census is not a true census, but only samples smaller organizations.

The QCEW is the single most comprehensive source of wage and employment data by industry and is based on state unemployment-insurance filings. This is the BEA's major source for wage data and accounts for about 95 percent of its wage estimates. Unfortunately, the published data do not disaggregate the private ownership category into nonprofit and for-profit. In addition, religious organizations and religious-affiliated organizations (mostly schools) are not required to participate in unemployment insurance, and so many are missing from the data. The BEA's wage and employment estimates are larger than QCEW figures because the BEA includes wages for workers not covered by unemployment insurance and estimates wages earned but not reported to the government.

Nonprofits that file Form 990 or Form 990-EZ report wages to the IRS. Small nonprofits and religious organizations are not required to file with the IRS. IRS data are based on the filers' different fiscal years rather than a calendar year. The IRS releases two files containing wage data. The Statistics of Income (SOI) file is carefully reviewed by the IRS for data quality. It contains all large organizations and a sample of small ones. The sample organizations are weighted so that the sum of the SOI file preserves certain totals in the overall population, but this weighting does not preserve totals by industry. As the sample changes from year to year, we observe large fluctuations in wages by industry in the SOI data, particularly among smaller industries, but these fluctuations are an artifact of the sampling and weighting.

The other file released by the IRS is the Return Transaction File (RTF). Although comprehensive, the RTF is not checked for accuracy. Our review found a variety of errors where wages from a given Form 990 were off by a factor of 1,000 or more. Both IRS files contain the most recent return filed by an organization. Organizations filing late may be represented in these datasets by a prior year's return. In addition, employment numbers are requested on Form 990 but until recently, not on Form 990-EZ.

No single dataset is sufficient to produce estimates of nonprofit wages and employment by industry. Each has its strengths and weaknesses. The method we developed attempts to use the strengths of each, while minimizing its weaknesses.

For industries where the Economic Census reports information on whether establishments are taxable or tax exempt, the basic approach is to multiply the tax-exempt share from the Economic Census by the value for the whole private industry from the QCEW. Wage data reported to the IRS are used for the remaining industries.

# Nonprofit Industries in the Economic Census

The industries with a nonprofit breakout in the Economic Census are NAICS 54 (professional, scientific, and technical services), 61 (educational services), 62 (health care and social assistance), 71 (arts, entertainment, and recreation), and 81 (other services, except government). The first step was to calculate the tax-exempt share of wages by industry from the Economic Census.

The percentage of wages that was tax exempt from the 1997 census was used for 1990 to 1997. The percentage from the 2002 census was used from 2002 forward. Percentages for 1998 to 2001 were calculated using linear interpolation between the 1997 and 2002 percentages. We considered using the percentage of wages that was tax exempt from the 1992 census for 1990 to 1994, but decided against it. The NAICS version of the 1992 census was missing extensive data on nonprofits, while the older version using the Standard Industrial Classification suppressed most tax-exempt data for confidentiality.

For general medical and surgical hospitals (NAICS 6221), psychiatric and substance abuse hospitals (NAICS 6222), and specialty (except psychiatric and substance abuse) hospitals (NAICS 6223), we removed government hospitals from the census totals before calculating the nonprofit percentage. For the 1997 census, we could not remove government hospitals in NAICS 6223 because they had not been reported separately, so they remain in the nonprofit total.

Parts of industries 61 (other services, except government) and 81 (other services, except government) are excluded from the census, requiring us to identify alternative sources for the tax-exempt share. For junior colleges (NAICS 6112), and colleges and universities (NAICS 6113), the nonprofit percentage was estimated using data on total employment from the Integrated Postsecondary Education Data System of the National Center for Education Statistics (NCES). The NCES Private School Survey contained no information on nonprofit versus for-profit status, so all private elementary and secondary schools (NAICS 6111) were assumed to be nonprofit. Finally, 100 percent of labor unions and similar labor organizations (NAICS 81393), political organizations (NAICS 81394), and religious organizations (NAICS 8131) were assumed to be nonprofit.

We then obtained QCEW private wages at the six-digit NAICS level. Multiplying these wages by the corresponding tax-exempt shares yielded the estimates of wages covered by unemployment insurance in tables 2.10 and 2.11.

We performed most calculations at the six-digit NAICS level and then aggregated them. In 1997, however, data were suppressed to protect organizations' identities, requiring us to combine cosmetology and barber schools (NAICS 611511) and flight training (NAICS 611512).

Our calculations revealed an implausible discontinuity in two NAICS industries 541710 (physical, engineering, and biological research services) and 541720 (research and development in the social sciences and humanities). As a result, we elected to substitute IRS-based estimates for these industries, as discussed below.

For most of the industries in tables 2.10 and 2.11, the wages covered by unemployment insurance are equivalent to the total reported wages for the industry. In a few industries, however, a significant number of nonprofit employees are not covered by unemployment insurance: elementary and secondary schools (NAICS 6111), junior colleges (NAICS 6112), colleges and universities (NAICS 6113), and religious organizations (NAICS 8131). For these, we estimated total reported wages by replacing the QCEW private wages by wage estimates from the Census Bureau's County Business Patterns. These results are shown in table 2.5.

Finally, we attempted to measure total wages, including the BEA's imputation for unreported wages, by multiplying our nonprofit percentages by BEA wages by industry. These calculations were carried out at the two-digit level because BEA publishes only these. These are the wage estimates reported in table 2.1.

## Industries with No Nonprofit Breakout in the Economic Census

The remaining industries, excepting NAICS 54 (professional, scientific, and technical services), have no nonprofit breakout in the Economic Census. For these, we calculated two wage estimates. The first is total reported wages, calculated directly from IRS sources. We used the Core Files at the National Center for Charitable Statistics (NCCS), which are based on the IRS RTFs. We used the sum of lines 25 (officers' compensation) and 26 (other wages and salaries) from the schedule of functional expenses for organizations filing Form 990 and the compensation line from Form 990-EZ. Both 501c(3) and 501(c) other files were used. To clean the Core Files, we initially replaced all RTF records with the same SOI records where available. The NTEE industry classification codes were carefully reviewed. Wage outliers were identified, individually investigated, and manually corrected by reference to the original Form 990 when available or by interpolation between other years when not.

Wages were totaled by two-digit NAICS industries by reclassifying the NTEE core codes according to the scheme shown in table 2.15. This resulted in the numbers reported in table 2.6.

Experimental efforts to develop wage estimates for years prior to 1998 used a variety of approaches, none of which resulted in stable, plausible estimates. The same method would not work for earlier years because the variable for line 26 (other wages and salaries) was not included in the files released by the IRS.

To capture unreported wages, reported wages as developed above were divided by QCEW private wages by industry, yielding the nonprofit share of wages. This percentage was then multiplied by BEA wages by industry, resulting in total wages for these industries. These results appear in table 2.1. No estimate of wages covered by unemployment insurance is provided for these industries.

## Employment Estimates

Employment estimates for industries covered by the Economic Census were developed analogously to wages. There are two differences. First, the nonprofit share of employment from the Economic Census was used instead of the share of wages, and the share was multiplied by private employment in the industry, rather than by wages. Second, because the BEA does not provide an estimate of employment in NPISHs, only two employment estimates were calculated: nonprofit employment covered by unemployment insurance and total reported nonprofit employment.

For the remaining industries, we multiplied the nonprofit share of wages by QCEW private employment. This method is limited because it assumes that wages in the non-profit and for-profit portions of a given industry are similar. If nonprofit wages are significantly lower, for example, nonprofit employment will be underestimated.

We considered using IRS data on employment as an alternative approach. Comparisons of the wages and employment reported on the same Forms 990 suggested that employment was being underreported to the IRS. Using the employment numbers reported to the IRS also resulted in lower estimated employment than the estimates from the wage-share method, so this method offered no correction of the suspected underestimation problem.

While we recognize the limitations of the wage-share approach, we chose it as the best available at this time. Nonprofit employment data remain the largest missing pieces of nonprofit data.

The Johns Hopkins Center for Civil Society Studies has estimated 2004 nonprofit employment by industry for public charities only, based on access to QCEW microdata (Salamon and Sokolowski 2006). Public charities are a subset of the total number of nonprofits we had estimated. The two estimates are compared in table 2.14. For most of the industries, the differences in the two estimates are plausible because one is an estimate for only public charities. Clearly, though, the estimates for industries 51 (information) and 54 (professional, scientific, and technical services) are not compatible. Potential explanations for the incompatibility include the following:

- Nonprofit wage levels may be much lower in these industries than for-profit ones, resulting in a significant underestimate by the wage-share method.
- IRS data are based on legal entities. The QCEW data are based on establishments. A single entity may have multiple establishments, and a single establishment may have multiple legal entities. Where there are multiple establishments or entities, they may be classified into different industry categories. As a result, the IRS and the QCEW could be classifying the same organization in different industries.
- IRS data are coded according to the NTEE. The QCEW data are coded according to the NAICS. Our conversion from NTEE to NAICS maps one NTEE code into one NAICS code. This may have underestimated some NAICS industries and inflated others.
- Coding the entities according to NTEE could be in error. This is an ongoing issue being addressed at NCCS.
- Coding at the Bureau of Labor Statistics (BLS) according to NAICS could be in error. We have no access to source data to test this.
- Many small organizations use professional accounting firms to report and file. In fall 2006, a researcher at Johns Hopkins reported a conversation with a BLS analyst

who suggested that these organizations may then be counted in the same NAICS industry as the accounting firm, industry 54. We have no data on the extent of this problem.[1]

Investigating the differences suggested that classification was clearly one source of the problem, but that the wage-share method was also responsible to some degree.

Ideally, the BLS would modify its data collection and reporting for the QCEW to distinguish private nonprofits from private for-profits in all industries. Such an approach would provide an excellent basis for estimating nonprofit wages and employment. We would need only to correct for the organizations not covered by unemployment insurance and for unreported wages.

---

1. Personal telephone conversation with S. Wojciech Sokolowski, senior research associate for the Comparative Nonprofit Sector Project and the Nonprofit Employment Data Project, Johns Hopkins University, December 2006. The authors contacted Sokolowski to discuss differences in the studies that could account for the incompatible results. Sokolowski concluded, based on a conversation with a BLS analyst, that this is the possible source of the difference.

# 3

# Trends in Private Giving and Volunteering

Americans are generous people who make large donations of time and money to help worthy causes. Most of these donations are made to or through nonprofit organizations. In fact, the nonprofit sector is distinguished from the business and government sectors by the substantial part such gifts play. This chapter presents a variety of statistics that paint a picture of giving and volunteering in the United States.

## Individual Giving

- Total private giving reached $295 billion in 2006 and more than doubled from 1996 to 2006.

- Total private giving as a percentage of national income achieved a record level in 1999 and again in 2000, reaching 2.61 percent in 2000. Each year since 2000 has exceeded the long-standing prior record set in 1971.

- Total private giving as a percentage of nonprofit outlays hit bottom in 1995 at 24.8 percent then increased steadily to 34.2 percent in 2000. After 2000, it declined to 28.7 percent in 2003, but rebounded somewhat in 2004 and 2005, reaching 30.9 percent.

- In constant 2006 dollars, per capita individual contributions have been on a general upward trend from 1965. From 1995 to 2000, they increased at a dramatic rate, rising to $720 in 2000. After declines in 2001 and 2002, they have set new records in each of the last three years.

## Volunteering

- In 2006, 26.7 percent of the population said they had volunteered at some time during the previous year, which translates into 61.2 million volunteers.

- About 6.5 percent of the population volunteers on an average day, which translated into more than 15 million volunteers per day in 2006, each of whom spent 2.31 hours volunteering that day.
- The average volunteer served 207 hours in 2006.
- In total, about 12.9 billion hours were volunteered in 2006.
- Assuming a full-time employee works 1,700 hours per year, those volunteer hours were the equivalent of 7.6 million full-time employees.
- Assuming those employees would have earned the average private nonfarm hourly wage, they would have earned $215.6 billion in 2006.

# Foundation and Corporate Giving

- Foundation giving in 2005 was $36.4 billion. This was a 197 percent increase from 10 years earlier.
- The United States had 71,095 active independent, corporate, and community foundations in 2005—a 77 percent increase from 10 years earlier.
- According to the Giving USA Foundation (2007), corporations, including corporate foundations, donated $12.7 billion in 2006. That was up 69 percent from 10 years earlier.
- The Conference Board's 2006 Corporate Contributions Report (Muirhead 2007) found that corporations' median contribution of domestic pretax income was 1 percent in 2005. The median contribution of corporate sales was 0.08 percent.

# Individual Giving

Each year, the Giving USA Foundation publishes *Giving USA,* which has become the established source for information on private giving and its components: cash and in-kind gifts from living persons, personal bequests, foundation giving, and corporate giving.

Table 3.1 shows private giving and how it compares with national income and nonprofit outlays.

- Private giving reached $295 billion in 2006.
- Private giving more than doubled from 1996 to 2006.
- Private giving as a percentage of national income achieved a record level in 1999 and again in 2000, reaching 2.61 percent in 2000. Private giving each year since 2000 has exceeded the long-standing prior record set in 1971, 2.33 percent (see also figure 3.1).
- Private giving as a percent of nonprofit outlays hit bottom in 1995 at 24.8, then increased steadily to 34.2 percent in 2000. After 2000, it declined to 28.7 percent in 2003 but rebounded somewhat in 2004 and 2005, reaching 30.9 percent (see also figure 3.2).

**Table 3.1.** Private Contributions to Nonprofit Organizations by National Income and Nonprofit Outlays, 1965–2006

| | $ Billions | | | Private Giving as a % of | |
|---|---|---|---|---|---|
| | Private giving | National income | Nonprofit outlays | National income | Nonprofit outlays |
| 1965 | 14.71 | 653.4 | — | 2.25 | — |
| 1966 | 15.79 | 711.0 | — | 2.22 | — |
| 1967 | 17.03 | 751.9 | — | 2.26 | — |
| 1968 | 18.85 | 823.2 | — | 2.29 | — |
| 1969 | 20.66 | 889.7 | — | 2.32 | — |
| 1970 | 21.04 | 930.9 | — | 2.26 | — |
| 1971 | 23.44 | 1,008.1 | — | 2.33 | — |
| 1972 | 24.44 | 1,111.2 | — | 2.20 | — |
| 1973 | 25.59 | 1,247.4 | — | 2.05 | — |
| 1974 | 26.88 | 1,342.1 | — | 2.00 | — |
| 1975 | 28.56 | 1,445.9 | — | 1.98 | — |
| 1976 | 31.85 | 1,611.8 | — | 1.98 | — |
| 1977 | 35.21 | 1,798.9 | — | 1.96 | — |
| 1978 | 38.57 | 2,027.4 | — | 1.90 | — |
| 1979 | 43.11 | 2,249.1 | — | 1.92 | — |
| 1980 | 48.63 | 2,439.3 | — | 1.99 | — |
| 1981 | 55.28 | 2,742.4 | — | 2.02 | — |
| 1982 | 59.11 | 2,864.3 | — | 2.06 | — |
| 1983 | 63.21 | 3,084.2 | — | 2.05 | — |
| 1984 | 68.58 | 3,482.3 | — | 1.97 | — |
| 1985 | 71.69 | 3,723.4 | — | 1.93 | — |
| 1986 | 83.25 | 3,902.3 | — | 2.13 | — |
| 1987 | 82.20 | 4,173.7 | — | 1.97 | — |
| 1988 | 88.04 | 4,549.4 | — | 1.94 | — |
| 1989 | 98.30 | 4,826.6 | — | 2.04 | — |
| 1990 | 100.52 | 5,089.1 | — | 1.98 | — |
| 1991 | 104.92 | 5,227.9 | — | 2.01 | — |
| 1992 | 111.79 | 5,512.8 | 430.7 | 2.03 | 26.0 |
| 1993 | 116.86 | 5,773.4 | 457.0 | 2.02 | 25.6 |
| 1994 | 120.29 | 6,122.3 | 480.7 | 1.96 | 25.0 |

*(continued)*

**Table 3.1.** Private Contributions to Nonprofit Organizations by National Income and Nonprofit Outlays, 1965–2006 *(continued)*

|      | $ Billions | | | Private Giving as a % of | |
| --- | --- | --- | --- | --- | --- |
|      | Private giving | National income | Nonprofit outlays | National income | Nonprofit outlays |
| 1995 | 123.68 | 6,453.9 | 499.6 | 1.92 | 24.8 |
| 1996 | 139.10 | 6,840.1 | 528.4 | 2.03 | 26.3 |
| 1997 | 162.99 | 7,292.2 | 551.9 | 2.24 | 29.5 |
| 1998 | 176.80 | 7,752.8 | 591.7 | 2.28 | 29.9 |
| 1999 | 202.74 | 8,236.7 | 625.7 | 2.46 | 32.4 |
| 2000 | 229.71 | 8,795.2 | 672.6 | 2.61 | 34.2 |
| 2001 | 231.08 | 8,979.8 | 725.3 | 2.57 | 31.9 |
| 2002 | 231.54 | 9,229.3 | 778.2 | 2.51 | 29.8 |
| 2003 | 236.28 | 9,632.3 | 823.4 | 2.45 | 28.7 |
| 2004 | 259.02 | 10,255.9 | 865.8 | 2.53 | 29.9 |
| 2005 | 283.05 | 10,887.6 | 915.2 | 2.60 | 30.9 |
| 2006 | 295.02 | 11,655.6 | — | 2.53 | — |

*Sources:* Private giving from Giving USA Foundation, *Giving USA* (2007); national income from U.S. Department of Commerce, Bureau of Economic Analysis, National Income and Product Accounts, table 1.13 (2007); nonprofit outlays from U.S. Department of Commerce, Bureau of Economic Analysis, National Income and Product Accounts, table 2.9 (2006).
— = no data available

Table 3.2 shows private contributions by type of nonprofit.

- Religion receives more donations than any other area (see also figure 3.3), but the share going to religion peaked in 1985 and has been declining since.
- The shares going to health and human services organizations declined steadily from 1974 to 1990, but have remained fairly stable since.
- The share of donations to foundations grew dramatically from 4.2 percent in 1978 when data were first collected to a peak of 14.2 percent in 1999.
- The shares to public-society benefit, environmental, and international organizations have been steadily increasing.

## Giving by Living Individuals

Giving by living individuals represents the largest share of private giving, ranging from about 75 to 85 percent of private giving since 1965. When personal bequests are considered, the share of giving by individuals is even higher.

**Figure 3.1.**  Private Giving Compared with National Income, 1965–2006 (percent)

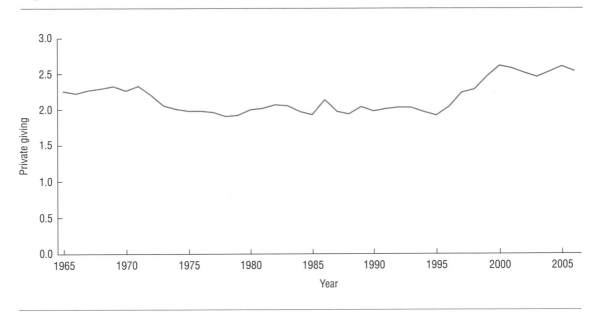

*Source:* Authors' calculations based on private giving from Giving USA Foundation, *Giving USA* (2007) and national income from U.S. Department of Commerce, Bureau of Economic Analysis, National Income and Product Accounts, table 1.13 (2007).

**Figure 3.2.**  Private Contributions in Current Dollars and as a Percentage of Nonprofit Outlays, 1992–2005

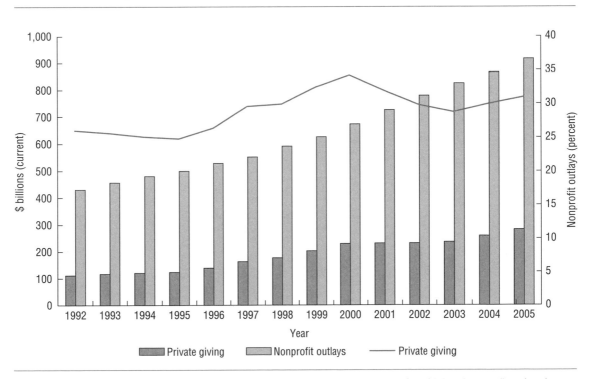

*Source:* Authors calculations based on private giving from Giving USA Foundation, *Giving USA* (2007) and nonprofit outlays from U.S. Department of Commerce, Bureau of Economic Analysis, National Income and Product Accounts, table 2.9 (2006).

**Table 3.2.** Distribution of Private Contributions to Nonprofit Organizations by Type of Nonprofit, 1966–2006

| | $ Billions Total | Religion | Education | Health | Human services | Arts, culture, humanities | Public-society benefit % | Environment or animals | International affairs | Gifts to foundations | Unallocated |
|---|---|---|---|---|---|---|---|---|---|---|---|
| 1966 | 15.79 | 45.7 | 13.0 | 16.5 | 19.1 | 3.4 | 2.5 | — | — | — | -0.3 |
| 1967 | 17.03 | 44.5 | 12.5 | 16.4 | 18.6 | 3.3 | 2.4 | — | — | — | 2.3 |
| 1968 | 18.85 | 44.7 | 12.6 | 16.4 | 16.3 | 3.2 | 2.3 | — | — | — | 4.5 |
| 1969 | 20.66 | 43.7 | 12.3 | 16.3 | 14.6 | 3.5 | 2.7 | — | — | — | 6.9 |
| 1970 | 21.04 | 44.4 | 12.4 | 17.2 | 14.0 | 3.1 | 2.2 | — | — | — | 6.8 |
| 1971 | 23.44 | 43.0 | 11.7 | 16.7 | 12.9 | 4.3 | 2.9 | — | — | — | 8.5 |
| 1972 | 24.44 | 41.3 | 12.2 | 16.7 | 14.6 | 4.5 | 3.4 | — | — | — | 7.3 |
| 1973 | 25.59 | 41.1 | 13.0 | 17.7 | 15.1 | 4.9 | 2.4 | — | — | — | 5.7 |
| 1974 | 26.88 | 44.0 | 12.6 | 18.8 | 18.5 | 5.4 | 3.3 | — | — | — | -2.7 |
| 1975 | 28.56 | 44.9 | 11.2 | 18.0 | 17.7 | 5.2 | 4.3 | — | — | — | -1.2 |
| 1976 | 31.85 | 44.5 | 11.3 | 16.3 | 16.1 | 4.8 | 4.6 | — | — | — | 2.3 |
| 1977 | 35.21 | 48.2 | 11.0 | 15.0 | 14.8 | 5.2 | 3.7 | — | — | — | 2.0 |
| 1978 | 38.57 | 47.6 | 11.2 | 13.7 | 13.7 | 4.8 | 3.9 | — | — | 4.2 | 0.8 |
| 1979 | 43.11 | 46.8 | 10.9 | 12.6 | 12.4 | 4.6 | 4.2 | — | — | 5.1 | 3.3 |
| 1980 | 48.63 | 45.7 | 10.4 | 11.4 | 11.1 | 4.4 | 4.7 | — | — | 4.1 | 8.2 |
| 1981 | 55.28 | 45.3 | 10.7 | 10.3 | 9.9 | 4.1 | 3.9 | — | — | 4.3 | 11.4 |
| 1982 | 59.11 | 47.5 | 10.4 | 9.7 | 9.4 | 4.6 | 4.1 | — | — | 6.8 | 7.6 |
| 1983 | 63.21 | 50.4 | 10.6 | 9.2 | 8.9 | 3.9 | 3.9 | — | — | 4.3 | 8.8 |
| 1984 | 68.58 | 51.8 | 10.6 | 8.5 | 8.3 | 3.7 | 4.2 | — | — | 4.9 | 8.0 |

| Year | | | | | | | | | | | |
|------|------|------|------|------|------|------|------|------|------|------|------|
| 1985 | 71.69 | 53.3 | 11.2 | 8.0 | 7.8 | 3.8 | 4.5 | — | — | 6.6 | 4.7 |
| 1986 | 83.25 | 50.1 | 11.3 | 7.0 | 6.8 | 3.6 | 4.5 | — | — | 6.0 | 10.7 |
| 1987 | 82.20 | 52.9 | 11.9 | 7.3 | 7.0 | 3.8 | 5.2 | 1.3 | 1.0 | 6.3 | 3.3 |
| 1988 | 88.04 | 51.3 | 11.5 | 6.9 | 6.5 | 3.8 | 5.8 | 1.3 | 1.0 | 4.5 | 7.5 |
| 1989 | 98.30 | 48.6 | 11.3 | 6.6 | 6.4 | 3.8 | 7.1 | 1.4 | 1.7 | 4.5 | 8.6 |
| 1990 | 100.52 | 49.5 | 11.6 | 7.3 | 6.4 | 4.0 | 7.3 | 1.5 | 2.2 | 3.8 | 6.2 |
| 1991 | 104.92 | 47.7 | 11.8 | 7.4 | 7.1 | 4.1 | 7.9 | 1.6 | 2.0 | 4.3 | 6.2 |
| 1992 | 111.79 | 45.6 | 11.6 | 7.6 | 7.5 | 4.0 | 7.6 | 1.5 | 2.1 | 4.5 | 7.9 |
| 1993 | 116.86 | 45.3 | 12.2 | 7.5 | 7.5 | 4.2 | 7.4 | 1.7 | 1.9 | 5.4 | 7.1 |
| 1994 | 120.29 | 46.9 | 11.7 | 7.6 | 7.4 | 3.9 | 8.3 | 1.7 | 2.3 | 5.3 | 4.9 |
| 1995 | 123.68 | 47.0 | 12.6 | 11.3 | 7.9 | 4.6 | 9.1 | 1.9 | 2.4 | 6.8 | -3.5 |
| 1996 | 139.10 | 44.5 | 13.3 | 10.2 | 7.5 | 4.6 | 8.1 | 1.9 | 2.6 | 9.1 | -1.7 |
| 1997 | 162.99 | 39.7 | 12.5 | 7.8 | 7.7 | 4.5 | 7.9 | 1.9 | 2.6 | 8.6 | 6.8 |
| 1998 | 176.80 | 38.6 | 13.5 | 7.5 | 8.8 | 5.6 | 7.9 | 2.0 | 2.9 | 11.3 | 2.0 |
| 1999 | 202.74 | 35.1 | 13.4 | 7.5 | 8.8 | 4.6 | 6.4 | 2.1 | 3.2 | 14.2 | 4.6 |
| 2000 | 229.71 | 33.5 | 12.9 | 7.2 | 8.7 | 4.6 | 6.7 | 2.1 | 3.1 | 10.8 | 10.5 |
| 2001 | 231.08 | 34.6 | 14.2 | 7.9 | 9.4 | 4.9 | 7.1 | 2.3 | 3.6 | 11.1 | 4.9 |
| 2002 | 231.54 | 35.8 | 12.9 | 7.7 | 10.5 | 4.7 | 7.8 | 2.3 | 3.8 | 8.3 | 6.3 |
| 2003 | 236.28 | 35.8 | 12.6 | 8.7 | 9.9 | 4.6 | 6.9 | 2.3 | 4.2 | 9.2 | 5.8 |
| 2004 | 259.02 | 34.0 | 13.0 | 7.8 | 9.4 | 4.5 | 7.3 | 2.1 | 4.5 | 7.8 | 9.6 |
| 2005 | 283.05 | 32.7 | 13.2 | 7.3 | 11.5 | 4.0 | 7.2 | 2.3 | 4.4 | 9.7 | 7.7 |
| 2006 | 295.02 | 32.8 | 13.9 | 6.9 | 10.0 | 4.2 | 7.3 | 2.2 | 3.8 | 10.0 | 8.8 |

Source: Giving USA Foundation, Giving USA (2007).
— = no data available

**Figure 3.3.** Distribution of Private Contributions by Recipient Area, 2006 (percent)

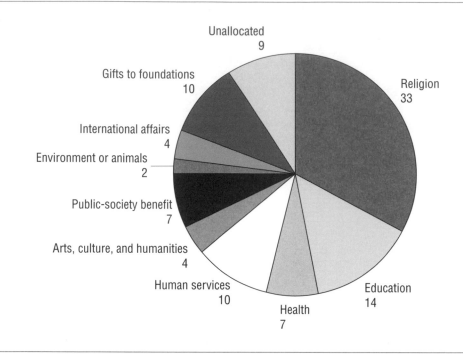

Unallocated
9

Gifts to foundations
10

International affairs
4

Environment or animals
2

Public-society benefit
7

Arts, culture, and humanities
4

Human services
10

Health
7

Education
14

Religion
33

*Source:* Giving USA Foundation, *Giving USA* (2007).

- Giving by living individuals reached $222.9 billion in 2006. Personal bequests added another $22.9 billion. (See table 3.3.)
- The share of giving from living individuals declined from 1965 to 1971, then rose until peaking in 1979, then declined until 2001. In recent years, it has rebounded somewhat. (See figure 3.4.)
- Giving from foundations has followed an almost opposite trend to that of giving by living individuals, although at a lower share. (See figure 3.4.)
- In constant 2006 dollars, per capita individual contributions have been on a general upward trend from 1965. From 1995 to 2000, they increased at a dramatic rate, peaking at $720 in 2000. After declines in 2001 and 2002, they have set new records in each of the last three years. (See table 3.4 and figure 3.5.)
- Within each income range, a higher percentage of itemizers than nonitemizers gives to charity, and itemizers give a higher percentage of their income. (See table 3.6.)
- The amount people give is more closely related to their income than to other demographic characteristics such as age, marital status, or race/ethnicity. Within each income range, the percentage that gives increases with age, as does the average amount donated. Unlike age, marital status and race/ethnicity do not appear systematically related to charitable giving once income differences are taken into account (see table 3.7). Prior studies have noted that church attendance is a good predictor of charitable giving, but our sources did not include that variable.

**Table 3.3.** Private Contributions to Nonprofit Organizations by Source, 1965–2006

| | Total Private Giving | | Gifts by Living Individuals | | Personal Bequests | | Gifts by Foundations | | Gifts by Corporations | |
|---|---|---|---|---|---|---|---|---|---|---|
| | $ billions | % | $ billions | % | $ billions | % | $ billions | % | $ billions | % |
| 1965 | 14.7 | 100.0 | 11.8 | 80.4 | 1.0 | 6.9 | 1.1 | 7.7 | 0.7 | 5.0 |
| 1966 | 15.8 | 100.0 | 12.4 | 78.8 | 1.3 | 8.3 | 1.3 | 7.9 | 0.8 | 5.0 |
| 1967 | 17.0 | 100.0 | 13.4 | 78.7 | 1.4 | 8.2 | 1.4 | 8.2 | 0.8 | 4.8 |
| 1968 | 18.9 | 100.0 | 14.8 | 78.2 | 1.6 | 8.5 | 1.6 | 8.5 | 0.9 | 4.8 |
| 1969 | 20.7 | 100.0 | 15.9 | 77.1 | 2.0 | 9.7 | 1.8 | 8.7 | 0.9 | 4.5 |
| 1970 | 21.0 | 100.0 | 16.2 | 76.9 | 2.1 | 10.1 | 1.9 | 9.0 | 0.8 | 3.9 |
| 1971 | 23.4 | 100.0 | 17.6 | 75.3 | 3.0 | 12.8 | 2.0 | 8.3 | 0.9 | 3.6 |
| 1972 | 24.4 | 100.0 | 19.4 | 79.3 | 2.1 | 8.6 | 2.0 | 8.2 | 1.0 | 4.0 |
| 1973 | 25.6 | 100.0 | 20.5 | 80.2 | 2.0 | 7.8 | 2.0 | 7.8 | 1.1 | 4.1 |
| 1974 | 26.9 | 100.0 | 21.6 | 80.4 | 2.1 | 7.7 | 2.1 | 7.8 | 1.1 | 4.1 |
| 1975 | 28.6 | 100.0 | 23.5 | 82.4 | 2.2 | 7.8 | 1.7 | 5.8 | 1.2 | 4.0 |
| 1976 | 31.9 | 100.0 | 26.3 | 82.6 | 2.3 | 7.2 | 1.9 | 6.0 | 1.3 | 4.2 |
| 1977 | 35.2 | 100.0 | 29.6 | 83.9 | 2.1 | 6.0 | 2.0 | 5.7 | 1.5 | 4.4 |
| 1978 | 38.6 | 100.0 | 32.1 | 83.2 | 2.6 | 6.7 | 2.2 | 5.6 | 1.7 | 4.4 |
| 1979 | 43.1 | 100.0 | 36.6 | 84.9 | 2.2 | 5.2 | 2.2 | 5.2 | 2.1 | 4.8 |
| 1980 | 48.6 | 100.0 | 40.7 | 83.7 | 2.9 | 5.9 | 2.8 | 5.8 | 2.3 | 4.6 |
| 1981 | 55.3 | 100.0 | 46.0 | 83.2 | 3.6 | 6.5 | 3.1 | 5.6 | 2.6 | 4.8 |
| 1982 | 59.1 | 100.0 | 47.6 | 80.6 | 5.2 | 8.8 | 3.2 | 5.3 | 3.1 | 5.3 |
| 1983 | 63.2 | 100.0 | 52.1 | 82.4 | 3.9 | 6.1 | 3.6 | 5.7 | 3.7 | 5.8 |
| 1984 | 68.6 | 100.0 | 56.5 | 82.3 | 4.0 | 5.9 | 4.0 | 5.8 | 4.1 | 6.0 |
| 1985 | 71.7 | 100.0 | 57.4 | 80.1 | 4.8 | 6.7 | 4.9 | 6.8 | 4.6 | 6.5 |
| 1986 | 83.3 | 100.0 | 67.1 | 80.6 | 5.7 | 6.8 | 5.4 | 6.5 | 5.0 | 6.0 |
| 1987 | 82.2 | 100.0 | 64.5 | 78.5 | 6.6 | 8.0 | 5.9 | 7.2 | 5.2 | 6.3 |
| 1988 | 88.0 | 100.0 | 70.0 | 79.5 | 6.6 | 7.5 | 6.2 | 7.0 | 5.3 | 6.1 |
| 1989 | 98.3 | 100.0 | 79.5 | 80.8 | 6.8 | 7.0 | 6.6 | 6.7 | 5.5 | 5.6 |
| 1990 | 100.5 | 100.0 | 81.0 | 80.6 | 6.8 | 6.8 | 7.2 | 7.2 | 5.5 | 5.4 |
| 1991 | 104.9 | 100.0 | 84.3 | 80.3 | 7.7 | 7.3 | 7.7 | 7.4 | 5.3 | 5.0 |
| 1992 | 111.8 | 100.0 | 87.7 | 78.5 | 9.5 | 8.5 | 8.6 | 7.7 | 5.9 | 5.3 |
| 1993 | 116.9 | 100.0 | 92.0 | 78.7 | 8.9 | 7.6 | 9.5 | 8.2 | 6.5 | 5.5 |
| 1994 | 120.3 | 100.0 | 92.5 | 76.9 | 11.1 | 9.3 | 9.7 | 8.0 | 7.0 | 5.8 |

*(continued)*

**Table 3.3.** Private Contributions to Nonprofit Organizations by Source, 1965–2006 *(continued)*

| | Total Private Giving | | Gifts by Living Individuals | | Personal Bequests | | Gifts by Foundations | | Gifts by Corporations | |
|---|---|---|---|---|---|---|---|---|---|---|
| | $ billions | % | $ billions | % | $ billions | % | $ billions | % | $ billions | % |
| 1995 | 123.7 | 100.0 | 95.4 | 77.1 | 10.4 | 8.4 | 10.6 | 8.5 | 7.4 | 5.9 |
| 1996 | 139.1 | 100.0 | 107.6 | 77.3 | 12.0 | 8.6 | 12.0 | 8.6 | 7.5 | 5.4 |
| 1997 | 163.0 | 100.0 | 124.2 | 76.2 | 16.3 | 10.0 | 13.9 | 8.5 | 8.6 | 5.3 |
| 1998 | 176.8 | 100.0 | 138.4 | 78.3 | 13.0 | 7.3 | 17.0 | 9.6 | 8.5 | 4.8 |
| 1999 | 202.7 | 100.0 | 154.6 | 76.3 | 17.4 | 8.6 | 20.5 | 10.1 | 10.2 | 5.0 |
| 2000 | 229.7 | 100.0 | 174.5 | 76.0 | 19.9 | 8.7 | 24.6 | 10.7 | 10.7 | 4.7 |
| 2001 | 231.1 | 100.0 | 172.4 | 74.6 | 19.8 | 8.6 | 27.2 | 11.8 | 11.7 | 5.0 |
| 2002 | 231.5 | 100.0 | 172.9 | 74.7 | 20.9 | 9.0 | 27.0 | 11.7 | 10.8 | 4.7 |
| 2003 | 236.3 | 100.0 | 180.2 | 76.3 | 18.2 | 7.7 | 26.8 | 11.4 | 11.1 | 4.7 |
| 2004 | 259.0 | 100.0 | 200.8 | 77.5 | 18.5 | 7.1 | 28.4 | 11.0 | 11.4 | 4.4 |
| 2005 | 283.1 | 100.0 | 213.5 | 75.4 | 23.4 | 8.3 | 32.4 | 11.5 | 13.8 | 4.9 |
| 2006 | 295.0 | 100.0 | 222.9 | 75.6 | 22.9 | 7.8 | 36.5 | 12.4 | 12.7 | 4.3 |

*Source:* Giving USA Foundation, *Giving USA* (2007).

# Estimates of Giving Based on IRS Records

The IRS Statistics of Income Division maintains and publishes a variety of data useful for tracking trends in individual giving. It publishes information on estate tax returns, showing the number and size of charitable deductions. It also publishes information on charitable deductions taken by personal income tax filers who itemize deductions.
Table 3.8 shows the data from estate tax returns.

- The number of returns and the gross value of estates both peaked in 2000.
- The number of bequests peaked in 2001; the value of bequests peaked in 2005. (See also figure 3.7.)
- The value of bequests in constant dollars has been on an upward trend throughout the period covered by our data, although it retreated briefly in 2003 and 2004.
- The percentage of estate value given to charity was fairly steady from 1995 to 2004, averaging 7.6 percent, a larger share than observed in prior years but much below the 2005 value of 10.7 percent.

**Figure 3.4.** Private Giving by Living Individuals and Foundations, 1965–2006 (percent)

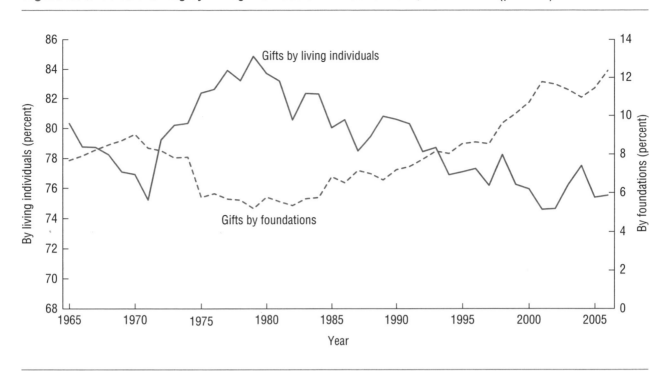

*Source:* Giving USA Foundation, *Giving USA* (2007).

Table 3.9 contains statistics of individual giving broken out by whether the givers itemized deductions on their personal income tax returns. Nonitemizers' contributions are estimated by subtracting itemizers' contributions from the total individual giving found in table 3.3. The assumption is that those who do not file tax returns do not make charitable contributions. Some trends noted below may be a result of the late 1990s stock market boom and the bust of the early 2000s.

- From 1985 to 2005, the average itemizer's adjusted gross income has been four times larger than the average nonitemizer's, but the average contribution has been eight times larger, so the percentage of income given by itemizers has been approximately twice that of nonitemizers.
- From 1985 to 2005, approximately half as many filers have itemized as have not, so that in total, all itemizers gave only four times as much as all nonitemizers, even though their average contribution was eight times larger. This suggests that itemizers account for approximately four-fifths of individual contributions.
- Contributions as a percent of adjusted gross income rose from 1995 to 2004, falling only in 2005.
- From 1985 to 2005, cash contributions accounted for 79 percent of itemizers' contributions on average. (See table 3.10.)

**Table 3.4.** Per Capita Contributions and Individual Contributions to Nonprofit Organizations, 1965–2006

| | Private Giving ($ billions) | | Population (midyear, millions) | Per Capita Individual Giving | | Total personal income ($ billions) | Individual giving as % of personal income |
|------|-------|----------------|--------|-----|--------|---------|------|
| | Total | By individuals | | $ | 2006 $ | | |
| 1965 | 14.7 | 11.8 | 194.3 | 61 | 315 | 555.7 | 2.1 |
| 1966 | 15.8 | 12.4 | 196.6 | 63 | 318 | 603.9 | 2.1 |
| 1967 | 17.0 | 13.4 | 198.7 | 67 | 329 | 648.3 | 2.1 |
| 1968 | 18.9 | 14.8 | 200.7 | 73 | 344 | 712.0 | 2.1 |
| 1969 | 20.7 | 15.9 | 202.7 | 79 | 350 | 778.5 | 2.0 |
| 1970 | 21.0 | 16.2 | 205.1 | 79 | 334 | 838.8 | 1.9 |
| 1971 | 23.4 | 17.6 | 207.7 | 85 | 342 | 903.5 | 2.0 |
| 1972 | 24.4 | 19.4 | 209.9 | 92 | 357 | 992.7 | 2.0 |
| 1973 | 25.6 | 20.5 | 211.9 | 97 | 355 | 1,110.7 | 1.8 |
| 1974 | 26.9 | 21.6 | 213.9 | 101 | 339 | 1,222.6 | 1.8 |
| 1975 | 28.6 | 23.5 | 216.0 | 109 | 334 | 1,335.0 | 1.8 |
| 1976 | 31.9 | 26.3 | 218.0 | 121 | 350 | 1,474.8 | 1.8 |
| 1977 | 35.2 | 29.6 | 220.2 | 134 | 366 | 1,633.2 | 1.8 |
| 1978 | 38.6 | 32.1 | 222.6 | 144 | 367 | 1,837.7 | 1.7 |
| 1979 | 43.1 | 36.6 | 225.1 | 163 | 382 | 2,062.2 | 1.8 |
| 1980 | 48.6 | 40.7 | 227.7 | 179 | 385 | 2,307.9 | 1.8 |
| 1981 | 55.3 | 46.0 | 230.0 | 200 | 394 | 2,591.3 | 1.8 |
| 1982 | 59.1 | 47.6 | 232.2 | 205 | 381 | 2,775.3 | 1.7 |
| 1983 | 63.2 | 52.1 | 234.3 | 222 | 397 | 2,960.7 | 1.8 |
| 1984 | 68.6 | 56.5 | 236.3 | 239 | 412 | 3,289.5 | 1.7 |
| 1985 | 71.7 | 57.4 | 238.5 | 241 | 402 | 3,526.7 | 1.6 |
| 1986 | 83.3 | 67.1 | 240.7 | 279 | 456 | 3,722.4 | 1.8 |
| 1987 | 82.2 | 64.5 | 242.8 | 266 | 423 | 3,947.4 | 1.6 |
| 1988 | 88.0 | 70.0 | 245.0 | 286 | 440 | 4,253.7 | 1.6 |
| 1989 | 98.3 | 79.5 | 247.3 | 321 | 477 | 4,587.8 | 1.7 |
| 1990 | 100.5 | 81.0 | 250.1 | 324 | 463 | 4,878.6 | 1.7 |
| 1991 | 104.9 | 84.3 | 253.5 | 332 | 459 | 5,051.0 | 1.7 |
| 1992 | 111.8 | 87.7 | 256.9 | 341 | 461 | 5,362.0 | 1.6 |
| 1993 | 116.9 | 92.0 | 260.3 | 353 | 466 | 5,558.5 | 1.7 |

*(continued)*

**Table 3.4.** Per Capita Contributions and Individual Contributions to Nonprofit Organizations, 1965–2006 *(continued)*

| | Private Giving ($ billions) | | Population (midyear, millions) | Per Capita Individual Giving | | Total personal income ($ billions) | Individual giving as % of personal income |
| | Total | By individuals | | $ | 2006 $ | | |
|------|-------|------------|-------|-----|-------|----------|-----|
| 1994 | 120.3 | 92.5  | 263.4 | 351 | 454 | 5,842.5  | 1.6 |
| 1995 | 123.7 | 95.4  | 266.6 | 358 | 453 | 6,152.3  | 1.5 |
| 1996 | 139.1 | 107.6 | 269.7 | 399 | 495 | 6,520.6  | 1.6 |
| 1997 | 163.0 | 124.2 | 272.9 | 455 | 556 | 6,915.1  | 1.8 |
| 1998 | 176.8 | 138.4 | 276.1 | 501 | 605 | 7,423.0  | 1.9 |
| 1999 | 202.7 | 154.6 | 279.3 | 554 | 659 | 7,802.4  | 2.0 |
| 2000 | 229.7 | 174.5 | 282.4 | 618 | 720 | 8,429.7  | 2.1 |
| 2001 | 231.1 | 172.4 | 285.3 | 604 | 688 | 8,724.1  | 2.0 |
| 2002 | 231.5 | 172.9 | 288.2 | 600 | 671 | 8,881.9  | 1.9 |
| 2003 | 236.3 | 180.2 | 291.1 | 619 | 678 | 9,163.6  | 2.0 |
| 2004 | 259.0 | 200.8 | 293.9 | 683 | 728 | 9,727.2  | 2.1 |
| 2005 | 283.1 | 213.5 | 296.6 | 720 | 742 | 10,301.1 | 2.1 |
| 2006 | 295.0 | 222.9 | 299.8 | 743 | 743 | 10,983.4 | 2.0 |

*Sources:* Private and individual giving from Giving USA Foundation, *Giving USA* (2007); population from Chairman of the Council of Economic Advisers, *Economic Report of the President,* table B-34 (2007); personal income from U.S. Department of Commerce, Bureau of Economic Analysis, National Income and Product Accounts, table 2.1 (2007).
*Note:* Figures for giving were deflated using the GDP deflator from U.S. Department of Commerce, Bureau of Economic Analysis, National Income and Product Accounts, table 1.1.4 (2007).

- The percentage of itemizers' contributions represented by cash contributions declined from a high of 88 percent in 1987 to a low of 70 percent in 2000. Since then, it has rebounded somewhat. (See table 3.10 and figure 3.8.)
- From 1985 to 2005, 89 percent of itemizers took a charitable deduction. (See table 3.11.)
- In constant dollars, the average charitable deduction by itemizers was on an increasing trend until 2000. After declining for two years, the average size increased each year from 2003 to 2005, setting a new record in 2005. (See table 3.11.)
- From 1993 to 2005, the average itemizer with adjusted gross income over $1 million took a charitable deduction equal to 4.5 percent of adjusted gross income. (See table 3.12.)
- In constant dollars, the average charitable deduction by an itemizer whose adjusted gross income was over $1 million peaked in 2000 and has not yet returned to that level, although it has been increasing since 2002. (See table 3.12.)

**Figure 3.5.** Per Capita Individual Charitable Contributions, 1965–2006

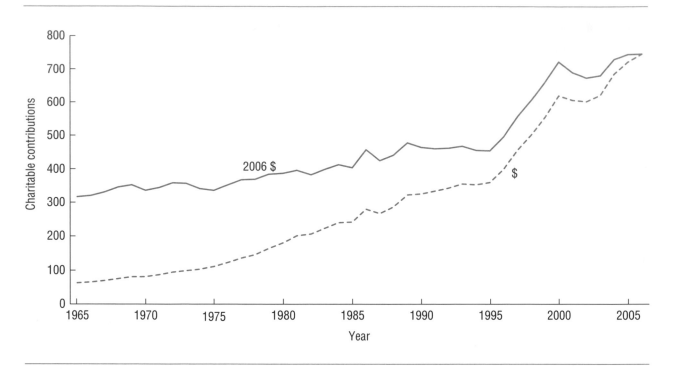

*Source:* Private and individual giving from Giving USA Foundation, *Giving USA* (2007); population from Chairman of the Council of Economic Advisers, *Economic Report of the President*, table B-34 (2007); personal income from U.S. Department of Commerce, Bureau of Economic Analysis, National Income and Product Accounts, table 2.1 (2007).

**Table 3.5.** Household Charitable Giving by Recipient Organization, 2002

| Type of nonprofit | Estimated household giving ($ billions) | Households that gave (%) | Average gift ($) |
|---|---|---|---|
| Religion | 92.0 | 45 | 1,703 |
| To help needy | 15.9 | 29 | 457 |
| Combined purposes | 15.4 | 27 | 476 |
| Health | 7.5 | 21 | 298 |
| Education | 7.5 | 15 | 416 |
| Youth/Families | 2.5 | 11 | 192 |
| Arts | 2.3 | 9 | 215 |
| Environment | 1.5 | 8 | 157 |
| Community | 1.0 | 6 | 139 |
| International | 1.4 | 4 | 293 |
| Other | 3.6 | 8 | 374 |
| Any charity[a] | n.a. | 67 | 1,872 |

*Source:* Center on Philanthropy at Indiana University, Center on Philanthropy Panel Study (2006).
a. Only households that gave at least $25 total were included.
n.a. = not applicable

**Figure 3.6.** Distribution of Total Estimated Household Giving, 2002 (percent)

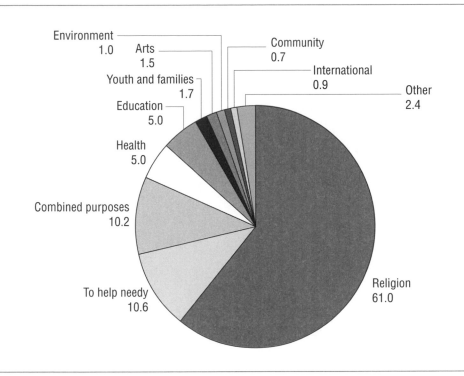

Environment
1.0
Arts
1.5
Youth and families
1.7
Education
5.0
Health
5.0
Combined purposes
10.2
To help needy
10.6
Community
0.7
International
0.9
Other
2.4
Religion
61.0

*Source:* Center on Philanthropy at Indiana University, Center on Philanthropy Panel Study (2006).

# Volunteering

Just as important to many nonprofits as gifts of cash or goods is the time so many people give. Of course, the volunteer experience is usually rewarding too, but that doesn't detract from the immense value these gifts of time and skill provide to nonprofits and the people they serve. Estimating the economic value of such volunteering is one major purpose of this section.

Table 3.13 provides key indicators from the two major government surveys that collect data on volunteering, the Current Population Survey (CPS) and the American Time Use Survey (ATUS), and uses them to estimate the economic value of volunteering.

The CPS asks people about their volunteering during the previous year.

- In 2006, 26.7 percent of the civilian population 16 and older said they had volunteered during the previous year.
- That translated into 61.2 million volunteers in 2006.
- Asked to remember how many hours they had volunteered the previous year, volunteers' median response was 52 hours.
- The rate and number of volunteers was down slightly in 2006, after three stable years. This decline was observed across all demographic groups. (See also table 3.15.)

**Table 3.6.** Household Charitable Giving by Income Range and Itemizer Status, 2002

| Income | Average | | | Itemizers | | | Nonitemizers | | |
|---|---|---|---|---|---|---|---|---|---|
| | % that give | Average yearly donation ($) | Donation as % of income | % that give | Average yearly donation ($) | Donation as % of donation income | % that give | Average yearly donation ($) | Donation as % of income |
| **Total charitable giving** | | | | | | | | | |
| <$50,000 | 54 | 1,153 | 3.6 | 100 | 2,056 | 5.0 | 46 | 829 | 2.9 |
| $50,000–$100,000 | 80 | 1,823 | 2.6 | 100 | 2,342 | 3.2 | 63 | 1,127 | 1.7 |
| >$100,000 | 92 | 3,459 | 1.6 | 100 | 4,035 | 1.6 | 78 | 2,085 | 1.5 |
| All | 67 | 1,872 | 2.2 | 100 | 2,816 | 2.3 | 52 | 1,056 | 2.1 |
| **Religious giving** | | | | | | | | | |
| <$50,000 | 37 | 1,140 | 3.5 | 75 | 1,879 | 4.6 | 30 | 838 | 2.9 |
| $50,000–$100,000 | 54 | 1,791 | 2.6 | 72 | 2,259 | 3.1 | 39 | 1,061 | 1.6 |
| >$100,000 | 62 | 2,761 | 1.1 | 68 | 3,222 | 1.1 | 48 | 1,542 | 1.1 |
| All | 45 | 1,703 | 1.8 | 71 | 2,458 | 1.8 | 34 | 974 | 1.9 |
| **Secular giving** | | | | | | | | | |
| <$50,000 | 42 | 490 | 1.5 | 87 | 749 | 1.8 | 34 | 380 | 1.3 |
| $50,000–$100,000 | 69 | 710 | 1.0 | 88 | 820 | 1.1 | 54 | 558 | 0.8 |
| >$100,000 | 86 | 1,744 | 0.8 | 95 | 1,923 | 0.7 | 69 | 1,284 | 0.9 |
| All | 56 | 863 | 0.9 | 90 | 1,180 | 0.9 | 41 | 552 | 1.0 |

*Source:* Center on Philanthropy at Indiana University, Center on Philanthropy Panel Study (2006).

*Notes:* All averages are for donors who gave more than $25 to any charity. Data in the leftmost three columns reflect all analyzed cases. Donations as a percentage of income is the average donation divided by the average income. Not all analyzed cases are included in the breakout by itemization status because of some cases where itemization status was not known. Income is averaged for 2001 and 2002 because giving is often a result of the prior year's financial results and the current year's financial position. One case is excluded because total giving exceeded 120 percent of income.

**Table 3.7.** Household Charitable Giving by Income and by Age, Marital Status, and Race/Ethnicity, 2002

| Income | Total Charitable Giving | | | | Religious Giving | | | | Secular Giving | | | |
|---|---|---|---|---|---|---|---|---|---|---|---|---|
| | <$50K | $50K–$100K | >$100K | All | <$50K | $50K–$100K | >$100K | All | <$50K | $50K–$100K | >$100K | All |
| **All households** | | | | | | | | | | | | |
| % that give | 54 | 80 | 92 | 67 | 37 | 54 | 62 | 45 | 42 | 69 | 86 | 56 |
| Average yearly donation ($) | 1,153 | 1,823 | 3,459 | 1,872 | 1,140 | 1,791 | 2,761 | 1,703 | 490 | 710 | 1,744 | 863 |
| Donation as % of income | 3.6 | 2.6 | 1.6 | 2.2 | 3.5 | 2.6 | 1.1 | 1.8 | 1.5 | 1.0 | 0.8 | 0.9 |
| **Age 18–39** | | | | | | | | | | | | |
| % who give | 44 | 73 | 84 | 61 | 31 | 45 | 56 | 40 | 32 | 61 | 77 | 50 |
| Average yearly donation ($) | 841 | 1,436 | 2,273 | 1,459 | 967 | 1,797 | 1,830 | 1,505 | 212 | 394 | 1,144 | 564 |
| Donation as % of income | 2.2 | 2.1 | 1.5 | 1.8 | 2.5 | 2.5 | 1.3 | 1.9 | 0.5 | 0.6 | 0.8 | 0.7 |
| **Age 40–64** | | | | | | | | | | | | |
| % who give | 56 | 82 | 93 | 73 | 38 | 56 | 64 | 49 | 44 | 71 | 87 | 62 |
| Average yearly donation ($) | 1,208 | 2,040 | 3,752 | 2,234 | 1,126 | 2,008 | 2,939 | 1,972 | 579 | 778 | 1,833 | 1,043 |
| Donation as % of income | 3.3 | 2.9 | 1.5 | 2.0 | 3.1 | 2.8 | 1.0 | 1.6 | 1.5 | 1.1 | 0.7 | 0.9 |
| **Age 65+** | | | | | | | | | | | | |
| % who give | 68 | 92 | 96 | 74 | 57 | 75 | 73 | 61 | 51 | 86 | 89 | 60 |
| Average yearly donation ($) | 1,452 | 2,087 | 5,140 | 1,889 | 1,344 | 1,686 | 3,584 | 1,586 | 453 | 775 | 2,593 | 736 |
| Donation as % of income | 5.4 | 3.0 | 3.3 | 3.9 | 4.9 | 2.5 | 2.3 | 3.3 | 1.6 | 1.1 | 1.6 | 1.4 |
| **Married couples, widows, widowers** | | | | | | | | | | | | |
| % who give | 64 | 83 | 93 | 77 | 51 | 61 | 64 | 58 | 47 | 72 | 86 | 65 |
| Average yearly donation ($) | 1,483 | 2,029 | 3,697 | 2,286 | 1,422 | 1,948 | 2,944 | 1,996 | 474 | 691 | 1,808 | 960 |
| Donation as % of income | 4.3 | 2.8 | 1.6 | 2.2 | 4.1 | 2.7 | 1.1 | 1.8 | 1.3 | 1.0 | 0.7 | 0.8 |

*(continued)*

**Table 3.7.** Household Charitable Giving by Income and by Age, Marital Status, and Race/Ethnicity, 2002 *(continued)*

| Income | Total Charitable Giving | | | | Religious Giving | | | | Secular Giving | | | |
|---|---|---|---|---|---|---|---|---|---|---|---|---|
| | <$50K | $50K–$100K | >$100K | All | <$50K | $50K–$100K | >$100K | All | <$50K | $50K–$100K | >$100K | All |
| **Never-married women** | | | | | | | | | | | | |
| % who give | 40 | 83 | 95 | 48.0 | 20 | 46 | 34 | 24 | 34 | 76 | 95 | 43 |
| Average yearly donation ($) | 772 | 1,099 | 3,867 | 970 | 795 | 969 | 1,266 | 860 | 434 | 618 | 3,412 | 603 |
| Donation as % of income | 2.7 | 1.8 | 2.6 | 2.3 | 2.7 | 1.6 | 1.4 | 2.1 | 1.5 | 1.0 | 2.3 | 1.4 |
| **Never-married men** | | | | | | | | | | | | |
| % who give | 39 | 59 | 94 | 46 | 18 | 20 | 48 | 20 | 32 | 49 | 90 | 39 |
| Average yearly donation ($) | 841 | 939 | 1,582 | 976 | 513 | 643 | 1,380 | 693 | 738 | 867 | 923 | 796 |
| Donation as % of income | 2.8 | 1.5 | 1.2 | 1.8 | 1.7 | 1.1 | 1.0 | 1.3 | 2.4 | 1.3 | 0.7 | 1.4 |
| **All other marital status (divorced, annulled, separated)** | | | | | | | | | | | | |
| % who give | 52 | 73 | 84 | 59 | 30 | 39 | 49 | 34 | 42 | 63 | 77 | 49 |
| Average yearly donation ($) | 714 | 1,361 | 1,874 | 1,001 | 617 | 1,270 | 1,150 | 839 | 439 | 799 | 1,298 | 628 |
| Donation as % of income | 2.5 | 2.1 | 1.4 | 2.1 | 2.2 | 2.0 | 0.9 | 1.8 | 1.5 | 1.3 | 1.0 | 1.2 |
| **Caucasian/White** | | | | | | | | | | | | |
| % who give | 60 | 82 | 93 | 72 | 39 | 55 | 61 | 48 | 48 | 73 | 87 | 62 |
| Average yearly donation ($) | 1,225 | 1,914 | 3,553 | 1,996 | 1,218 | 1,883 | 2,768 | 1,803 | 523 | 739 | 1,850 | 929 |
| Donation as % of income | 3.7 | 2.7 | 1.5 | 2.2 | 3.6 | 2.7 | 1.0 | 1.7 | 1.5 | 1.0 | 0.8 | 0.9 |

**African American/Black**

| | | | | | | | | | | | | |
|---|---|---|---|---|---|---|---|---|---|---|---|---|
| % who give | 40 | 73 | 90 | 49 | 29 | 55 | 74 | 36 | 29 | 58 | 81 | 37 |
| Average yearly donation ($) | 978 | 1,697 | 3,891 | 1,453 | 968 | 1,691 | 3,759 | 1,460 | 369 | 525 | 910 | 474 |
| Donation as % of income | 3.5 | 2.6 | 3.6 | 3.1 | 3.5 | 2.6 | 3.4 | 3.1 | 1.3 | 0.8 | 0.8 | 1.0 |

**Latino/Hispanic**

| | | | | | | | | | | | | |
|---|---|---|---|---|---|---|---|---|---|---|---|---|
| % who give | 34 | 69 | 89 | 43 | 29 | 53 | 63 | 35 | 17 | 42 | 73 | 24 |
| Average yearly donation ($) | 694 | 965 | 2,872 | 948 | 750 | 978 | 2,732 | 952 | 136 | 360 | 1,155 | 335 |
| Donation as % of income | 2.4 | 1.5 | 2.1 | 1.9 | 2.6 | 1.4 | 2.1 | 2.0 | 0.5 | 0.6 | 0.9 | 0.6 |

**Asian/Pacific Islander**

| | | | | | | | | | | | | |
|---|---|---|---|---|---|---|---|---|---|---|---|---|
| % who give | 47 | 86 | 92 | 74 | 34 | 66 | 45 | 48 | 36 | 62 | 87 | 60 |
| Average yearly donation ($) | 491 | 1,087 | 2,542 | 1,449 | 498 | 1,198 | 3,449 | 1,618 | 179 | 237 | 917 | 498 |
| Donation as % of income | 1.2 | 1.5 | 1.8 | 1.7 | 1.3 | 1.6 | 2.4 | 2.0 | 0.4 | 0.3 | 0.7 | 0.5 |

**All other race/Ethnicity**

| | | | | | | | | | | | | |
|---|---|---|---|---|---|---|---|---|---|---|---|---|
| % who give | 47 | 73 | 100 | 61 | 29 | 36 | 94 | 39 | 34 | 54 | 85 | 46 |
| Average yearly donation ($) | 1,265 | 1,154 | 1,198 | 1,214 | 1,168 | 757 | 546 | 879 | 738 | 1,035 | 806 | 854 |
| Donation as % of income | 3.7 | 1.9 | 0.9 | 1.9 | 3.8 | 1.3 | 0.4 | 1.3 | 2.0 | 1.7 | 0.6 | 1.3 |

*Source*: Center on Philanthropy at Indiana University, Center on Philanthropy Panel Study (2006).
*Notes*: All averages are for donors who gave more than $25 to any charity. Donations as a percentage of income is the average donation divided by the average income. Not all analyzed cases are included in the demographic breakouts because some respondents did not answer all questions. Income is averaged for 2001 and 2002 because giving is often a result of the prior year's financial results and the current year's financial position. One case is excluded because reported total giving exceeded 120 percent of income.

**Table 3.8.** Estate Tax Returns and Charitable Bequests, Selected Years, 1987–2005

| Year | Returns | Gross Estate $ billions | Gross Estate $ billions (2005) | Bequests | % of returns | Value of Bequests $ billions | Value of Bequests $ billions (2005) | % of gross estate |
|------|---------|-------------|------------------|----------|--------------|-------------|------------------|-------------------|
| 1987 | 45,113  | 66.6  | 102.8 | 8,967  | 19.9 | 4.0  | 4.0  | 6.0  |
| 1990 | 50,367  | 87.1  | 120.6 | 9,709  | 19.3 | 5.5  | 5.5  | 6.3  |
| 1992 | 59,176  | 98.9  | 129.4 | 11,053 | 18.7 | 6.8  | 6.8  | 6.9  |
| 1993 | 60,211  | 103.7 | 132.6 | 11,119 | 18.5 | 7.3  | 7.3  | 7.0  |
| 1994 | 68,595  | 117.0 | 146.5 | 11,869 | 17.3 | 9.3  | 9.3  | 7.9  |
| 1995 | 69,755  | 117.7 | 144.4 | 13,039 | 18.7 | 8.7  | 8.7  | 7.4  |
| 1996 | 79,321  | 137.4 | 165.4 | 14,233 | 17.9 | 10.2 | 10.2 | 7.4  |
| 1997 | 90,006  | 162.3 | 192.2 | 15,575 | 17.3 | 14.3 | 14.3 | 8.8  |
| 1998 | 97,856  | 173.8 | 203.6 | 16,982 | 17.4 | 10.9 | 10.9 | 6.2  |
| 1999 | 103,979 | 196.4 | 226.8 | 17,554 | 16.9 | 14.6 | 14.6 | 7.4  |
| 2000 | 108,322 | 217.4 | 245.7 | 18,011 | 16.6 | 16.1 | 16.1 | 7.4  |
| 2001 | 106,885 | 214.8 | 237.1 | 18,652 | 17.5 | 16.1 | 16.1 | 7.5  |
| 2002 | 98,356  | 211.2 | 229.0 | 16,104 | 16.4 | 17.8 | 17.8 | 8.4  |
| 2003 | 66,042  | 194.5 | 206.6 | 12,492 | 18.9 | 14.6 | 14.6 | 7.5  |
| 2004 | 62,718  | 192.6 | 198.9 | 11,599 | 18.5 | 15.0 | 15.0 | 7.8  |
| 2005 | 45,070  | 184.7 | 184.7 | 8,785  | 19.5 | 19.8 | 19.8 | 10.7 |

*Source:* U.S. Department of the Treasury, Internal Revenue Service, SOI Tax Stats—Estate Tax Statistics (1987, 1990, 1992–2005).
*Note:* Figures for giving were deflated using the GDP deflator from U.S. Department of Commerce, Bureau of Economic Analysis, National Income and Product Accounts, table 1.1.4 (2007).

The ATUS is different. Administered throughout the year, it asks in great detail how people spent the last 24 hours. By this approach, the survey shows volunteer activity on an average day.

- About 6.5 percent of the adult population volunteers on an average day.
- That translated into more than 15 million volunteers per day in 2006.
- The average person who volunteered spent 2.31 hours volunteering that day.
- In total, about 12.9 billion hours were volunteered in 2006.
- Assuming a full-time employee works 1,700 hours per year, those volunteer hours were the equivalent of 7.6 million full-time employees.
- Assuming those employees would have earned the average private nonfarm hourly wage, volunteers' time was worth $215.6 billion in 2005.
- According to this survey, volunteering increased slightly from 2003 to 2005 but declined in 2006.

**Figure 3.7.** Number and Value of Charitable Bequests by Year Filed, 1987–2005

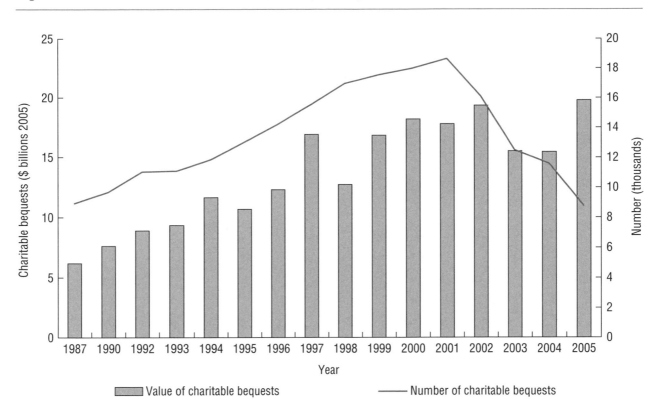

Source: U.S. Department of the Treasury, Internal Revenue Service, SOI Tax Stats—Estate Tax Statistics (1987, 1990, 1992–2005). Constant dollar values are authors' calculations using the GDP deflator from U.S. Department of Commerce, Bureau of Economic Analysis, National Income and Product Accounts, table 1.1.4 (2007).

■ Combining data from the two surveys yields the average annual volunteer hours per volunteer—207—in 2006.

The CPS also records the types of organizations people volunteered for and demographic information about volunteers. When people volunteered for more than one organization, they were asked to choose one as their "main" organization.

■ The type of organization most frequently mentioned was religious, followed by educational or youth service organizations. (See table 3.14 and figure 3.9.)

■ The only other type of organization mentioned by more than 10 percent of respondents is social or community service organizations. (See table 3.14 and figure 3.9.)

■ Women are more likely to volunteer than men. (See table 3.15.)

■ The peak ages for volunteering have been from 35 to 44, although 45- to 54-year-olds showed the same propensity in 2006. (See table 3.15.)

■ College graduates are more likely to volunteer than those with less schooling. (See table 3.15.)

**Table 3.9.** Estimates of Individual Charitable Contributions by Tax-Itemization Status, 1985–2005

| | Returns | AGI ($ millions) | AGI per return | Charitable contributions ($ millions) | Per return | As % of AGI |
|---|---|---|---|---|---|---|
| **1985** | | | | | | |
| All | 101,660,287 | 2,305,952 | 22,683 | 57,390 | 565 | 2.49 |
| Itemizer | 39,848,184 | 1,582,587 | 39,715 | 47,963 | 1,204 | 3.03 |
| Nonitemizer | 61,812,103 | 723,365 | 11,703 | 9,427 | 153 | 1.30 |
| **1986** | | | | | | |
| All | 103,045,170 | 2,481,681 | 24,083 | 67,090 | 651 | 2.70 |
| Itemizer | 40,667,008 | 1,725,714 | 42,435 | 53,816 | 1,323 | 3.12 |
| Nonitemizer | 62,378,162 | 755,967 | 12,119 | 13,274 | 213 | 1.76 |
| **1987** | | | | | | |
| All | 106,996,270 | 2,772,824 | 25,915 | 64,530 | 603 | 2.33 |
| Itemizer | 35,627,790 | 1,799,048 | 50,496 | 49,624 | 1,393 | 2.76 |
| Nonitemizer | 71,368,480 | 973,776 | 13,644 | 14,906 | 209 | 1.53 |
| **1988** | | | | | | |
| All | 109,708,280 | 3,083,020 | 28,102 | 69,980 | 638 | 2.27 |
| Itemizer | 31,902,985 | 1,887,494 | 59,164 | 50,949 | 1,597 | 2.70 |
| Nonitemizer | 77,805,295 | 1,195,526 | 15,366 | 19,031 | 245 | 1.59 |
| **1989** | | | | | | |
| All | 112,135,673 | 3,256,359 | 29,039 | 79,450 | 709 | 2.44 |
| Itemizer | 31,972,317 | 1,971,222 | 61,654 | 55,459 | 1,735 | 2.81 |
| Nonitemizer | 80,163,356 | 1,285,137 | 16,031 | 23,991 | 299 | 1.87 |
| **1990** | | | | | | |
| All | 113,717,136 | 3,405,428 | 29,946 | 81,040 | 713 | 2.38 |
| Itemizer | 32,174,938 | 2,046,651 | 63,610 | 57,243 | 1,779 | 2.80 |
| Nonitemizer | 81,542,198 | 1,358,777 | 16,663 | 23,797 | 292 | 1.75 |
| **1991** | | | | | | |
| All | 114,730,124 | 3,464,524 | 30,197 | 84,270 | 735 | 2.43 |
| Itemizer | 32,489,919 | 2,056,805 | 63,306 | 60,574 | 1,864 | 2.95 |
| Nonitemizer | 82,240,205 | 1,407,719 | 17,117 | 23,696 | 288 | 1.68 |
| **1992** | | | | | | |
| All | 113,604,503 | 3,629,129 | 31,945 | 87,700 | 772 | 2.42 |
| Itemizer | 32,540,614 | 2,183,969 | 67,115 | 63,843 | 1,962 | 2.92 |
| Nonitemizer | 81,063,889 | 1,445,160 | 17,827 | 23,857 | 294 | 1.65 |

*(continued)*

**Table 3.9.** Estimates of Individual Charitable Contributions by Tax-Itemization Status, 1985–2005 *(continued)*

| | Returns | AGI ($ millions) | AGI per return | Charitable contributions ($ millions) | Per return | As % of AGI |
|---|---|---|---|---|---|---|
| **1993** | | | | | | |
| All | 114,601,819 | 3,723,340 | 32,489 | 92,000 | 803 | 2.47 |
| Itemizer | 32,821,464 | 2,241,087 | 68,281 | 68,354 | 2,083 | 3.05 |
| Nonitemizer | 81,780,355 | 1,482,253 | 18,125 | 23,646 | 289 | 1.60 |
| **1994** | | | | | | |
| All | 115,943,131 | 3,907,518 | 33,702 | 92,520 | 798 | 2.37 |
| Itemizer | 33,017,754 | 2,342,834 | 70,957 | 70,545 | 2,137 | 3.01 |
| Nonitemizer | 82,925,377 | 1,564,684 | 18,869 | 21,975 | 265 | 1.40 |
| **1995** | | | | | | |
| All | 118,218,327 | 4,189,354 | 35,437 | 95,360 | 807 | 2.28 |
| Itemizer | 34,007,717 | 2,542,781 | 74,771 | 74,992 | 2,205 | 2.95 |
| Nonitemizer | 84,210,610 | 1,646,573 | 19,553 | 20,368 | 242 | 1.24 |
| **1996** | | | | | | |
| All | 120,351,208 | 4,535,974 | 37,689 | 107,560 | 894 | 2.37 |
| Itemizer | 35,414,589 | 2,812,927 | 79,428 | 86,159 | 2,433 | 3.06 |
| Nonitemizer | 84,936,619 | 1,723,048 | 20,286 | 21,401 | 252 | 1.24 |
| **1997** | | | | | | |
| All | 122,421,991 | 4,969,950 | 40,597 | 124,200 | 1,015 | 2.50 |
| Itemizer | 36,624,595 | 3,130,184 | 85,467 | 99,192 | 2,708 | 3.17 |
| Nonitemizer | 85,797,396 | 1,839,766 | 21,443 | 25,008 | 291 | 1.36 |
| **1998** | | | | | | |
| All | 124,770,662 | 5,415,973 | 43,407 | 138,350 | 1,109 | 2.55 |
| Itemizer | 38,186,186 | 3,466,035 | 90,767 | 109,240 | 2,861 | 3.15 |
| Nonitemizer | 86,584,476 | 1,949,938 | 22,521 | 29,110 | 336 | 1.49 |
| **1999** | | | | | | |
| All | 127,075,145 | 5,855,468 | 46,079 | 154,630 | 1,217 | 2.64 |
| Itemizer | 40,244,305 | 3,853,151 | 95,744 | 125,799 | 3,126 | 3.26 |
| Nonitemizer | 86,830,840 | 2,002,317 | 23,060 | 28,831 | 332 | 1.44 |

*(continued)*

**Table 3.9.** Estimates of Individual Charitable Contributions by Tax-Itemization Status, 1985–2005 *(continued)*

| | Returns | AGI ($ millions) | AGI per return | Charitable contributions ($ millions) | Per return | As % of AGI |
|---|---|---|---|---|---|---|
| **2000** | | | | | | |
| All | 129,373,500 | 6,365,377 | 49,202 | 174,510 | 1,349 | 2.74 |
| Itemizer | 42,534,320 | 4,294,262 | 100,960 | 140,682 | 3,307 | 3.28 |
| Nonitemizer | 86,839,180 | 2,071,115 | 23,850 | 33,828 | 390 | 1.63 |
| **2001** | | | | | | |
| All | 130,255,237 | 6,170,604 | 47,373 | 172,400 | 1,324 | 2.79 |
| Itemizer | 44,562,308 | 4,164,470 | 93,453 | 139,241 | 3,125 | 3.34 |
| Nonitemizer | 85,692,929 | 2,006,134 | 23,411 | 33,159 | 387 | 1.65 |
| **2002** | | | | | | |
| All | 130,076,443 | 6,033,586 | 46,385 | 172,870 | 1,329 | 2.87 |
| Itemizer | 45,647,551 | 4,080,678 | 89,395 | 140,571 | 3,079 | 3.44 |
| Nonitemizer | 84,428,892 | 1,952,907 | 23,131 | 32,299 | 383 | 1.65 |
| **2003** | | | | | | |
| All | 130,423,626 | 6,207,109 | 47,592 | 180,190 | 1,382 | 2.90 |
| Itemizer | 43,949,591 | 4,103,653 | 93,372 | 145,702 | 3,315 | 3.55 |
| Nonitemizer | 86,474,035 | 2,103,455 | 24,325 | 34,488 | 399 | 1.64 |
| **2004** | | | | | | |
| All | 132,226,042 | 6,788,805 | 51,342 | 200,790 | 1,519 | 2.96 |
| Itemizer | 46,335,237 | 4,643,404 | 100,213 | 165,564 | 3,573 | 3.57 |
| Nonitemizer | 85,890,805 | 2,145,402 | 24,978 | 35,226 | 410 | 1.64 |
| **2005** | | | | | | |
| All | 134,372,678 | 7,422,496 | 55,238 | 213,470 | 1,589 | 2.88 |
| Itemizer | 47,755,427 | 5,185,666 | 108,588 | 183,391 | 3,840 | 3.54 |
| Nonitemizer | 86,617,251 | 2,236,830 | 25,824 | 30,079 | 347 | 1.34 |

*Sources:* Giving USA Foundation, *Giving USA* (2007); U.S. Department of the Treasury, Internal Revenue Service, SOI Tax Stats—Individual Income Tax Returns Publication 1304 (Complete Report) (1985–2005).
AGI = adjusted gross income
*Note:* Nonitemizer contributions are calculated as the difference between individual giving from table 3.3 and itemizer giving.

**Table 3.10.** Distribution of Itemizers' Cash and Noncash Charitable Contributions, 1985–2005

| | Total Charitable Contributions | | Cash Contributions | | Noncash Contributions | |
|---|---|---|---|---|---|---|
| | $ thousands | % | $ thousands | % | $ thousands | % |
| 1985 | 47,962,848 | 100.0 | 41,371,619 | 86.3 | 6,591,229 | 13.7 |
| 1986 | 53,815,978 | 100.0 | 43,168,816 | 80.2 | 10,647,169 | 19.8 |
| 1987 | 49,623,906 | 100.0 | 43,448,099 | 87.6 | 6,175,807 | 12.4 |
| 1988 | 50,949,273 | 100.0 | 42,834,342 | 84.1 | 6,711,616 | 13.2 |
| 1989 | 55,459,205 | 100.0 | 46,553,194 | 83.9 | 7,550,914 | 13.6 |
| 1990 | 57,242,767 | 100.0 | 48,485,664 | 84.7 | 7,494,016 | 13.1 |
| 1991 | 60,573,565 | 100.0 | 51,277,927 | 84.7 | 9,681,786 | 16.0 |
| 1992 | 63,843,281 | 100.0 | 53,647,612 | 84.0 | 9,632,779 | 15.1 |
| 1993 | 68,354,293 | 100.0 | 55,784,521 | 81.6 | 12,278,893 | 18.0 |
| 1994 | 70,544,542 | 100.0 | 56,229,759 | 79.7 | 14,739,299 | 20.9 |
| 1995 | 74,991,519 | 100.0 | 59,589,837 | 79.5 | 13,521,937 | 18.0 |
| 1996 | 86,159,305 | 100.0 | 65,658,168 | 76.2 | 21,298,819 | 24.7 |
| 1997 | 99,191,962 | 100.0 | 72,425,402 | 73.0 | 27,961,174 | 28.2 |
| 1998 | 109,240,078 | 100.0 | 80,114,372 | 73.3 | 29,255,985 | 26.8 |
| 1999 | 125,798,548 | 100.0 | 88,276,422 | 70.2 | 38,286,580 | 30.4 |
| 2000 | 140,681,631 | 100.0 | 98,247,539 | 69.8 | 47,256,104 | 33.6 |
| 2001 | 139,241,476 | 100.0 | 104,747,173 | 75.2 | 37,997,546 | 27.3 |
| 2002 | 140,571,365 | 100.0 | 108,130,267 | 76.9 | 34,293,125 | 24.4 |
| 2003 | 145,702,137 | 100.0 | 110,336,696 | 75.7 | 38,041,067 | 26.1 |
| 2004 | 165,564,388 | 100.0 | 122,874,926 | 74.2 | 43,373,209 | 26.2 |
| 2005 | 183,390,686 | 100.0 | 139,054,112 | 75.8 | 48,056,520 | 26.2 |

*Source:* U.S. Department of the Treasury, Internal Revenue Service, SOI Tax Stats—Individual Income Tax Returns Publication 1304 (Complete Report), table 2.1 (1985–2005).
*Note:* Due to treatment of tax-year carryovers by the IRS, the sum of cash and noncash contributions may not equal total contributions.

**Figure 3.8.** Cash and Noncash Charitable Contributions, 1985–2005 (percent)

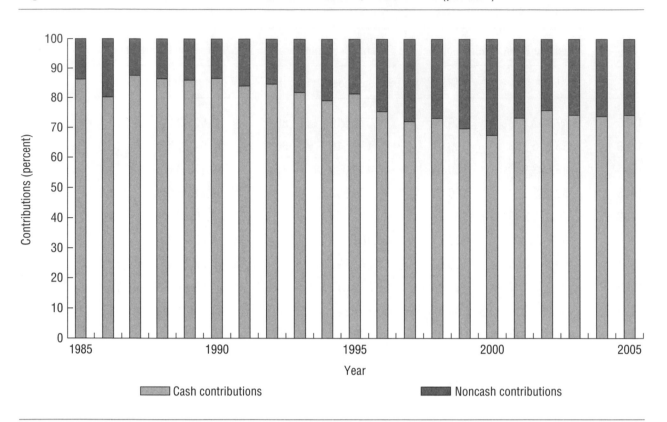

*Source:* U.S. Department of the Treasury, Internal Revenue Service, SOI Tax Stats—Individual Income Tax Returns Publication 1304 (Complete Report), table 2.1 (1985–2005).

- Part-time employees are more likely to volunteer than those with any other employment status. (See table 3.15.)
- A married person with a spouse present is more likely to volunteer than someone with any other marital status. (See table 3.15.)

Instead of focusing on types of organizations, the ATUS asks about types of activities to demonstrate how nonprofits are putting their volunteers to use. (Travel and waiting associated with volunteering are tracked as separate categories.)

- Measured as the average amount of time across all volunteers, the largest single use of volunteers is for administration and support. This includes fundraising, office work, computer use, phone calls, writing, editing, and reading. (See table 3.16 and figure 3.10.)
- The second largest use is for social service and care. This includes preparing food and cleaning up, collecting and delivering clothing or other goods, providing direct care or services, teaching, leading, counseling, and mentoring. (See table 3.16 and figure 3.10.)

**Table 3.11.** Average Charitable Deduction for All Tax Returns and for Itemizers with Charitable Deductions, 1985–2005

| | Returns | | Total Charitable Deductions | | Average Charitable Contribution | | | |
| | | | | | All Returns | | With Charitable Deductions | |
| | All | With charitable deductions | $ millions | $ millions 2005 | $ | $ 2005 | $ | $ 2005 |
|---|---|---|---|---|---|---|---|---|
| 1985 | 39,848,184 | 36,228,636 | 47,963 | 87,056 | 1,204 | 2,185 | 1,324 | 2,403 |
| 1986 | 40,667,008 | 36,857,590 | 53,816 | 95,897 | 1,323 | 2,358 | 1,460 | 2,602 |
| 1987 | 35,627,790 | 32,229,545 | 49,624 | 85,313 | 1,393 | 2,395 | 1,540 | 2,647 |
| 1988 | 31,902,985 | 29,110,570 | 50,949 | 84,111 | 1,597 | 2,636 | 1,750 | 2,889 |
| 1989 | 31,972,317 | 29,132,485 | 55,459 | 87,348 | 1,735 | 2,732 | 1,904 | 2,998 |
| 1990 | 32,174,938 | 29,230,264 | 57,243 | 85,536 | 1,779 | 2,658 | 1,958 | 2,926 |
| 1991 | 32,489,919 | 29,551,348 | 60,574 | 86,858 | 1,864 | 2,673 | 2,050 | 2,939 |
| 1992 | 32,540,614 | 29,603,407 | 63,843 | 88,871 | 1,962 | 2,731 | 2,157 | 3,002 |
| 1993 | 32,821,464 | 29,799,001 | 68,354 | 92,385 | 2,083 | 2,815 | 2,294 | 3,100 |
| 1994 | 33,017,754 | 29,848,727 | 70,545 | 92,965 | 2,137 | 2,816 | 2,363 | 3,115 |
| 1995 | 34,007,717 | 30,540,637 | 74,992 | 96,101 | 2,205 | 2,826 | 2,455 | 3,147 |
| 1996 | 35,414,589 | 31,591,983 | 86,159 | 107,246 | 2,433 | 3,028 | 2,727 | 3,395 |
| 1997 | 36,624,595 | 32,612,634 | 99,192 | 120,699 | 2,708 | 3,296 | 3,042 | 3,701 |
| 1998 | 38,186,186 | 33,835,992 | 109,240 | 130,887 | 2,861 | 3,428 | 3,229 | 3,868 |
| 1999 | 40,244,305 | 35,523,471 | 125,799 | 147,470 | 3,126 | 3,664 | 3,541 | 4,151 |
| 2000 | 42,534,320 | 37,524,825 | 140,682 | 159,554 | 3,307 | 3,751 | 3,749 | 4,252 |
| 2001 | 44,562,308 | 39,386,782 | 139,241 | 153,551 | 3,125 | 3,446 | 3,535 | 3,899 |
| 2002 | 45,647,551 | 40,399,695 | 140,571 | 152,605 | 3,079 | 3,343 | 3,480 | 3,777 |
| 2003 | 43,949,591 | 38,626,902 | 145,702 | 154,650 | 3,315 | 3,519 | 3,772 | 4,004 |
| 2004 | 46,335,237 | 40,623,426 | 165,564 | 171,174 | 3,573 | 3,694 | 4,076 | 4,214 |
| 2005 | 47,755,427 | 41,381,465 | 183,391 | 183,391 | 3,840 | 3,840 | 4,432 | 4,432 |

*Sources:* U.S. Department of the Treasury, Internal Revenue Service, SOI Tax Stats—Individual Income Tax Returns Publication 1304 (Complete Report) (1985–2005). Constant dollar values are authors' calculations, using the consumer price index for urban consumers, all items, U.S. city average, from the Bureau of Labor Statistics, with the 2005 figure as the baseline for comparison (i.e., rebased to 2005 = 100).

**Table 3.12.** Charitable Contributions from Itemizers with Adjusted Gross Income of $1 Million or More, 1993–2005

| Year | Returns | % of all returns with contribution deductions | $ Thousands | | Average Contribution | | Contributions as a % of AGI | Cash Contributions | | Noncash Contributions | |
|------|---------|---------|---------|---------|---------|---------|---------|---------|------|---------|------|
| | | | AGI | Total contributions | $ | $ 2005 | | $ thousands | % | $ thousands | % |
| 1993 | 62,392 | 0.21 | 163,049,402 | 7,050,906 | 113,010 | 152,739 | 4.3 | 3,907,828 | 54.5 | 3,265,085 | 45.5 |
| 1994 | 64,814 | 0.22 | 172,014,314 | 7,872,412 | 121,462 | 160,064 | 4.6 | 3,882,070 | 48.7 | 4,092,446 | 51.3 |
| 1995 | 80,362 | 0.26 | 214,365,387 | 8,845,408 | 110,070 | 141,054 | 4.1 | 4,667,770 | 59.6 | 3,168,163 | 40.4 |
| 1996 | 102,129 | 0.32 | 296,349,836 | 13,648,238 | 133,637 | 166,344 | 4.6 | 5,808,136 | 43.7 | 7,479,736 | 56.3 |
| 1997 | 132,072 | 0.40 | 397,475,502 | 18,618,418 | 140,972 | 171,538 | 4.7 | 7,365,764 | 38.8 | 11,641,343 | 61.2 |
| 1998 | 155,879 | 0.46 | 496,505,525 | 21,141,556 | 135,628 | 162,504 | 4.3 | 9,299,041 | 45.3 | 11,238,947 | 54.7 |
| 1999 | 186,729 | 0.53 | 610,730,186 | 27,245,122 | 145,907 | 171,043 | 4.5 | 10,208,251 | 38.9 | 16,021,218 | 61.1 |
| 2000 | 218,949 | 0.58 | 770,956,226 | 32,633,045 | 149,044 | 169,038 | 4.2 | 12,384,192 | 32.9 | 25,304,866 | 67.1 |
| 2001 | 178,520 | 0.45 | 547,369,318 | 24,932,570 | 139,663 | 154,015 | 4.6 | 11,772,323 | 43.0 | 15,576,513 | 57.0 |
| 2002 | 155,055 | 0.38 | 447,482,537 | 20,811,652 | 134,221 | 145,711 | 4.7 | 11,159,827 | 53.1 | 9,843,792 | 46.9 |
| 2003 | 165,399 | 0.43 | 503,009,522 | 24,196,568 | 146,292 | 155,276 | 4.8 | 12,169,102 | 49.8 | 12,255,944 | 50.2 |
| 2004 | 219,411 | 0.54 | 718,083,999 | 34,123,211 | 155,522 | 160,791 | 4.8 | 17,231,783 | 50.4 | 16,958,795 | 49.6 |
| 2005 | 278,701 | 0.67 | 970,597,258 | 45,412,078 | 162,942 | 162,942 | 4.5 | 25,960,921 | 54.6 | 21,547,363 | 45.4 |

*Sources:* U.S. Department of the Treasury, Internal Revenue Service, SOI Tax Stats—Individual Income Tax Returns Publication 1304 (Complete Report) (1985–2005). Constant dollar values are authors' calculations, using the consumer price index for urban consumers, all items, U.S. city average, from the Bureau of Labor Statistics, with the 2005 figure as the baseline for comparison (i.e., rebased to 2005 = 100).
AGI = adjusted gross income

**Table 3.13.** Number, Hours, and Dollar Value of Volunteers, 2002–2006

|  | 2002 | 2003 | 2004 | 2005 | 2006 |
|---|---|---|---|---|---|
| **Per year** | | | | | |
| % of population volunteering | 27.4 | 28.8 | 28.8 | 28.8 | 26.7 |
| Volunteers (thousands) | 59,783 | 63,791 | 64,542 | 65,357 | 61,199 |
| Hours volunteered (thousands) | — | 12,634,799 | 13,747,007 | 13,510,436 | 12,864,875 |
| Average hours per volunteer | — | 195 | 210 | 204 | 207 |
| Median hours per volunteer | 52 | 52 | 52 | 50 | 52 |
| **Per average day** | | | | | |
| % of population volunteering | — | 6.3 | 6.9 | 7.1 | 6.5 |
| Volunteers (thousands) | — | 14,201 | 15,705 | 16,471 | 15,228 |
| Hours per day per volunteer | — | 2.44 | 2.40 | 2.25 | 2.31 |
| Population (thousands) | — | 225,295 | 228,123 | 230,427 | 233,122 |
| Volunteer hours' equivalent in full-time employees (thousands) | — | 7,432 | 8,086 | 7,947 | 7,568 |
| Assigned hourly wages for volunteers ($) | — | 15.37 | 15.69 | 16.13 | 16.76 |
| Assigned value of volunteer time ($ thousands) | — | 193,944,166 | 215,415,595 | 217,653,117 | 215,615,300 |

*Sources:* Authors' calculations based on per year figures from U.S. Department of Labor, Bureau of Labor Statistics, Current Population Survey (2002–2006); per average day figures from U.S. Department of Labor, Bureau of Labor Statistics, American Time Use Survey (2003–2006); hourly wages from U.S. Department of Labor, Bureau of Labor Statistics, Current Employment Statistics (2007).
— = data not available

**Table 3.14.** Volunteers by Main Type of Organization, 2002–2006 (percent)

| Main type of organization | 2002 | 2003 | 2004 | 2005 | 2006 |
|---|---|---|---|---|---|
| All | 27.4 | 28.8 | 28.8 | 28.8 | 26.7 |
| Civic, political, professional, or international | 6.1 | 6.4 | 7.0 | 6.4 | 6.1 |
| Educational or youth service | 27.2 | 27.4 | 27.0 | 26.2 | 26.4 |
| Environmental or animal care | 1.6 | 1.7 | 1.7 | 1.8 | 1.6 |
| Hospital or other health | 8.6 | 8.2 | 7.5 | 7.7 | 8.1 |
| Public safety | 1.4 | 1.2 | 1.5 | 1.3 | 1.3 |
| Religious | 33.9 | 34.6 | 34.4 | 34.8 | 35.0 |
| Social or community service | 12.1 | 11.8 | 12.4 | 13.4 | 12.7 |
| Sport, hobby, cultural, or arts | 4.0 | 4.1 | 3.6 | 3.3 | 3.7 |
| Other | 3.5 | 3.1 | 3.3 | 3.5 | 3.4 |
| Not determined | 1.5 | 1.5 | 1.6 | 1.7 | 1.5 |

*Source:* U.S. Department of Labor, Bureau of Labor Statistics, Current Population Survey, Volunteer Supplement (2002–2006).

**Figure 3.9.** Volunteers by Their Main Organization, 2002–2006 (percent)

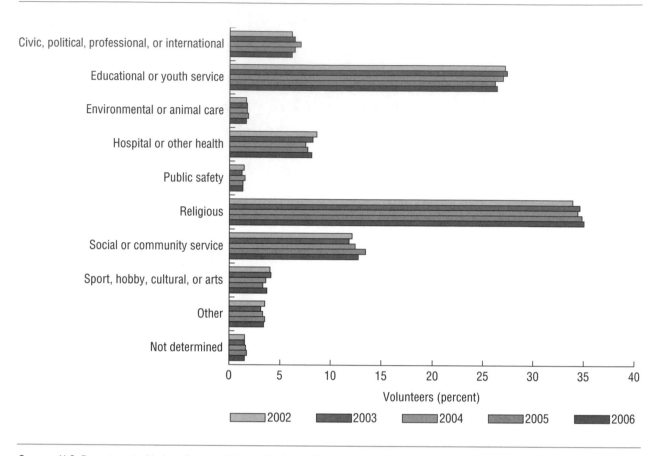

*Source:* U.S. Department of Labor, Bureau of Labor Statistics, Current Population Survey (2002–2006).

■ If the percentage of volunteers who performed each activity is considered instead of the average time, travel emerges as the most common activity, even though the total time engaged in travel is less than in many other categories. (See table 3.16, table 3.17, and figure 3.11.)

As a final look at volunteering, consider the American Heritage Time Use Study (AHTUS), an attempt to create historical data compatible with the ATUS by manipulating datasets from past studies, each using unique samples, data definitions, and methodologies. Table 3.18 provides statistics similar to those in table 3.13, but for a period spanning four decades. The numbers reported here are from a preliminary version of the AHTUS and therefore subject to change. To maximize comparability across the studies, the 2003 data are reported somewhat differently than in table 3.13. The most important differences are that table 3.18 excludes 15- to 17-year-olds and travel associated with volunteering, but includes civic obligations and participation. The percentage of the population that volunteers and the average hours per volunteer are similar

**Table 3.15.** Volunteers by Demographic Group, 2002–2006 (percent)

| | 2002 | 2003 | 2004 | 2005 | 2006 |
|---|---|---|---|---|---|
| Total | 27.4 | 28.8 | 28.8 | 28.8 | 26.7 |
| Gender | | | | | |
| Male | 23.6 | 25.1 | 25.0 | 25.0 | 23.0 |
| Female | 31.0 | 32.2 | 32.4 | 32.4 | 30.1 |
| Race/Ethnicity | | | | | |
| White | 29.2 | 30.6 | 30.5 | 30.4 | 28.3 |
| Black or African American | 19.1 | 20.0 | 20.8 | 22.1 | 19.2 |
| Asian | — | 18.7 | 19.3 | 20.7 | 18.5 |
| Hispanic or Latino | 15.5 | 15.7 | 14.5 | 15.4 | 13.9 |
| Age | | | | | |
| 16 and older | 27.4 | 28.8 | 28.8 | 28.8 | 26.7 |
| 16–24 | 21.9 | 24.1 | 24.2 | 24.4 | 21.7 |
| 25–34 | 24.8 | 26.5 | 25.8 | 25.3 | 23.1 |
| 35–44 | 34.1 | 34.7 | 34.2 | 34.5 | 31.2 |
| 45–54 | 31.3 | 32.7 | 32.8 | 32.7 | 31.2 |
| 55–64 | 27.5 | 29.2 | 30.1 | 30.2 | 27.9 |
| 65 and older | 22.7 | 23.7 | 24.6 | 24.8 | 23.8 |
| Education | | | | | |
| Less than high school diploma | 10.1 | 9.9 | 9.6 | 10.0 | 9.3 |
| High school graduate, no college | 21.2 | 21.7 | 21.6 | 21.2 | 19.2 |
| Less than a bachelor's degree | 32.8 | 34.1 | 34.2 | 33.7 | 30.9 |
| College graduate | 43.3 | 45.6 | 45.7 | 45.8 | 43.3 |
| Employment | | | | | |
| Civilian labor force | 29.3 | 30.9 | 30.9 | 31.1 | 28.5 |
| Employed | 29.5 | 31.2 | 31.2 | 31.3 | 28.7 |
| Full-time | 28.3 | 29.6 | 29.6 | 29.8 | 27.3 |
| Part-time | 35.4 | 38.4 | 38.5 | 38.2 | 35.5 |
| Unemployed | 25.1 | 26.7 | 25.6 | 26.4 | 23.8 |
| Not in the labor force | 23.7 | 24.6 | 24.7 | 24.4 | 23.1 |
| Marital status | | | | | |
| Single, never married | 21.2 | 22.8 | 23.2 | 23.0 | 20.3 |
| Married, spouse present | 32.7 | 34.0 | 33.9 | 34.1 | 32.2 |
| Other marital status | 22.1 | 22.5 | 22.9 | 23.1 | 21.3 |

*Source:* U.S. Department of Labor, Bureau of Labor Statistics, Current Population Survey, Volunteer Supplement (2002–2006).
— = data not available

**Table 3.16.** Distribution of Average Annual Volunteer Hours by Activity, 2003–2006

|  | 2003 | 2004 | 2005 | 2006 |
|---|---|---|---|---|
| Administrative and support | 28.0 | 24.8 | 24.4 | 20.6 |
| Social service and care | 21.1 | 22.7 | 20.2 | 17.8 |
| Maintenance, building, and cleanup | 6.1 | 6.0 | 3.7 | 5.7 |
| Performing and cultural activities | 5.9 | 4.3 | 9.1 | 6.9 |
| Meetings, conferences, and training | 11.2 | 11.1 | 11.1 | 10.6 |
| Public health and safety | 1.3 | 2.4 | 1.1 | 0.9 |
| Waiting | 0.0 | 0.0 | 0.1 | 0.3 |
| Other | 15.3 | 17.0 | 17.9 | 22.9 |
| Travel | 11.1 | 11.6 | 12.3 | 14.2 |
| Total | 100.0 | 100.0 | 100.0 | 100.0 |

*Source:* Authors' calculations based on U.S. Department of Labor, Bureau of Labor Statistics, American Time Use Survey (2003–2006).
*Note:* Waiting was not a separate category in 2003, so wait time was distributed across the other categories.

**Figure 3.10.** Distribution of Average Volunteer Time by Activity, 2006 (percent)

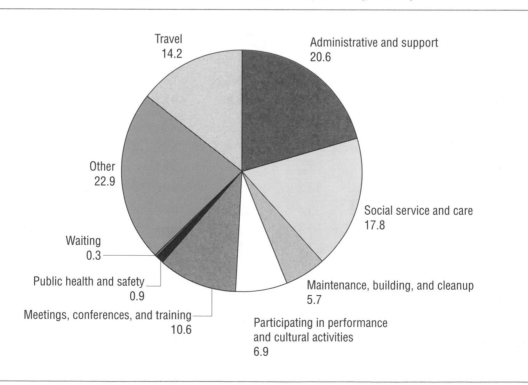

*Source:* U.S. Department of Labor, Bureau of Labor Statistics, American Time Use Survey (2006).

**Table 3.17.** Volunteers by Activity, 2003–2006 (percent)

|  | 2003 | 2004 | 2005 | 2006 |
|---|---|---|---|---|
| Administrative and support | 43.6 | 44.1 | 40.4 | 37.3 |
| Social service and care | 25.6 | 28.1 | 27.5 | 23.8 |
| Maintenance, building, and cleanup | 7.5 | 8.5 | 5.5 | 6.7 |
| Performing and cultural activities | 7.2 | 5.5 | 9.7 | 8.9 |
| Meetings, conferences, and training | 13.2 | 12.5 | 11.9 | 13.1 |
| Public health and safety | 1.8 | 2.3 | 1.6 | 1.3 |
| Waiting | 0.0 | 0.3 | 0.5 | 2.0 |
| Other | 21.3 | 20.2 | 20.7 | 25.3 |
| Travel | 63.6 | 65.0 | 60.9 | 65.7 |

*Source:* Authors' calculations based on U.S. Department of Labor, Bureau of Labor Statistics, American Time Use Survey (2003–2006).
*Notes:* Multiple responses were allowed. Waiting was not a separate category in 2003, so wait time was distributed across the other categories.

**Figure 3.11.** Volunteers by Activity, 2006 (percent)

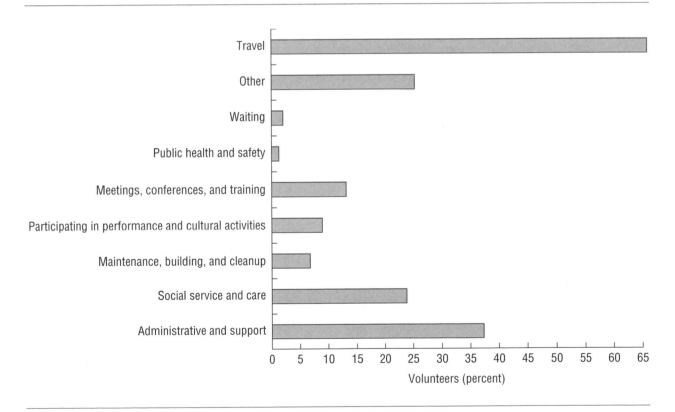

*Source:* U.S. Department of Labor, Bureau of Labor Statistics, American Time Use Survey (2006).

**Table 3.18.** Number, Hours, and Dollar Value of Volunteers, 1965–2003, Selected Years

|  | 1965–1966 | 1975 | 1985 | 1992–1994 | 2003 |
|---|---|---|---|---|---|
| **Per average day** |  |  |  |  |  |
| % of population volunteering | 7.0 | 8.5 | 11.8 | 3.7 | 6.8 |
| Volunteers (thousands) | 8,467 | 12,409 | 20,226 | 6,880 | 14,364 |
| Hours per day per volunteer | 2.05 | 2.23 | 1.28 | 2.46 | 2.12 |
| **Per year** |  |  |  |  |  |
| Hours volunteered (thousands) | 6,320,916 | 10,105,699 | 9,465,752 | 6,167,027 | 11,094,664 |
| Volunteer hours' equivalent in full-time employees (thousands) | 3,718 | 5,945 | 5,568 | 3,628 | 6,526 |
| Population (thousands) | 120,654 | 146,393 | 170,954 | 187,824 | 211,814 |
| Assigned hourly wages for volunteers ($) | 2.68 | 4.73 | 8.73 | 11.04 | 15.35 |
| Total assigned value of volunteer time ($ thousands) | 16,940,055 | 47,799,958 | 82,636,014 | 68,063,426 | 170,303,088 |

*Sources:* Population from U.S. Department of Labor, Bureau of Labor Statistics, Current Population Survey (2007), except for 2003, which is calculated from U.S. Department of Labor, Bureau of Labor Statistics, American Time Use Survey (2003); wages from U.S. Department of Labor, Bureau of Labor Statistics, Current Employment Statistics, private nonfarm hourly wage (2007); authors' calculations using Centre for Time Use Research, American Heritage Time Use Study, Release 1 (May 2006).

*Notes:* American Time Use Survey numbers in this table differ from table 3.13 because 15- to 17-year-olds are excluded here to make the numbers compatible with the other studies. The numbers here include civic obligations and participation, but exclude travel associated with volunteering. Despite significant effort to make the numbers from the five studies comparable, methodological differences remain, so that differences may reflect different methods rather than behavioral change across time. In particular, the 1992–1994 participation rate is believed to be low because that study collected significantly fewer episodes per diary than the others. The methodological reasons the 1985 participation rate is high and the average hours per volunteer is low are unknown; however, these offset each other so that the estimate for total annual hours volunteered in 1985 is in line with the other studies. Conclusions and calculations are those of the authors, and may not reflect the views of the creators or funders of the American Heritage Time Use Study or the collectors of the original surveys harmonized in this dataset.

for 1965, 1975, and 2003. The differences in 1985 and 1992 likely reflect methodological differences, but the factors cannot be isolated. In the future, the AHTUS will expand with additional studies and with changes to this preliminary version.

## Giving by Foundations

The recognized source of information on giving by foundations is the Foundation Center. Their research (2007) reveals the following:

■ Foundation giving in 2005 was $36.4 billion. This was a 197 percent increase from 10 years earlier. (See table 3.19 and figure 3.12.)

■ There were 71,095 active foundations in the United States in 2005. This was a 77 percent increase from 10 years earlier. (See table 3.19.)

**Table 3.19.** Grants Made, Gifts Received, and Assets Held by Foundations, 1975–2005

| | Grantmaking Foundations | | Grants Made | | Gifts Received | | Assets | |
|---|---|---|---|---|---|---|---|---|
| | Number | % of 1975[a] | $ billions | % of 1975[a] | $ billions | % of 1978[b] | $ billions | % of 1975[a] |
| 1975 | 21,877 | 100.0 | 1.94 | 100.0 | — | — | 30.13 | 100.0 |
| 1976 | 21,447 | 98.0 | 2.23 | 114.6 | — | — | 34.78 | 115.5 |
| 1977 | 22,152 | 101.3 | 2.35 | 120.7 | — | — | 35.37 | 117.4 |
| 1978 | 22,484 | 102.8 | 2.55 | 131.0 | 1.61 | 100.0 | 37.27 | 123.7 |
| 1979 | 22,535 | 103.0 | 2.85 | 146.4 | 2.21 | 137.5 | 41.59 | 138.1 |
| 1980 | 22,088 | 101.0 | 3.43 | 176.6 | 1.98 | 123.3 | 48.17 | 159.9 |
| 1981 | 21,967 | 100.4 | 3.79 | 195.1 | 2.39 | 148.6 | 47.57 | 157.9 |
| 1982 | 23,770 | 108.7 | 4.49 | 230.9 | 4.00 | 248.7 | 58.67 | 194.7 |
| 1983 | 24,261 | 110.9 | 4.48 | 230.3 | 2.71 | 168.1 | 67.87 | 224.3 |
| 1984 | 24,859 | 113.6 | 5.04 | 259.3 | 3.36 | 208.6 | 74.05 | 245.8 |
| 1985 | 25,639 | 117.2 | 6.03 | 309.9 | 5.18 | 321.7 | 102.06 | 338.8 |
| 1986 | — | — | — | — | — | — | — | — |
| 1987 | 27,661 | 126.4 | 6.66 | 342.4 | 4.96 | 307.9 | 115.44 | 383.2 |
| 1988 | 30,338 | 138.7 | 7.42 | 381.3 | 5.16 | 320.4 | 122.08 | 405.2 |
| 1989 | 31,990 | 146.2 | 7.91 | 406.8 | 5.52 | 343.0 | 137.54 | 456.5 |
| 1990 | 32,401 | 148.1 | 8.68 | 446.1 | 4.97 | 308.8 | 142.48 | 472.9 |
| 1991 | 33,356 | 152.5 | 9.21 | 473.6 | 5.47 | 339.5 | 162.91 | 540.7 |
| 1992 | 35,765 | 163.5 | 10.21 | 524.9 | 6.18 | 383.8 | 176.82 | 586.9 |
| 1993 | 37,571 | 171.7 | 11.11 | 571.4 | 7.76 | 481.8 | 189.21 | 628.0 |
| 1994 | 38,807 | 177.4 | 11.29 | 580.5 | 8.08 | 502.0 | 195.79 | 649.8 |
| 1995 | 40,140 | 183.5 | 12.26 | 630.5 | 10.26 | 637.3 | 226.74 | 752.5 |
| 1996 | 41,588 | 190.1 | 13.84 | 711.4 | 16.02 | 995.0 | 267.58 | 888.1 |
| 1997 | 44,146 | 201.8 | 15.99 | 821.9 | 15.83 | 983.4 | 329.91 | 1,095.0 |
| 1998 | 46,832 | 214.1 | 19.46 | 1,000.4 | 22.57 | 1,402.1 | 385.05 | 1,278.0 |
| 1999 | 50,201 | 229.5 | 23.32 | 1,199.1 | 32.08 | 1,992.3 | 448.61 | 1,489.0 |
| 2000 | 56,582 | 258.6 | 27.56 | 1,417.2 | 27.61 | 1,715.1 | 486.09 | 1,613.3 |
| 2001 | 61,810 | 282.5 | 30.50 | 1,568.4 | 28.71 | 1,783.5 | 467.34 | 1,551.1 |
| 2002 | 64,843 | 296.4 | 30.43 | 1,564.7 | 22.16 | 1,376.6 | 435.19 | 1,444.4 |
| 2003 | 66,398 | 303.5 | 30.31 | 1,558.4 | 24.86 | 1,544.0 | 476.71 | 1,582.2 |
| 2004 | 67,736 | 309.6 | 31.84 | 1,641.2 | 23.99 | 1,490.0 | 510.48 | 1,694.3 |
| 2005 | 71,095 | 325.0 | 36.40 | 1,876.4 | 31.47 | 1,954.3 | 550.55 | 1,827.3 |

*Source:* Foundation Center, Research Studies: National Trends (2007).
*Notes:* Grants made include grants, scholarships, employee-matching gifts, and other amounts separated as "grants and contributions paid during the year" on Form 990-PF. Asset figures represent the market value of assets.
a. Percentages are calculated using the 1975 figure as the baseline for comparison (i.e., rebased to 1975 = 100).
b. Percentages are calculated using the 1978 figure as the baseline for comparison (i.e., rebased to 1978 = 100).
— = data not available

**Figure 3.12.** Number of Foundations and Amount of Grants Made by Year, 1994–2005

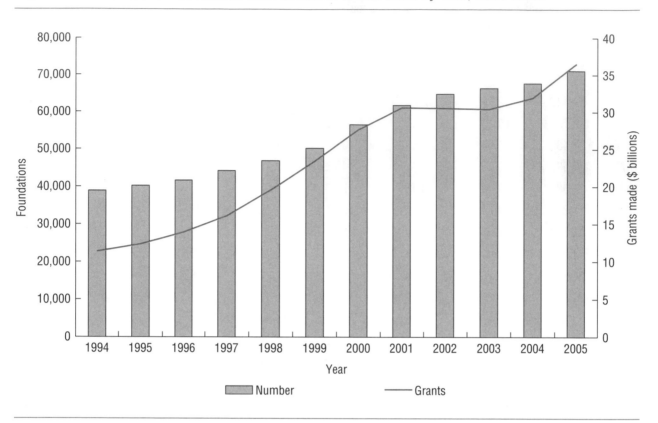

*Source:* Foundation Center, Research Studies: National Trends (2007).

- Foundation assets reached $550.6 billion in 2005. This was a 143 percent increase from 10 years earlier. (See table 3.19.)
- In 2005, 88.7 percent of foundations were independent foundations, 6.6 percent were operating foundations, 3.7 percent were corporate foundations, and 1.0 percent were community foundations. (See table 3.20 and figure 3.13.)
- Independent foundations held 82.7 percent of the assets held by foundations in 2005. Community foundations held 8.1 percent of the assets, operating foundations held 5.9 percent, and corporate foundations held just 3.2 percent. (See table 3.20 and figure 3.13.)
- In 2005, independent foundations accounted for 69.2 percent of the dollar value of grants made, corporate foundations and operating foundations each for 11 percent, and community foundations for 8.8 percent. (See table 3.20.)
- In 2004, the 233 largest foundations held 49.9 percent of all foundation assets and accounted for 35.5 percent of the dollar value of grants made. At the small end of the spectrum, the 64 percent of foundations with under $1 million in assets each accounted for only 2.3 percent of all foundation assets, but 10.9 percent of the dollar value of grants made. (See table 3.21.)
- The decade from 1990 to 1999 saw the greatest increase in the number of foundations with assets over $1 million, with an average of 822 being created each year.

**Table 3.20.** Number of Foundations, Grants Made, Gifts Received, and Assets by Type of Foundation, 2000–2005

| | Foundations | | Grants Made | | Gifts Received | | Assets | |
|---|---|---|---|---|---|---|---|---|
| | Number | % | $ millions | % | $ millions | % | $ millions | % |
| **2000** | | | | | | | | |
| Independent | 50,532 | 89.3 | 21,346 | 77.4 | 19,156 | 69.4 | 408,749 | 84.1 |
| Corporate | 2,018 | 3.6 | 2,985 | 10.8 | 2,902 | 10.5 | 15,899 | 3.3 |
| Operating | 3,472 | 6.1 | 1,066 | 3.9 | 1,727 | 6.3 | 30,973 | 6.4 |
| Community | 560 | 1.0 | 2,166 | 7.9 | 3,829 | 13.9 | 30,464 | 6.3 |
| Total | 56,582 | 100.0 | 27,563 | 100.0 | 27,614 | 100.0 | 486,085 | 100.0 |
| **2001** | | | | | | | | |
| Independent | 55,120 | 89.2 | 23,705 | 77.7 | 20,539 | 71.5 | 403,526 | 84.6 |
| Corporate | 2,170 | 3.5 | 3,284 | 10.8 | 3,040 | 10.6 | 15,578 | 3.3 |
| Operating | 3,918 | 6.3 | 1,110 | 3.6 | 1,950 | 6.8 | 27,384 | 5.7 |
| Community | 602 | 1.0 | 2,403 | 7.9 | 3,185 | 11.1 | 30,301 | 6.4 |
| Total | 61,810 | 100.0 | 30,502 | 100.0 | 28,714 | 100.0 | 467,336 | 100.0 |
| **2002** | | | | | | | | |
| Independent | 57,834 | 89.2 | 23,254 | 76.4 | 13,952 | 62.9 | 364,143 | 83.7 |
| Corporate | 2,362 | 3.6 | 3,457 | 11.4 | 3,002 | 13.5 | 14,428 | 3.3 |
| Operating | 3,986 | 6.1 | 1,195 | 3.9 | 2,035 | 9.2 | 26,847 | 6.2 |
| Community | 661 | 1.0 | 2,526 | 8.3 | 3,175 | 14.3 | 29,772 | 6.8 |
| Total | 64,843 | 100.0 | 30,432 | 100.0 | 22,163 | 100.0 | 435,190 | 100.0 |
| **2003** | | | | | | | | |
| Independent | 58,991 | 88.8 | 22,568 | 74.5 | 15,846 | 63.7 | 399,138 | 83.7 |
| Corporate | 2,549 | 3.8 | 3,466 | 11.4 | 3,234 | 13.0 | 15,447 | 3.2 |
| Operating | 4,159 | 6.3 | 1,744 | 5.8 | 2,302 | 9.3 | 27,975 | 5.9 |
| Community | 699 | 1.1 | 2,532 | 8.4 | 3,476 | 14.0 | 34,153 | 7.2 |
| Total | 66,398 | 100.0 | 30,309 | 100.0 | 24,858 | 100.0 | 476,713 | 100.0 |
| **2004** | | | | | | | | |
| Independent | 60,031 | 88.6 | 23,334 | 73.3 | 13,655 | 56.9 | 425,103 | 83.3 |
| Corporate | 2,596 | 3.8 | 3,430 | 10.8 | 3,667 | 15.3 | 16,645 | 3.3 |
| Operating | 4,409 | 6.5 | 2,164 | 6.8 | 2,808 | 11.7 | 29,951 | 5.9 |
| Community | 700 | 1.0 | 2,916 | 9.2 | 3,859 | 16.1 | 38,782 | 7.6 |
| Total | 67,736 | 100.0 | 31,844 | 100.0 | 23,989 | 100.0 | 510,481 | 100.0 |

*(continued)*

**Table 3.20.** Number of Foundations, Grants Made, Gifts Received, and Assets by Type of Foundation, 2000–2005 *(continued)*

| | Foundations | | Grants Made | | Gifts Received | | Assets | |
|---|---|---|---|---|---|---|---|---|
| | Number | % | $ millions | % | $ millions | % | $ millions | % |
| **2005** | | | | | | | | |
| Independent | 63,059 | 88.7 | 25,199 | 69.2 | 17,366 | 55.2 | 455,570 | 82.7 |
| Corporate | 2,607 | 3.7 | 3,996 | 11.0 | 4,008 | 12.7 | 17,795 | 3.2 |
| Operating | 4,722 | 6.6 | 3,990 | 11.0 | 4,505 | 14.3 | 32,603 | 5.9 |
| Community | 707 | 1.0 | 3,217 | 8.8 | 5,587 | 17.8 | 44,583 | 8.1 |
| Total | 71,095 | 100.0 | 36,403 | 100.0 | 31,465 | 100.0 | 550,552 | 100.0 |

*Source:* Foundation Center, Research Studies: National Trends (2007).
*Notes:* Grants made include grants, scholarships, and employee-matching gifts. They do not include program-related investments (such as loans, loan guarantees, equity investments, and other investments made by foundations to organizations to forward their charitable purposes), set-asides, or program expenses. Asset figures represent the market value of assets.

**Figure 3.13.** Distribution of Foundations by Number, Assets, and Grants, 2005 (percent)

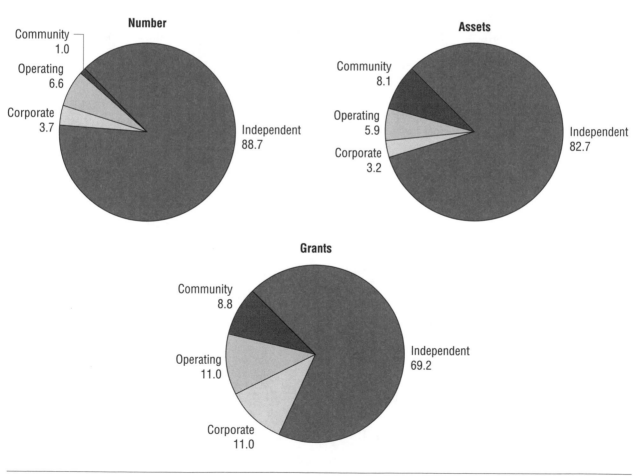

*Source:* Foundation Center, Research Studies: National Trends (2007).

**Table 3.21.** Grants by Foundation Assets, 2002–2004

| Assets ($ millions) | Foundations | | Grants Made | | Assets | |
|---|---|---|---|---|---|---|
| | Number | % | $ thousands | % | $ thousands | % |
| **2002** | | | | | | |
| 250 or more | 202 | 0.3 | 10,591,925 | 34.8 | 210,772,484 | 48.4 |
| 50–249.9 | 865 | 1.3 | 5,852,752 | 19.2 | 87,250,757 | 20.0 |
| 10–49.9 | 3,361 | 5.2 | 5,486,975 | 18.0 | 71,547,145 | 16.4 |
| 1–9.9 | 17,203 | 26.5 | 5,669,998 | 18.6 | 53,949,246 | 12.3 |
| Under 1 | 43,212 | 66.6 | 2,830,149 | 9.2 | 11,670,839 | 2.7 |
| Total | 64,843 | 100.0 | 30,431,799 | 100.0 | 435,190,471 | 100.0 |
| **2003** | | | | | | |
| 250 or more | 207 | 0.3 | 10,521,494 | 34.7 | 237,735,202 | 49.9 |
| 50–249.9 | 908 | 1.3 | 5,974,240 | 19.7 | 92,458,500 | 19.4 |
| 10–49.9 | 3,617 | 5.4 | 5,307,777 | 17.5 | 77,346,419 | 16.2 |
| 1–9.9 | 18,410 | 27.7 | 5,499,923 | 18.2 | 57,342,778 | 12.0 |
| Under 1 | 43,256 | 65.2 | 3,005,401 | 10.0 | 11,830,215 | 2.5 |
| Total | 66,398 | 100.0 | 30,308,835 | 100.0 | 476,713,115 | 100.0 |
| **2004** | | | | | | |
| 250 or more | 233 | 0.3 | 11,306,943 | 35.5 | 254,909,427 | 49.9 |
| 50–249.9 | 997 | 1.5 | 5,732,432 | 18.0 | 100,942,795 | 19.7 |
| 10–49.9 | 3,895 | 5.8 | 5,362,931 | 16.8 | 82,226,337 | 16.1 |
| 1–9.9 | 19,369 | 28.6 | 5,947,989 | 18.7 | 60,516,897 | 11.9 |
| Under 1 | 43,242 | 63.8 | 3,493,610 | 10.9 | 11,885,451 | 2.3 |
| Total | 67,736 | 100.0 | 31,843,907 | 100.0 | 510,480,908 | 100.0 |

*Source:* Foundation Center, Research Studies: National Trends (2006).
*Notes:* Grants made include grants, scholarships, and employee-matching gifts. They do not include program-related investments (such as loans, loan guarantees, equity investments, and other investments made by foundations to organizations to forward their charitable purposes), set-asides, or program expenses. Asset figures represent the market value of assets.

That was more than double the 1980 to 1989 pace of 398 per year. From 2000 to 2004, an average of 536 foundations worth over $1 million were created each year. In all periods, the majority of these were independent foundations. (See table 3.22.)

■ In 2005, 80 percent of the dollars given by foundations went to organizations in four areas: education (26.6 percent), health (23.1 percent), human services (16.4 percent), and arts and culture (13.9 percent). (See table 3.23.)

**Table 3.22.** Number of Larger Foundations Created by Year, through 2004

| Decade created | All | | Independent | | Corporate | | Community | | Operating | |
|---|---|---|---|---|---|---|---|---|---|---|
| | Number | Annual average | Number | Annual average | Number | Annual average | Number | Annual average | Number | Annual average |
| Before 1900 | 88 | — | 72 | — | 0 | — | 0 | — | 16 | — |
| 1900–1909 | 23 | 2 | 19 | 2 | 0 | — | 0 | — | 4 | — |
| 1910–1919 | 76 | 8 | 54 | 5 | 1 | — | 17 | 2 | 4 | — |
| 1920–1929 | 160 | 16 | 127 | 13 | 6 | 1 | 21 | 2 | 6 | 1 |
| 1930–1939 | 192 | 19 | 176 | 18 | 7 | 1 | 4 | 0 | 5 | 1 |
| 1940–1949 | 719 | 72 | 623 | 62 | 57 | 6 | 21 | 2 | 18 | 2 |
| 1950–1959 | 1,752 | 175 | 1,436 | 144 | 259 | 26 | 33 | 3 | 24 | 2 |
| 1960–1969 | 1,768 | 177 | 1,541 | 154 | 144 | 14 | 54 | 5 | 29 | 3 |
| 1970–1979 | 1,080 | 108 | 880 | 88 | 91 | 9 | 81 | 8 | 28 | 3 |
| 1980–1989 | 3,976 | 398 | 3,439 | 344 | 308 | 31 | 129 | 13 | 100 | 10 |
| 1990–1999 | 8,219 | 822 | 7,259 | 726 | 448 | 45 | 203 | 20 | 309 | 31 |
| 2000–2004 | 2,682 | 536 | 2,349 | 470 | 198 | 40 | 19 | 4 | 116 | 23 |
| Unknown | 1,262 | — | 1,079 | — | 53 | — | 34 | — | 96 | — |
| Total | 21,997 | — | 19,054 | — | 1,572 | — | 616 | — | 755 | — |

*Source:* Foundation Center, Research Studies: National Trends (2006).
*Notes:* Data included are for foundations with at least $1 million in assets or making grants of $100,000 or more in 2003–2004. The sum of individual items may not equal column totals due to rounding. Data are incomplete for 2000–2004.
— = data not available

**Table 3.23.** Number and Value of Grants Made by Foundations, by Major Categories, 2001–2005

| | Grants | | Value of Grants | | |
|---|---|---|---|---|---|
| | Number | % | $ thousands | % | Average value ($) |
| **2001** | | | | | |
| Arts and culture | 18,412 | 14.7 | 2,047,972 | 12.2 | 111,230 |
| Education | 25,629 | 20.5 | 4,492,540 | 26.8 | 175,291 |
| Environment and animals | 7,587 | 6.1 | 1,043,896 | 6.2 | 137,590 |
| Health | 15,550 | 12.5 | 3,434,967 | 20.5 | 220,898 |
| Human services | 30,933 | 24.8 | 2,312,124 | 13.8 | 74,746 |
| International and foreign affairs | 3,014 | 2.4 | 398,816 | 2.4 | 132,321 |
| Public and societal benefit | 15,368 | 12.3 | 1,826,594 | 10.9 | 118,857 |
| Science and social science | 4,521 | 3.6 | 837,652 | 5.0 | 185,280 |
| Religion | 3,729 | 3.0 | 351,396 | 2.1 | 94,233 |
| Other | 101 | 0.1 | 17,348 | 0.1 | 171,762 |
| Total | 124,844 | 100.0 | 16,763,304 | 100.0 | 134,274 |
| **2002** | | | | | |
| Arts and culture | 18,674 | 14.6 | 1,945,785 | 12.2 | 104,198 |
| Education | 26,490 | 20.7 | 4,209,352 | 26.4 | 158,903 |
| Environment and animals | 7,830 | 6.1 | 943,136 | 5.9 | 120,452 |
| Health | 15,188 | 11.9 | 2,920,053 | 18.3 | 192,261 |
| Human services | 33,250 | 26.0 | 2,349,813 | 14.8 | 70,671 |
| International and foreign affairs | 3,025 | 2.4 | 413,422 | 2.6 | 136,668 |
| Public and societal benefit | 15,480 | 12.1 | 1,821,082 | 11.4 | 117,641 |
| Science and social science | 3,767 | 2.9 | 877,904 | 5.5 | 233,051 |
| Religion | 3,912 | 3.1 | 429,336 | 2.7 | 109,748 |
| Other | 112 | 0.1 | 15,012 | 0.1 | 134,036 |
| Total | 127,728 | 100.0 | 15,924,895 | 100.0 | 124,678 |
| **2003** | | | | | |
| Arts and culture | 17,881 | 14.8 | 1,790,269 | 12.5 | 100,121 |
| Education | 24,531 | 20.3 | 3,505,713 | 24.5 | 142,910 |
| Environment and animals | 7,393 | 6.1 | 892,321 | 6.2 | 120,698 |
| Health | 14,604 | 12.1 | 2,798,070 | 19.5 | 191,596 |
| Human services | 30,960 | 25.6 | 2,232,212 | 15.6 | 72,100 |
| International and foreign affairs | 2,562 | 2.1 | 360,802 | 2.5 | 140,828 |

*(continued)*

**Table 3.23.** Number and Value of Grants Made by Foundations, by Major Categories, 2001–2005 *(continued)*

| | Grants | | Value of Grants | | |
|---|---|---|---|---|---|
| | Number | % | $ thousands | % | Average value ($) |
| Public and societal benefit | 15,674 | 13.0 | 1,825,760 | 12.7 | 116,483 |
| Science and social science | 3,512 | 2.9 | 565,594 | 3.9 | 161,046 |
| Religion | 3,498 | 2.9 | 340,003 | 2.4 | 97,199 |
| Other | 106 | 0.1 | 12,647 | 0.1 | 119,311 |
| Total | 120,721 | 100.0 | 14,323,389 | 100.0 | 118,649 |
| **2004** | | | | | |
| Arts and culture | 18,516 | 14.6 | 1,979,541 | 12.8 | 106,910 |
| Education | 25,689 | 20.3 | 3,625,448 | 23.4 | 141,128 |
| Environment and animals | 7,374 | 5.8 | 813,320 | 5.3 | 110,296 |
| Health | 16,208 | 12.8 | 3,447,203 | 22.3 | 212,685 |
| Human services | 32,294 | 25.5 | 2,146,396 | 13.9 | 66,464 |
| International and foreign affairs | 2,796 | 2.2 | 419,965 | 2.7 | 150,202 |
| Public and societal benefit | 16,097 | 12.7 | 2,004,661 | 13.0 | 124,536 |
| Science and social science | 3,521 | 2.8 | 669,690 | 4.3 | 190,199 |
| Religion | 3,907 | 3.1 | 362,044 | 2.3 | 92,665 |
| Other | 95 | 0.1 | 9,329 | 0.1 | 98,200 |
| Total | 126,497 | 100.0 | 15,477,595 | 100.0 | 122,355 |
| **2005** | | | | | |
| Arts and culture | 18,698 | 14.3 | 2,054,627 | 13.9 | 109,885 |
| Education | 26,114 | 19.9 | 3,936,636 | 26.6 | 150,748 |
| Environment and animals | 8,195 | 6.3 | 1,040,153 | 7.0 | 126,925 |
| Health | 17,138 | 13.1 | 3,417,483 | 23.1 | 199,410 |
| Human services | 34,085 | 26.0 | 2,425,458 | 16.4 | 71,159 |
| International and foreign affairs | 3,430 | 2.6 | 591,214 | 4.0 | 172,366 |
| Public and societal benefit | 15,785 | 12.1 | 183,368 | 1.2 | 11,617 |
| Science and social science | 3,402 | 2.6 | 709,075 | 4.8 | 208,429 |
| Religion | 4,011 | 3.1 | 408,826 | 2.8 | 101,926 |
| Other | 103 | 0.1 | 10,918 | 0.1 | 106,000 |
| Total | 130,961 | 100.0 | 14,777,758 | 100.0 | 112,841 |

*Source:* Foundation Center, Research Studies: National Trends (2007).
*Notes:* Major categories are defined by the National Taxonomy of Exempt Entities. The sum of individual items may not equal column totals due to rounding.

# Giving by Corporations

The final component of private giving is that by corporations. Corporate contributions can be made directly by the corporation or through a corporate foundation. Both kinds of contributions are reported below.

- According to the Giving USA Foundation (2007), corporations donated $12.7 billion in 2006. That was up 69 percent from 10 years earlier, but down 7.6 percent from 2005. Since these estimates are based on IRS deductions, they exclude certain in-kind contributions that are not tax deductible. (See table 3.3)
- According to the Foundation Center (2007), corporate foundation giving was $4.0 billion in 2005, up 16.5 percent from $3.4 billion in 2004. (See table 3.20.)
- The Conference Board's 2006 Corporate Contributions Report (Muirhead 2007) found that corporations' median contribution of domestic pretax income was 1 percent in 2005. The median contribution of corporate sales was 0.08 percent.
- According to the same study, 56 percent of corporate contributions go to health and human services. Education is second, receiving 15 percent.
- Muirhead (2007) also reported that among industries, pharmaceutical companies donated the largest share of U.S. contributions in 2005. The majority of these are noncash donations.
- Among 130 companies participating in both the 2004 and 2005 Corporate Contributions Reports (Muirhead 2004, 2005), giving increased 18 percent from 2004 to 2005, and the median contribution increased from $10.7 million in 2004 to $12.5 million in 2005.
- Among Corporate Contributions Report respondents, 53 percent of contributions in 2005 were noncash. Noncash contributions also exceeded cash contributions in 2004.

# Conclusion

Giving and volunteering provide vital resources to the nonprofit sector. Private giving represents about 2.5 percent of national income and about 30 percent of nonprofit outlays. Living individuals make three-fourths of all private contributions, and personal bequests add another 7 to 8 percentage points. Foundations and corporations round out the total. Over the last 25 years, the share of individual giving has declined somewhat while that of foundations has increased, perhaps suggesting that more living individuals are giving through foundations. Certainly, foundations have been growing significantly in number, grants, and assets. Individuals who itemize tax deductions account for four-fifths of individual contributions and give about twice the percentage of their income as nonitemizers. Volunteers contribute the equivalent of 7.6 million full-time employees, on top of the sector's 12.9 million paid employees (see table 2.2). On an average day, 6.5 percent of the population, or 15 million people, volunteers 2.31 hours each. Over the course of the year, a little over one-fourth of the population, or 61 million people, volunteers an average of 207 hours each.

# Technical Notes

Per day values in table 3.13 are based on author calculations and do not match published numbers from the American Time Use Survey (ATUS), because the ATUS includes travel time only in major categories and not in subcategories, thus excluding travel time associated with volunteering. Table 3.13 includes all time in the 2006 ATUS activity codes 15xxxx (volunteering) and 1815xx (travel associated with volunteering), and the analogous codes for 2003–2005. Participation rates are calculated by summing the weights (*TUFINLWGT*) for all respondents with any time in the above categories and dividing by the sum of the weights of all respondents. The number of volunteers is calculated by summing the weights for all respondents with volunteer time and dividing by 365.

Hours per day per volunteer result from a two-step process: Average minutes across the whole population are calculated by multiplying each respondent's minutes in the above categories by that respondent's weight, summing those products, and dividing by the sum of the weights of all respondents. This is converted to hours per day by dividing by 60, and to hours per day per volunteer by dividing by the volunteer participation rate calculated above. These are standard calculations, documented in ATUS codebooks.

The per year calculations in the bottom of table 3.13 are also author calculations. Population is calculated by dividing the sum of *TUFINLWGT* by 365. Total annual volunteer hours is calculated by multiplying population times the percent of population volunteering on an average day times 365, times the average hours volunteered per day per volunteer. Full time equivalent employment is calculated by dividing total annual volunteer hours per year by 1,700 working hours per full-time employee per year. Total assigned value of volunteer time is total annual volunteer hours times the average private nonfarm hourly wage.

The calculation of average annual hours per volunteer requires making an assumption about 15-year-olds' annual volunteer participation rates. Total volunteer hours per year is available from the ATUS only. The number of volunteers per year is available only from the volunteer supplement to the CPS. One cannot be simply divided by the other because, although both are based on the CPS sample, the ATUS includes those 15 years old and older, while the CPS volunteer supplement includes only those 16 years old and older. If we use the number of volunteers from the CPS volunteer supplement, we overestimate average hours per volunteer, because 15-year-olds are included in total volunteer hours but not total volunteers. If we try to apply the percentage of population volunteering from the CPS volunteer supplement to the ATUS total population, we underestimate average hours per volunteer, because young people volunteer at a lower rate than average, so we would be overestimating the number of volunteers. We can identify the number of volunteers among 15-year-olds in ATUS, but only for an average day, not for the year.

Thus, the basic approach is to estimate the number of 15-year-old volunteers, add it to the CPS volunteer supplement total, and then divide that into total volunteer hours for the year. We calculate the implied 16-and-over population in the CPS by dividing the number of volunteers by the volunteer participation rate. The 15-and-over population is already calculated from the ATUS above. Subtracting the first from the second yields the number of 15-year-olds. The number of 15-year-old volunteers per year is estimated by multiplying the number of 15-year-olds by the annual volunteering rate of 16- to 24-year-olds from the CPS volunteer supplement. The number of 15-year-old volunteers is added to the number of volunteers 16 and older from the CPS volunteer supplement, resulting in total annual volunteers 15 and older. Finally, total annual volunteer hours is divided by the annual number of volunteers 15 and older, resulting in average annual hours per volunteer 15 and older.

Table 3.16 is also based on author calculations using the ATUS. The categories shown correspond to the activity codes given above—15xxxx and 1815xx—summed to the four-digit level. For each category shown, each respondent's time was multiplied by that respondent's weight (*TUFINLWGT*) and the results summed. The sum was divided by the sum of weights of all volunteers, even those who did not perform that particular activity on the diary day. The result is the average minutes per day per volunteer for each activity. Converted to hours, these totals would sum to the average hours volunteered per volunteer per day in table 3.13.

Table 3.17 is also based on author calculations using the ATUS. Participation rates for each activity are calculated by summing *TUFINLWGT* of respondents who reported any time in that activity and dividing by the sum of the weights of all volunteers.

The source for table 3.18 is author calculations based on the AHTUS. Figures in this table are based on a preliminary release of the dataset, Release 1 (May 2006). To maximize comparability among the studies, we combined AHTUS main activity codes 41 through 48. All ATUS 15xxxx codes map into AHTUS Main41, so this is a broader measure that includes civic obligations and participation. Figures in this table exclude travel associated with volunteering, because it could not be separated from travel associated with worship. The table also excludes 15- to 17-year-olds, because the AHTUS does. A small number of records were erroneously excluded from the 2003 data in this initial release, accounting for less than 1 percent of 2003 records. We believe the effect of the exclusion on the results reported here to be minimal.

Individual respondents were weighted to exclude poor-quality diaries and to match the age and gender composition of the CPS sample in the appropriate year (*INFLTWT*). We rescaled these weights to achieve full population size, as calculated below.

We calculated the average volunteer minutes across the population by multiplying total time in Main41–Main48 by the rescaled *INFLTWT* for each respondent, summing the results, and dividing that by the sum of the weights across all respondents. This was then divided by 60 to get hours volunteered per day for the entire population.

Volunteer participation rates were calculated by summing the weights of respondents with any volunteer time and dividing by the sum of the weights of all respondents. The number of volunteers was calculated by multiplying participation rates by population.

Hours per day per volunteer were calculated by dividing the hours per day volunteered across the entire population by the volunteer participation rate.

Population in table 3.18 was estimated using the CPS, except for 2003, which was calculated from the ATUS. For the other years, reported population age 16 and over was averaged with reported population age 20 and over, resulting in estimated population 18 and over. To match the study periods, 1965 and 1966 were averaged together, as were 1975 and 1976, and 1992 to 1994. For 2003, weights (*TU04FWGT*) for respondents age 18 and over were summed and the result divided by 365.

Total annual volunteer hours is population, times 365, times the percentage of the population volunteering per average day, times the hours volunteered per volunteer per day. Full-time equivalent employment is total annual volunteer hours divided by 1,700 working hours per full-time employee. The assigned value of volunteer time is total annual volunteer hours times the average private nonfarm hourly wage.

Despite significant effort to make the numbers from the five studies comparable, methodological differences remain; apparent trends may reflect different methods rather than behavioral change across time. In particular, the 1992–1994 participation rate is believed to be low because that study collected significantly fewer episodes per diary than the others. We believe the 1985 participation rate to be high and the average hours per volunteer low for methodological reasons unknown, however, these offset each other so that the estimate for total annual hours volunteered in 1985 is in line with the other studies.

# 4

# Financial Trends

In this chapter, we first "follow the money" to gain an understanding of the nonprofit sector's revenue and outlays (consumption expenditures and transfer payments) and how these have been changing over time. As in chapter 1, our basic source data come from the BEA's National Income and Product Accounts, and thus are limited to NPISHs. Second, we turn to a different source of data, the IRS Forms 990, to explore more detailed revenue trends exclusively for 501(c)(3) public charities.

## Trends in Revenues

In 2006, NPISH revenue was $1,006.7 billion, a 5.7 percent increase over 2005 (figure 4.1). From 1992 to 2006, revenue grew at a compound annual rate of 6.0 percent.

Nonprofits raise revenue in three major ways. Most of the sector's revenue comes from fees for services, such as hospital charges and school tuition. The BEA refers to these as sales receipts; this also includes membership dues and fees. The second largest source of revenue is contributions, such as grants and other donations. The BEA calls these transfer receipts. Finally, nonprofits have asset income, including interest, dividends, and rental income. Figure 4.2 shows the distribution of 2006 revenue among these three categories. Sales receipts accounted for 69.7 percent of nonprofit revenue, transfer receipts for 25.9 percent, and asset income for just 4.5 percent of revenue.

BEA sales receipts and transfer receipts contain a mixture of funds from public and private sources. Although the BEA does separate government transfer receipts from those from private sources, it does not publish a similar breakout of sales receipts. Past almanacs included a table showing public and private revenue sources separately. We provide that information for all reporting public charities in table 5.5, and for seven subsectors in tables 5.12 through 5.18.

**Figure 4.1.** Revenue of Nonprofit Institutions Serving Households, 1992–2006 ($ billions)

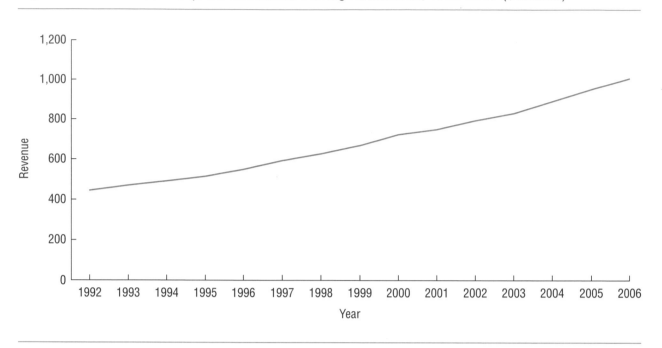

*Source:* U.S. Department of Commerce, Bureau of Economic Analysis, National Income and Product Accounts, table 2.9 (2007).

**Figure 4.2.** Sources of Revenue for Nonprofit Institutions Serving Households, 2006 (percent)

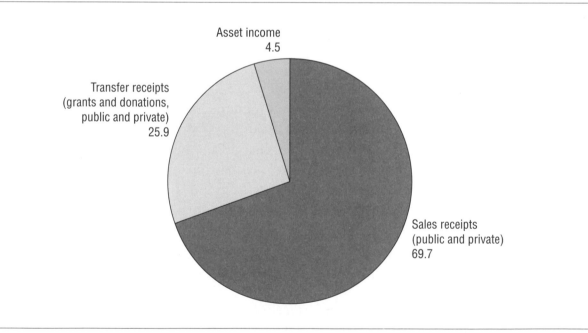

*Source:* U.S. Department of Commerce, Bureau of Economic Analysis, National Income and Product Accounts, table 2.9 (2007).

Figure 4.3 shows the value of all these components over time, plus a linear trend line for sales receipts. Most revenue growth in the nonprofit sector has been the result of increased sales receipts—the only source of growth from 1992 to 1995, and from 2000 to 2003. From 1996 to 2000, somewhat less than half the revenue growth came from increased transfer receipts.

Transfer receipts stopped increasing during a period of significant stock market decline. Asset income was essentially no higher at the end of the period than at the beginning and reflected neither the stock market boom nor the bust. Interestingly, the increase in transfer receipts came at the same time as an increase in the trend for sales receipts. This suggests that the increased transfer receipts were used to expand service provision rather than to reduce fees charged for existing services. When transfer receipts stopped growing in 2001, the trend in sales receipts increased again, suggesting that nonprofits attempted to maintain their expanded service provision, despite fewer transfer receipts, by increasing their fees.

With its major components growing at widely different rates, the composition of revenue has changed dramatically over time. Figure 4.4 shows the trend in the share of the three major components over time. Asset income, which provided almost 8 percent of revenue in 1992, was down to 4.5 percent by 2006. Transfer receipts, which had been fairly steady at about 21 percent of revenue, rose steadily to 28 percent of revenue before declining to 26 percent in 2006. Obviously, stock market values

**Figure 4.3.** Revenue for Nonprofit Institutions Serving Households by Source, 1992–2006 ($ billions)

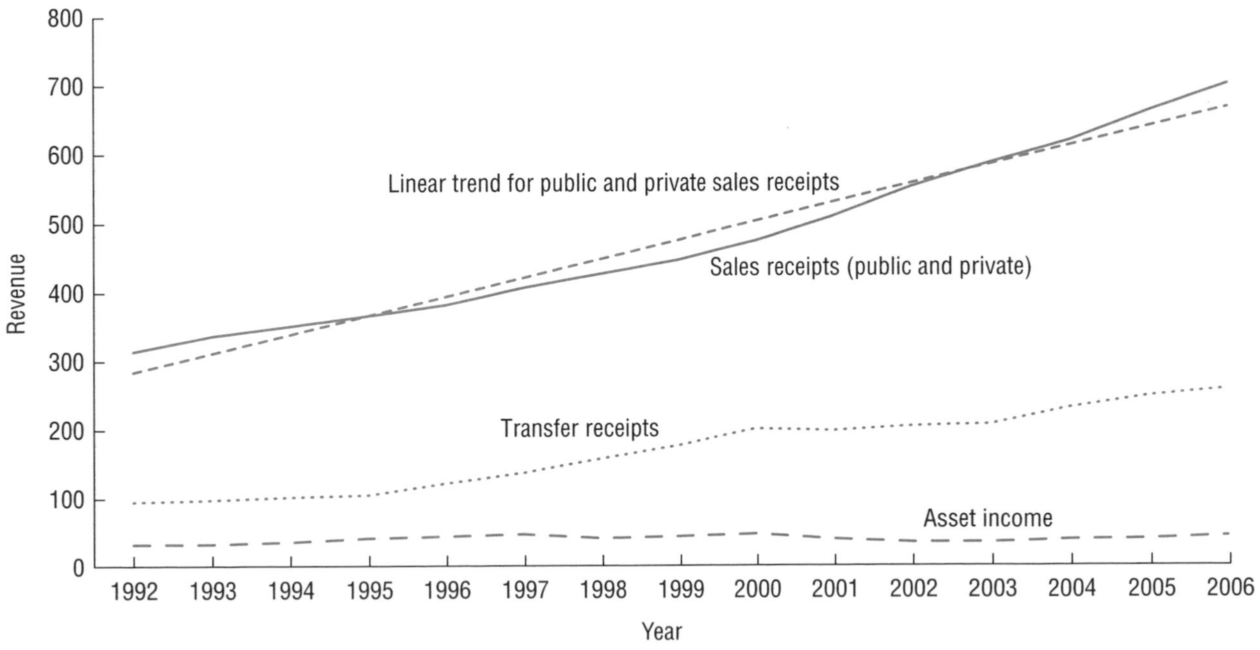

*Source:* U.S. Department of Commerce, Bureau of Economic Analysis, National Income and Product Accounts, table 2.9 (2007), except linear trend line, which is calculated by the authors.

**Figure 4.4.** Types of Revenue for Nonprofit Institutions Serving Households, 1992–2006 (percent)

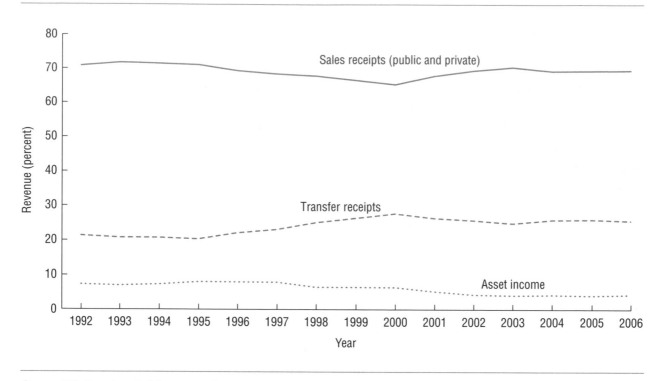

*Source:* U.S. Department of Commerce, Bureau of Economic Analysis, National Income and Product Accounts, table 2.9 (2007).

affect both asset income and transfer receipts. Sales receipts declined steadily as a percent of revenue until 2000, when they reached a low of 66 percent. Since then, they have returned to the levels observed at the beginning of the period. This suggests that the increase in transfer receipts has substituted for the decline in asset income. From a management point of view, this means a shift from unrestricted dollars controlled by the nonprofit to contributed dollars, which often have severe restrictions on how they can be spent. The effect is likely to be a reduction in nonprofits' financial flexibility.

Figure 4.5 shows the trend in transfer receipts by the source of the funds. Although government transfers have been increasing over time, almost the entire increase has come from households. Yet, as figure 4.6 shows, the household share has been remarkably steady, fluctuating between 85 and 90 percent. Figure 4.6 also shows that transfers from business have been declining slightly, offsetting the slightly increased transfers from government.

Figure 4.7 shows the relative shares in 2006 of the three types of asset income: interest, dividends, and rental income. Interest income accounted for 58.8 percent of asset income, dividend income for 36.4 percent, and rental income for just 4.9 percent. Figure 4.8 shows that from 1992 to 2006, interest and dividend income fluctuated dramatically but with no clear trend—although both have increased the last few years. The key point is that none of the three components of asset income is growing enough to keep pace with

**Figure 4.5.** Transfer Receipts for Nonprofit Organizations Serving Households by Source, 1992–2006 ($ billions)

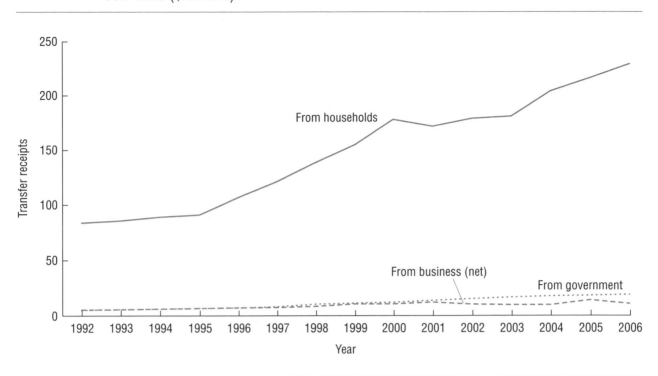

*Source:* U.S. Department of Commerce, Bureau of Economic Analysis, National Income and Product Accounts, table 2.9 (2007).

**Figure 4.6.** Transfer Receipts for Nonprofit Institutions Serving Households by Source, 1992–2006 (percent)

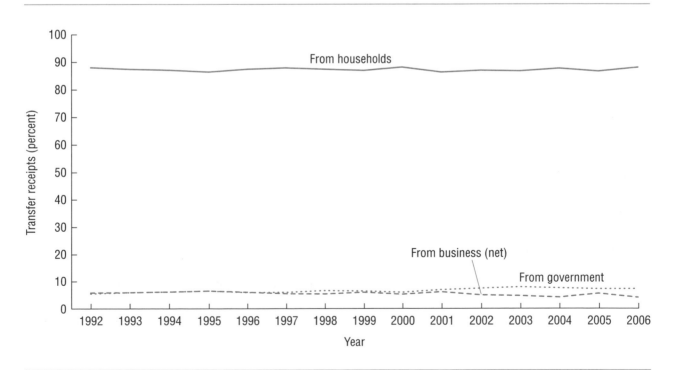

*Source:* U.S. Department of Commerce, Bureau of Economic Analysis, National Income and Product Accounts, table 2.9 (2007).

**Figure 4.7.** Asset Income for Nonprofit Institutions Serving Households by Source, 2006 (percent)

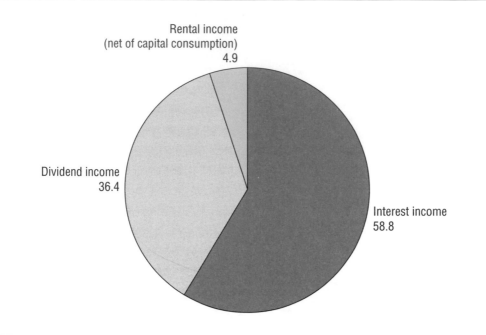

Rental income
(net of capital consumption)
4.9

Dividend income
36.4

Interest income
58.8

*Source:* U.S. Department of Commerce, Bureau of Economic Analysis, National Income and Product Accounts, table 2.9 (2007).

**Figure 4.8.** Asset Income for Nonprofit Institutions Serving Households by Source,
1992–2006 ($ billions)

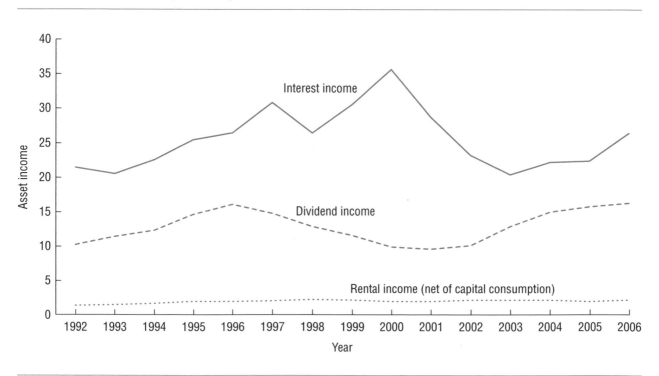

*Source:* U.S. Department of Commerce, Bureau of Economic Analysis, National Income and Product Accounts, table 2.9 (2007).

the growing nonprofit sector, suggesting that the sector may be becoming increasingly undercapitalized.

## Trends in Outlays

Nonprofits can do three things with their funds: spend them, give them away, or invest them. Figure 4.9 shows how the sector used its funds in 2006. Of the total, 88.7 percent was spent directly, 8.0 percent was given away, and just 3.3 percent was left over to invest or as a buffer for cash flow.

Figure 4.10 shows the value of these components over time. Both consumption expenditures and transfer payments have been growing steadily, but saving, after increasing temporarily in the late 1990s, has declined to the levels of the early 1990s. The decline in savings could partially explain the concurrent decline in revenue from asset income discussed above, but stock market and other macroeconomic conditions could also be factors.

Figure 4.11 shows the trend in these three different uses of funds over time. Transfer payments grew steadily over the period. The temporary increase in saving was mirrored in a temporary decline in the share consumed. There may also be a very slight downward trend in the share consumed, mirroring the increase in transfer payments. The very low share for savings suggests that after a brief respite during the late 1990s, nonprofits are living close to the margin.

**Figure 4.9.** Uses of Funds by Nonprofit Institutions Serving Households, 2006 (percent)

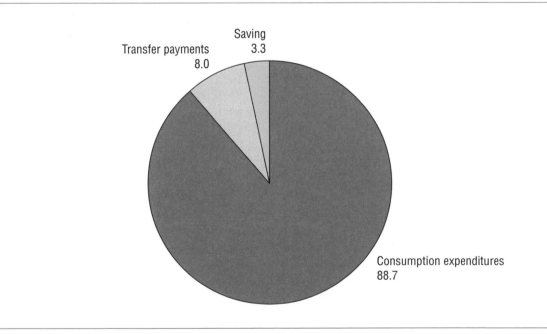

*Source:* U.S. Department of Commerce, Bureau of Economic Analysis, National Income and Product Accounts, table 2.9 (2007).

**Figure 4.10.** Outlays from Nonprofit Institutions Serving Households by Use, 1992–2006 ($ billions)

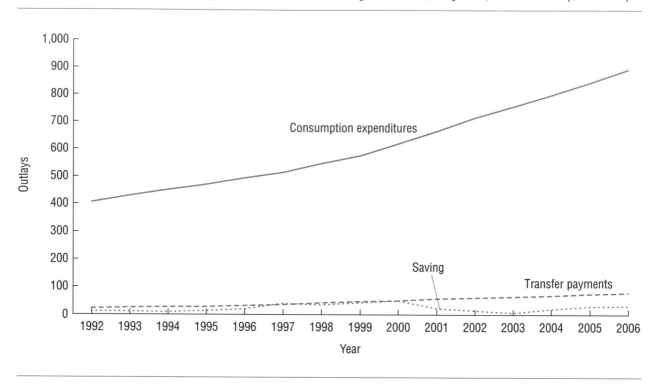

*Source:* U.S. Department of Commerce, Bureau of Economic Analysis, National Income and Product Accounts, table 2.9 (2007).

**Figure 4.11.** Outlays from Nonprofit Institutions Serving Households by Use, 1992–2006 (percent)

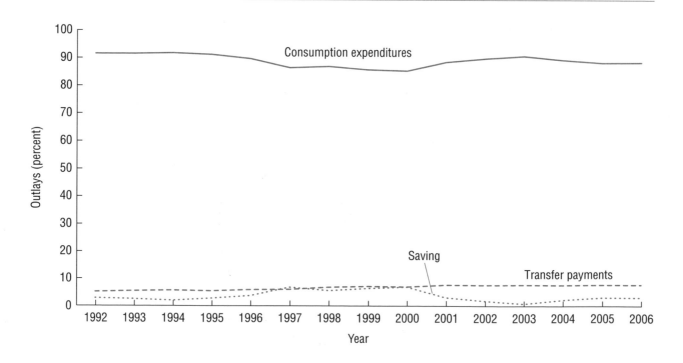

*Source:* U.S. Department of Commerce, Bureau of Economic Analysis, National Income and Product Accounts, table 2.9 (2007).

Figure 4.12 shows how the nonprofit sector's 2006 consumption expenditures were divided among five areas defined by the BEA. The specific industries included in each of these five areas are shown in table 4.3. The names of the categories are self-explanatory except personal business, which includes offices of lawyers, labor unions, and part of professional associations. Medical care accounted for 59.1 percent of expenditures in 2006. The second largest area was religious and welfare activities at 19.8 percent. Education and research accounted for 14.9 percent.

Figure 4.13 shows how these shares have been changing over time—or perhaps more accurately, how they have not been changing. Recreation appears to be declining slightly but steadily. Medical care and religious and welfare activities have fluctuated but exhibit no clear trend. However, consumption in all five areas has grown, as shown in figure 4.14.

Transfer payments by NPISHs are divided into three categories. The largest category is transfers to households. This includes benefits paid to members, specific assistance to individuals, and grants and allocations. The second largest category is transfers from the United States to the rest of the world, such as assistance provided by relief organizations. Finally, the BEA treats the excise taxes paid by grantmaking foundations as transfer payments to government. Figure 4.15 shows the shares of each of these categories in 2006. Transfers to households accounted for 86.0 percent of all transfer payments, net transfers overseas, 13.4 percent, and excise taxes, just 0.6 percent.

**Figure 4.12.** Consumption Expenditures for Nonprofit Institutions Serving Households by Subsector, 2006 (percent)

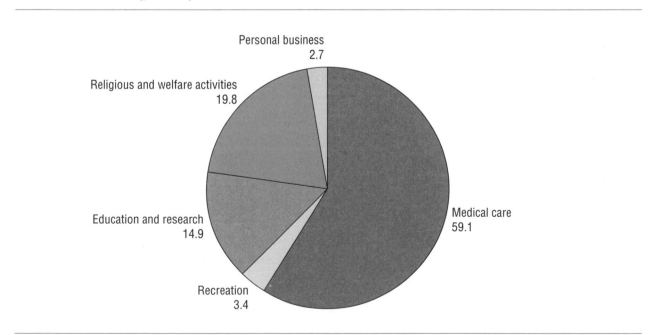

*Source:* U.S. Department of Commerce, Bureau of Economic Analysis, National Income and Product Accounts, table 2.9 (2007).

**Figure 4.13.** Consumption Expenditures for Nonprofit Institutions Serving Households by Subsector, 1992–2006 (percent)

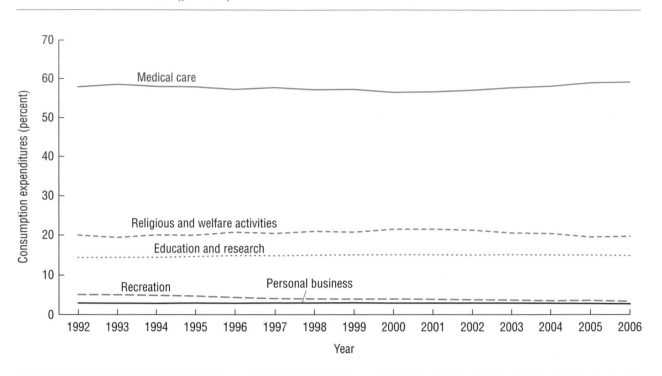

*Source:* U.S. Department of Commerce, Bureau of Economic Analysis, National Income and Product Accounts, table 2.9 (2007).

**Figure 4.14.** Consumption Expenditures for Nonprofit Subsectors, 1992–2006 ($ billions)

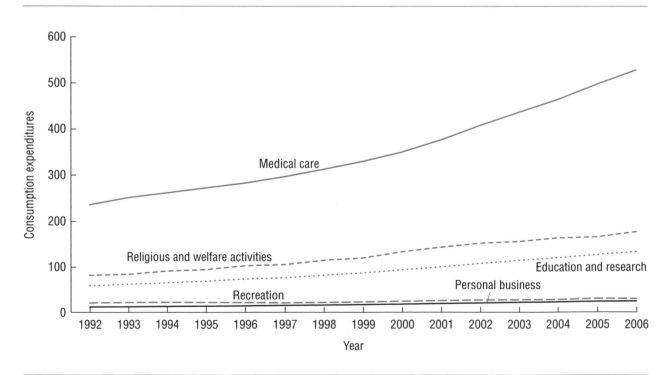

*Source:* U.S. Department of Commerce, Bureau of Economic Analysis, National Income and Product Accounts, table 2.9 (2007).

**Figure 4.15.** Transfer Payments from Nonprofit Institutions Serving Households by Recipient, 2006 (percent)

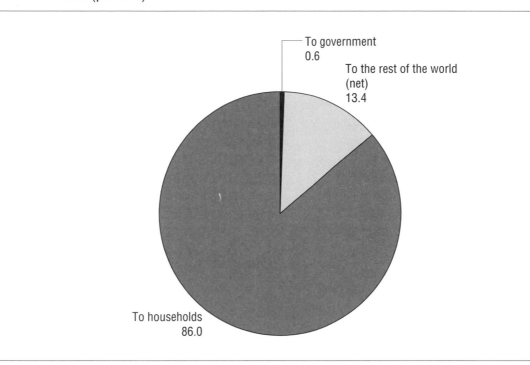

To government
0.6

To the rest of the world
(net)
13.4

To households
86.0

*Source:* U.S. Department of Commerce, Bureau of Economic Analysis, National Income and Product Accounts, table 2.9 (2007).

Figure 4.16 shows the dollar trend in these three components of transfer payments. Transfers to both households and the rest of the world have been growing; transfers to government have been flat, although there was a temporary increase during the late 1990s. Figure 4.17 shows the shares in these components over time. In the late 1990s, there appears to have been a reduction in the share going to households and a concomitant increase in the share going to the rest of the world, but trends have been fairly steady since that time.

For convenience, tables 4.1 and 4.2 show the BEA data on NPISH revenues and outlays, on which this chapter is based.

## Conclusion

Analysis of nonprofit revenues and outlays reveals that the sector is growing steadily, and that the relative sizes of five subsectors remain stable. Despite growing revenues and outlays, however, nonprofit saving has been declining. Apparently, as a result, asset income has not been growing. Increased transfer receipts (contributions) have been making up the difference. The data suggest that the sector may be becoming increasingly undercapitalized and that its financial flexibility may be declining as restricted contributions substitute for unrestricted asset income.

**Figure 4.16.** Transfer Payments from Nonprofit Institutions Serving Households by Recipient, 1992–2006 ($ billions)

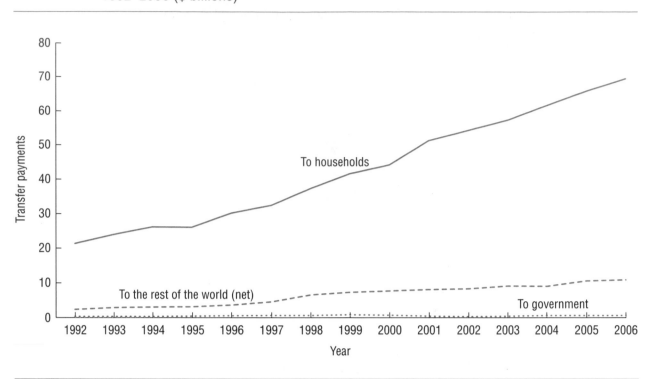

*Source:* U.S. Department of Commerce, Bureau of Economic Analysis, National Income and Product Accounts, table 2.9 (2007).

**Figure 4.17.** Transfer Payments from Nonprofit Institutions Serving Households by Recipient, 1992–2006 (percent)

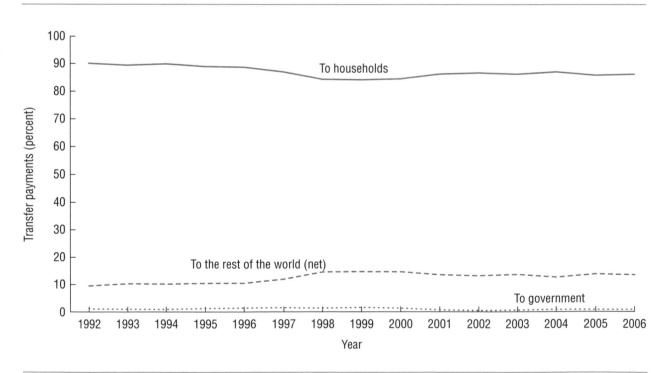

*Source:* U.S. Department of Commerce, Bureau of Economic Analysis, National Income and Product Accounts, table 2.9 (2007).

**Table 4.1.** Revenues for Nonprofit Institutions Serving Households ($ billions)

| | 1992 | 1993 | 1994 | 1995 | 1996 | 1997 | 1998 | 1999 | 2000 | 2001 | 2002 | 2003 | 2004 | 2005 | 2006 |
|---|---|---|---|---|---|---|---|---|---|---|---|---|---|---|---|
| Sales receipts (public and private)[a] | 315.3 | 337.6 | 351.9 | 366.9 | 382.5 | 407.4 | 427.5 | 447.6 | 474.7 | 510.1 | 552.8 | 587.5 | 619.7 | 662.5 | 701.2 |
| Medical care | 235.2 | 252.2 | 261.5 | 270.4 | 279.9 | 297.5 | 311.1 | 324.6 | 342.5 | 368.3 | 403.1 | 430.1 | 454.0 | 487.9 | 518.1 |
| Recreation | 12.6 | 13.6 | 14.2 | 15.0 | 15.2 | 15.7 | 16.7 | 17.6 | 18.5 | 19.5 | 20.1 | 20.9 | 22.0 | 24.0 | 25.6 |
| Education and research | 32.3 | 34.4 | 36.4 | 38.6 | 41.8 | 44.8 | 47.2 | 49.6 | 52.7 | 56.2 | 60.6 | 64.6 | 68.5 | 73.0 | 76.4 |
| Religious and welfare activities | 22.2 | 24.2 | 26.2 | 28.7 | 30.9 | 33.9 | 36.4 | 38.8 | 42.4 | 46.5 | 48.8 | 51.5 | 54.1 | 56.1 | 59.0 |
| Personal business | 12.9 | 13.2 | 13.6 | 14.2 | 14.6 | 15.4 | 16.1 | 17.0 | 18.5 | 19.6 | 20.1 | 20.4 | 21.1 | 21.6 | 22.1 |
| Transfer receipts | 95.7 | 98.5 | 102.8 | 105.7 | 122.7 | 138.3 | 158.9 | 178.2 | 202.1 | 199.1 | 205.9 | 208.7 | 232.9 | 249.8 | 260.4 |
| From government | 5.5 | 6.1 | 6.6 | 7.1 | 7.6 | 8.6 | 10.9 | 11.9 | 12.6 | 14.3 | 15.8 | 17.1 | 18.2 | 18.7 | 19.6 |
| From business (net) | 5.8 | 6.1 | 6.6 | 7.1 | 7.7 | 7.9 | 8.9 | 11.1 | 11.1 | 12.7 | 10.8 | 10.3 | 10.2 | 14.5 | 11.3 |
| From households[b] | 84.4 | 86.3 | 89.7 | 91.5 | 107.5 | 121.8 | 139.1 | 155.2 | 178.4 | 172.2 | 179.3 | 181.3 | 204.5 | 216.7 | 229.5 |
| Asset income | 33.2 | 33.6 | 36.7 | 42.2 | 44.7 | 47.9 | 41.8 | 44.5 | 47.7 | 40.5 | 35.7 | 35.7 | 39.6 | 40.4 | 45.1 |
| Interest income | 21.5 | 20.6 | 22.6 | 25.5 | 26.5 | 30.9 | 26.5 | 30.6 | 35.7 | 28.8 | 23.3 | 20.5 | 22.3 | 22.5 | 26.5 |
| Dividend income | 10.3 | 11.5 | 12.4 | 14.7 | 16.2 | 14.9 | 13.0 | 11.7 | 10.0 | 9.7 | 10.2 | 13.0 | 15.1 | 15.9 | 16.4 |
| Rental income (net of capital consumption) | 1.4 | 1.5 | 1.7 | 2.0 | 2.0 | 2.1 | 2.3 | 2.2 | 2.0 | 2.0 | 2.2 | 2.2 | 2.2 | 2.0 | 2.2 |
| Total | 444.2 | 469.6 | 491.4 | 514.8 | 550.0 | 593.7 | 628.1 | 670.3 | 724.4 | 749.8 | 794.3 | 831.9 | 892.3 | 952.8 | 1,006.7 |

*Source:* U.S. Department of Commerce, Bureau of Economic Analysis, National Income and Product Accounts, table 2.9 (2006).

*Note:* Estimates in this table exclude nonprofit institutions serving business and government.

a. Sales receipts excludes unrelated sales, secondary sales, and sales to business, government, and the rest of the world, and includes membership dues and fees. A significant portion of sales comes from public funding sources, such as Medicare and Medicaid.

b. Transfer receipts from households includes individual contributions and bequests from households, but excludes transfers between nonprofits.

**Table 4.2.** Outlays from Nonprofit Institutions Serving Households ($ billions)

| | 1992 | 1993 | 1994 | 1995 | 1996 | 1997 | 1998 | 1999 | 2000 | 2001 | 2002 | 2003 | 2004 | 2005 | 2006 |
|---|---|---|---|---|---|---|---|---|---|---|---|---|---|---|---|
| Consumption expenditures[a] | 407.1 | 430.3 | 451.7 | 470.4 | 494.5 | 514.7 | 547.5 | 576.3 | 620.3 | 665.8 | 715.5 | 756.9 | 799.4 | 844.3 | 893.1 |
| Medical care | 235.3 | 251.3 | 261.7 | 272.1 | 282.8 | 297.1 | 312.9 | 330.0 | 350.3 | 376.7 | 407.9 | 436.5 | 464.1 | 497.4 | 528.2 |
| Recreation | 20.3 | 21.3 | 21.7 | 21.9 | 21.3 | 20.8 | 21.6 | 22.6 | 24.5 | 25.9 | 27.0 | 27.9 | 28.2 | 30.4 | 30.2 |
| Education and research | 58.3 | 61.8 | 64.9 | 68.7 | 73.5 | 76.3 | 82.0 | 86.9 | 93.7 | 100.4 | 107.6 | 114.7 | 120.3 | 127.0 | 133.5 |
| Religious and welfare activities | 81.3 | 83.5 | 90.5 | 93.9 | 102.6 | 105.2 | 114.8 | 119.7 | 133.6 | 143.4 | 152.2 | 155.8 | 163.8 | 165.9 | 176.9 |
| Personal business | 11.9 | 12.4 | 12.9 | 13.8 | 14.3 | 15.3 | 16.2 | 17.2 | 18.1 | 19.5 | 20.8 | 22.0 | 22.9 | 23.6 | 24.4 |
| Transfer payments | 23.6 | 26.7 | 29.0 | 29.2 | 33.9 | 37.2 | 44.2 | 49.4 | 52.3 | 59.5 | 62.7 | 66.5 | 70.8 | 76.7 | 80.7 |
| To government[b] | 0.2 | 0.2 | 0.2 | 0.3 | 0.4 | 0.5 | 0.5 | 0.7 | 0.6 | 0.3 | 0.2 | 0.3 | 0.5 | 0.5 | 0.5 |
| To the rest of the world (net) | 2.2 | 2.7 | 2.9 | 3.0 | 3.5 | 4.4 | 6.4 | 7.2 | 7.6 | 8.0 | 8.2 | 9.0 | 8.9 | 10.5 | 10.8 |
| To households[c] | 21.2 | 23.8 | 26.0 | 25.9 | 30.0 | 32.3 | 37.2 | 41.5 | 44.1 | 51.2 | 54.2 | 57.2 | 61.5 | 65.7 | 69.4 |
| Total NPISH outlays | 430.7 | 457.0 | 480.7 | 499.6 | 528.4 | 551.9 | 591.7 | 625.7 | 672.6 | 725.3 | 778.2 | 823.4 | 870.2 | 921.0 | 973.8 |
| NPISH saving | 13.5 | 12.6 | 10.6 | 15.2 | 21.6 | 41.8 | 36.5 | 44.6 | 51.9 | 24.5 | 16.2 | 8.5 | 22.1 | 31.8 | 32.9 |
| Transfer payments between NPISHs[d] | 25.4 | 26.8 | 26.2 | 27.7 | 32.1 | 35.6 | 41.8 | 47.0 | 54.5 | 58.5 | 59.4 | 61.7 | 64.0 | 70.5 | 77.3 |

*Source:* U.S. Department of Commerce, Bureau of Economic Analysis, National Income and Product Accounts, table 2.9 (2006).
NPISH = nonprofit institutions serving households
*Note:* Estimates in this table exclude nonprofit institutions serving business and government.
a. Consumption expenditures is net of unrelated sales, secondary sales, and sales to business, government, and the rest of the world.
b. Transfer payments to government consists of excise taxes paid by private foundations.
c. Transfer payments to households includes benefits paid to members, specific assistance to individuals, and grants and allocations.
d. Transfer payments between NPISHs includes grants and allocations made by nonprofit institutions that indirectly support households through the support of other nonprofit institutions, plus their payments to affiliates.

**Table 4.3.** NAICS Industries Included in Bureau of Economic Analysis Consumption Categories

Medical care
| | |
|---|---|
| 621410 | Family planning centers |
| 621420 | Outpatient mental health and substance abuse centers |
| 621491 | HMO medical centers |
| 621492 | Kidney dialysis centers |
| 621493 | Freestanding ambulatory surgical and emergency centers |
| 621498 | All other outpatient care centers |
| 621610 | Home health care services |
| 621910 | Ambulance services |
| 621991 | Blood and organ bank services |
| 621999 | All other miscellaneous ambulatory health care services |
| 622110 | General medical and surgical hospitals |
| 622210 | Psychiatric and substance abuse hospitals |
| 622310 | Specialty hospitals (except psychiatric and substance abuse) hospitals |
| 623110 | Nursing care facilities |
| 623210 | Residential mental retardation facilities |
| 623311 | Continuing care retirement communities |

Recreation
| | |
|---|---|
| 611610 | Fine arts schools |
| 611620 | Sports and recreation instruction |
| 711110 | Theater companies and dinner theaters |
| 711120 | Dance companies |
| 711130 | Musical groups and artists |
| 711190 | Other performing arts companies |
| 711310 | Promoters of performing arts, sports, and similar events with facilities |
| 711320 | Promoters of performing arts, sports, and similar events without facilities |
| 713910 | Golf courses and country clubs |
| 713940 | Fitness and recreational sports centers |
| 713990 | All other amusement and recreation industries |
| 813410 | Civic and social organizations |
| 813920 | Professional organizations |
| 813990 | Other similar organizations (except business, professional, labor, and political organizations) |

Education and research
| | |
|---|---|
| 541710 | Research and development in the physical, engineering, and life sciences |
| 541720 | Research and development in the social sciences and humanities |
| 611110 | Elementary and secondary schools |
| 611210 | Junior colleges |
| 611310 | Colleges, universities, and professional schools |
| 611410 | Business and secretarial schools |
| 611420 | Computer training |
| 611430 | Professional and management development training |
| 611511 | Cosmetology and barber schools |
| 611519 | Other technical and trade schools |
| 611512 | Flight training |
| 611610 | Fine arts schools |

*(continued)*

**Table 4.3.** NAICS Industries Included in Bureau of Economic Analysis Consumption Categories
*(continued)*

| | |
|---|---|
| 611630 | Language schools |
| 611691 | Exam preparation and tutoring |
| 611692 | Automobile driving schools |
| 611699 | All other miscellaneous schools and instruction |
| 611710 | Educational support services |
| 624410 | Child day care services |
| 813211 | Grantmaking foundations |

Religious and welfare activities

| | |
|---|---|
| 623220 | Residential mental health and substance abuse facilities |
| 623312 | Homes for the elderly |
| 623990 | Other residential care facilities |
| 624110 | Child and youth services |
| 624120 | Services for the elderly and persons with disabilities |
| 624190 | Other individual and family services |
| 624210 | Community food services |
| 624221 | Temporary shelters |
| 624229 | Other community housing services |
| 624230 | Emergency and other relief services |
| 624310 | Vocational rehabilitation services |
| 624411 | Child day care services |
| 712110 | Museums |
| 712120 | Historical sites |
| 712130 | Zoos and botanical gardens |
| 712190 | Nature parks and other similar institutions |
| 813110 | Religious organizations |
| 813211 | Grantmaking foundations |
| 813212 | Voluntary health organizations |
| 813219 | Other grantmaking and giving services |
| 813311 | Human rights organizations |
| 813312 | Environment, conservation, and wildlife organizations |
| 813319 | Other social advocacy organizations |
| 813410 | Civic and social organizations |
| 813940 | Political organizations |
| 813990 | Other similar organizations (except business, professional, labor, and political organizations) |

Personal business

| | |
|---|---|
| 541110 | Offices of lawyers |
| 813920 | Professional organizations |
| 813930 | Labor organizations and similar labor organizations |

*Source:* Private communication from analysts at the Bureau of Economic Analysis, August 2006.
NAICS = North American Industry Classification System

# Revenue Trends for 501(c)(3) Public Charities

After adjusting for inflation, revenue received by 501(c)(3) public charities grew by nearly 100 percent in the 13-year period from 1992 through 2005 (table 4.4). Growth was relatively uniform across all major subsectors with the exception of the international subsector (which saw revenues increase by 240.33 percent) and supporting organizations—a category that includes organizations from all of the other categories—which had a relatively modest gain of only 52.58 percent. All other subsectors grew between 83.57 percent (higher education) and 134.54 percent (environment and animals).

The appendix to this chapter provides the detailed numbers in both current and constant dollars for 1992, 1995, 1997, 2000, 2002, and 2005. This unusual mix of years makes these numbers readily comparable to sources such as the Economic Census, which was last updated in 1997 and 2002, and provides data for the more typical five-year periods starting with 1995.

Table 4.4. Cumulative Percentage Change of Public Charity Revenues as Measured in Constant Dollars, 1992–2005

| | Total | Private contributions | Private payments | Government grants and payments | Investment income | Other revenue |
|---|---|---|---|---|---|---|
| Arts, culture, and humanities | 89.48 | 118.69 | 68.48 | 89.66 | 71.12 | 63.59 |
| Education | 90.23 | 94.80 | 70.80 | 95.72 | 206.20 | 45.49 |
| Higher education | 83.57 | 69.55 | 66.20 | 71.77 | 225.89 | 36.12 |
| Other education | 122.21 | 187.22 | 93.90 | 217.72 | 100.65 | 79.73 |
| Environment and animals | 134.54 | 207.40 | 75.98 | 176.12 | 134.34 | 46.75 |
| Health care | 101.03 | 74.47 | 114.19 | 82.62 | 152.30 | 99.57 |
| Hospitals | 96.10 | 105.66 | 110.22 | 75.74 | 154.55 | 128.02 |
| Other health care | 119.71 | 54.09 | 126.41 | 130.18 | 146.09 | 32.59 |
| Human services | 105.59 | 104.68 | 130.84 | 93.17 | 71.71 | 48.12 |
| International | 240.33 | 302.16 | 124.40 | 159.38 | 122.80 | 24.85 |
| Other operating public charities | 112.95 | 142.80 | 100.49 | 176.55 | 26.05 | 34.83 |
| Supporting public charities | 52.58 | 133.15 | −32.39 | 179.50 | 159.55 | 50.22 |
| Total | 96.47 | 123.29 | 90.89 | 90.07 | 151.24 | 64.70 |

*Source:* Calculations by the National Center for Charitable Statistics based on U.S. Department of the Treasury, Internal Revenue Service, Statistics of Income Division, Exempt Organizations Sample Files, public charities only.
*Notes:* Only operating organizations are included in categories other than supporting public charities. For a detailed discussion on the methodology, see http://nccs.urban.org/database/overview.cfm. The numbers reported in this section will not be identical to the revenues reported in chapter 5 due to differences in the data sources and methodology.

**Table 4.5.** Annual Percentage Change of Public Charity Revenues as Measured in Constant Dollars, 1992–2005

|  | Total | Private contributions | Private payments | Government grants and payments | Investment income | Other revenue |
|---|---|---|---|---|---|---|
| Arts, culture, and humanities | 5.04 | 6.20 | 4.09 | 5.05 | 4.22 | 3.86 |
| Education | 5.07 | 5.26 | 4.20 | 5.30 | 8.99 | 2.93 |
| Higher education | 4.78 | 4.14 | 3.99 | 4.25 | 9.51 | 2.40 |
| Other education | 6.33 | 8.45 | 5.23 | 9.30 | 5.50 | 4.61 |
| Environment and animals | 6.78 | 9.02 | 4.44 | 8.13 | 6.77 | 2.99 |
| Health care | 5.52 | 4.37 | 6.03 | 4.74 | 7.38 | 5.46 |
| Hospitals | 5.32 | 5.70 | 5.88 | 4.43 | 7.45 | 6.55 |
| Other health care | 6.24 | 3.38 | 6.49 | 6.62 | 7.17 | 2.19 |
| Human services | 5.70 | 5.66 | 6.65 | 5.20 | 4.25 | 3.07 |
| International | 9.88 | 11.30 | 6.41 | 7.61 | 6.36 | 1.72 |
| Other operating public charities | 5.99 | 7.06 | 5.50 | 8.14 | 1.80 | 2.33 |
| Supporting public charities | 3.30 | 6.73 | −2.97 | 8.23 | 7.61 | 3.18 |
| Total | 5.33 | 6.37 | 5.10 | 5.06 | 7.34 | 3.91 |

*Source:* Calculations by the National Center for Charitable Statistics based on U.S. Department of the Treasury, Internal Revenue Service, Statistics of Income Division, Exempt Organizations Sample Files, public charities only.

*Notes:* Only operating organizations are included in categories other than supporting public charities. For a detailed discussion on the methodology, see http://nccs.urban.org/database/overview.cfm. The numbers reported in this section will not be identical to the revenues reported in chapter 5 due to differences in the data sources and methodology.

All major types of revenue for the nonprofit sector grew during this period. Investment income, which includes sales of securities, interest, and dividends, grew fastest with cumulative real growth of 151.24 percent, or an average of 7.34 per year (table 4.5). Private contributions were second, with growth of 123.29 percent (6.37 percent per year). Both private payments and government grants and payments had cumulative real growth of 90.00 percent, or more than 5.00 percent per year. (Private payments include ticket sales in the arts, tuition in education, and patient fees provided by private parties in health care.) The "other revenue" category grew the slowest. This includes miscellaneous revenue, membership dues, and net special events income. Chapter 5 discusses the distribution of the different types of revenue in greater detail.

Private contributions to international organizations quadrupled in real terms, substantially faster than any other revenue source.

# Revenue by Source and Type of Public Charity, 1992–2005

| | $ (Billions) | | | | | | Constant $ (2000, Billions) | | | | | |
|---|---|---|---|---|---|---|---|---|---|---|---|---|
| | Total | Private contributions | Private payments | Government grants and payments | Investment income | Other revenue | Total | Private contributions | Private payments | Government grants and payments | Investment income | Other revenue |
| **2005** | | | | | | | | | | | | |
| Arts, culture, and humanities | 22.67 | 9.62 | 6.61 | 2.83 | 2.09 | 1.52 | 20.88 | 8.86 | 6.09 | 2.60 | 1.92 | 1.40 |
| Education | 189.79 | 23.89 | 106.32 | 23.03 | 32.24 | 4.31 | 174.79 | 22.00 | 97.92 | 21.21 | 29.69 | 3.97 |
| Higher education | 151.58 | 16.33 | 86.27 | 16.90 | 28.92 | 3.17 | 139.61 | 15.04 | 79.45 | 15.56 | 26.63 | 2.92 |
| Other education | 38.20 | 7.56 | 20.04 | 6.13 | 3.32 | 1.14 | 35.18 | 6.96 | 18.46 | 5.65 | 3.06 | 1.05 |
| Environment and animals | 10.51 | 5.04 | 2.50 | 1.28 | 0.78 | 0.93 | 9.68 | 4.64 | 2.30 | 1.18 | 0.71 | 0.85 |
| Health care | 672.50 | 16.20 | 379.14 | 245.51 | 19.73 | 11.92 | 619.36 | 14.92 | 349.18 | 226.11 | 18.17 | 10.98 |
| Hospitals | 518.96 | 7.55 | 280.85 | 206.38 | 14.62 | 9.56 | 477.95 | 6.95 | 258.66 | 190.07 | 13.47 | 8.81 |
| Other health care | 153.54 | 8.65 | 98.29 | 39.13 | 5.10 | 2.36 | 141.40 | 7.97 | 90.52 | 36.04 | 4.70 | 2.18 |
| Human services | 143.29 | 22.61 | 59.01 | 52.05 | 3.82 | 5.80 | 131.97 | 20.82 | 54.35 | 47.93 | 3.52 | 5.34 |
| International | 19.84 | 14.29 | 1.12 | 3.95 | 0.38 | 0.11 | 18.28 | 13.16 | 1.03 | 3.64 | 0.35 | 0.10 |
| Other operating public charities | 40.77 | 9.08 | 14.06 | 12.81 | 3.63 | 1.19 | 37.54 | 8.36 | 12.95 | 11.80 | 3.34 | 1.10 |
| Supporting public charities | 96.67 | 43.05 | 21.22 | 9.56 | 18.25 | 4.60 | 89.03 | 39.65 | 19.54 | 8.80 | 16.81 | 4.24 |
| Total | 1,196.04 | 143.77 | 589.97 | 351.01 | 80.91 | 30.38 | 1,101.53 | 132.41 | 543.35 | 323.27 | 74.51 | 27.98 |
| **2002** | | | | | | | | | | | | |
| Arts, culture, and humanities | 18.64 | 8.10 | 6.03 | 2.76 | 0.44 | 1.30 | 17.90 | 7.78 | 5.79 | 2.65 | 0.43 | 1.25 |
| Education | 132.96 | 19.23 | 84.70 | 19.20 | 6.65 | 3.17 | 127.66 | 18.47 | 81.33 | 18.44 | 6.38 | 3.05 |
| Higher education | 103.34 | 13.38 | 68.16 | 13.84 | 5.88 | 2.08 | 99.22 | 12.85 | 65.44 | 13.28 | 5.65 | 2.00 |
| Other education | 29.62 | 5.85 | 16.54 | 5.37 | 0.76 | 1.09 | 28.44 | 5.62 | 15.88 | 5.15 | 0.73 | 1.05 |

|  | | | | | | | | | | | |
|---|---|---|---|---|---|---|---|---|---|---|---|
| Environment and animals | 7.35 | 3.57 | 1.91 | 1.00 | 0.11 | 0.76 | 7.06 | 3.43 | 1.84 | 0.96 | 0.11 | 0.73 |
| Health care | 518.54 | 13.80 | 292.17 | 199.15 | 3.66 | 9.76 | 497.88 | 13.25 | 280.53 | 191.21 | 3.52 | 9.37 |
| Hospitals | 401.12 | 6.39 | 215.95 | 167.95 | 3.02 | 7.82 | 385.14 | 6.13 | 207.34 | 161.26 | 2.90 | 7.50 |
| Other health care | 117.42 | 7.42 | 76.22 | 31.20 | 0.65 | 1.94 | 112.75 | 7.12 | 73.19 | 29.95 | 0.62 | 1.86 |
| Human services | 124.10 | 18.77 | 51.50 | 47.59 | 1.41 | 4.83 | 119.16 | 18.02 | 49.45 | 45.70 | 1.36 | 4.64 |
| International | 12.34 | 8.21 | 0.86 | 3.06 | 0.11 | 0.09 | 11.84 | 7.88 | 0.82 | 2.94 | 0.11 | 0.09 |
| Other operating public charities | 28.03 | 7.58 | 10.03 | 8.56 | 0.88 | 0.98 | 26.92 | 7.28 | 9.63 | 8.22 | 0.84 | 0.94 |
| Supporting public charities | 64.05 | 32.28 | 16.98 | 8.64 | 1.99 | 4.15 | 61.50 | 30.99 | 16.30 | 8.30 | 1.92 | 3.98 |
| Total | 906.02 | 111.55 | 464.18 | 289.97 | 15.27 | 25.05 | 869.92 | 107.11 | 445.69 | 278.42 | 14.66 | 24.05 |
| **2000** | | | | | | | | | | | | |
| Arts, culture, and humanities | 20.19 | 8.97 | 5.68 | 2.48 | 1.87 | 1.20 | 20.19 | 8.97 | 5.68 | 2.48 | 1.87 | 1.20 |
| Education | 131.82 | 20.22 | 72.35 | 15.63 | 20.72 | 2.90 | 131.82 | 20.22 | 72.35 | 15.63 | 20.72 | 2.90 |
| Higher education | 105.40 | 14.82 | 58.43 | 11.62 | 18.59 | 1.93 | 105.40 | 14.82 | 58.43 | 11.62 | 18.59 | 1.93 |
| Other education | 26.42 | 5.40 | 13.92 | 4.01 | 2.13 | 0.97 | 26.42 | 5.40 | 13.92 | 4.01 | 2.13 | 0.97 |
| Environment and animals | 7.62 | 3.87 | 1.65 | 0.82 | 0.54 | 0.73 | 7.62 | 3.87 | 1.65 | 0.82 | 0.54 | 0.73 |
| Health care | 441.49 | 13.84 | 243.33 | 164.81 | 12.06 | 7.45 | 441.49 | 13.84 | 243.33 | 164.81 | 12.06 | 7.45 |
| Hospitals | 338.02 | 6.06 | 174.11 | 142.32 | 9.71 | 5.82 | 338.02 | 6.06 | 174.11 | 142.32 | 9.71 | 5.82 |
| Other health care | 103.47 | 7.77 | 69.22 | 22.49 | 2.35 | 1.63 | 103.47 | 7.77 | 69.22 | 22.49 | 2.35 | 1.63 |
| Human services | 109.35 | 17.93 | 42.28 | 41.12 | 3.37 | 4.64 | 109.35 | 17.93 | 42.28 | 41.12 | 3.37 | 4.64 |
| International | 9.43 | 6.45 | 0.74 | 1.82 | 0.33 | 0.09 | 9.43 | 6.45 | 0.74 | 1.82 | 0.33 | 0.09 |
| Other operating public charities | 24.39 | 6.89 | 8.73 | 4.96 | 2.90 | 0.91 | 24.39 | 6.89 | 8.73 | 4.96 | 2.90 | 0.91 |
| Supporting public charities | 78.05 | 34.29 | 18.32 | 6.58 | 15.30 | 3.56 | 78.05 | 34.29 | 18.32 | 6.58 | 15.30 | 3.56 |
| Total | 822.35 | 112.46 | 393.10 | 238.21 | 57.11 | 21.48 | 822.35 | 112.46 | 393.10 | 238.21 | 57.11 | 21.48 |

*(continued)*

|  | $ (Billions) | | | | | | Constant $ (2000, Billions) | | | | | |
|---|---|---|---|---|---|---|---|---|---|---|---|---|
|  | Total | Private contributions | Private payments | Government grants and payments | Investment income | Other revenue | Total | Private contributions | Private payments | Government grants and payments | Investment income | Other revenue |
| **1997** | | | | | | | | | | | | |
| Arts, culture, and humanities | 15.70 | 6.16 | 4.74 | 1.59 | 2.15 | 1.06 | 16.42 | 6.44 | 4.96 | 1.66 | 2.25 | 1.11 |
| Education | 114.53 | 16.19 | 61.60 | 12.53 | 21.21 | 3.00 | 119.81 | 16.94 | 64.44 | 13.10 | 22.19 | 3.14 |
| Higher education | 91.86 | 12.25 | 49.76 | 9.74 | 17.89 | 2.22 | 96.10 | 12.82 | 52.06 | 10.19 | 18.71 | 2.32 |
| Other education | 22.67 | 3.94 | 11.84 | 2.79 | 3.32 | 0.79 | 23.72 | 4.12 | 12.38 | 2.92 | 3.48 | 0.82 |
| Environment and animals | 5.63 | 2.38 | 1.28 | 0.55 | 0.73 | 0.69 | 5.89 | 2.49 | 1.34 | 0.57 | 0.76 | 0.72 |
| Health care | 364.55 | 12.59 | 179.75 | 149.45 | 15.48 | 7.28 | 381.37 | 13.17 | 188.04 | 156.34 | 16.19 | 7.62 |
| Hospitals | 274.70 | 4.39 | 122.49 | 131.47 | 11.58 | 4.77 | 287.38 | 4.59 | 128.14 | 137.53 | 12.12 | 4.99 |
| Other health care | 89.84 | 8.20 | 57.26 | 17.98 | 3.89 | 2.51 | 93.99 | 8.58 | 59.90 | 18.81 | 4.07 | 2.63 |
| Human services | 88.28 | 12.68 | 33.27 | 35.07 | 3.58 | 3.68 | 92.35 | 13.27 | 34.80 | 36.68 | 3.75 | 3.85 |
| International | 6.39 | 3.71 | 0.84 | 1.51 | 0.24 | 0.10 | 6.69 | 3.88 | 0.87 | 1.58 | 0.25 | 0.10 |
| Other operating public charities | 21.67 | 5.55 | 6.64 | 4.00 | 4.23 | 1.25 | 22.67 | 5.80 | 6.95 | 4.19 | 4.42 | 1.30 |
| Supporting public charities | 69.02 | 24.49 | 22.29 | 4.34 | 14.51 | 3.39 | 72.20 | 25.62 | 23.32 | 4.54 | 15.18 | 3.55 |
| Total | 685.76 | 83.74 | 310.41 | 209.04 | 62.12 | 20.45 | 717.40 | 87.61 | 324.74 | 218.68 | 64.98 | 21.39 |
| **1995** | | | | | | | | | | | | |
| Arts, culture, and humanities | 11.64 | 4.27 | 3.66 | 1.50 | 1.38 | 0.84 | 12.63 | 4.63 | 3.97 | 1.63 | 1.49 | 0.91 |
| Education | 98.00 | 12.75 | 55.72 | 11.47 | 15.54 | 2.53 | 106.32 | 13.83 | 60.44 | 12.44 | 16.86 | 2.75 |
| Higher education | 78.95 | 9.78 | 45.62 | 8.80 | 12.99 | 1.76 | 85.65 | 10.61 | 49.49 | 9.55 | 14.09 | 1.91 |
| Other education | 19.05 | 2.96 | 10.09 | 2.67 | 2.55 | 0.78 | 20.67 | 3.22 | 10.95 | 2.89 | 2.77 | 0.84 |
| Environment and animals | 4.69 | 1.81 | 1.19 | 0.51 | 0.43 | 0.76 | 5.09 | 1.96 | 1.29 | 0.55 | 0.47 | 0.82 |

| | | | | | | | | | | | | |
|---|---|---|---|---|---|---|---|---|---|---|---|---|
| Health care | 330.34 | 17.04 | 156.36 | 140.42 | 10.45 | 6.08 | 358.37 | 18.48 | 169.63 | 152.33 | 11.33 | 6.59 |
| Hospitals | 249.65 | 3.39 | 112.25 | 122.01 | 7.98 | 4.02 | 270.83 | 3.68 | 121.77 | 132.36 | 8.66 | 4.36 |
| Other health care | 80.69 | 13.64 | 44.11 | 18.41 | 2.46 | 2.06 | 87.53 | 14.80 | 47.85 | 19.97 | 2.67 | 2.23 |
| Human services | 72.83 | 9.48 | 26.53 | 31.12 | 2.59 | 3.11 | 79.01 | 10.29 | 28.78 | 33.76 | 2.81 | 3.38 |
| International | 5.80 | 3.01 | 0.51 | 1.95 | 0.19 | 0.13 | 6.29 | 3.27 | 0.56 | 2.12 | 0.21 | 0.14 |
| Other operating public charities | 20.86 | 5.34 | 6.58 | 4.09 | 3.91 | 0.94 | 22.63 | 5.79 | 7.14 | 4.43 | 4.24 | 1.02 |
| Supporting public charities | 58.07 | 18.58 | 22.73 | 4.05 | 9.28 | 3.43 | 63.00 | 20.15 | 24.66 | 4.39 | 10.07 | 3.72 |
| Total | 602.24 | 72.27 | 273.28 | 195.11 | 43.77 | 17.81 | 653.33 | 78.40 | 296.47 | 211.66 | 47.48 | 19.32 |
| **1992** | | | | | | | | | | | | |
| Arts, culture, and humanities | 9.52 | 3.50 | 3.12 | 1.19 | 0.97 | 0.74 | 11.02 | 4.05 | 3.61 | 1.37 | 1.12 | 0.86 |
| Education | 79.41 | 9.76 | 49.54 | 9.37 | 8.38 | 2.36 | 91.88 | 11.29 | 57.33 | 10.84 | 9.70 | 2.73 |
| Higher education | 65.72 | 7.67 | 41.31 | 7.83 | 7.06 | 1.85 | 76.05 | 8.87 | 47.81 | 9.06 | 8.17 | 2.14 |
| Other education | 13.68 | 2.09 | 8.23 | 1.54 | 1.32 | 0.51 | 15.83 | 2.42 | 9.52 | 1.78 | 1.52 | 0.59 |
| Environment and animals | 3.57 | 1.30 | 1.13 | 0.37 | 0.26 | 0.50 | 4.13 | 1.51 | 1.31 | 0.43 | 0.30 | 0.58 |
| Health care | 266.25 | 7.39 | 140.88 | 107.00 | 6.22 | 4.76 | 308.09 | 8.55 | 163.02 | 123.82 | 7.20 | 5.50 |
| Hospitals | 210.63 | 2.92 | 106.33 | 93.47 | 4.57 | 3.34 | 243.73 | 3.38 | 123.04 | 108.16 | 5.29 | 3.86 |
| Other health care | 55.62 | 4.47 | 34.55 | 13.53 | 1.65 | 1.42 | 64.36 | 5.17 | 39.98 | 15.66 | 1.91 | 1.64 |
| Human services | 55.47 | 8.79 | 20.35 | 21.45 | 1.77 | 3.12 | 64.19 | 10.17 | 23.54 | 24.81 | 2.05 | 3.61 |
| International | 4.64 | 2.83 | 0.40 | 1.21 | 0.14 | 0.07 | 5.37 | 3.27 | 0.46 | 1.40 | 0.16 | 0.08 |
| Other operating public charities | 15.24 | 2.98 | 5.58 | 3.69 | 2.29 | 0.70 | 17.63 | 3.44 | 6.46 | 4.27 | 2.65 | 0.81 |
| Supporting public charities | 50.43 | 14.70 | 24.98 | 2.72 | 5.60 | 2.44 | 58.35 | 17.00 | 28.90 | 3.15 | 6.48 | 2.82 |
| Total | 484.53 | 51.25 | 245.98 | 146.99 | 25.63 | 14.68 | 560.66 | 59.30 | 284.63 | 170.08 | 29.66 | 16.99 |

*Source:* Calculations by the National Center for Charitable Statistics based on U.S. Internal Revenue Service, Statistics of Income Division, Exempt Organizations Sample Files, public charities only.

*Notes:* Only operating organizations are included in categories other than supporting public charities. The numbers reported in this section will not be identical to the revenues reported in chapter 5 due to differences in the data sources and methodology.

# The Size, Scope, and Finances of Public Charities

While chapter 1 discusses the size of the nonprofit sector, this chapter examines the size, scope, and financial condition of organizations exempt from taxation under section 501(c)(3) of the Internal Revenue Code, most of which are known as public charities. We begin with a review of the larger nonprofit sector as discussed in chapter 1, and then go on to discuss public charities in detail—including a look at these organizations by subsector and state.

## Overview of the Nonprofit Sector

Approximately 1.4 million nonprofit organizations were registered with the IRS in 2005 (table 5.1). This figure includes a diverse group of organizations, both in size and mission, which range from hospitals and human service organizations to advocacy groups and chambers of commerce. The vast majority—and those holding most of the sector's revenues and assets—are registered with the IRS as 501(c)(3) public charities.

Organizations are eligible for tax-exempt status under section 501(c)(3) if their purpose includes assisting the poor and underprivileged; advancing religion, education, health, science, art, or culture; protecting the environment; or other purposes beneficial to the community. Many organizations receiving public charity status must also receive a substantial proportion of their income, directly or indirectly, from the general public or from the government (also called "public support"). Public charities and religious congregations can receive fully tax-deductible contributions. (The nation's approximately 350,000 religious congregations are also considered public charities, but they are not required to register with the IRS, although about half do so) (Weitzman et al. 2002).

Private foundations are also exempt under section 501(c)(3). A founding individual, a family, or a corporation usually endows these organizations. Typically, foundations

**Table 5.1.** Size and Financial Scope of the Nonprofit Sector, 1995–2005

| | 1995 | 2000 | 2005 | % change, 1995–2005 | % change, 1995–2005 (inflation adjusted) |
|---|---|---|---|---|---|
| All nonprofits | 1.1 million | 1.3 million | 1.4 million | 27.3 | — |
| Reporting nonprofits | 431,567 | 428,154 | 530,376[a] | 22.9 | — |
| Revenues ($) | 802 billion | 1.1 trillion | 1.6 trillion | 96.9 | 54.6 |
| Expenses ($) | 729 billion | 984 billion | 1.4 trillion | 96.4 | 54.2 |
| Assets ($) | 1.5 trillion | 2.4 trillion | 3.4 trillion | 125.6 | 77.1 |
| Public charities, 501(c)(3) | 572,660 | 690,326 | 876,164 | 53.0 | — |
| Reporting public charities | 187,038 | 245,749 | 310,683 | 66.1 | — |
| Revenues ($) | 573 billion | 811 billion | 1.1 trillion | 99.5 | 56.6 |
| Expenses ($) | 530 billion | 731 billion | 1.1 trillion | 98.7 | 56.0 |
| Assets ($) | 843 billion | 1.4 trillion | 2.0 trillion | 134.3 | 83.9 |

*Sources:* Urban Institute, National Center for Charitable Statistics, NCCS-GuideStar National Nonprofit Research Database: Special Research Version (2005), Core Files (1995, 2000, 2005); IRS Business Master Files, Exempt Organizations (1996, 2001, 2006).
*Notes:* Reporting public charities include only organizations that both reported (filed IRS Forms 990) and were required to do so. The following were excluded: foreign organizations, government-associated organizations, organizations without state identifiers, and organizations excluded by the authors' discretion. Organizations not required to report include religious congregations and organizations with less than $25,000 in gross receipts.
a. The total number of reporting nonprofit organizations in this chapter differs from the figure in chapter 1 because mutual benefit organizations (NTEE = Y) are not included in this chapter's count of reporting public charities.
— = data not available

fund 501(c)(3) public charities, although they may also provide scholarships, support government activities, or operate programs.

Additional types of nonprofit organizations include social welfare organizations (501(c)(4)), labor and agricultural associations (501(c)(5)), business leagues (501(c)(6)), fraternal beneficiary societies (501(c)(8)), and others.

Of the 1.4 million nonprofit organizations registered with the IRS in 2005, over half a million collected more than $25,000 in gross receipts and are therefore required to file a Form 990 annually. These "reporting organizations" accounted for approximately $1.6 trillion in revenue and $3.4 trillion in assets in 2005, the latest year for which complete data are available (table 5.1).

As displayed in table 5.1, the number of nonprofit organizations registered with the IRS grew by 27.3 percent from 1995 to 2005. Over this same time, the number of reporting nonprofit organizations grew by 22.9 percent. In contrast, the number of public charities registered with the IRS grew at almost twice that rate, while the number of reporting public charities grew nearly threefold.

The finances of reporting nonprofit organizations also grew at a healthy rate from 1995 to 2005. While the U.S. GDP increased by approximately 35 percent over this period after adjusting for inflation (Bureau of Economic Analysis 2007), revenues and assets for reporting nonprofits grew by at least 54 percent—a difference of nearly 20 percentage points. Total assets, in particular, rose dramatically, with an inflation-adjusted increase of 77.1 percent.

# Reporting Public Charities

The remainder of this chapter will focus on reporting public charities, those 501(c)(3) organizations that are considered charitable in scope, rely primarily on support from the general public or the government, and are required to file Form 990 with the IRS. Table 5.2 outlines the registration and filing requirements.

Typically, congregations, most religious primary and secondary schools, and other religious organizations are not required to apply for tax-exempt status with the IRS, so most do not register. All financial figures for reporting organizations given in this chapter exclude religious congregations, regardless of whether they filed a Form 990.

## Reporting Public Charities by Size and Age

Public charities reported a total of $1.1 trillion in expenses and $2.0 trillion in total assets for 2005. However, these total dollar figures are dominated by the largest organizations, primarily hospitals and higher education institutions, which account for more than half of total expenses and assets of all public charities.

**Table 5.2.** Registration and Filing Requirements for 501(c)(3) Organizations

| | One-time registration for tax exemption | Annual reporting to IRS on Form 990 |
|---|---|---|
| Nonreligious public charities | | |
| Less than $5,000 in annual gross receipts | Optional | Optional |
| $5,000–$24,999 in annual gross receipts | Required | Optional |
| $25,000 or more in annual gross receipts | Required | Required |
| Religious public charities | | |
| Congregations, religious primary and secondary schools, denominations, and integrated auxiliaries | Optional | Optional |
| Religiously affiliated hospitals, universities, human service organizations, and others | Required to follow nonreligious public charity regulations | Required to follow nonreligious public charity regulations |
| Private foundations | Required regardless of size | Required regardless of size |

*Source:* U.S. Internal Revenue Service.

**Figure 5.1.** Number and Expenses of Reporting Public Charities, 2005

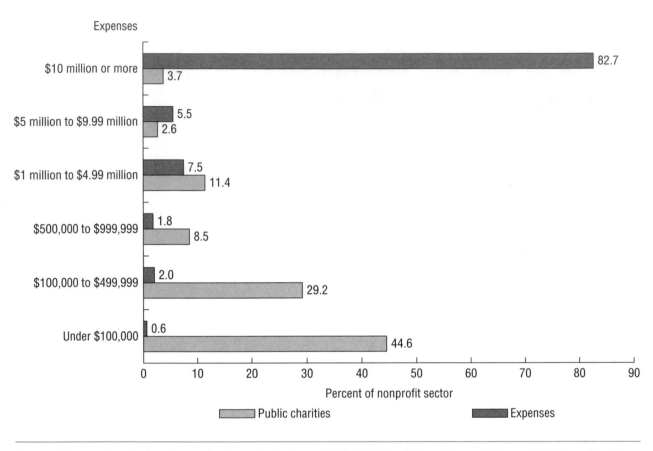

*Source:* Urban Institute, National Center for Charitable Statistics, NCCS-GuideStar National Nonprofit Research Database: Special Research Version (2005).

As shown in figure 5.1, the majority of public charities report less than $500,000 in expenses. In 2005, 44.6 percent of public charities reported less than $100,000 in expenses and another 29.2 percent reported expenses between $100,000 and $499,999. Only 17.7 percent of public charities reported over $1 million in expenses, with 3.7 percent reporting $10 million or more. Also exhibited in figure 5.1, organizations with under $1 million in total expenses, while accounting for over 80 percent of public charities, account for just 4.4 percent of the total expenses of all public charities.

Not surprisingly, the larger organizations tend to be older—69 percent of organizations with $10 million or more in total expenses report a founding date prior to 1985. Half of all organizations with less than $500,000 in total expenses report a founding date of 1993 or later (table 5.3).

## Reporting Public Charities by Subsector

Human service public charities, which include organizations that provide job training, legal aid, housing, youth development services, disaster assistance, and food distribution

**Table 5.3.** Reporting Public Charities by Founding Date, 2005 (percent)

| Expenses | Unknown | Before 1940 | 1940–1954 | 1955–1969 | 1970–1984 | 1985–1992 | 1993–2005 | Total |
|---|---|---|---|---|---|---|---|---|
| Under $100,000 | 0.8 | 0.2 | 2.9 | 6.6 | 15.9 | 15.8 | 57.9 | 100.0 |
| $100,000–$499,999 | 0.7 | 0.3 | 3.1 | 6.2 | 20.2 | 18.7 | 50.7 | 100.0 |
| $500,000–$999,999 | 0.8 | 0.6 | 4.8 | 8.0 | 26.8 | 20.1 | 38.9 | 100.0 |
| $1 million–$4.9 million | 0.9 | 1.4 | 7.6 | 11.5 | 29.8 | 17.4 | 31.3 | 100.0 |
| $5 million–$9.9 million | 1.0 | 2.9 | 11.9 | 16.6 | 28.7 | 15.1 | 23.7 | 100.0 |
| $10 million or more | 0.7 | 8.0 | 21.0 | 16.4 | 23.9 | 11.7 | 18.2 | 100.0 |
| All | 0.8 | 0.8 | 4.5 | 7.8 | 20.3 | 17.0 | 48.8 | 100.0 |

*Source:* Urban Institute, National Center for Charitable Statistics, NCCS-GuideStar National Nonprofit Research Database: Special Research Version (2005).
*Notes:* Reporting public charities include only organizations that both reported (filed IRS Forms 990) and were required to do so. The following were excluded: foreign organizations, government-associated organizations, organizations without state identifiers, and organizations excluded by the authors' discretion. Organizations not required to report include religious congregations and organizations with less than $25,000 in gross receipts.

programs, account for nearly one-third of public charities. Education public charities, which include higher education institutions and elementary and secondary schools, as well as education support organizations, account for the second largest proportion of organizations with 18.7 percent. (See chapter 5, appendix B, for a complete listing of the types of organizations within each subsector.)

We also can distinguish operating public charities from supporting public charities. Supporting public charities primarily distribute funds to operating public charities. Such charities can support a particular operating public charity or a group of public charities. Supporting organizations account for 12.9 percent (40,005) of all public charities.

The education subsector has many supporting public charities. These organizations include parent and teacher groups, alumni associations, and scholarship organizations. The "other" category, which includes civil rights and advocacy groups, philanthropy and voluntarism organizations, and religion-related organizations, also includes many support organizations. These supporting organizations include community foundations and federated giving programs such as the United Way (table 5.4).

## Finances of Reporting Public Charities

In 2005, public charities reported total revenues of $1.1 trillion. Fees for services and goods, which include tuition payments, hospital patient revenues including Medicare and Medicaid, and ticket sales, accounted for 70.3 percent of revenue. Private contributions, which include individual contributions and grants from foundations and

**Table 5.4.** Reporting Public Charities by Subsector, 2005

| Subsector | Operating public charities | % | Supporting public charities | % | All public charities | % |
|---|---|---|---|---|---|---|
| Arts, culture, and humanities | 34,077 | 12.6 | 1,763 | 4.4 | 35,840 | 11.5 |
| Education | 45,145 | 16.7 | 12,846 | 32.1 | 57,991 | 18.7 |
| Environment and animals | 12,533 | 4.6 | 866 | 2.2 | 13,399 | 4.3 |
| Health | 35,441 | 13.1 | 5,802 | 14.5 | 41,243 | 13.3 |
| Human services | 97,282 | 35.9 | 3,154 | 7.9 | 100,436 | 32.3 |
| International and foreign affairs | 4,631 | 1.7 | 444 | 1.1 | 5,075 | 1.6 |
| Other | 41,569 | 15.4 | 15,130 | 37.8 | 56,699 | 18.2 |
| Total | 270,678 | 100.0 | 40,005 | 100.0 | 310,683 | 100.0 |

*Source:* Urban Institute, National Center for Charitable Statistics, NCCS-GuideStar National Nonprofit Research Database: Special Research Version (2005).
*Notes:* Reporting public charities include only organizations that both reported (filed IRS Forms 990) and were required to do so. The following were excluded: foreign organizations, government-associated organizations, organizations without state identifiers, and organizations excluded by the authors' discretion. Organizations not required to report include religious congregations and organizations with less than $25,000 in gross receipts. Categories are as defined by the National Taxonomy of Exempt Entities (see chapter 5, appendix B, for more detail).

corporations, accounted for 12.3 percent; 9.0 percent of total revenue was from government grants. Investment income and other income, which includes dues and assessments, rental income, and income from special events, accounted for 5.4 percent and 2.9 percent of revenue respectively (figure 5.2).

Excluding hospitals and higher education institutions changes the distribution of sources of revenue substantially, as shown in figure 5.3. In contrast, the remaining organizations are less dependent on fees for services and goods and more dependent on private contributions and government grants, also known as public support.

Table 5.5 gives a detailed view of public charities' revenues, expenses, and assets. As displayed, differences between operating and supporting organizations are apparent in their distribution of revenues and expenses. Supporting organizations report relying more heavily on private contributions than do operating organizations (37.5 percent vs. 10.2 percent) and less on fees for services and goods (42.2 percent vs. 72.7 percent). Supporting organizations also report a greater percentage of income as investment income than do operating organizations (14.1 percent vs. 4.7 percent).

Public charities reported total expenses of $1.1 trillion in 2005, 92.2 percent of which were operating expenses. Personnel costs, including wages, salaries, and benefits, accounted for nearly half of all operating expenses. Other expenses accounted for the second largest proportion of operating expenses at 30.7 percent (see text box).

Operating expenses for supporting organizations and operating organizations also differ. Supporting organizations report spending less on personnel costs than do

**Figure 5.2.** Sources of Revenue for Reporting Public Charities, 2005 (percent)

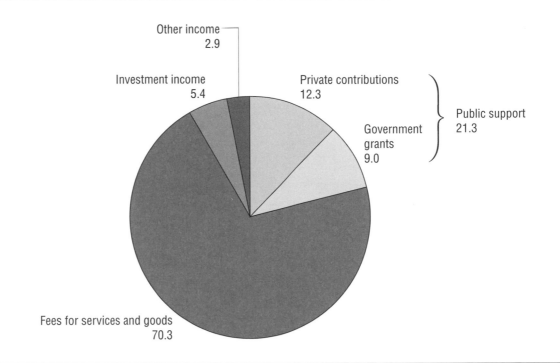

Other income
2.9

Investment income
5.4

Private contributions
12.3

Government grants
9.0

Public support
21.3

Fees for services and goods
70.3

*Source:* Urban Institute, National Center for Charitable Statistics, NCCS-GuideStar National Nonprofit Research Database: Special Research Version (2005).

**Figure 5.3.** Sources of Revenue for Reporting Public Charities, Excluding Hospitals and Higher Education, 2005 (percent)

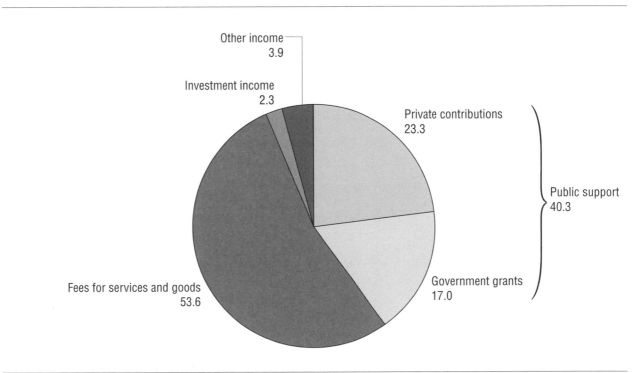

Other income
3.9

Investment income
2.3

Private contributions
23.3

Public support
40.3

Government grants
17.0

Fees for services and goods
53.6

*Source:* Urban Institute, National Center for Charitable Statistics, NCCS-GuideStar National Nonprofit Research Database: Special Research Version (2005).

**Table 5.5.** Revenues and Expenses for Reporting Public Charities, 2005

| | All Organizations | | Operating Organizations | | Supporting Organizations | |
|---|---|---|---|---|---|---|
| Number of organizations | 310,683 | | 270,678 | | 40,005 | |
| | $ millions | % | $ millions | % | $ millions | % |
| Public support | 243,710.8 | 21.3[a] | 207,549.0 | 19.6[a] | 36,161.7 | 41.2 |
| Private contributions | 140,931.6 | 12.3 | 108,042.2 | 10.2 | 32,889.4 | 37.5 |
| Direct contributions | 123,669.5 | 10.8 | 93,969.5 | 8.9 | 29,700.0 | 33.9 |
| Indirect contributions | 17,262.1 | 1.5 | 14,072.6 | 1.3 | 3,189.4 | 3.6 |
| Government grants | 102,779.2 | 9.0 | 99,506.9 | 9.4 | 3,272.3 | 3.7 |
| Fees for services and goods | 804,817.6 | 70.3 | 767,790.9 | 72.7 | 37,026.7 | 42.2 |
| Program service revenue[b] | 799,693.3 | 69.9 | 762,940.5 | 72.2 | 36,752.8 | 41.9 |
| Net income from sales of inventory | 5,124.3 | 0.4 | 4,850.4 | 0.5 | 273.9 | 0.3 |
| Investment income | 61,929.7 | 5.4 | 49,554.8 | 4.7 | 12,374.9 | 14.1 |
| Dividends | 18,338.8 | 1.6 | 13,854.7 | 1.3 | 4,484.1 | 5.1 |
| Interest | 5,471.0 | 0.5 | 4,787.2 | 0.5 | 683.8 | 0.8 |
| Net gain on sale of assets | 34,904.8 | 3.1 | 28,490.5 | 2.7 | 6,414.3 | 7.3 |
| Other investment income | 3,215.1 | 0.3 | 2,422.3 | 0.2 | 792.8 | 0.9 |
| Other income | 33,564.1 | 2.9 | 31,458.9 | 3.0 | 2,105.1 | 2.4 |
| Dues and assessments | 8,528.8 | 0.7 | 8,214.2 | 0.8 | 314.5 | 0.4 |
| Net income from special events | 3,773.3 | 0.3 | 3,217.6 | 0.3 | 555.7 | 0.6 |
| Other (includes net rental and other) | 21,262.0 | 1.9 | 20,027.1 | 1.9 | 1,234.8 | 1.4 |
| Total revenue | 1,144,022.2 | 100.0 | 1,056,353.7 | 100.0 | 87,668.5 | 100.0 |
| Paid personnel | 457,234.9 | 47.1[c] | 447,274.6 | 48.4[c] | 9,960.3 | 21.5 |
| Wages and salaries | 369,338.6 | 38.0 | 361,472.8 | 39.1 | 7,865.8 | 17.0 |
| Compensation of officers | 13,887.1 | 1.4 | 13,037.6 | 1.4 | 849.5 | 1.8 |
| Other wages and salaries | 355,451.5 | 36.6 | 348,435.2 | 37.7 | 7,016.3 | 15.2 |
| Fringe benefits and payroll taxes | 87,896.3 | 9.1 | 85,801.8 | 9.3 | 2,094.5 | 4.5 |
| Pension plan contributions | 14,053.0 | 1.4 | 13,720.9 | 1.5 | 332.1 | 0.7 |
| Other employee benefits | 48,563.9 | 5.0 | 47,269.7 | 5.1 | 1,294.1 | 2.8 |
| Payroll taxes | 25,279.4 | 2.6 | 24,811.2 | 2.7 | 468.2 | 1.0 |
| Supplies | 86,637.3 | 8.9 | 84,244.1 | 9.1 | 2,393.2 | 5.2 |
| Communications (printing, phone, etc.) | 19,953.7 | 2.1 | 19,153.6 | 2.1 | 800.1 | 1.7 |
| Professional fees | 10,534.1 | 1.1 | 9,903.7 | 1.1 | 630.4 | 1.4 |

*(continued)*

**Table 5.5.** Revenues and Expenses for Reporting Public Charities, 2005 *(continued)*

| | All Organizations | | Operating Organizations | | Supporting Organizations | |
|---|---|---|---|---|---|---|
| Number of organizations | 310,683 | | 270,678 | | 40,005 | |
| | $ millions | % | $ millions | % | $ millions | % |
| Occupancy | 25,458.0 | 2.6 | 24,636.4 | 2.7 | 821.6 | 1.8 |
| Equipment rental and maintenance | 13,434.7 | 1.4 | 13,183.7 | 1.4 | 251.1 | 0.5 |
| Interest | 15,983.7 | 1.6 | 15,506.2 | 1.7 | 477.5 | 1.0 |
| Depreciation and depletion | 43,505.8 | 4.5 | 42,362.9 | 4.6 | 1,143.0 | 2.5 |
| Other | 298,416.1 | 30.7 | 268,588.9 | 29.0 | 29,827.2 | 64.4 |
| Total current operating expenses | 971,158.4 | 100.0 | 924,854.0 | 100.0 | 46,304.4 | 100.0 |
| Plus grants and benefits | 78,157.2 | 7.4[d] | 55,114.3 | 5.6[d] | 23,042.9 | 32.4 |
| Grants and allocations | 60,269.2 | 5.7 | 37,973.2 | 3.9 | 22,296.0 | 31.3 |
| Specific assistance to individuals | 11,107.0 | 1.1 | 10,379.3 | 1.1 | 727.7 | 1.0 |
| Benefits paid to members | 6,781.1 | 0.6 | 6,761.8 | 0.7 | 19.3 | 0.0 |
| Plus payments to affiliates | 4,171.7 | 0.4 | 2,319.2 | 0.2 | 1,852.5 | 2.6 |
| Total expenses | 1,053,487.3 | 100.0 | 982,287.5 | 100.0 | 71,199.9 | 100.0 |
| Net income (revenue − expenses) | 90,534.9 | 7.9[a] | 74,066.2 | 7.0[a] | 16,468.7 | 18.8 |
| Total assets | 1,975,791.8 | 187.5[d] | 1,708,998.7 | 174.0[d] | 266,793.1 | 374.7 |
| Total liabilities | 755,356.9 | 71.7 | 708,891.3 | 72.2 | 46,465.6 | 65.3 |
| Net assets (assets − liabilities) | 1,220,434.9 | 115.8 | 1,000,107.4 | 101.8 | 220,327.5 | 309.4 |

*Source:* Urban Institute, National Center for Charitable Statistics, NCCS-GuideStar National Nonprofit Research Database: Special Research Version (2005).

*Notes:* Authors' calculations are based on U.S. Internal Revenue Service Forms 990 and 990-EZ, classified according to the National Taxonomy of Exempt Entities–Core Codes, and adjusted by the National Center for Charitable Statistics and Independent Sector. Reporting public charities include only organizations that both reported (filed IRS Forms 990) and were required to do so. The following were excluded: foreign organizations, government-associated organizations, organizations without state identifiers, and organizations excluded by the authors' discretion. Organizations not required to report include religious congregations and organizations with less than $25,000 in gross receipts. The table includes separate analyses for operating public charities and supporting organizations to clarify the distribution of funds and to avoid double-counting the financial information for supporting organizations (see chapter 5, appendix A, for a detailed description of the methodology). The sum of the dollar amounts may not equal due to rounding.

a. Percentages for revenue items and net income are expressed as percentages of total revenue.

b. Program service revenue figures may include sizable income via government contracts, which the data source is unable to differentiate from funds raised via the public (i.e., fees for services).

c. Percentages for current operating expense items are expressed as percentages of total current operating expenses.

d. Percentages for other expense items, assets, and liabilities are expressed as percentages of total expenses.

## Other Expenses

The IRS Form 990 separates expenses into 21 line items plus several lines for other expenses. While these 21 line items are intended to cover most expenses nonprofit organizations are likely to incur, such as grants and allocations, compensation, legal fees, accounting fees, supplies, and equipment rental, more than 80 percent of reporting public charities classified some expense as "other" in 2004. Such other expenses accounted for 28.3 percent of total expenses.

In a recent examination of a random sample of 106 organizations, Golladay and Pollak (2003) found that as much as 20 percent of expenses reported as other could be allocated to the existing line items on the Form 990. They also found that two types of expenses were commonly listed under other expenses—consulting and insurance. Consulting, which includes any skilled services other than accounting or legal, accounted for 38 percent of other expenses in their sample. Insurance expenses accounted for about 2 percent of other expenses, but were listed by over half of the organizations in the sample as an other expense.

operating organizations (21.5 percent vs. 48.4 percent), but spend much more in other expenses (64.4 percent vs. 29.0 percent). However, these may include consulting fees and other costs for personnel functions.

In addition to operating expenses, supporting organizations report distributing nearly $22.3 billion, or 31.3 percent of total expenses, in grants and allocations (table 5.5). Most of this $22.3 billion is probably included as revenue for the operating charities that receive it as contributions, so these funds may be counted twice. These grants, however, only represent 2.1 percent of total revenue for all reporting public charities.

## Growth in the Number of Reporting Public Charities, 1995–2005

The number of public charities grew from 187,038 in 1995 to 310,683 in 2005, an increase of 66.1 percent. Growth in individual subsectors over the same 10-year period varied widely. Health organizations increased by a modest 27.7 percent, while the number of environment and animal organizations more than doubled (table 5.6).

The three smallest subsectors exhibited the greatest growth over the 10-year period— environment and animals increased by 120.1 percent, for an average annual increase of 8.2 percent; international and foreign affairs grew by 105.4 percent, for an average annual increase of 7.5 percent; and religion-related organizations increased by 101.3 percent, for an average annual increase of 7.2 percent.

Human services, the largest subsector, increased 58.1 percent from 1995 to 2005. Within this category the growth was greatest for public safety and disaster-preparedness organizations and recreation and sports organizations—both of these categories more than doubled.

**Table 5.6.** Change in the Number of Reporting Public Charities by Category, 1995, 2000, and 2005

| | Reporting Public Charities | | | Total % Change | Average Annual % Change | | |
|---|---|---|---|---|---|---|---|
| | 1995 | 2000 | 2005 | 1995–2005 | 1995–2005 | 1995–2000 | 2000–2005 |
| All public charities | 187,038 | 245,749 | 310,683 | 66.1 | 5.2 | 5.6 | 4.8 |
| Arts, culture, and humanities | 21,277 | 28,489 | 35,840 | 68.4 | 5.4 | 6.0 | 4.7 |
| Performing arts organizations | 7,284 | 9,642 | 12,416 | 70.5 | 5.5 | 5.8 | 5.2 |
| Historical societies and related | 2,868 | 4,174 | 5,236 | 82.6 | 6.2 | 7.8 | 4.6 |
| Museums and museum activities | 2,129 | 2,827 | 3,380 | 58.8 | 4.7 | 5.8 | 3.6 |
| Other arts, culture, and humanities | 8,996 | 11,846 | 14,808 | 64.6 | 5.1 | 5.7 | 4.6 |
| Education | 30,509 | 43,094 | 57,991 | 90.1 | 6.6 | 7.2 | 6.1 |
| Higher education institutions | 1,869 | 1,988 | 2,112 | 13.0 | 1.2 | 1.2 | 1.2 |
| Student services and organizations | 3,525 | 5,647 | 8,175 | 131.9 | 8.8 | 9.9 | 7.7 |
| Elementary and secondary education | 7,678 | 9,483 | 11,675 | 52.1 | 4.3 | 4.3 | 4.2 |
| Other education | 17,437 | 25,976 | 36,029 | 106.6 | 7.5 | 8.3 | 6.8 |
| Environment and animals | 6,088 | 9,529 | 13,399 | 120.1 | 8.2 | 9.4 | 7.1 |
| Environment | 3,591 | 5,638 | 7,587 | 111.3 | 7.8 | 9.4 | 6.1 |
| Animal related | 2,497 | 3,891 | 5,812 | 132.8 | 8.8 | 9.3 | 8.4 |
| Health | 32,289 | 36,502 | 41,243 | 27.7 | 2.5 | 2.5 | 2.5 |
| Nursing services | 2,447 | 2,520 | 2,513 | 2.7 | 0.3 | 0.6 | -0.1 |
| Hospitals and primary treatment facilities | 4,992 | 5,032 | 5,045 | 1.1 | 0.1 | 0.2 | 0.1 |
| Treatment facilities—outpatient | 1,654 | 2,020 | 2,343 | 41.7 | 3.5 | 4.1 | 3.0 |
| Mental health | 6,990 | 7,561 | 8,496 | 21.5 | 2.0 | 1.6 | 2.4 |

*(continued)*

**Table 5.6.** Change in the Number of Reporting Public Charities by Category, 1995, 2000, and 2005 *(continued)*

| | Reporting Public Charities | | | Total % Change | Average Annual % Change | | |
|---|---|---|---|---|---|---|---|
| | 1995 | 2000 | 2005 | 1995–2005 | 1995–2005 | 1995–2000 | 2000–2005 |
| Disease-specific—general | 6,057 | 7,574 | 9,463 | 56.2 | 4.6 | 4.6 | 4.6 |
| Medical research | 905 | 1,129 | 1,400 | 54.7 | 4.5 | 4.5 | 4.4 |
| Other health | 9,244 | 10,666 | 11,983 | 29.6 | 2.6 | 2.9 | 2.4 |
| Human services | 63,528 | 81,043 | 100,436 | 58.1 | 4.7 | 5.0 | 4.4 |
| Crime and legal related | 3,818 | 4,956 | 6,044 | 58.3 | 4.7 | 5.4 | 4.0 |
| Employment and job related | 3,036 | 3,511 | 3,872 | 27.5 | 2.5 | 2.9 | 2.0 |
| Food, agriculture, and nutrition | 1,923 | 2,335 | 2,982 | 55.1 | 4.5 | 4.0 | 5.0 |
| Housing and shelter | 9,855 | 13,280 | 15,882 | 61.2 | 4.9 | 6.1 | 3.6 |
| Public safety and disaster preparedness | 2,191 | 3,455 | 5,068 | 131.3 | 8.7 | 9.5 | 8.0 |
| Recreation and sports | 11,904 | 17,439 | 24,519 | 106.0 | 7.5 | 7.9 | 7.1 |
| Youth development | 4,515 | 5,443 | 6,501 | 44.0 | 3.7 | 3.8 | 3.6 |
| Children and youth services | 5,372 | 6,219 | 7,016 | 30.6 | 2.7 | 3.0 | 2.4 |
| Family services | 3,392 | 3,988 | 4,585 | 35.2 | 3.1 | 3.3 | 2.8 |
| Residential and custodial care | 4,654 | 5,032 | 5,388 | 15.8 | 1.5 | 1.6 | 1.4 |

| | | | | | | |
|---|---|---|---|---|---|---|
| Services promoting independence | 5,920 | 6,766 | 7,813 | 32.0 | 2.8 | 2.7 | 2.9 |
| Other human services | 6,948 | 8,619 | 10,766 | 55.0 | 4.5 | 4.4 | 4.5 |
| International and foreign affairs | 2,471 | 3,843 | 5,075 | 105.4 | 7.5 | 9.2 | 5.7 |
| Public and societal benefit | 21,440 | 29,508 | 37,677 | 75.7 | 5.8 | 6.6 | 5.0 |
| Civil rights and advocacy | 1,259 | 1,681 | 2,062 | 63.8 | 5.1 | 6.0 | 4.2 |
| Community improvement | 8,289 | 11,500 | 14,607 | 76.2 | 5.8 | 6.8 | 4.9 |
| Philanthropy and voluntarism | 8,038 | 11,456 | 14,595 | 81.6 | 6.1 | 7.3 | 5.0 |
| Science and technology | 1,271 | 1,469 | 1,760 | 38.5 | 3.3 | 2.9 | 3.7 |
| Social science | 587 | 674 | 769 | 31.0 | 2.7 | 2.8 | 2.7 |
| Other public and societal benefit | 1,996 | 2,728 | 3,884 | 94.6 | 6.9 | 6.4 | 7.3 |
| Religion related | 9,242 | 13,717 | 18,600 | 101.3 | 7.2 | 8.2 | 6.3 |
| Unknown, unclassified | 194 | 24 | 422 | 117.5 | 8.1 | −34.2 | 77.4 |

*Source:* Urban Institute, National Center for Charitable Statistics, NCCS-GuideStar National Nonprofit Research Database: Special Research Version (2005).
*Notes:* Reporting public charities include only organizations that both reported (filed IRS Forms 990) and were required to do so. The following were excluded: foreign organizations, government-associated organizations, organizations without state identifiers, and organizations excluded by the authors' discretion. Organizations not required to report include religious congregations and organizations with less than $25,000 in gross receipts. Categories are as defined by the National Taxonomy of Exempt Entities (see chapter 5, appendix B, for more detail).

As mentioned above, health exhibited the least amount of growth in the number of public charities, with an increase of 27.7 percent from 1995 to 2005. In this subsector, hospitals and nursing services showed the least growth (1.1 percent and 2.7 percent, respectively), and medical research and disease-specific organizations showed the most, around 55 percent.

## Growth in Revenue of Reporting Public Charities

Table 5.7 displays the growth in total revenue by subsector between 1995 and 2005. As displayed, total revenue grew from $573 billion in 1995 to $1.1 trillion in 2005, an increase of 99.5 percent, for an average annual growth rate of 7.2 percent. This represents a 56.6 percent inflation-adjusted increase over the 10-year period.

Growth in total revenue across subsectors ranged from 80.6 percent for arts, culture, and humanities organizations to 224.3 percent for international and foreign affairs organizations. Much like the trend in the number of public charities, the smaller subsectors exhibited the greatest growth in revenue. International and foreign affairs increased in revenue by 224.3 percent (155.1 percent after adjusting for inflation), while environment and animal organizations' revenue increased by 141.7 percent (89.7 percent after adjusting for inflation).

Human services, the largest subsector in number of organizations, also exhibited a large increase in revenue—growing from $67 billion in 1995 to $148 billion in 2005. This is a 73.9 percent increase after adjusting for inflation. Health organizations, which accounted for nearly 60 percent of total revenues of all reporting public charities, showed modest growth in total revenue, with a 92.3 percent increase over the 10-year period (50.9 percent after adjusting for inflation).

## Growth in Public Support for Reporting Public Charities

Table 5.8 displays the growth in public support for reporting public charities from 1995 to 2005. Public support is a major component of revenue for many public charities and consists of private contributions from individuals, foundations, corporations, and other public charities, as well as government grants. It does not include government contracts and program service revenue.

Public support increased from $107 billion in 1995 to $244 billion in 2005, an increase of 128.3 percent, or an inflation-adjusted 79.2 percent. Public support, while growing at a high rate over the 10-year period, showed greater growth between 1995 and 2000 (an average annual growth rate of 10.2 percent) than between 2000 and 2005 (an average annual growth rate of 7.0 percent). Public support grew at a higher rate than total revenue (table 5.7), indicating that the proportion of revenue attributed to public support grew over the 10-year period.

International and foreign affairs organizations saw the greatest growth in public support from 1995 to 2005 with a 256.1 percent increase (179.6 percent after adjusting for inflation). Environment and animal-related organizations also saw large growth in public support, increasing from $2.6 billion in 1995 to $7.2 billion in 2005. Arts, culture,

**Table 5.7.** Change in Total Revenue for Reporting Public Charities by Category, 1995, 2000, and 2005

| | $ Millions | | | Total % Change | Average Annual % Change | | | |
|---|---|---|---|---|---|---|---|---|
| | 1995 | 2000 | 2005 | 1995–2005 | 1995–2005 | 1995–2000 | 2000–2005 | |
| All public charities | 573,319 | 811,362 | 1,144,022 | 99.5 | 7.2 | 7.2 | 7.1 | |
| Arts, culture, and humanities | 15,148 | 24,256 | 27,355 | 80.6 | 6.1 | 9.9 | 2.4 | |
| Performing arts organizations | 4,317 | 6,526 | 7,807 | 80.8 | 6.1 | 8.6 | 3.6 | |
| Historical societies and related | 998 | 1,789 | 2,027 | 103.2 | 7.3 | 12.4 | 2.5 | |
| Museums and museum activities | 3,176 | 6,046 | 6,287 | 98.0 | 7.1 | 13.7 | 0.8 | |
| Other arts, culture, and humanities | 6,657 | 9,895 | 11,234 | 68.7 | 5.4 | 8.2 | 2.6 | |
| Education | 95,289 | 146,236 | 188,178 | 97.5 | 7.0 | 8.9 | 5.2 | |
| Higher education institutions | 71,496 | 103,873 | 130,722 | 82.8 | 6.2 | 7.8 | 4.7 | |
| Student services and organizations | 2,571 | 4,048 | 4,919 | 91.3 | 6.7 | 9.5 | 4.0 | |
| Elementary and secondary education | 11,916 | 20,846 | 28,833 | 142.0 | 9.2 | 11.8 | 6.7 | |
| Other education | 9,306 | 17,470 | 23,704 | 154.7 | 9.8 | 13.4 | 6.3 | |
| Environment and animals | 4,823 | 8,830 | 11,658 | 141.7 | 9.2 | 12.9 | 5.7 | |
| Environment | 2,734 | 5,346 | 6,970 | 154.9 | 9.8 | 14.3 | 5.4 | |
| Animal related | 2,088 | 3,484 | 4,688 | 124.5 | 8.4 | 10.8 | 6.1 | |
| Health | 349,606 | 458,397 | 672,131 | 92.3 | 6.8 | 5.6 | 8.0 | |
| Nursing services | 13,818 | 16,211 | 21,202 | 53.4 | 4.4 | 3.2 | 5.5 | |
| Hospitals and primary treatment facilities | 262,943 | 328,558 | 492,498 | 87.3 | 6.5 | 4.6 | 8.4 | |
| Treatment facilities—outpatient | 17,641 | 31,969 | 44,075 | 149.8 | 9.6 | 12.6 | 6.6 | |
| Mental health | 12,235 | 17,435 | 23,577 | 92.7 | 6.8 | 7.3 | 6.2 | |
| Disease-specific—general | 8,563 | 12,539 | 18,404 | 114.9 | 8.0 | 7.9 | 8.0 | |
| Medical research | 4,431 | 6,501 | 9,342 | 110.8 | 7.7 | 8.0 | 7.5 | |
| Other health | 29,974 | 45,183 | 63,033 | 110.3 | 7.7 | 8.6 | 6.9 | |

*(continued)*

**Table 5.7.** Change in Total Revenue for Reporting Public Charities by Category, 1995, 2000, and 2005 *(continued)*

| | $ Millions | | | Total % Change | Average Annual % Change | | |
| --- | --- | --- | --- | --- | --- | --- | --- |
| | 1995 | 2000 | 2005 | 1995–2005 | 1995–2005 | 1995–2000 | 2000–2005 |
| Human services | 66,811 | 107,352 | 148,099 | 121.7 | 8.3 | 9.9 | 6.6 |
| Crime and legal related | 2,856 | 4,292 | 5,695 | 99.4 | 7.1 | 8.5 | 5.8 |
| Employment and job related | 5,144 | 8,113 | 11,164 | 117.0 | 8.1 | 9.5 | 6.6 |
| Food, agriculture, and nutrition | 1,338 | 3,638 | 5,206 | 289.2 | 14.6 | 22.2 | 7.4 |
| Housing and shelter | 6,418 | 10,552 | 16,350 | 154.8 | 9.8 | 10.5 | 9.2 |
| Public safety and disaster preparedness | 571 | 900 | 1,557 | 172.9 | 10.6 | 9.5 | 11.6 |
| Recreation and sports | 4,432 | 7,183 | 9,703 | 118.9 | 8.2 | 10.1 | 6.2 |
| Youth development | 2,873 | 4,669 | 5,890 | 105.0 | 7.4 | 10.2 | 4.8 |
| Children and youth services | 5,075 | 8,158 | 10,649 | 109.9 | 7.7 | 10.0 | 5.5 |
| Family services | 3,023 | 4,585 | 5,716 | 89.1 | 6.6 | 8.7 | 4.5 |
| Residential and custodial care | 14,364 | 20,256 | 28,385 | 97.6 | 7.0 | 7.1 | 7.0 |
| Services promoting independence | 9,247 | 14,112 | 19,859 | 114.8 | 7.9 | 8.8 | 7.1 |
| Other human services | 11,471 | 20,895 | 27,925 | 143.4 | 9.3 | 12.7 | 6.0 |

| | | | | | | | |
|---|---|---|---|---|---|---|---|
| International and foreign affairs | 7,040 | 11,471 | 22,827 | 224.3 | 12.5 | 10.3 | 14.8 |
| Public and societal benefit | 29,761 | 47,591 | 63,362 | 112.9 | 7.8 | 9.8 | 5.9 |
| Civil rights and advocacy | 809 | 1,384 | 1,913 | 136.6 | 9.0 | 11.3 | 6.7 |
| Community improvement | 6,579 | 9,801 | 12,845 | 95.2 | 6.9 | 8.3 | 5.6 |
| Philanthropy and voluntarism | 13,669 | 23,144 | 25,906 | 89.5 | 6.6 | 11.1 | 2.3 |
| Science and technology | 4,610 | 6,487 | 11,915 | 158.5 | 10.0 | 7.1 | 12.9 |
| Social science | 727 | 1,122 | 1,558 | 114.1 | 7.9 | 9.0 | 6.8 |
| Other public and societal benefit | 3,367 | 5,654 | 9,224 | 174.0 | 10.6 | 10.9 | 10.3 |
| Religion related | 4,788 | 7,222 | 10,304 | 115.2 | 8.0 | 8.6 | 7.4 |
| Unknown, unclassified | 53 | 7 | 109 | 104.0 | 7.4 | −32.8 | 71.6 |

*Source:* Urban Institute, National Center for Charitable Statistics, NCCS-GuideStar National Nonprofit Research Database: Special Research Version (2005).
*Notes:* Reporting public charities include only organizations that both reported (filed IRS Forms 990) and were required to do so. The following were excluded: foreign organizations, government-associated organizations, organizations without state identifiers, and organizations excluded by the authors' discretion. Organizations not required to report include religious congregations and organizations with less than $25,000 in gross receipts. Categories are as defined by the National Taxonomy of Exempt Entities (see chapter 5, appendix B, for more detail).

**Table 5.8.** Change in Public Support for Reporting Public Charities by Category, 1995, 2000, and 2005

| | $ Millions | | | Total % Change | Average Annual % Change | | |
|---|---|---|---|---|---|---|---|
| | 1995 | 2000 | 2005 | 1995–2005 | 1995–2005 | 1995–2000 | 2000–2005 |
| All public charities | 106,762 | 173,463 | 243,711 | 128.3 | 8.6 | 10.2 | 7.0 |
| Arts, culture, and humanities | 7,293 | 12,233 | 14,586 | 100.0 | 7.2 | 10.9 | 3.6 |
| Performing arts organizations | 1,717 | 2,781 | 3,452 | 101.0 | 7.2 | 10.1 | 4.4 |
| Historical societies and related | 473 | 945 | 1,212 | 156.1 | 9.9 | 14.8 | 5.1 |
| Museums and museum activities | 1,670 | 3,327 | 3,766 | 125.5 | 8.5 | 14.8 | 2.5 |
| Other arts, culture, and humanities | 3,433 | 5,179 | 6,156 | 79.3 | 6.0 | 8.6 | 3.5 |
| Education | 23,286 | 36,474 | 50,482 | 116.8 | 8.0 | 9.4 | 6.7 |
| Higher education institutions | 16,097 | 21,886 | 27,853 | 73.0 | 5.6 | 6.3 | 4.9 |
| Student services and organizations | 680 | 1,427 | 2,242 | 229.7 | 12.7 | 16.0 | 9.5 |
| Elementary and secondary education | 2,799 | 5,732 | 8,448 | 201.9 | 11.7 | 15.4 | 8.1 |
| Other education | 3,710 | 7,429 | 11,939 | 221.8 | 12.4 | 14.9 | 10.0 |
| Environment and animals | 2,591 | 5,275 | 7,242 | 179.5 | 10.8 | 15.3 | 6.5 |
| Environment | 1,606 | 3,427 | 4,565 | 184.2 | 11.0 | 16.4 | 5.9 |
| Animal related | 985 | 1,847 | 2,677 | 171.8 | 10.5 | 13.4 | 7.7 |
| Health | 23,036 | 35,824 | 49,708 | 115.8 | 8.0 | 9.2 | 6.8 |
| Nursing services | 797 | 1,063 | 1,130 | 41.8 | 3.6 | 5.9 | 1.2 |
| Hospitals and primary treatment facilities | 5,831 | 8,823 | 12,531 | 114.9 | 8.0 | 8.6 | 7.3 |
| Treatment facilities—outpatient | 1,607 | 2,380 | 3,329 | 107.2 | 7.6 | 8.2 | 6.9 |
| Mental health | 4,702 | 6,636 | 8,082 | 71.9 | 5.6 | 7.1 | 4.0 |
| Disease-specific—general | 4,297 | 6,755 | 9,621 | 123.9 | 8.4 | 9.5 | 7.3 |
| Medical research | 1,631 | 3,008 | 4,543 | 178.5 | 10.8 | 13.0 | 8.6 |
| Other health | 4,171 | 7,159 | 10,472 | 151.0 | 9.6 | 11.4 | 7.9 |

| Category | | | | | | |
|---|---|---|---|---|---|---|
| Human services | 26,011 | 43,509 | 57,832 | 122.3 | 8.3 | 10.8 | 5.9 |
| Crime and legal related | 1,738 | 2,730 | 3,631 | 108.9 | 7.6 | 9.5 | 5.9 |
| Employment and job related | 2,233 | 3,356 | 4,500 | 101.6 | 7.3 | 8.5 | 6.0 |
| Food, agriculture, and nutrition | 959 | 3,095 | 4,392 | 358.2 | 16.4 | 26.4 | 7.3 |
| Housing and shelter | 2,235 | 3,597 | 4,958 | 121.9 | 8.3 | 10.0 | 6.6 |
| Public safety and disaster preparedness | 228 | 388 | 828 | 264.0 | 13.8 | 11.3 | 16.4 |
| Recreation and sports | 1,471 | 2,252 | 2,920 | 98.5 | 7.1 | 8.9 | 5.3 |
| Youth development | 1,303 | 2,416 | 3,338 | 156.1 | 9.9 | 13.1 | 6.7 |
| Children and youth services | 2,259 | 3,835 | 4,844 | 114.4 | 7.9 | 11.2 | 4.8 |
| Family services | 1,449 | 2,266 | 2,776 | 91.5 | 6.7 | 9.3 | 4.1 |
| Residential and custodial care | 2,004 | 2,809 | 3,114 | 55.4 | 4.5 | 7.0 | 2.1 |
| Services promoting independence | 4,373 | 6,433 | 8,682 | 98.6 | 7.1 | 8.0 | 6.2 |
| Other human services | 5,761 | 10,330 | 13,849 | 140.4 | 9.2 | 12.4 | 6.0 |
| International and foreign affairs | 5,716 | 9,693 | 20,356 | 256.1 | 13.5 | 11.1 | 16.0 |
| Public and societal benefit | 16,313 | 25,983 | 36,958 | 126.6 | 8.5 | 9.8 | 7.3 |
| Civil rights and advocacy | 628 | 1,063 | 1,499 | 138.7 | 9.1 | 11.1 | 7.1 |
| Community improvement | 4,058 | 6,079 | 8,067 | 98.8 | 7.1 | 8.4 | 5.8 |
| Philanthropy and voluntarism | 9,264 | 14,988 | 18,288 | 97.4 | 7.0 | 10.1 | 4.1 |
| Science and technology | 1,152 | 1,679 | 5,385 | 367.4 | 16.7 | 7.8 | 26.3 |
| Social science | 342 | 604 | 1,018 | 197.8 | 11.5 | 12.1 | 11.0 |
| Other public and societal benefit | 868 | 1,569 | 2,701 | 211.1 | 12.0 | 12.6 | 11.5 |
| Religion related | 2,489 | 4,468 | 6,486 | 160.6 | 10.0 | 12.4 | 7.7 |
| Unknown, unclassified | 26 | 5 | 62 | 141.3 | 9.2 | −27.5 | 64.5 |

*Source:* Urban Institute, National Center for Charitable Statistics, NCCS-GuideStar National Nonprofit Research Database: Special Research Version (2005).
*Notes:* Reporting public charities include only organizations that both reported (filed IRS Forms 990) and were required to do so. The following were excluded: foreign organizations, government-associated organizations, organizations without state identifiers, and organizations excluded by the authors' discretion. Organizations not required to report include religious congregations and organizations with less than $25,000 in gross receipts. Categories are as defined by the National Taxonomy of Exempt Entities (see chapter 5, appendix B, for more detail).

and humanities organizations showed the least growth with a 100.0 percent increase (an inflation-adjusted 57.0 percent).

Human service charities received the largest share of public support among all public charities over the 10-year period, representing nearly a quarter of public support among all public charities. However, these organizations showed relatively average growth in public support compared with other subsectors, with an inflation-adjusted growth rate of 74.5 percent. Within the human service subsector, two types of organizations saw huge increases in public support—food, agriculture, and nutrition organizations and public safety and disaster preparedness organizations more than tripled in the amount of public support received over the 10-year period.

## Growth in Expenses of Reporting Public Charities

The growth in total expenses for reporting public charities from 1995 to 2005 is shown in table 5.9. As displayed, total expenses for public charities grew from $530 billion in 1995 to $1.1 trillion in 2005, a 56.0 percent inflation-adjusted increase. This is similar to the growth in total revenues over this same time.

International and foreign affairs expenses grew from nearly $7 billion in 1995 to nearly $21 billion in 2005. This was the largest percent increase among the subsectors. Environment and animal organizations and human service organizations represented the second and third largest increases, growing by 140.7 percent and 123.4 percent respectively (an inflation-adjusted 88.9 percent and 75.4 percent). While health organizations account for 60 percent of total reporting public charities' expenses, the category exhibited one of the lowest increases in expenses with an increase of 93.2 percent (51.7 percent after adjusting for inflation).

## Growth in Assets of Reporting Public Charities

Table 5.10 displays the growth in assets for reporting public charities from 1995 to 2005. Total assets increased from $843 billion in 1995 to nearly $2 trillion in 2005, an increase of 134.3 percent (an 84.0 percent inflation-adjusted increase). A great deal of this growth took place between 1995 and 2000, with an average annual growth rate at nearly twice the rate between 2000 and 2005.

International and foreign affairs organizations and environment and animal organizations showed the greatest increase in assets over the 10-year period. International organizations increased from $6 billion in 1995 to $18 billion in 2005, while environment and animal organizations increased from $11 billion 1995 to $32 billion in 2005. Although health organizations held the highest percentage of assets in the nonprofit sector, they exhibited the least growth in total assets, increasing at an average annual rate of 7.5 percent.

Table 5.11 displays the growth in net assets, total assets minus liabilities, over the 10-year period. As displayed, net assets grew from $516 billion in 1995 to $1.2 trillion

**Table 5.9.** Change in Total Expenses for Reporting Public Charities by Category, 1995, 2000, and 2005

| | $ Millions | | | Total % Change | Average Annual % Change | | | |
| --- | --- | --- | --- | --- | --- | --- | --- | --- |
| | 1995 | 2000 | 2005 | 1995–2005 | 1995–2005 | 1995–2000 | 2000–2005 |
| All public charities | 530,278 | 730,761 | 1,053,487 | 98.7 | 7.1 | 6.6 | 7.6 |
| Arts, culture, and humanities | 13,142 | 19,004 | 23,927 | 82.1 | 6.2 | 7.7 | 4.7 |
| Performing arts organizations | 3,937 | 5,619 | 7,187 | 82.6 | 6.2 | 7.4 | 5.0 |
| Historical societies and related | 766 | 1,207 | 1,562 | 103.9 | 7.4 | 9.5 | 5.3 |
| Museums and museum activities | 2,390 | 3,808 | 4,929 | 106.2 | 7.5 | 9.8 | 5.3 |
| Other arts, culture, and humanities | 6,049 | 8,370 | 10,248 | 69.4 | 5.4 | 6.7 | 4.1 |
| Education | 85,084 | 109,173 | 158,679 | 86.5 | 6.4 | 5.1 | 7.8 |
| Higher education institutions | 64,594 | 75,957 | 110,004 | 70.3 | 5.5 | 3.3 | 7.7 |
| Student services and organizations | 2,143 | 2,748 | 4,039 | 88.5 | 6.5 | 5.1 | 8.0 |
| Elementary and secondary education | 10,528 | 16,308 | 25,772 | 144.8 | 9.4 | 9.1 | 9.6 |
| Other education | 7,819 | 14,161 | 18,864 | 141.3 | 9.2 | 12.6 | 5.9 |
| Environment and animals | 4,075 | 6,736 | 9,807 | 140.7 | 9.2 | 10.6 | 7.8 |
| Environment | 2,229 | 3,845 | 5,683 | 154.9 | 9.8 | 11.5 | 8.1 |
| Animal related | 1,845 | 2,890 | 4,124 | 123.5 | 8.4 | 9.4 | 7.4 |
| Health | 329,837 | 443,172 | 637,323 | 93.2 | 6.8 | 6.1 | 7.5 |
| Nursing services | 13,460 | 15,978 | 20,788 | 54.4 | 4.4 | 3.5 | 5.4 |
| Hospitals and primary treatment facilities | 248,624 | 320,225 | 468,000 | 88.2 | 6.5 | 5.2 | 7.9 |
| Treatment facilities—outpatient | 17,394 | 32,979 | 43,339 | 149.2 | 9.6 | 13.7 | 5.6 |
| Mental health | 11,760 | 16,702 | 22,929 | 95.0 | 6.9 | 7.3 | 6.5 |
| Disease-specific—general | 8,187 | 11,799 | 17,342 | 111.8 | 7.8 | 7.6 | 8.0 |
| Medical research | 2,874 | 4,637 | 6,806 | 136.8 | 9.0 | 10.0 | 8.0 |
| Other health | 27,540 | 40,853 | 58,119 | 111.0 | 7.8 | 8.2 | 7.3 |

*(continued)*

**Table 5.9.** Change in Total Expenses for Reporting Public Charities by Category, 1995, 2000, and 2005 *(continued)*

| | $ Millions | | | Total % Change | Average Annual % Change | | |
| --- | --- | --- | --- | --- | --- | --- | --- |
| | 1995 | 2000 | 2005 | 1995–2005 | 1995–2005 | 1995–2000 | 2000–2005 |
| Human services | 63,200 | 100,258 | 141,215 | 123.4 | 8.4 | 9.7 | 7.1 |
| Crime and legal related | 2,734 | 4,050 | 5,418 | 98.2 | 7.1 | 8.2 | 6.0 |
| Employment and job related | 4,952 | 7,755 | 10,824 | 118.6 | 8.1 | 9.4 | 6.9 |
| Food, agriculture, and nutrition | 1,277 | 3,475 | 4,999 | 291.3 | 14.6 | 22.2 | 7.5 |
| Housing and shelter | 5,869 | 9,697 | 15,503 | 164.2 | 10.2 | 10.6 | 9.8 |
| Public safety and disaster preparedness | 498 | 788 | 1,348 | 170.7 | 10.5 | 9.6 | 11.3 |
| Recreation and sports | 4,108 | 6,526 | 9,056 | 120.4 | 8.2 | 9.7 | 6.8 |
| Youth development | 2,640 | 3,952 | 5,202 | 97.1 | 7.0 | 8.4 | 5.7 |
| Children and youth services | 4,920 | 7,798 | 10,391 | 111.2 | 7.8 | 9.6 | 5.9 |
| Family services | 2,901 | 4,346 | 5,503 | 89.7 | 6.6 | 8.4 | 4.8 |
| Residential and custodial care | 13,643 | 19,046 | 27,420 | 101.0 | 7.2 | 6.9 | 7.6 |
| Services promoting independence | 8,953 | 13,515 | 19,257 | 115.1 | 8.0 | 8.6 | 7.3 |
| Other human services | 10,705 | 19,312 | 26,293 | 145.6 | 9.4 | 12.5 | 6.4 |

| | | | | | | |
|---|---|---|---|---|---|---|
| International and foreign affairs | 6,742 | 10,661 | 20,535 | 204.6 | 11.8 | 9.6 | 14.0 |
| Public and societal benefit | 23,851 | 35,571 | 53,052 | 122.4 | 8.3 | 8.3 | 8.3 |
| Civil rights and advocacy | 772 | 1,238 | 1,798 | 133.0 | 8.8 | 9.9 | 7.7 |
| Community improvement | 6,185 | 8,891 | 11,915 | 92.6 | 6.8 | 7.5 | 6.0 |
| Philanthropy and voluntarism | 8,876 | 13,850 | 18,698 | 110.7 | 7.7 | 9.3 | 6.2 |
| Science and technology | 4,350 | 5,584 | 11,251 | 158.6 | 10.0 | 5.1 | 15.0 |
| Social science | 667 | 984 | 1,428 | 114.0 | 7.9 | 8.1 | 7.7 |
| Other public and societal benefit | 3,001 | 5,023 | 7,963 | 165.3 | 10.3 | 10.9 | 9.7 |
| Religion related | 4,294 | 6,181 | 8,867 | 106.5 | 7.5 | 7.6 | 7.5 |
| Unknown, unclassified | 53 | 4 | 83 | 55.8 | 4.5 | −39.4 | 80.3 |

*Source:* Urban Institute, National Center for Charitable Statistics, NCCS-GuideStar National Nonprofit Research Database: Special Research Version (2005).
*Notes:* Reporting public charities include only organizations that both reported (filed IRS Forms 990) and were required to do so. The following were excluded: foreign organizations, government-associated organizations, organizations without state identifiers, and organizations excluded by the authors' discretion. Organizations not required to report include religious congregations and organizations with less than $25,000 in gross receipts. Categories are as defined by the National Taxonomy of Exempt Entities (see chapter 5, appendix B, for more detail).

**Table 5.10.** Change in Total Assets for Reporting Public Charities by Category, 1995, 2000, and 2005

| | $ Millions | | | Total % Change | Average Annual % Change | | |
|---|---|---|---|---|---|---|---|
| | 1995 | 2000 | 2005 | 1995–2005 | 1995–2005 | 1995–2000 | 2000–2005 |
| All public charities | 843,174 | 1,432,919 | 1,975,792 | 134.3 | 8.9 | 11.2 | 6.6 |
| Arts, culture, and humanities | 32,828 | 59,901 | 81,885 | 149.4 | 9.6 | 12.8 | 6.5 |
| Performing arts organizations | 6,142 | 11,137 | 16,060 | 161.5 | 10.1 | 12.6 | 7.6 |
| Historical societies and related | 3,588 | 6,348 | 8,429 | 134.9 | 8.9 | 12.1 | 5.8 |
| Museums and museum activities | 12,091 | 23,436 | 32,570 | 169.4 | 10.4 | 14.2 | 6.8 |
| Other arts, culture, and humanities | 11,007 | 18,979 | 24,826 | 125.5 | 8.5 | 11.5 | 5.5 |
| Education | 213,483 | 406,739 | 571,643 | 167.8 | 10.4 | 13.8 | 7.0 |
| Higher education institutions | 159,417 | 305,448 | 421,542 | 164.4 | 10.2 | 13.9 | 6.7 |
| Student services and organizations | 11,768 | 11,360 | 18,262 | 55.2 | 4.5 | –0.7 | 10.0 |
| Elementary and secondary education | 23,094 | 48,316 | 72,296 | 213.0 | 12.1 | 15.9 | 8.4 |
| Other education | 19,204 | 41,615 | 59,543 | 210.1 | 12.0 | 16.7 | 7.4 |
| Environment and animals | 11,494 | 21,911 | 31,607 | 175.0 | 10.6 | 13.8 | 7.6 |
| Environment | 7,294 | 14,040 | 20,882 | 186.3 | 11.1 | 14.0 | 8.3 |
| Animal related | 4,199 | 7,871 | 10,725 | 155.4 | 9.8 | –13.4 | 6.4 |
| Health | 401,758 | 605,292 | 826,158 | 105.6 | 7.5 | 8.5 | 6.4 |
| Nursing services | 12,729 | 19,001 | 21,754 | 70.9 | 5.5 | 8.3 | 2.7 |
| Hospitals and primary treatment facilities | 300,007 | 433,341 | 608,836 | 102.9 | 7.3 | 7.6 | 7.0 |
| Treatment facilities—outpatient | 10,547 | 17,611 | 21,674 | 105.5 | 7.5 | 10.8 | 4.2 |
| Mental health | 8,554 | 13,616 | 18,742 | 119.1 | 8.2 | 9.7 | 6.6 |
| Disease-specific—general | 7,807 | 13,874 | 18,628 | 138.6 | 9.1 | 12.2 | 6.1 |
| Medical research | 15,861 | 26,675 | 32,004 | 101.8 | 7.3 | 11.0 | 3.7 |
| Other health | 46,253 | 81,173 | 104,521 | 126.0 | 8.5 | 11.9 | 5.2 |

| | | | | | | |
|---|---|---|---|---|---|---|
| Human services | 94,065 | 162,693 | 223,041 | 137.1 | 9.0 | 11.6 | 6.5 |
| Crime and legal related | 2,030 | 3,536 | 4,951 | 143.8 | 9.3 | 11.7 | 7.0 |
| Employment and job related | 3,416 | 6,185 | 8,540 | 150.0 | 9.6 | 12.6 | 6.7 |
| Food, agriculture, and nutrition | 908 | 1,793 | 2,732 | 201.1 | 11.7 | 14.6 | 8.8 |
| Housing and shelter | 20,334 | 35,067 | 52,796 | 159.6 | 10.0 | 11.5 | 8.5 |
| Public safety and disaster preparedness | 1,220 | 2,230 | 3,650 | 199.2 | 11.6 | 12.8 | 10.4 |
| Recreation and sports | 5,107 | 9,042 | 13,188 | 158.2 | 10.0 | 12.1 | 7.8 |
| Youth development | 4,678 | 8,374 | 10,731 | 129.4 | 8.7 | 12.4 | 5.1 |
| Children and youth services | 2,920 | 5,463 | 6,891 | 136.0 | 9.0 | 13.3 | 4.8 |
| Family services | 2,371 | 4,129 | 5,298 | 123.5 | 8.4 | 11.7 | 5.1 |
| Residential and custodial care | 29,136 | 45,319 | 59,413 | 103.9 | 7.4 | 9.2 | 5.6 |
| Services promoting independence | 7,248 | 12,130 | 16,435 | 126.8 | 8.5 | 10.8 | 6.3 |
| Other human services | 14,697 | 29,424 | 38,415 | 161.4 | 10.1 | 14.9 | 5.5 |
| International and foreign affairs | 6,139 | 11,096 | 18,341 | 198.8 | 11.6 | 12.6 | 10.6 |
| Public and societal benefit | 74,087 | 148,821 | 200,315 | 170.4 | 10.5 | 15.0 | 6.1 |
| Civil rights and advocacy | 626 | 1,367 | 1,989 | 217.7 | 12.3 | 16.9 | 7.8 |
| Community improvement | 8,752 | 16,548 | 23,048 | 163.4 | 10.2 | 13.6 | 6.9 |
| Philanthropy and voluntarism | 44,334 | 94,517 | 110,794 | 149.9 | 9.6 | 16.3 | 3.2 |
| Science and technology | 6,849 | 10,609 | 13,485 | 96.9 | 7.0 | 9.1 | 4.9 |
| Social science | 1,157 | 2,094 | 2,904 | 151.1 | 9.6 | 12.6 | 6.8 |
| Other public and societal benefit | 12,369 | 23,686 | 48,094 | 288.8 | 14.5 | 13.9 | 15.2 |
| Religion related | 9,291 | 16,462 | 22,650 | 143.8 | 9.3 | 12.1 | 6.6 |
| Unknown, unclassified | 30 | 4 | 152 | 414.3 | 17.8 | −34.7 | 112.6 |

*Source:* Urban Institute, National Center for Charitable Statistics, NCCS-GuideStar National Nonprofit Research Database: Special Research Version (2005).
*Notes:* Reporting public charities include only organizations that both reported (filed IRS Forms 990) and were required to do so. The following were excluded: foreign organizations, government-associated organizations, organizations without state identifiers, and organizations excluded by the authors' discretion. Organizations not required to report include religious congregations and organizations with less than $25,000 in gross receipts. Categories are as defined by the National Taxonomy of Exempt Entities (see chapter 5, appendix B, for more detail).

**Table 5.11.** Change in Net Assets for Reporting Public Charities by Category, 1995, 2000, and 2005

| | $ Millions | | | Total % Change | Average Annual % Change | | |
|---|---|---|---|---|---|---|---|
| | 1995 | 2000 | 2005 | 1995–2005 | 1995–2005 | 1995–2000 | 2000–2005 |
| All public charities | 515,647 | 946,222 | 1,220,435 | 136.7 | 9.0 | 12.9 | 5.2 |
| Arts, culture, and humanities | 25,871 | 51,208 | 66,566 | 157.3 | 9.9 | 14.6 | 5.4 |
| Performing arts organizations | 4,140 | 8,939 | 12,139 | 193.2 | 11.4 | 16.6 | 6.3 |
| Historical societies and related | 3,212 | 5,761 | 7,445 | 131.8 | 8.8 | 12.4 | 5.3 |
| Museums and museum activities | 10,294 | 20,996 | 27,696 | 169.1 | 10.4 | 15.3 | 5.7 |
| Other arts, culture, and humanities | 8,225 | 15,511 | 19,286 | 134.5 | 8.9 | 13.5 | 4.5 |
| Education | 160,170 | 326,829 | 413,407 | 158.1 | 9.9 | 15.3 | 4.8 |
| Higher education institutions | 122,059 | 245,064 | 300,100 | 145.9 | 9.4 | 15.0 | 4.1 |
| Student services and organizations | 4,203 | 8,111 | 11,182 | 166.1 | 10.3 | 14.1 | 6.6 |
| Elementary and secondary education | 18,179 | 38,469 | 53,839 | 196.2 | 11.5 | 16.2 | 7.0 |
| Other education | 15,730 | 35,185 | 48,287 | 207.0 | 11.9 | 17.5 | 6.5 |
| Environment and animals | 8,223 | 17,830 | 25,315 | 207.8 | 11.9 | 16.7 | 7.3 |
| Environment | 5,043 | 11,398 | 16,802 | 233.2 | 12.8 | 17.7 | 8.1 |
| Animal related | 3,180 | 6,431 | 8,513 | 167.7 | 10.3 | 15.1 | 5.8 |
| Health | 214,662 | 331,597 | 440,835 | 105.4 | 7.5 | 9.1 | 5.9 |
| Nursing services | 4,601 | 7,666 | 9,308 | 102.3 | 7.3 | 10.8 | 4.0 |
| Hospitals and primary treatment facilities | 152,608 | 221,742 | 299,253 | 96.1 | 7.0 | 7.8 | 6.2 |
| Treatment facilities—outpatient | 4,301 | 5,582 | 9,573 | 122.6 | 8.3 | 5.4 | 11.4 |
| Mental health | 4,657 | 7,899 | 11,108 | 138.5 | 9.1 | 11.1 | 7.1 |
| Disease-specific—general | 4,817 | 9,547 | 11,952 | 148.1 | 9.5 | 14.7 | 4.6 |
| Medical research | 13,280 | 22,258 | 26,020 | 95.9 | 7.0 | 10.9 | 3.2 |
| Other health | 30,399 | 56,901 | 73,621 | 142.2 | 9.2 | 13.4 | 5.3 |

| | | | | | | | |
|---|---|---|---|---|---|---|---|
| Human services | 43,877 | 85,137 | 109,578 | 149.7 | 9.6 | 14.2 | 5.2 |
| Crime and legal related | 1,374 | 2,620 | 3,593 | 161.6 | 10.1 | 13.8 | 6.5 |
| Employment and job related | 2,242 | 4,116 | 5,533 | 146.8 | 9.5 | 12.9 | 6.1 |
| Food, agriculture, and nutrition | 722 | 1,526 | 2,301 | 218.7 | 12.3 | 16.2 | 8.5 |
| Housing and shelter | 3,615 | 8,947 | 13,232 | 266.1 | 13.9 | 19.9 | 8.1 |
| Public safety and disaster preparedness | 975 | 1,784 | 2,914 | 198.7 | 11.6 | 12.8 | 10.3 |
| Recreation and sports | 3,492 | 6,664 | 9,794 | 180.5 | 10.9 | 13.8 | 8.0 |
| Youth development | 4,037 | 7,517 | 9,405 | 133.0 | 8.8 | 13.2 | 4.6 |
| Children and youth services | 1,962 | 3,780 | 4,602 | 134.6 | 8.9 | 14.0 | 4.0 |
| Family services | 1,730 | 3,160 | 3,878 | 124.1 | 8.4 | 12.8 | 4.2 |
| Residential and custodial care | 9,212 | 15,945 | 18,246 | 98.1 | 7.1 | 11.6 | 2.7 |
| Services promoting independence | 4,320 | 7,841 | 10,181 | 135.7 | 9.0 | 12.7 | 5.4 |
| Other human services | 10,196 | 21,238 | 25,899 | 154.0 | 9.8 | 15.8 | 4.0 |
| International and foreign affairs | 4,202 | 8,538 | 14,261 | 239.4 | 13.0 | 15.2 | 10.8 |
| Public and societal benefit | 51,605 | 111,869 | 133,012 | 157.7 | 9.9 | 16.7 | 3.5 |
| Civil rights and advocacy | 402 | 1,038 | 1,527 | 280.2 | 14.3 | 20.9 | 8.0 |
| Community improvement | 4,738 | 9,344 | 12,774 | 169.6 | 10.4 | 14.5 | 6.5 |
| Philanthropy and voluntarism | 38,086 | 86,125 | 98,276 | 158.0 | 9.9 | 17.7 | 2.7 |
| Science and technology | 4,406 | 7,960 | 9,740 | 121.0 | 8.3 | 12.6 | 4.1 |
| Social science | 799 | 1,674 | 2,079 | 160.2 | 10.0 | 15.9 | 4.4 |
| Other public and societal benefit | 3,174 | 5,728 | 8,615 | 171.4 | 10.5 | 12.5 | 8.5 |
| Religion related | 7,030 | 13,214 | 17,382 | 147.2 | 9.5 | 13.5 | 5.6 |
| Unknown, unclassified | 6 | 1 | 80 | 1,161.3 | 28.8 | −26.6 | 126.3 |

*Source:* Urban Institute, National Center for Charitable Statistics, NCCS-GuideStar National Nonprofit Research Database: Special Research Version (2005).
*Notes:* Reporting public charities include only organizations that both reported (filed IRS Forms 990) and were required to do so. The following were excluded: foreign organizations, government-associated organizations, organizations without state identifiers, and organizations excluded by the authors' discretion. Organizations not required to report include religious congregations and organizations with less than $25,000 in gross receipts. Categories are as defined by the National Taxonomy of Exempt Entities (see chapter 5, appendix B, for more detail).

in 2005, a 136.7 percent increase (an 85.8 percent inflation-adjusted increase). This is slightly higher than the increase in total assets (table 5.10).

International and foreign affairs organizations exhibited the greatest increase in net assets over the 10-year period. Net assets for these organizations increased from $4 billion in 1995 to $14 billion in 2005, an increase of 239.4 percent (an inflation-adjusted 166.4 percent). Environment and animal organizations also displayed a large increase in net assets, growing 141.7 percent after adjusting for inflation.

## Reporting Public Charities by Major Subsector

Below is a more in-depth look at reporting public charities by subsector. For each subsector, we first give a financial snapshot for 2005. We then go on to break the subsector into its component parts, or industries, and discuss the proportion of each subsector's resources belonging to each industry. Two key measures of financial health, net margin and net assets to expenses ratio, are also discussed.

The net margin equals net income (total revenue minus total expenses) divided by total revenue. This measure describes the amount of "profit" the organization produced (i.e., its financial cushion). Since revenues may vary depending on the timing of grants and donations, this measure often fluctuates significantly for individual organizations from one year to the next.

The net assets to expense ratio is net assets (assets minus liabilities) divided by total expenses. This ratio is a measure of the ability of an organization to continue functioning if it should fall on difficult financial times and run a deficit. If the net assets are available as cash (e.g., in a checking or short-term savings account), those funds can be used to cover expenses directly. In other instances, the organizations may be able to sell assets such as land or buildings or use them as collateral on a loan to sustain its programs.

### Arts, Culture, and Humanities

The arts, culture, and humanities subsector includes museums, performing arts groups, folklife organizations, historical societies, and supporting organizations such as local art agencies. In 2005, arts, culture, and humanities organizations accounted for 11.5 percent of all reporting public charities but only 2.3 percent of total expenses and 4.1 percent of total assets.

Arts, culture, and humanities public charities reported $27.4 billion in total revenue and $23.9 billion in total expenses in 2005 (table 5.12). Figure 5.4 displays the sources of revenue for these organizations. As displayed, private contributions, which include contributions from individuals as well as grants from foundations, corporations, and other public charities, accounted for 40.8 percent of total revenue. This subsector is the third most dependent on private contributions behind international and foreign affairs and environment and animals.

Wages, salaries, and other personnel costs account for 39.7 percent of total operating expenses for arts, culture, and humanities public charities, while another 39.6 percent

**Table 5.12.** Revenues and Expenses for Reporting Public Charities in Arts, Culture, and Humanities, 2005

| | All Organizations | | Operating Organizations | | Supporting Organizations | |
|---|---|---|---|---|---|---|
| Number of organizations | 35,840 | | 34,077 | | 1,763 | |
| | $ millions | % | $ millions | % | $ millions | % |
| Public support | 14,585.8 | 53.3[a] | 13,857.2 | 53.0[a] | 728.6 | 59.8 |
| Private contributions | 11,156.2 | 40.8 | 10,487.6 | 40.1 | 668.6 | 54.9 |
| Direct contributions | 10,689.9 | 39.1 | 10,030.1 | 38.4 | 659.8 | 54.2 |
| Indirect contributions | 466.3 | 1.7 | 457.5 | 1.8 | 8.8 | 0.7 |
| Government grants | 3,429.6 | 12.5 | 3,369.6 | 12.9 | 60.0 | 4.9 |
| Fees for services and goods | 8,552.9 | 31.3 | 8,383.7 | 32.1 | 169.2 | 13.9 |
| Program service revenue[b] | 7,780.1 | 28.4 | 7,626.8 | 29.2 | 153.3 | 12.6 |
| Net income from sales of inventory | 772.8 | 2.8 | 756.9 | 2.9 | 15.9 | 1.3 |
| Investment income | 2,111.0 | 7.7 | 1,851.6 | 7.1 | 259.4 | 21.3 |
| Dividends | 781.4 | 2.9 | 670.9 | 2.6 | 110.6 | 9.1 |
| Interest | 175.5 | 0.6 | 155.1 | 0.6 | 20.4 | 1.7 |
| Net gain on sale of assets | 1,104.2 | 4.0 | 980.2 | 3.8 | 124.0 | 10.2 |
| Other investment income | 49.9 | 0.2 | 45.5 | 0.2 | 4.4 | 0.4 |
| Other income | 2,105.3 | 7.7 | 2,044.9 | 7.8 | 60.5 | 5.0 |
| Dues and assessments | 988.1 | 3.6 | 961.6 | 3.7 | 26.5 | 2.2 |
| Net income from special events | 354.0 | 1.3 | 335.4 | 1.3 | 18.6 | 1.5 |
| Other (includes net rental and other) | 763.2 | 2.8 | 747.9 | 2.9 | 15.3 | 1.3 |
| Total revenue | 27,355.0 | 100.0 | 26,137.4 | 100.0 | 1,217.6 | 100.0 |
| Paid personnel | 8,896.8 | 39.7[c] | 8,726.6 | 40.0[c] | 170.2 | 28.8 |
| Wages and salaries | 7,399.4 | 33.0 | 7,253.6 | 33.2 | 145.7 | 24.6 |
| Compensation of officers | 906.6 | 4.0 | 880.0 | 4.0 | 26.6 | 4.5 |
| Other wages and salaries | 6,492.8 | 28.9 | 6,373.6 | 29.2 | 119.2 | 20.1 |
| Fringe benefits and payroll taxes | 1,497.4 | 6.7 | 1,473.0 | 6.7 | 24.4 | 4.1 |
| Pension plan contributions | 243.6 | 1.1 | 240.5 | 1.1 | 3.1 | 0.5 |
| Other employee benefits | 705.7 | 3.1 | 695.2 | 3.2 | 10.5 | 1.8 |
| Payroll taxes | 548.2 | 2.4 | 537.4 | 2.5 | 10.8 | 1.8 |
| Supplies | 365.1 | 1.6 | 356.1 | 1.6 | 9.0 | 1.5 |
| Communications (printing, phone, etc.) | 947.8 | 4.2 | 925.2 | 4.2 | 22.6 | 3.8 |
| Professional fees | 758.2 | 3.4 | 736.3 | 3.4 | 21.9 | 3.7 |

*(continued)*

**Table 5.12.** Revenues and Expenses for Reporting Public Charities in Arts, Culture, and Humanities, 2005 *(continued)*

| | All Organizations | | Operating Organizations | | Supporting Organizations | |
|---|---|---|---|---|---|---|
| Number of organizations | 35,840 | | 34,077 | | 1,763 | |
| | $ millions | % | $ millions | % | $ millions | % |
| Occupancy | 877.8 | 3.9 | 860.7 | 3.9 | 17.1 | 2.9 |
| Equipment rental and maintenance | 281.6 | 1.3 | 275.2 | 1.3 | 6.4 | 1.1 |
| Interest | 229.1 | 1.0 | 219.7 | 1.0 | 9.5 | 1.6 |
| Depreciation and depletion | 1,182.8 | 5.3 | 1,150.9 | 5.3 | 31.9 | 5.4 |
| Other | 8,892.0 | 39.6 | 8,588.9 | 39.3 | 303.1 | 51.2 |
| Total current operating expenses | 22,431.2 | 100.0 | 21,839.6 | 100.0 | 591.6 | 100.0 |
| Plus grants and benefits | 1,406.0 | 5.9[d] | 1,072.1 | 4.7[d] | 333.9 | 35.6 |
| Grants and allocations | 1,367.0 | 5.7 | 1,034.8 | 4.5 | 332.2 | 35.4 |
| Specific assistance to individuals | 28.1 | 0.1 | 26.9 | 0.1 | 1.2 | 0.1 |
| Benefits paid to members | 10.9 | 0.0 | 10.4 | 0.0 | 0.5 | 0.1 |
| Plus payments to affiliates | 89.4 | 0.4 | 77.3 | 0.3 | 12.1 | 1.3 |
| Total expenses | 23,926.6 | 100.0 | 22,989.1 | 100.0 | 937.5 | 100.0 |
| Net income (revenue − expenses) | 3,428.4 | 12.5[a] | 3,148.4 | 12.0[a] | 280.0 | 23.0 |
| Total assets | 81,884.6 | 342.2[d] | 75,026.3 | 326.4[d] | 6,858.3 | 731.5 |
| Total liabilities | 15,319.1 | 64.0 | 14,369.8 | 62.5 | 949.3 | 101.3 |
| Net assets (assets − liabilities) | 66,565.5 | 278.2 | 60,656.5 | 263.8 | 5,909.0 | 630.3 |

*Source:* Urban Institute, National Center for Charitable Statistics, NCCS-GuideStar National Nonprofit Research Database: Special Research Version (2005).

*Notes:* Authors' calculations are based on U.S. Internal Revenue Service Forms 990 and 990-EZ, classified according to the National Taxonomy of Exempt Entities–Core Codes, and adjusted by the National Center for Charitable Statistics and Independent Sector. Reporting public charities include only organizations that both reported (filed IRS Forms 990) and were required to do so. The following were excluded: foreign organizations, government-associated organizations, organizations without state identifiers, and organizations excluded by the authors' discretion. Organizations not required to report include religious congregations and organizations with less than $25,000 in gross receipts. The table includes separate analyses for operating public charities and supporting organizations to clarify the distribution of funds and to avoid double-counting the financial information for supporting organizations (see chapter 5, appendix A, for a detailed description of the methodology). Categories are as defined by the National Taxonomy of Exempt Entities (see chapter 5, appendix B, for more detail). The sum of the dollar amounts may not equal due to rounding.

a. Percentages for revenue items and net income are expressed as percentages of total revenue.

b. Program service revenue figures may include sizable income via government contracts, which the data source is unable to differentiate from funds raised via the public (i.e., fees for services).

c. Percentages for current operating expense items are expressed as percentages of total current operating expenses.

d. Percentages for other expense items, assets, and liabilities are expressed as percentages of total expenses.

**Figure 5.4.** Sources of Revenue for Arts, Culture, and Humanities Reporting Public Charities, 2005 (percent)

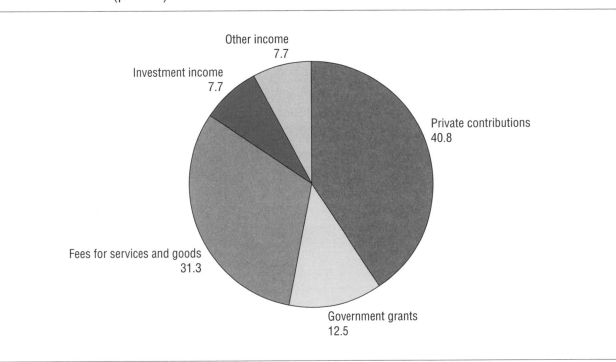

Other income
7.7

Investment income
7.7

Private contributions
40.8

Fees for services and goods
31.3

Government grants
12.5

*Source:* Urban Institute, National Center for Charitable Statistics, NCCS-GuideStar National Nonprofit Research Database: Special Research Version (2005).

are classified as other expenses (table 5.12). These two types of expenses account for the greatest proportions of operating expenses across all subsectors.

The arts, culture, and humanities subsector reported net income of $3.4 billion, for a net margin of 12.5 percent—the third highest net margin when compared with other subsectors. Additionally, these organizations held $81.9 billion in total assets and had net assets (assets minus liabilities) of $66.6 billion. The arts, culture, and humanities subsector had the highest net assets to expense ratio—278.2 percent.

Figure 5.5 displays the number, assets, revenues, and expenses of organizations within the arts, culture, and humanities subsector. Such organizations classified as other account for 41.3 percent of the sector. The "other" category includes arts services organizations, arts education organizations, media and communications organizations, and arts councils and agencies. These organizations also account for the greatest proportion of revenue and expenses within the subsector, with 41.1 percent of revenues and 42.8 percent of expenses. Performing arts organizations account for the second largest percentage of public charities, revenues, and expenses—holding 34.6 percent of organizations, 28.5 percent of revenues, and 30.0 percent of expenses. Museums account for the smallest number of reporting public charities in the arts, culture, and humanities subsector, but hold 39.8 percent of total assets.

Net income among the organizations within the subsector ranged from a high of $1.4 billion for museums to $465 million for historical societies. However, when we look

**Figure 5.5.** Number, Assets, Revenues, and Expenses of Arts, Culture, and Humanities Public Charities, 2005

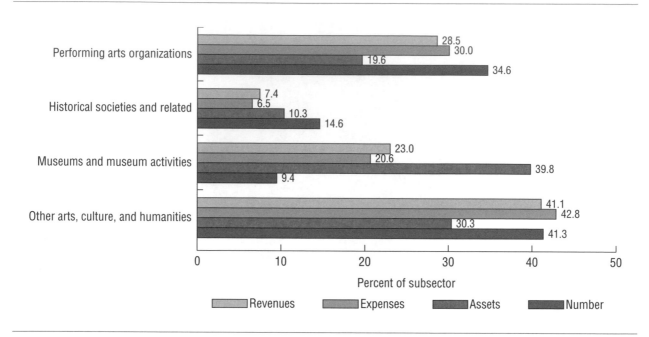

*Source:* Urban Institute, National Center for Charitable Statistics, NCCS-GuideStar National Nonprofit Research Database: Special Research Version (2005).

at the net margins for these organizations, historical societies report the highest with a margin of 22.9 percent, followed by museums with 21.6 percent, other arts, culture, and humanities organizations with 8.8 percent, and finally, performing arts organizations with 7.9 percent.

Net assets within the arts, culture, and humanities subsector range from $7.4 billion for historical societies to $27.7 billion for museums. The net assets to expense ratio also varies. Museums report the highest with net assets of 561.9 percent of expenses, followed by historical societies with 476.5 percent, other with 188.2 percent, and finally performing arts organizations with 168.9 percent.

## Education

The education subsector includes higher education institutions, student service organizations, elementary and secondary education institutions, libraries, and parent-teacher groups. In 2005, the 57,991 education public charities accounted for 18.7 percent of public charities. Education organizations accounted for 15.1 percent of total expenses and 28.9 percent of total assets for all public charities.

Education public charities reported $188 billion in total revenue and $159 billion in total expenses in 2005 (table 5.13). Figure 5.6 displays the sources of revenue for education organizations. Fees for services and goods, primarily tuition payments, account for 55.9 percent of total revenue for education public charities, making it the second most dependent subsector, behind health, on this type of revenue source. Private contributions

**Table 5.13.** Revenues and Expenses for Reporting Public Charities in Education, 2005

| | All Organizations | | Operating Organizations | | Supporting Organizations | |
|---|---|---|---|---|---|---|
| Number of organizations | 57,991 | | 45,145 | | 12,846 | |
| | $ millions | % | $ millions | % | $ millions | % |
| Public support | 50,481.7 | 26.8[a] | 44,978.6 | 25.1[a] | 5,503.1 | 60.8[a] |
| Private contributions | 28,056.5 | 14.9 | 23,850.9 | 13.3 | 4,205.6 | 46.5 |
| Direct contributions | 26,076.4 | 13.9 | 22,367.0 | 12.5 | 3,709.5 | 41.0 |
| Indirect contributions | 1,980.0 | 1.1 | 1,483.9 | 0.8 | 496.1 | 5.5 |
| Government grants | 22,425.3 | 11.9 | 21,127.7 | 11.8 | 1,297.5 | 14.3 |
| Fees for services and goods | 105,202.0 | 55.9 | 103,734.3 | 57.9 | 1,467.7 | 16.2 |
| Program service revenue[b] | 104,449.5 | 55.5 | 103,074.0 | 57.5 | 1,375.6 | 15.2 |
| Net income from sales of inventory | 752.5 | 0.4 | 660.3 | 0.4 | 92.2 | 1.0 |
| Investment income | 26,591.0 | 14.1 | 25,148.2 | 14.0 | 1,442.8 | 15.9 |
| Dividends | 6,643.9 | 3.5 | 5,886.1 | 3.3 | 757.8 | 8.4 |
| Interest | 1,190.7 | 0.6 | 1,060.2 | 0.6 | 130.6 | 1.4 |
| Net gain on sale of assets | 18,040.0 | 9.6 | 17,587.3 | 9.8 | 452.7 | 5.0 |
| Other investment income | 716.3 | 0.4 | 614.7 | 0.3 | 101.6 | 1.1 |
| Other income | 5,903.5 | 3.1 | 5,267.7 | 2.9 | 635.8 | 7.0 |
| Dues and assessments | 1,030.4 | 0.5 | 923.6 | 0.5 | 106.7 | 1.2 |
| Net income from special events | 838.6 | 0.4 | 612.4 | 0.3 | 226.2 | 2.5 |
| Other (includes net rental and other) | 4,034.6 | 2.1 | 3,731.7 | 2.1 | 302.9 | 3.3 |
| Total revenue | 188,178.2 | 100.0 | 179,128.8 | 100.0 | 9,049.4 | 100.0 |
| Paid personnel | 75,609.9 | 53.8[c] | 74,509.0 | 54.5[c] | 1,100.9 | 29.5[c] |
| Wages and salaries | 61,131.4 | 43.5 | 60,214.9 | 44.0 | 916.4 | 24.6 |
| Compensation of officers | 2,289.3 | 1.6 | 2,221.6 | 1.6 | 67.7 | 1.8 |
| Other wages and salaries | 58,842.0 | 41.9 | 57,993.3 | 42.4 | 848.7 | 22.8 |
| Fringe benefits and payroll taxes | 14,478.5 | 10.3 | 14,294.0 | 10.5 | 184.5 | 4.9 |
| Pension plan contributions | 3,149.5 | 2.2 | 3,115.1 | 2.3 | 34.4 | 0.9 |
| Other employee benefits | 7,514.9 | 5.4 | 7,418.3 | 5.4 | 96.7 | 2.6 |
| Payroll taxes | 3,814.1 | 2.7 | 3,760.7 | 2.8 | 53.3 | 1.4 |
| Supplies | 6,939.7 | 4.9 | 6,837.4 | 5.0 | 102.2 | 2.7 |
| Communications (printing, phone, etc.) | 4,675.8 | 3.3 | 4,549.1 | 3.3 | 126.7 | 3.4 |
| Professional fees | 2,144.7 | 1.5 | 2,078.6 | 1.5 | 66.1 | 1.8 |

*(continued)*

**Table 5.13.** Revenues and Expenses for Reporting Public Charities in Education, 2005 *(continued)*

| | All Organizations | | Operating Organizations | | Supporting Organizations | |
|---|---|---|---|---|---|---|
| Number of organizations | 57,991 | | 45,145 | | 12,846 | |
| | $ millions | % | $ millions | % | $ millions | % |
| Occupancy | 5,671.6 | 4.0 | 5,566.0 | 4.1 | 105.6 | 2.8 |
| Equipment rental and maintenance | 2,064.5 | 1.5 | 2,039.7 | 1.5 | 24.8 | 0.7 |
| Interest | 2,577.3 | 1.8 | 2,518.8 | 1.8 | 58.5 | 1.6 |
| Depreciation and depletion | 7,540.8 | 5.4 | 7,459.0 | 5.5 | 81.8 | 2.2 |
| Other | 33,208.4 | 23.6 | 31,147.4 | 22.8 | 2,061.0 | 55.3 |
| Total current operating expenses | 140,432.7 | 100.0 | 136,705.1 | 100.0 | 3,727.6 | 100.0 |
| Plus grants and benefits | 17,776.2 | 11.2[d] | 15,727.4 | 10.3[d] | 2,048.8 | 34.2[d] |
| Grants and allocations | 17,240.3 | 10.9 | 15,224.9 | 10.0 | 2,015.4 | 33.7 |
| Specific assistance to individuals | 438.7 | 0.3 | 411.1 | 0.3 | 27.6 | 0.5 |
| Benefits paid to members | 97.1 | 0.1 | 91.4 | 0.1 | 5.8 | 0.1 |
| Plus payments to affiliates | 470.3 | 0.3 | 260.0 | 0.2 | 210.3 | 3.5 |
| Total expenses | 158,679.2 | 100.0 | 152,692.5 | 100.0 | 5,986.8 | 100.0 |
| Net income (revenue − expenses) | 29,499.0 | 15.7[a] | 26,436.3 | 14.8[a] | 3,062.6 | 33.8[a] |
| Total assets | 571,643.1 | 360.3[d] | 536,495.9 | 351.4[d] | 35,147.2 | 587.1[d] |
| Total liabilities | 158,235.6 | 99.7 | 152,150.3 | 99.6 | 6,085.3 | 101.6 |
| Net assets (assets − liabilities) | 413,407.5 | 260.5 | 384,345.6 | 251.7 | 29,061.9 | 485.4 |

*Source:* Urban Institute, National Center for Charitable Statistics, NCCS-GuideStar National Nonprofit Research Database: Special Research Version (2005).

*Notes:* Authors' calculations are based on U.S. Internal Revenue Service Forms 990 and 990-EZ, classified according to the National Taxonomy of Exempt Entities–Core Codes, and adjusted by the National Center for Charitable Statistics and Independent Sector. Reporting public charities include only organizations that both reported (filed IRS Forms 990) and were required to do so. The following were excluded: foreign organizations, government-associated organizations, organizations without state identifiers, and organizations excluded by the authors' discretion. Organizations not required to report include religious congregations and organizations with less than $25,000 in gross receipts. The table includes separate analyses for operating public charities and supporting organizations to clarify the distribution of funds and to avoid double-counting the financial information for supporting organizations (see chapter 5, appendix A, for a detailed description of the methodology). Categories are as defined by the National Taxonomy of Exempt Entities (see chapter 5, appendix B, for more detail). The sum of the dollar amounts may not equal due to rounding.
a. Percentages for revenue items and net income are expressed as percentages of total revenue.
b. Program service revenue figures may include sizable income via government contracts, which the data source is unable to differentiate from funds raised via the public (i.e., fees for services).
c. Percentages for current operating expense items are expressed as percentages of total current operating expenses.
d. Percentages for other expense items, assets, and liabilities are expressed as percentages of total expenses.

**Figure 5.6.** Sources of Revenue for Education Reporting Public Charities, 2005 (percent)

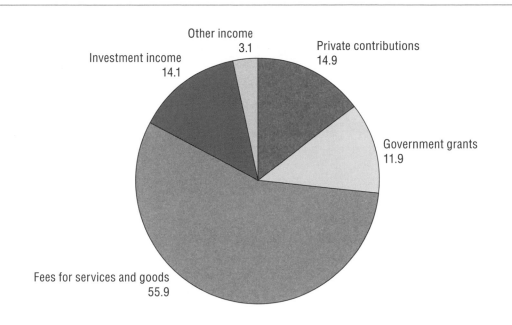

*Source:* Urban Institute, National Center for Charitable Statistics, NCCS-GuideStar National Nonprofit Research Database: Special Research Version (2005).

account for 14.9 percent of total revenue; among the subsectors, it is one of the least dependent on contributions.

As exhibited in table 5.13, wages, salaries, and other personnel costs account for 53.8 percent of total operating expenses, while another 23.6 percent of expenses are classified as other. This is consistent across all subsectors. Education organizations also distribute 10.9 percent of expenses as grants and allocations.

The education subsector reported net income of $29.5 billion, for a net margin of 15.7 percent—the second highest net margin when compared with other subsectors. Additionally, these organizations held $571.6 billion in total assets and had net assets (assets minus liabilities) of $413.4 billion. The education subsector had the second highest net assets to expense ratio—260.5 percent.

The number, assets, revenues, and expenses of organizations within the education subsector are displayed in figure 5.7. The "other" category, which includes special education programs, libraries, adult continuing education programs, and parent-teacher groups, accounts for 62.1 percent of these public charities. Elementary and secondary education organizations account for the second highest percent of public charities in the subsector—with one-fifth of all education organizations in this category. On the other hand, higher education organizations, which include colleges and universities, account for 3.6 percent of education reporting public charities but account for 73.7 percent of assets, 69.5 percent of revenues, and 69.3 percent of expenses.

Net income among organizations within the education subsector ranged from nearly $21 billion for higher education organizations to $881 million for student service

**Figure 5.7.** Number, Assets, Revenues, and Expenses of Education Public Charities, 2005

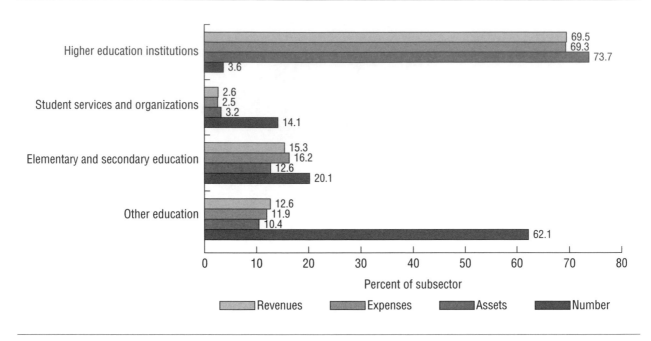

*Source:* Urban Institute, National Center for Charitable Statistics, NCCS-GuideStar National Nonprofit Research Database: Special Research Version (2005).

organizations. Other education organizations report the highest net margin with a margin of 20.4 percent. This is followed by student service organizations with 17.9 percent, higher education with 15.8 percent, and elementary and secondary schools with 10.6 percent.

Net assets among education organizations ranged from $11.2 billion for student services to $300.1 billion for higher education. Higher education institutions had net assets at least five times that of the other types of organizations in the education subsector. Student services organizations reported the highest net asset to expense ratio with of 276.9 percent, followed by higher education organizations with 272.8 percent, other education with 256.0 percent and finally elementary and secondary education with 208.9 percent.

## Environment and Animals

The environment and animals subsector includes environmental preservation organizations, recycling programs, pollution abatement programs, animal protection organizations, wildlife preservation organizations, and zoos. In 2005, environment and animal organizations accounted for 4.3 percent of all public charities, 0.9 percent of total expenses, and 1.6 percent of total assets for all public charities.

In 2005, these charities reported $11.7 billion in total revenues and $9.8 billion in total expenses (table 5.14). Figure 5.8 displays the sources of revenue for these organizations. As displayed, private contributions, which include contributions from individuals as well as grants from foundations, corporations, and other public charities, accounted for 48.0 percent of total revenue. The environment and animals subsector is the second most dependent subsector on private contributions, behind international and foreign

**Table 5.14.** Revenues and Expenses for Reporting Public Charities in the Environment and Animals, 2005

| | All Organizations | | Operating Organizations | | Supporting Organizations | |
|---|---|---|---|---|---|---|
| Number of organizations | 13,399 | | 12,533 | | 866 | |
| | $ millions | % | $ millions | % | $ millions | % |
| Public support | 7,241.8 | 62.1[a] | 6,824.4 | 62.3[a] | 417.5 | 59.3[a] |
| Private contributions | 5,599.6 | 48.0 | 5,228.1 | 47.7 | 371.5 | 52.8 |
| Direct contributions | 5,409.5 | 46.4 | 5,041.4 | 46.0 | 368.1 | 52.3 |
| Indirect contributions | 190.2 | 1.6 | 186.7 | 1.7 | 3.5 | 0.5 |
| Government grants | 1,642.2 | 14.1 | 1,596.3 | 14.6 | 45.9 | 6.5 |
| Fees for services and goods | 2,929.5 | 25.1 | 2,762.3 | 25.2 | 167.2 | 23.7 |
| Program service revenue[b] | 2,680.1 | 23.0 | 2,531.9 | 23.1 | 148.2 | 21.1 |
| Net income from sales of inventory | 249.3 | 2.1 | 230.3 | 2.1 | 19.0 | 2.7 |
| Investment income | 676.9 | 5.8 | 620.7 | 5.7 | 56.2 | 8.0 |
| Dividends | 255.1 | 2.2 | 223.1 | 2.0 | 32.0 | 4.6 |
| Interest | 84.7 | 0.7 | 79.8 | 0.7 | 4.9 | 0.7 |
| Net gain on sale of assets | 296.0 | 2.5 | 277.9 | 2.5 | 18.1 | 2.6 |
| Other investment income | 41.1 | 0.4 | 39.9 | 0.4 | 1.2 | 0.2 |
| Other income | 809.4 | 6.9 | 746.3 | 6.8 | 63.1 | 9.0 |
| Dues and assessments | 378.9 | 3.3 | 339.7 | 3.1 | 39.2 | 5.6 |
| Net income from special events | 164.3 | 1.4 | 156.8 | 1.4 | 7.5 | 1.1 |
| Other (includes net rental and other) | 266.2 | 2.3 | 249.8 | 2.3 | 16.4 | 2.3 |
| Total revenue | 11,657.6 | 100.0 | 10,953.7 | 100.0 | 704.0 | 100.0 |
| Paid personnel | 3,724.8 | 41.7[c] | 3,548.5 | 41.7[c] | 176.2 | 40.4[c] |
| Wages and salaries | 3,061.8 | 34.2 | 2,913.8 | 34.3 | 148.0 | 34.0 |
| Compensation of officers | 324.9 | 3.6 | 311.2 | 3.7 | 13.7 | 3.1 |
| Other wages and salaries | 2,736.8 | 30.6 | 2,602.5 | 30.6 | 134.3 | 30.8 |
| Fringe benefits and payroll taxes | 663.0 | 7.4 | 634.8 | 7.5 | 28.2 | 6.5 |
| Pension plan contributions | 106.7 | 1.2 | 103.0 | 1.2 | 3.8 | 0.9 |
| Other employee benefits | 330.4 | 3.7 | 316.5 | 3.7 | 13.9 | 3.2 |
| Payroll taxes | 225.9 | 2.5 | 215.3 | 2.5 | 10.6 | 2.4 |
| Supplies | 245.8 | 2.7 | 235.0 | 2.8 | 10.7 | 2.5 |
| Communications (printing, phone, etc.) | 478.2 | 5.3 | 466.9 | 5.5 | 11.3 | 2.6 |

*(continued)*

**Table 5.14.** Revenues and Expenses for Reporting Public Charities in the Environment and Animals, 2005 *(continued)*

| | All Organizations | | Operating Organizations | | Supporting Organizations | |
|---|---|---|---|---|---|---|
| Number of organizations | 13,399 | | 12,533 | | 866 | |
| | $ millions | % | $ millions | % | $ millions | % |
| Professional fees | 325.8 | 3.6 | 312.4 | 3.7 | 13.4 | 3.1 |
| Occupancy | 237.3 | 2.7 | 230.6 | 2.7 | 6.7 | 1.5 |
| Equipment rental and maintenance | 95.4 | 1.1 | 91.3 | 1.1 | 4.1 | 0.9 |
| Interest | 75.0 | 0.8 | 74.0 | 0.9 | 1.0 | 0.2 |
| Depreciation and depletion | 362.8 | 4.1 | 348.8 | 4.1 | 14.0 | 3.2 |
| Other | 3,396.4 | 38.0 | 3,198.1 | 37.6 | 198.3 | 45.5 |
| Total current operating expenses | 8,941.5 | 100.0 | 8,505.7 | 100.0 | 435.8 | 100.0 |
| Plus grants and benefits | 845.8 | 8.6[d] | 690.9 | 7.5[d] | 154.9 | 26.1[d] |
| Grants and allocations | 832.9 | 8.5 | 678.9 | 7.4 | 154.0 | 26.0 |
| Specific assistance to individuals | 10.7 | 0.1 | 10.5 | 0.1 | 0.2 | 0.0 |
| Benefits paid to members | 2.2 | 0.0 | 1.5 | 0.0 | 0.7 | 0.1 |
| Plus payments to affiliates | 19.4 | 0.2 | 17.8 | 0.2 | 1.6 | 0.3 |
| Total expenses | 9,806.7 | 100.0 | 9,214.4 | 100.0 | 592.3 | 100.0 |
| Net income (revenue − expenses) | 1,850.9 | 15.9[a] | 1,739.2 | 15.9[a] | 111.7 | 15.9[a] |
| Total assets | 31,607.3 | 322.3[d] | 29,593.2 | 321.2[d] | 2,014.1 | 340.0[d] |
| Total liabilities | 6,292.1 | 64.2 | 6,093.3 | 66.1 | 198.9 | 33.6 |
| Net assets (assets − liabilities) | 25,315.2 | 258.1 | 23,499.9 | 255.0 | 1,815.2 | 306.5 |

*Source:* Urban Institute, National Center for Charitable Statistics, NCCS-GuideStar National Nonprofit Research Database: Special Research Version (2005).

*Notes:* Authors' calculations are based on U.S. Internal Revenue Service Forms 990 and 990-EZ, classified according to the National Taxonomy of Exempt Entities–Core Codes, and adjusted by the National Center for Charitable Statistics and Independent Sector. Reporting public charities include only organizations that both reported (filed IRS Forms 990) and were required to do so. The following were excluded: foreign organizations, government-associated organizations, organizations without state identifiers, and organizations excluded by the authors' discretion. Organizations not required to report include religious congregations and organizations with less than $25,000 in gross receipts. The table includes separate analyses for operating public charities and supporting organizations to clarify the distribution of funds and to avoid double-counting the financial information for supporting organizations (see chapter 5, appendix A, for a detailed description of the methodology). Categories are as defined by the National Taxonomy of Exempt Entities (see chapter 5, appendix B, for more detail). The sum of the dollar amounts may not equal due to rounding.

a. Percentages for revenue items and net income are expressed as percentages of total revenue.

b. Program service revenue figures may include sizable income via government contracts, which the data source is unable to differentiate from funds raised via the public (i.e., fees for services).

c. Percentages for current operating expense items are expressed as percentages of total current operating expenses.

d. Percentages for other expense items, assets, and liabilities are expressed as percentages of total expenses.

**Figure 5.8.** Sources of Revenue for Environment and Animals Reporting Public Charities, 2005 (percent)

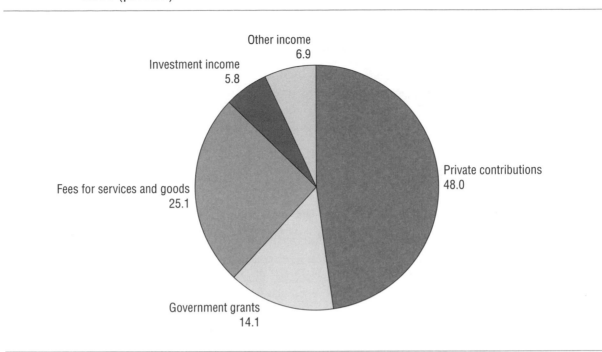

*Source:* Urban Institute, National Center for Charitable Statistics, NCCS-GuideStar National Nonprofit Research Database: Special Research Version (2005).

affairs. Another 25.1 percent of this subsector's revenue comes from fees for services and goods, which may include admission fees and educational program fees.

Wages, salaries, and other personnel costs account for 41.7 percent of operating expenses for environment and animal-related public charities, and another 38.0 percent is reported as other expenses (table 5.14). This distribution of operating expenses is consistent across all subsectors.

The environment and animals subsector reported net income of $1.9 billion, for a net margin of 15.9 percent—the highest net margin when compared with other subsectors. These organizations held $31.6 billion in total assets and had net assets (assets minus liabilities) of $25.3 billion. The environment and animals subsector had the third highest net asset to expense ratio—258.1 percent.

Figure 5.9 displays the number, assets, revenues, and expenses of environment and animal organizations. As shown, environmental public charities account for 56.6 percent of organizations in the environment and animals subsector. Environmental organizations also account for a larger proportion of revenue (59.8 percent), expenses (57.9 percent), and assets (66.1 percent) than animal-related organizations.

Environmental organizations reported $1.3 billion in net income, while animal-related organizations reported $564 million. In addition to having a higher net income, environmental organizations also report a higher net margin than animal-related organizations, 18.5 percent versus 12.0 percent.

**Figure 5.9.** Number, Assets, Revenues, and Expenses of Environment and
Animals Public Charities, 2005

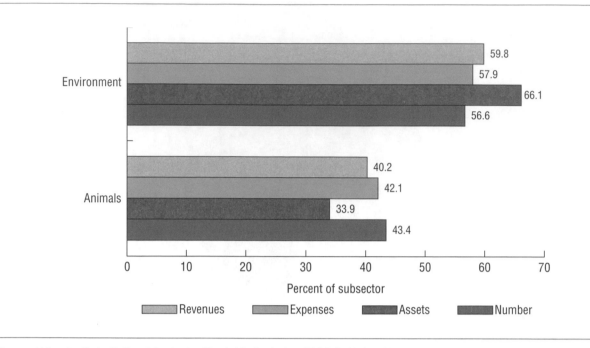

*Source:* Urban Institute, National Center for Charitable Statistics, NCCS-GuideStar National Nonprofit Research Database: Special
Research Version (2005).

Environmental organizations held nearly $17 billion in net assets, while animal-related organizations held $8.5 billion. In addition to having higher net assets, environment organizations also reported a higher net asset to expense ratio than animal-related organizations, 295.7 percent versus 206.4 percent.

## Health

The health subsector includes hospitals, nursing facilities, mental health organizations, and medical research organizations. In 2005, health organizations accounted for 13.3 percent of all public charities, 60.5 percent of total expenses, and 41.8 percent of total assets.

Health organizations reported $672.1 billion in total revenues and $637.3 billion in total expenses in 2005 (table 5.15). Figure 5.10 displays the sources of revenue for these organizations. As displayed, 87.5 percent of revenue for the health subsector comes from fees for services and goods, primarily patient revenues. Health is the most dependent subsector on fees for services and goods.

Wages, salaries, and other personnel costs account for 45.8 percent of total operating expenses for the health subsector. Another 31.6 percent of operating expenses are classified as other. The health subsector reports the smallest proportion of its expenses going to grants and benefits, with only 2.7 percent of funds going to grants, allocations, specific assistance paid to individuals, and benefits paid to members (table 5.15).

The health subsector reported net income of $34.8 billion, for a net margin of 5.2 percent—only human service reported a lower margin. These organizations held

**Table 5.15.** Revenues and Expenses for Reporting Public Charities in Health, 2005

| | All Organizations | | Operating Organizations | | Supporting Organizations | |
|---|---|---|---|---|---|---|
| Number of organizations | 41,243 | | 35,441 | | 5,802 | |
| | $ millions | % | $ millions | % | $ millions | % |
| Public support | 49,708.2 | 7.4[a] | 42,085.9 | 6.7[a] | 7,622.3 | 16.8[a] |
| Private contributions | 26,964.4 | 4.0 | 19,990.5 | 3.2 | 6,973.9 | 15.4 |
| Direct contributions | 20,255.5 | 3.0 | 14,910.3 | 2.4 | 5,345.2 | 11.8 |
| Indirect contributions | 6,708.9 | 1.0 | 5,080.2 | 0.8 | 1,628.7 | 3.6 |
| Government grants | 22,743.8 | 3.4 | 22,095.4 | 3.5 | 648.4 | 1.4 |
| Fees for services and goods | 588,186.4 | 87.5 | 555,135.2 | 88.6 | 33,051.2 | 73.1 |
| Program service revenue[b] | 587,128.6 | 87.4 | 554,163.5 | 88.4 | 32,965.1 | 72.9 |
| Net income from sales of inventory | 1,057.8 | 0.2 | 971.7 | 0.2 | 86.1 | 0.2 |
| Investment income | 19,607.2 | 2.9 | 15,722.8 | 2.5 | 3,884.4 | 8.6 |
| Dividends | 6,457.7 | 1.0 | 5,229.5 | 0.8 | 1,228.1 | 2.7 |
| Interest | 2,591.9 | 0.4 | 2,380.0 | 0.4 | 211.9 | 0.5 |
| Net gain on sale of assets | 8,803.4 | 1.3 | 6,752.3 | 1.1 | 2,051.1 | 4.5 |
| Other investment income | 1,754.2 | 0.3 | 1,361.0 | 0.2 | 393.2 | 0.9 |
| Other income | 14,629.2 | 2.2 | 13,948.2 | 2.2 | 681.0 | 1.5 |
| Dues and assessments | 1,143.8 | 0.2 | 1,115.0 | 0.2 | 28.8 | 0.1 |
| Net income from special events | 729.6 | 0.1 | 603.4 | 0.1 | 126.2 | 0.3 |
| Other (includes net rental and other) | 12,755.8 | 1.9 | 12,229.8 | 2.0 | 525.9 | 1.2 |
| Total revenue | 672,131.1 | 100.0 | 626,892.1 | 100.0 | 45,238.9 | 100.0 |
| Paid personnel | 282,788.2 | 45.8[c] | 277,099.3 | 47.6[c] | 5,688.9 | 16.4[c] |
| Wages and salaries | 227,249.4 | 36.8 | 222,900.4 | 38.3 | 4,348.9 | 12.5 |
| Compensation of officers | 5,115.4 | 0.8 | 4,815.1 | 0.8 | 300.4 | 0.9 |
| Other wages and salaries | 222,133.9 | 36.0 | 218,085.4 | 37.4 | 4,048.6 | 11.7 |
| Fringe benefits and payroll taxes | 55,538.8 | 9.0 | 54,198.9 | 9.3 | 1,340.0 | 3.9 |
| Pension plan contributions | 8,639.6 | 1.4 | 8,447.5 | 1.5 | 192.1 | 0.6 |
| Other employee benefits | 31,590.7 | 5.1 | 30,673.4 | 5.3 | 917.3 | 2.6 |
| Payroll taxes | 15,308.5 | 2.5 | 15,077.9 | 2.6 | 230.6 | 0.7 |
| Supplies | 72,860.2 | 11.8 | 70,710.9 | 12.1 | 2,149.3 | 6.2 |
| Communications (printing, phone, etc.) | 6,783.5 | 1.1 | 6,475.9 | 1.1 | 307.6 | 0.9 |
| Professional fees | 3,932.3 | 0.6 | 3,669.9 | 0.6 | 262.4 | 0.8 |

*(continued)*

**Table 5.15.** Revenues and Expenses for Reporting Public Charities in Health, 2005 *(continued)*

|  | All Organizations | | Operating Organizations | | Supporting Organizations | |
|---|---|---|---|---|---|---|
| Number of organizations | 41,243 | | 35,441 | | 5,802 | |
|  | $ millions | % | $ millions | % | $ millions | % |
| Occupancy | 10,905.7 | 1.8 | 10,476.1 | 1.8 | 429.6 | 1.2 |
| Equipment rental and maintenance | 8,958.0 | 1.5 | 8,809.5 | 1.5 | 148.5 | 0.4 |
| Interest | 8,856.9 | 1.4 | 8,607.1 | 1.5 | 249.8 | 0.7 |
| Depreciation and depletion | 27,224.0 | 4.4 | 26,478.8 | 4.5 | 745.2 | 2.1 |
| Other | 194,821.2 | 31.6 | 170,125.5 | 29.2 | 24,695.7 | 71.2 |
| Total current operating expenses | 617,130.2 | 100.0 | 582,453.1 | 100.0 | 34,677.2 | 100.0 |
| Plus grants and benefits | 17,246.3 | 2.7[d] | 12,733.2 | 2.1[d] | 4,513.2 | 11.1[d] |
| Grants and allocations | 9,584.9 | 1.5 | 5,129.7 | 0.9 | 4,455.2 | 11.0 |
| Specific assistance to individuals | 1,628.7 | 0.3 | 1,573.6 | 0.3 | 55.0 | 0.1 |
| Benefits paid to members | 6,032.8 | 0.9 | 6,029.8 | 1.0 | 3.0 | 0.0 |
| Plus payments to affiliates | 2,946.9 | 0.5 | 1,551.6 | 0.3 | 1,395.3 | 3.4 |
| Total expenses | 637,323.5 | 100.0 | 596,737.9 | 100.0 | 40,585.6 | 100.0 |
| Net income (revenue – expenses) | 34,807.6 | 5.2[a] | 30,154.3 | 4.8[a] | 4,653.3 | 10.3[a] |
| Total assets | 826,158.2 | 129.6[d] | 735,783.3 | 123.3[d] | 90,374.9 | 222.7[d] |
| Total liabilities | 385,323.7 | 60.5 | 362,566.0 | 60.8 | 22,757.7 | 56.1 |
| Net assets (assets – liabilities) | 440,834.6 | 69.2 | 373,217.3 | 62.5 | 67,617.2 | 166.6 |

*Source:* Urban Institute, National Center for Charitable Statistics, NCCS-GuideStar National Nonprofit Research Database: Special Research Version (2005).

*Notes:* Authors' calculations are based on U.S. Internal Revenue Service Forms 990 and 990-EZ, classified according to the National Taxonomy of Exempt Entities–Core Codes, and adjusted by the National Center for Charitable Statistics and Independent Sector. Reporting public charities include only organizations that both reported (filed IRS Forms 990) and were required to do so. The following were excluded: foreign organizations, government-associated organizations, organizations without state identifiers, and organizations excluded by the authors' discretion. Organizations not required to report include religious congregations and organizations with less than $25,000 in gross receipts. The table includes separate analyses for operating public charities and supporting organizations to clarify the distribution of funds and to avoid double-counting the financial information for supporting organizations (see chapter 5, appendix A, for a detailed description of the methodology). Categories are as defined by the National Taxonomy of Exempt Entities (see chapter 5, appendix B, for more detail). The sum of the dollar amounts may not equal due to rounding.

a. Percentages for revenue items and net income are expressed as percentages of total revenue.

b. Program service revenue figures may include sizable income via government contracts, which the data source is unable to differentiate from funds raised via the public (i.e., fees for services).

c. Percentages for current operating expense items are expressed as percentages of total current operating expenses.

d. Percentages for other expense items, assets, and liabilities are expressed as percentages of total expenses.

**Figure 5.10.** Sources of Revenue for Health Reporting Public Charities, 2005 (percent)

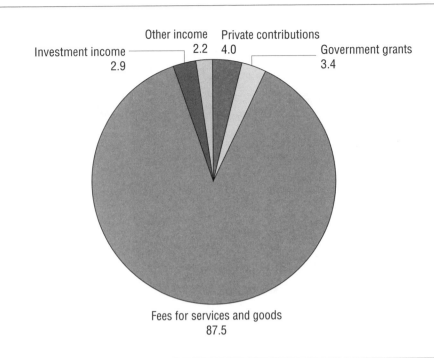

Investment income
2.9

Other income
2.2

Private contributions
4.0

Government grants
3.4

Fees for services and goods
87.5

*Source:* Urban Institute, National Center for Charitable Statistics, NCCS-GuideStar National Nonprofit Research Database: Special Research Version (2005).

$826.2 billion in total assets and had net assets (assets minus liabilities) of $440.8 billion. The heath subsector had a net asset to expense ratio of 69.2 percent—making it the subsector with the lowest ratio.

Figure 5.11 displays the number, assets, revenues, and expenses of public charities within the health subsector. As displayed, other health organizations, which include family planning organizations, blood banks, public health organizations, and patient and family support organizations, account for the greatest number. Disease-specific organizations, which include voluntary health organizations active in prevention and treatment of certain diseases such as cancer, report the second highest number of organizations within the health subsector. Examples of these types of organizations include the March of Dimes and the American Cancer Society. Hospitals and primary treatment facilities, however, account for nearly three-quarters of assets, expenses, and revenues.

Net income among all health organizations ranged from $414 million for nursing services to $24.5 billion for hospitals and primary treatment facilities. While most organizations in health had net margins ranging from 2.0 percent to 8.0 percent, medical research organizations reported a margin over three times that—27.1 percent.

Net assets within the health subsector varied dramatically—ranging from $9.3 billion for nursing facilities to $299.3 billion for hospitals and primary treatment facilities. The net assets to expense ratios also varied greatly among the types of organizations, ranging from a low of 22.1 percent for outpatient facilities to a high of 382.3 percent for medical research organizations.

**Figure 5.11.** Number, Assets, Revenues, and Expenses of Health Public Charities, 2005

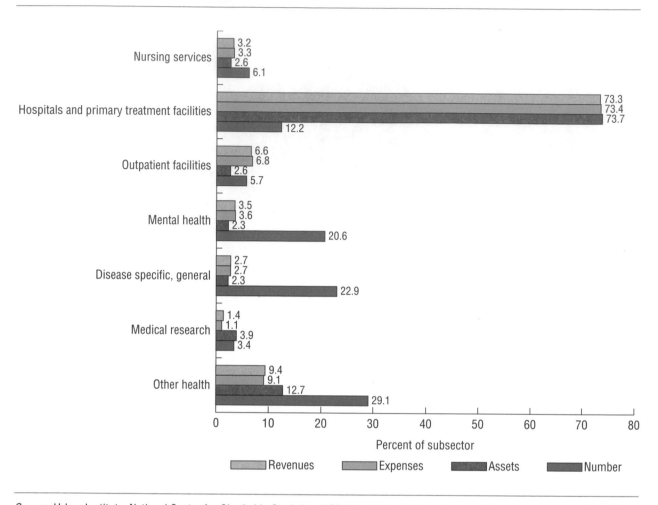

*Source:* Urban Institute, National Center for Charitable Statistics, NCCS-GuideStar National Nonprofit Research Database: Special Research Version (2005).

## Human Service

The 100,436 reporting public charities in the human service subsector account for 32.3 percent of all reporting public charities, making it the largest subsector in number of organizations. The human service subsector is also the most diverse subsector. It includes organizations ranging from soup kitchens to farmland preservation alliances to amateur sporting clubs. In 2005, human service organizations accounted for 11.3 percent of the sector's assets and 13.4 percent of its total expenses. However, these organizations are on average fairly small.

Human service public charities reported $148.1 billion in total revenue and $141.2 billion in total expenses in 2005 (table 5.16). Figure 5.12 displays the sources of revenue for these organizations. As shown, fees for services and goods account for 53.1 percent of revenue, making it the third most dependent subsector on fees behind health and education. Human service organizations also receive 22.7 percent of their

**Table 5.16.** Revenues and Expenses for Reporting Public Charities in Human Service, 2005

| | All Organizations 100,436 | | Operating Organizations 97,282 | | Supporting Organizations 3,154 | |
|---|---|---|---|---|---|---|
| Number of organizations | $ millions | % | $ millions | % | $ millions | % |
| Public support | 57,831.5 | 39.0[a] | 56,250.7 | 38.7[a] | 1,580.9 | 59.6[a] |
| Private contributions | 24,260.6 | 16.4 | 23,051.4 | 15.8 | 1,209.2 | 45.6 |
| Direct contributions | 20,678.0 | 14.0 | 19,544.9 | 13.4 | 1,133.1 | 42.7 |
| Indirect contributions | 3,582.6 | 2.4 | 3,506.5 | 2.4 | 76.1 | 2.9 |
| Government grants | 33,570.9 | 22.7 | 33,199.3 | 22.8 | 371.6 | 14.0 |
| Fees for services and goods | 78,702.8 | 53.1 | 78,210.9 | 53.8 | 491.9 | 18.5 |
| Program service revenue[b] | 76,918.9 | 51.9 | 76,444.3 | 52.6 | 474.6 | 17.9 |
| Net income from sales of inventory | 1,783.9 | 1.2 | 1,766.5 | 1.2 | 17.3 | 0.7 |
| Investment income | 4,239.1 | 2.9 | 3,788.3 | 2.6 | 450.8 | 17.0 |
| Dividends | 1,250.7 | 0.8 | 1,094.4 | 0.8 | 156.2 | 5.9 |
| Interest | 792.6 | 0.5 | 753.1 | 0.5 | 39.5 | 1.5 |
| Net gain on sale of assets | 1,895.6 | 1.3 | 1,685.1 | 1.2 | 210.4 | 7.9 |
| Other investment income | 300.2 | 0.2 | 255.6 | 0.2 | 44.6 | 1.7 |
| Other income | 7,325.9 | 4.9 | 7,197.6 | 4.9 | 128.4 | 4.8 |
| Dues and assessments | 3,938.7 | 2.7 | 3,920.1 | 2.7 | 18.6 | 0.7 |
| Net income from special events | 1,272.4 | 0.9 | 1,219.4 | 0.8 | 53.0 | 2.0 |
| Other (includes net rental and other) | 2,114.8 | 1.4 | 2,058.0 | 1.4 | 56.7 | 2.1 |
| Total revenue | 148,099.3 | 100.0 | 145,447.4 | 100.0 | 2,651.9 | 100.0 |
| Paid personnel | 64,723.7 | 50.4[c] | 64,335.8 | 50.6[c] | 387.9 | 32.4[c] |
| Wages and salaries | 53,222.1 | 41.5 | 52,902.7 | 41.6 | 319.5 | 26.6 |

(continued)

**Table 5.16.** Revenues and Expenses for Reporting Public Charities in Human Service, 2005 *(continued)*

| Number of organizations | All Organizations 100,436 | | Operating Organizations 97,282 | | Supporting Organizations 3,154 | |
|---|---|---|---|---|---|---|
| | $ millions | % | $ millions | % | $ millions | % |
| Compensation of officers | 3,244.7 | 2.5 | 3,189.4 | 2.5 | 55.3 | 4.6 |
| Other wages and salaries | 49,977.4 | 38.9 | 49,713.3 | 39.1 | 264.2 | 22.0 |
| Fringe benefits and payroll taxes | 11,501.6 | 9.0 | 11,433.2 | 9.0 | 68.4 | 5.7 |
| Pension plan contributions | 1,186.6 | 0.9 | 1,177.2 | 0.9 | 9.4 | 0.8 |
| Other employee benefits | 6,075.3 | 4.7 | 6,039.8 | 4.7 | 35.4 | 3.0 |
| Payroll taxes | 4,239.8 | 3.3 | 4,216.1 | 3.3 | 23.7 | 2.0 |
| Supplies | 4,636.6 | 3.6 | 4,610.9 | 3.6 | 25.8 | 2.1 |
| Communications (printing, phone, etc.) | 3,610.8 | 2.8 | 3,557.1 | 2.8 | 53.7 | 4.5 |
| Professional fees | 1,794.4 | 1.4 | 1,750.1 | 1.4 | 44.3 | 3.7 |
| Occupancy | 5,914.2 | 4.6 | 5,875.6 | 4.6 | 38.6 | 3.2 |
| Equipment rental and maintenance | 1,450.3 | 1.1 | 1,435.4 | 1.1 | 14.9 | 1.2 |
| Interest | 3,210.7 | 2.5 | 3,177.5 | 2.5 | 33.2 | 2.8 |
| Depreciation and depletion | 5,622.6 | 4.4 | 5,566.5 | 4.4 | 56.1 | 4.7 |
| Other | 37,427.5 | 29.2 | 36,883.1 | 29.0 | 544.3 | 45.4 |

| | | | | | | |
|---|---|---|---|---|---|---|
| Total current operating expenses | 128,391.0 | 100.0 | 127,192.2 | 100.0 | 1,198.8 | 100.0 |
| Plus grants and benefits | 12,447.6 | 8.8[d] | 11,661.4 | 8.4[d] | 786.2 | 38.0[d] |
| Grants and allocations | 6,622.0 | 4.7 | 5,872.5 | 4.2 | 749.4 | 36.2 |
| Specific assistance to individuals | 5,233.9 | 3.7 | 5,199.1 | 3.7 | 34.8 | 1.7 |
| Benefits paid to members | 591.8 | 0.4 | 589.8 | 0.4 | 2.0 | 0.1 |
| Plus payments to affiliates | 375.9 | 0.3 | 291.3 | 0.2 | 84.7 | 4.1 |
| Total expenses | 141,214.5 | 100.0 | 139,144.9 | 100.0 | 2,069.6 | 100.0 |
| Net income (revenue – expenses) | 6,884.8 | 4.6[a] | 6,302.5 | 4.3[a] | 582.2 | 22.0[a] |
| Total assets | 223,040.7 | 157.9[d] | 212,214.6 | 152.5[d] | 10,826.1 | 523.1[d] |
| Total liabilities | 113,462.7 | 80.3 | 111,687.7 | 80.3 | 1,774.9 | 85.8 |
| Net assets (assets – liabilities) | 109,578.1 | 77.6 | 100,526.9 | 72.2 | 9,051.2 | 437.3 |

*Source:* Urban Institute, National Center for Charitable Statistics, NCCS-GuideStar National Nonprofit Research Database: Special Research Version (2005).

*Notes:* Authors' calculations are based on U.S. Internal Revenue Service Forms 990 and 990-EZ, classified according to the National Taxonomy of Exempt Entities–Core Codes, and adjusted by the National Center for Charitable Statistics and Independent Sector. Reporting public charities include only organizations that both reported (filed IRS Forms 990) and were required to do so. The following were excluded: foreign organizations, government-associated organizations, organizations without state identifiers, and organizations excluded by the authors' discretion. Organizations not required to report include religious congregations and organizations with less than $25,000 in gross receipts. The table includes separate analyses for operating public charities and supporting organizations to clarify the distribution of funds and to avoid double-counting the financial information for supporting organizations (see chapter 5, appendix A, for a detailed description of the methodology). Categories are as defined by the National Taxonomy of Exempt Entities (see chapter 5, appendix B, for more detail). The sum of the dollar amounts may not equal due to rounding.

a. Percentages for revenue items and net income are expressed as percentages of total revenue.

b. Program service revenue figures may include sizable income via government contracts, which the data source is unable to differentiate from funds raised via the public (i.e., fees for services).

c. Percentages for current operating expense items are expressed as percentages of total current operating expenses.

d. Percentages for other expense items, assets, and liabilities are expressed as percentages of total expenses.

**Figure 5.12.** Sources of Revenue for Human Service Reporting Public Charities, 2005 (percent)

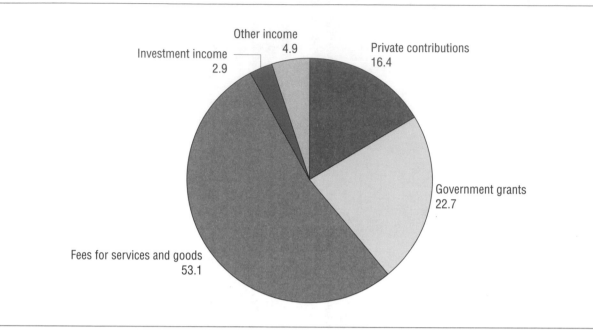

*Source:* Urban Institute, National Center for Charitable Statistics, NCCS-GuideStar National Nonprofit Research Database: Special Research Version (2005).

income from government grants, making it the subsector receiving the greatest proportion of its revenue from such grants.

As exhibited in table 5.16, wages, salaries, and other personnel costs account for 50.4 percent of total operating expenses for human service organizations. Another 29.2 percent of operating expenses are classified as other.

The human service subsector reported net income of $6.9 billion, for a net margin of 4.6 percent—the lowest net margin across all subsectors. These organizations held $223.0 billion in total assets and had net assets (assets minus liabilities) of $109.6 billion. The human service subsector had a net assets to expense ratio of 77.6 percent—making it the subsector with the third lowest ratio.

The number, assets, revenues, and expenses of reporting public charities in the human service subsector are displayed in figure 5.13. Recreation and sports organizations account for the greatest number of reporting public charities in this subsector, 24.4 percent. Housing and shelter organizations follow, with 15.8 percent.

Residential and custodial care organizations and other human service organizations (including multiservice organizations, financial counseling organizations, and transportation assistance programs) account for the highest proportion of revenues (around 19 percent each). Residential and custodial care organizations account for 26.6 percent of assets, housing and shelter organizations account for 23.7 percent of assets, and other human service organizations account for 17.2 percent of assets.

Among the types of human service organizations, net income ranged from $207 million for food, agriculture, and nutrition organizations to $1.6 billion for other human

**Figure 5.13.** Number, Assets, Revenues, and Expenses of Human Service Public Charities, 2005

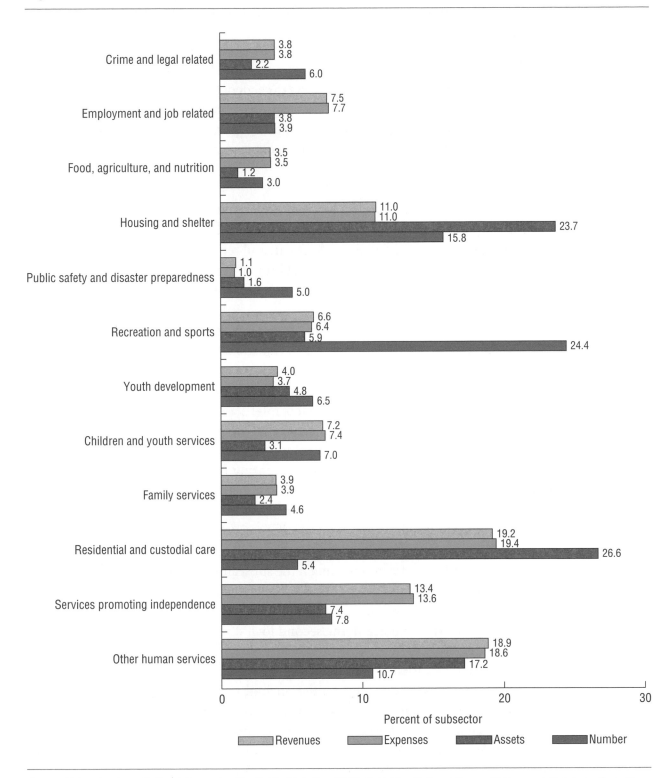

*Source:* Urban Institute, National Center for Charitable Statistics, NCCS-GuideStar National Nonprofit Research Database: Special Research Version (2005).

service organizations. The net margins across these organizations ranged from 2.4 percent for children and youth services organizations to 13.4 percent for public safety and disaster preparedness organizations.

Within the human service subsector, the net assets reported ranged from $2.3 billion for food, agriculture, and nutrition organizations to nearly $26 billion for other human services. Only three types of organizations exceeded 100 percent in their net assets to expense ratios—public safety and disaster preparedness with 216.2 percent, youth development with 180.8 percent, and recreation and sports with 108.1 percent. Children and youth services had the lowest net assets to expense ratio—44.3 percent.

## International and Foreign Affairs

The 5,075 international and foreign affairs public charities represented 1.6 percent of the total number of reporting public charities in 2005. This subsector includes international exchange programs, international development and relief services, international peace and security organizations, and international human rights organizations. These organizations accounted for 1.9 percent of total expenses for all reporting public charities and 0.9 percent of total assets.

International and foreign affairs public charities reported $22.8 billion in total revenue and $20.5 billion in total expenses (table 5.17). Figure 5.14 displays the sources of revenue for these organizations. As displayed, private contributions account for 67.3 percent of total revenue, making this the subsector most dependent on private contributions. Government grants account for 21.9 percent of international and foreign affairs revenue; the subsector is second only to human service in the proportion of revenue coming from government grants.

Like other subsectors, the majority of operating expenses for international and foreign affairs organizations are wages, salaries, other personnel costs, and other expenses. Unlike other subsectors, however, international public charities distribute 53.8 percent of their funds in grants, allocations, and specific assistance to individuals (table 5.17).

The international and foreign affairs subsector reported net income of $2.3 billion, for a net margin of 10.0 percent—making it the subsector with the third lowest margin. International and foreign affairs organizations reported $18.3 billion in total assets and $14.3 billion in net assets (assets minus liabilities). The net assets to expense ratio for these organizations is 69.5 percent, the second lowest ratio among all subsectors.

## Other Public Charities

The 56,699 public charities classified as other include public and societal benefit organizations involved in civil rights and advocacy, community improvement, philanthropy and voluntarism, science and technology, and social science. Religious-related organizations are also included in this category. As a group, these organizations account for 18.2 percent of public charities, 11.3 percent of total assets and 5.9 percent of total expenses.

These charities reported $73.8 billion in total revenue and $62.0 billion in total expenses in 2005 (table 5.18). Figure 5.15 displays the sources of revenue for these organizations. As shown, private contributions account for 40.0 percent and government

**Table 5.17.** Revenues and Expenses for Reporting Public Charities in International and Foreign Affairs, 2005

| | All Organizations | | Operating Organizations | | Supporting Organizations | |
| | 5,075 | | 4,631 | | 444 | |
| Number of organizations | $ millions | % | $ millions | % | $ millions | % |
|---|---|---|---|---|---|---|
| Public support | 20,355.5 | 89.2[a] | 18,097.9 | 88.9[a] | 2,257.7 | 91.6[a] |
| Private contributions | 15,357.8 | 67.3 | 13,234.5 | 65.0 | 2,123.3 | 86.2 |
| Direct contributions | 12,755.4 | 55.9 | 10,691.4 | 52.5 | 2,064.0 | 83.8 |
| Indirect contributions | 2,602.3 | 11.4 | 2,543.0 | 12.5 | 59.3 | 2.4 |
| Government grants | 4,997.8 | 21.9 | 4,863.4 | 23.9 | 134.4 | 5.5 |
| Fees for services and goods | 1,739.7 | 7.6 | 1,663.7 | 8.2 | 76.0 | 3.1 |
| Program service revenue[b] | 1,715.8 | 7.5 | 1,638.6 | 8.0 | 77.2 | 3.1 |
| Net income from sales of inventory | 23.9 | 0.1 | 25.1 | 0.1 | −1.1 | 0.0 |
| Investment income | 495.1 | 2.2 | 372.5 | 1.8 | 122.6 | 5.0 |
| Dividends | 222.1 | 1.0 | 180.1 | 0.9 | 42.0 | 1.7 |
| Interest | 56.5 | 0.2 | 39.5 | 0.2 | 17.0 | 0.7 |
| Net gain on sale of assets | 205.5 | 0.9 | 149.7 | 0.7 | 55.8 | 2.3 |
| Other investment income | 11.0 | 0.0 | 3.2 | 0.0 | 7.8 | 0.3 |
| Other income | 237.0 | 1.0 | 228.9 | 1.1 | 8.1 | 0.3 |
| Dues and assessments | 101.4 | 0.4 | 100.6 | 0.5 | 0.8 | 0.0 |
| Net income from special events | 38.1 | 0.2 | 34.1 | 0.2 | 4.0 | 0.2 |
| Other (includes net rental and other) | 97.5 | 0.4 | 94.2 | 0.5 | 3.3 | 0.1 |
| Total revenue | 22,827.3 | 100.0 | 20,362.9 | 100.0 | 2,464.4 | 100.0 |

*(continued)*

**Table 5.17.** Revenues and Expenses for Reporting Public Charities in International and Foreign Affairs, 2005 *(continued)*

| | All Organizations 5,075 | | Operating Organizations 4,631 | | Supporting Organizations 444 | |
|---|---|---|---|---|---|---|
| Number of organizations | $ millions | % | $ millions | % | $ millions | % |
| Paid personnel | 3,131.0 | 33.2c | 2,990.1 | 33.2c | 140.9 | 33.3c |
| Wages and salaries | 2,518.5 | 26.7 | 2,406.6 | 26.7 | 112.0 | 26.5 |
| Compensation of officers | 303.0 | 3.2 | 284.1 | 3.2 | 18.9 | 4.5 |
| Other wages and salaries | 2,215.5 | 23.5 | 2,122.4 | 23.5 | 93.1 | 22.0 |
| Fringe benefits and payroll taxes | 612.4 | 6.5 | 583.5 | 6.5 | 28.9 | 6.8 |
| Pension plan contributions | 106.8 | 1.1 | 101.1 | 1.1 | 5.6 | 1.3 |
| Other employee benefits | 365.4 | 3.9 | 349.2 | 3.9 | 16.2 | 3.8 |
| Payroll taxes | 140.3 | 1.5 | 133.2 | 1.5 | 7.1 | 1.7 |
| Supplies | 444.3 | 4.7 | 439.5 | 4.9 | 4.8 | 1.1 |
| Communications (printing, phone, etc.) | 959.5 | 10.2 | 905.2 | 10.0 | 54.2 | 12.8 |
| Professional fees | 280.9 | 3.0 | 261.4 | 2.9 | 19.5 | 4.6 |
| Occupancy | 338.1 | 3.6 | 322.0 | 3.6 | 16.1 | 3.8 |
| Equipment rental and maintenance | 84.7 | 0.9 | 82.5 | 0.9 | 2.2 | 0.5 |
| Interest | 37.7 | 0.4 | 35.0 | 0.4 | 2.7 | 0.6 |
| Depreciation and depletion | 162.4 | 1.7 | 154.5 | 1.7 | 7.9 | 1.9 |
| Other | 4,000.4 | 42.4 | 3,825.9 | 42.4 | 174.5 | 41.3 |

| | $ | % | $ | % | $ | % |
|---|---|---|---|---|---|---|
| Total current operating expenses | 9,438.8 | 100.0 | 9,016.1 | 100.0 | 422.7 | 100.0 |
| Plus grants and benefits | 11,051.6 | 53.8[d] | 9,406.6 | 51.0[d] | 1,645.0 | 79.2[d] |
| Grants and allocations | 7,988.8 | 38.9 | 6,847.1 | 37.1 | 1,141.7 | 55.0 |
| Specific assistance to individuals | 3,061.0 | 14.9 | 2,557.7 | 13.9 | 503.3 | 24.2 |
| Benefits paid to members | 1.8 | 0.0 | 1.8 | 0.0 | 0.0 | 0.0 |
| Plus payments to affiliates | 44.1 | 0.2 | 34.6 | 0.2 | 9.5 | 0.5 |
| Total expenses | 20,534.6 | 100.0 | 18,457.4 | 100.0 | 2,077.2 | 100.0 |
| Net income (revenue – expenses) | 2,292.7 | 10.0[a] | 1,905.5 | 9.4[a] | 387.2 | 15.7[a] |
| Total assets | 18,340.6 | 89.3[c] | 15,306.6 | 82.9[d] | 3,034.0 | 146.1[d] |
| Total liabilities | 4,079.1 | 19.9 | 3,655.3 | 19.8 | 423.8 | 20.4 |
| Net assets (assets – liabilities) | 14,261.5 | 69.5 | 11,651.3 | 63.1 | 2,610.2 | 125.7 |

*Source:* Urban Institute, National Center for Charitable Statistics, NCCS-GuideStar National Nonprofit Research Database: Special Research Version (2005).
*Notes:* Authors' calculations are based on U.S. Internal Revenue Service Forms 990 and 990-EZ, classified according to the National Taxonomy of Exempt Entities–Core Codes, and adjusted by the National Center for Charitable Statistics and Independent Sector. Reporting public charities include only organizations that both reported (filed IRS Forms 990) and were required to do so. The following were excluded: foreign organizations, government-associated organizations, organizations without state identifiers, and organizations excluded by the authors' discretion. Organizations not required to report include religious congregations and organizations with less than $25,000 in gross receipts. The table includes separate analyses for operating public charities and supporting organizations to clarify the distribution of funds and to avoid double-counting the financial information for supporting organizations (see chapter 5, appendix A, for a detailed description of the methodology). Categories are as defined by the National Taxonomy of Exempt Entities (see chapter 5, appendix B, for more detail). The sum of the dollar amounts may not equal due to rounding.
a. Percentages for revenue items and net income are expressed as percentages of total revenue.
b. Program service revenue figures may include sizable income via government contracts, which the data source is unable to differentiate from funds raised via the public (i.e., fees for services).
c. Percentages for current operating expense items are expressed as percentages of total current operating expenses.
d. Percentages for other expense items, assets, and liabilities are expressed as percentages of total expenses.

**Figure 5.14.** Sources of Revenue for International and Foreign Affairs Reporting Public Charities, 2005 (percent)

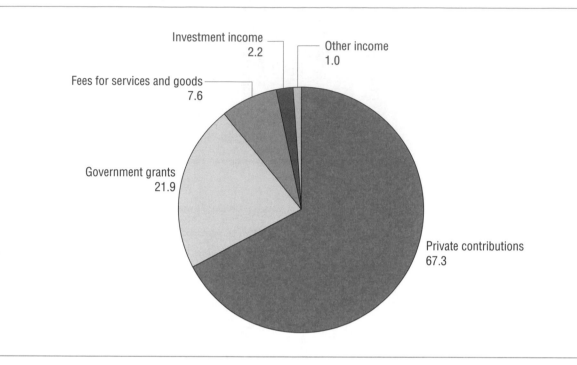

*Source:* Urban Institute, National Center for Charitable Statistics, NCCS-GuideStar National Nonprofit Research Database: Special Research Version (2005).

grants account for 18.9 percent of revenue. These organizations receive the third largest percent of funds from government grants behind human service and international and foreign affairs organizations.

Wages, salaries, and other personnel costs, along with other expenses, account for the largest percent of operating expenses for these organizations, at 41.4 percent. Grants and allocations account for 26.8 percent of total expenses, making it the second ranking group of organizations providing grants as a percentage of expenses (behind international and foreign affairs). The high percentage of grants is seen because this category includes federated giving programs and community foundations (table 5.18).

The net income reported by this group of organizations was $11.8 billion, for a net margin of 16.0 percent. These organizations report $223.1 billion in total assets and $150.5 billion in net assets. Their net assets to expenses ratio is 242.7 percent.

Figure 5.16 displays the number, assets, revenues, and expenses of reporting public charities in this other category. As displayed, religion-related organizations account for nearly one-third of organizations. However, philanthropy and voluntarism organizations, which include community foundations, voluntarism-promotion organizations, and fundraising organizations that cross subsectors, account for 49.7 percent of assets, 35.1 percent of revenues, and 30.2 percent of expenses.

Net income for organizations in this category ranged from $115 million for civil rights and advocacy groups to $7 billion for philanthropy and voluntarism organizations.

**Table 5.18.** Revenues and Expenses for Reporting Public Charities in Other Categories, 2005

| | All Organizations 56,699 | | Operating Organizations 41,569 | | Supporting Organizations 15,130 | |
|---|---|---|---|---|---|---|
| Number of organizations | $ millions | % | $ millions | % | $ millions | % |
| Public support | 43,506.1 | 59.0[a] | 25,454.4 | 53.7[a] | 18,051.8 | 68.5[a] |
| Private contributions | 29,536.5 | 40.0 | 12,199.2 | 25.7 | 17,337.3 | 65.8 |
| Direct contributions | 27,804.8 | 37.7 | 11,384.4 | 24.0 | 16,420.4 | 62.3 |
| Indirect contributions | 1,731.7 | 2.3 | 814.8 | 1.7 | 916.9 | 3.5 |
| Government grants | 13,969.6 | 18.9 | 13,255.2 | 27.9 | 714.5 | 2.7 |
| Fees for services and goods | 19,504.4 | 26.4 | 17,900.9 | 37.7 | 1,603.5 | 6.1 |
| Program service revenue[b] | 19,020.3 | 25.8 | 17,461.4 | 36.8 | 1,558.9 | 5.9 |
| Net income from sales of inventory | 484.1 | 0.7 | 439.5 | 0.9 | 44.6 | 0.2 |
| Investment income | 8,209.5 | 11.1 | 2,050.6 | 4.3 | 6,158.8 | 23.4 |
| Dividends | 2,727.9 | 3.7 | 570.6 | 1.2 | 2,157.3 | 8.2 |
| Interest | 579.1 | 0.8 | 319.6 | 0.7 | 259.5 | 1.0 |
| Net gain on sale of assets | 4,560.1 | 6.2 | 1,058.1 | 2.2 | 3,502.1 | 13.3 |
| Other investment income | 342.3 | 0.5 | 102.4 | 0.2 | 240.0 | 0.9 |
| Other income | 2,553.7 | 3.5 | 2,025.4 | 4.3 | 528.3 | 2.0 |
| Dues and assessments | 947.5 | 1.3 | 853.6 | 1.8 | 93.9 | 0.4 |
| Net income from special events | 376.3 | 0.5 | 256.1 | 0.5 | 120.2 | 0.5 |
| Other (includes net rental and other) | 1,229.9 | 1.7 | 915.7 | 1.9 | 314.2 | 1.2 |

(continued)

**Table 5.18.** Revenues and Expenses for Reporting Public Charities in Other Categories, 2005 *(continued)*

| | All Organizations 56,699 | | Operating Organizations 41,569 | | Supporting Organizations 15,130 | |
|---|---|---|---|---|---|---|
| Number of organizations | $ millions | % | $ millions | % | $ millions | % |
| Total revenue | 73,773.7 | 100.0 | 47,431.3 | 100.0 | 26,342.4 | 100.0 |
| Paid personnel | 18,360.6 | 41.4[c] | 16,065.2 | 41.0[c] | 2,295.4 | 43.7[c] |
| Wages and salaries | 14,756.1 | 33.2 | 12,880.8 | 32.9 | 1,875.3 | 35.7 |
| Compensation of officers | 1,703.1 | 3.8 | 1,336.1 | 3.4 | 366.9 | 7.0 |
| Other wages and salaries | 13,053.0 | 29.4 | 11,544.7 | 29.5 | 1,508.4 | 28.7 |
| Fringe benefits and payroll taxes | 3,604.5 | 8.1 | 3,184.4 | 8.1 | 420.1 | 8.0 |
| Pension plan contributions | 620.3 | 1.4 | 536.6 | 1.4 | 83.8 | 1.6 |
| Other employee benefits | 1,981.6 | 4.5 | 1,777.4 | 4.5 | 204.2 | 3.9 |
| Payroll taxes | 1,002.6 | 2.3 | 870.4 | 2.2 | 132.2 | 2.5 |
| Supplies | 1,145.6 | 2.6 | 1,054.2 | 2.7 | 91.5 | 1.7 |
| Communications (printing, phone, etc.) | 2,498.0 | 5.6 | 2,274.0 | 5.8 | 224.0 | 4.3 |
| Professional fees | 1,297.8 | 2.9 | 1,095.0 | 2.8 | 202.8 | 3.9 |
| Occupancy | 1,513.3 | 3.4 | 1,305.4 | 3.3 | 207.9 | 4.0 |
| Equipment rental and maintenance | 500.2 | 1.1 | 450.1 | 1.1 | 50.1 | 1.0 |
| Interest | 996.9 | 2.2 | 874.1 | 2.2 | 122.8 | 2.3 |
| Depreciation and depletion | 1,410.4 | 3.2 | 1,204.2 | 3.1 | 206.1 | 3.9 |
| Other | 16,670.2 | 37.6 | 14,820.0 | 37.9 | 1,850.2 | 35.2 |

| | | | | | |
|---|---|---|---|---|---|
| Total current operating expenses | 44,393.0 | 100.0 | 39,142.2 | 100.0 | 5,250.8 | 100.0 |
| Plus grants and benefits | 17,383.6 | 28.0[d] | 3,822.7 | 8.9[d] | 13,560.9 | 71.6[d] |
| Grants and allocations | 16,633.3 | 26.8 | 3,185.2 | 7.4 | 13,448.1 | 71.0 |
| Specific assistance to individuals | 705.8 | 1.1 | 600.3 | 1.4 | 105.5 | 0.6 |
| Benefits paid to members | 44.4 | 0.1 | 37.2 | 0.1 | 7.3 | 0.0 |
| Plus payments to affiliates | 225.6 | 0.4 | 86.5 | 0.2 | 139.1 | 0.7 |
| Total expenses | 62,002.2 | 100.0 | 43,051.4 | 100.0 | 18,950.9 | 100.0 |
| Net income (revenue − expenses) | 11,771.5 | 16.0[a] | 4,379.9 | 9.2[a] | 7,391.6 | 28.1[a] |
| Total assets | 223,117.2 | 359.9[d] | 104,578.7 | 242.9[d] | 118,538.5 | 625.5[d] |
| Total liabilities | 72,644.5 | 117.2 | 58,368.8 | 135.6 | 14,275.7 | 75.3 |
| Net assets (assets − liabilities) | 150,472.7 | 242.7 | 46,209.9 | 107.3 | 104,262.8 | 550.2 |

*Source:* Urban Institute, National Center for Charitable Statistics, NCCS-GuideStar National Nonprofit Research Database: Special Research Version (2005).

*Notes:* Authors' calculations are based on U.S. Internal Revenue Service Forms 990 and 990-EZ, classified according to the National Taxonomy of Exempt Entities–Core Codes, and adjusted by the National Center for Charitable Statistics and Independent Sector. Reporting public charities include only organizations that both reported (filed IRS Forms 990) and were required to do so. The following were excluded: foreign organizations, government-associated organizations, organizations without state identifiers, and organizations excluded by the authors' discretion. Organizations not required to report include religious congregations and organizations with less than $25,000 in gross receipts. The table includes separate analyses for operating public charities and supporting organizations to clarify the distribution of funds and to avoid double-counting the financial information for supporting organizations (see chapter 5, appendix A, for a detailed description of the methodology). Categories are as defined by the National Taxonomy of Exempt Entities (see chapter 5, appendix B, for more detail). The sum of the dollar amounts may not equal due to rounding.

a. Percentages for revenue items and net income are expressed as percentages of total revenue.

b. Program service revenue figures may include sizable income via government contracts, which the data source is unable to differentiate from funds raised via the public (i.e., fees for services).

c. Percentages for current operating expense items are expressed as percentages of total current operating expenses.

d. Percentages for other expense items, assets, and liabilities are expressed as percentages of total expenses.

**Figure 5.15.** Sources of Revenue for Other Reporting Public Charities, 2005 (percent)

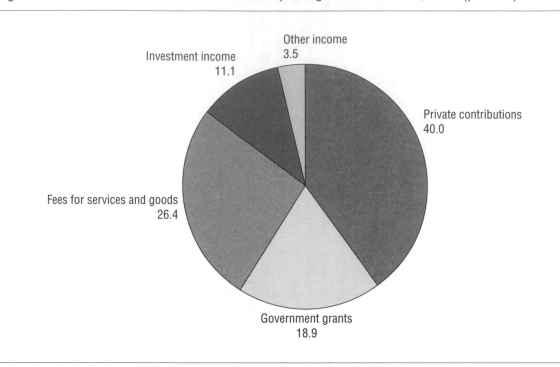

*Source:* Urban Institute, National Center for Charitable Statistics, NCCS-GuideStar National Nonprofit Research Database: Special Research Version (2005).

Philanthropy and voluntarism organizations also reported the highest net margins with 27.8 percent—this was twice the margin reported by the other types of organizations in this category. The net margins of the other organizations ranged from 5.6 percent for science and technology organizations to 13.9 percent for religion-related organizations.

Net assets for these organizations ranged from $1.5 billion for civil rights and advocacy groups to $98.3 billion for philanthropy and voluntarism organizations. The ratio of net assets to expenses showed great variation, ranging from 85.0 percent for civil rights and advocacy groups to 525.6 percent for philanthropy and voluntarism public charities.

## Reporting Public Charities by State

The number of public charities reported across the states varied widely, from a high of nearly 35,820 in California to a low of 888 in Wyoming. Not surprisingly, the number of reporting public charities in a state appears to be directly correlated with the population of the state. Highly populated states such as California and New York have the most charities, while less-populated states such as Wyoming and North Dakota have many fewer (table 5.19).

**Figure 5.16.** Number, Assets, Revenues, and Expenses for Other Public Charities, 2005

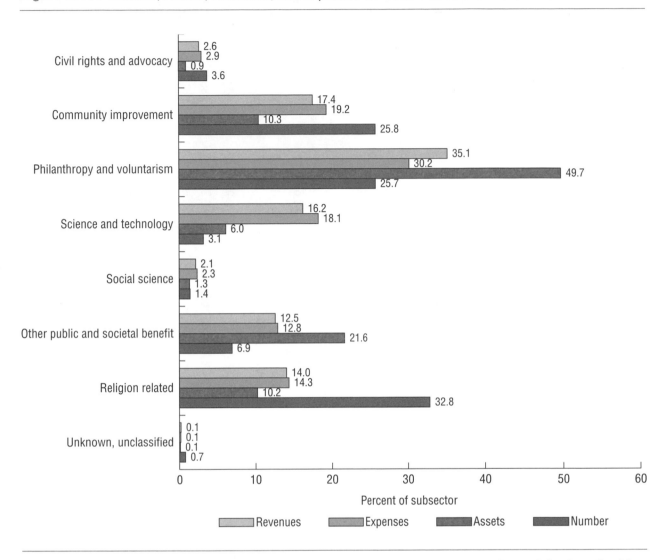

*Source:* Urban Institute, National Center for Charitable Statistics, NCCS-GuideStar National Nonprofit Research Database: Special Research Version (2005).

California, New York, Texas, Pennsylvania, Florida, Ohio, Illinois, Massachusetts, New Jersey, and Michigan report the most public charities, as well as the highest revenues and expenses. Nine of these states are also ranked in the top 10 in population. Connecticut and Virginia are added to this top 10 list in total assets reported by state, replacing New Jersey and Michigan.

While these figures give some insight into public charities across the states, a full picture of the nonprofit sector (reporting public charities only) is better examined by looking at the density of public charities by state (as measured by the number of reporting public charities divided by the population) and the expenses, revenues, and assets per resident (as measured by the total expenses, revenues, or assets divided by the

**Table 5.19.** Number, Revenue, Expenses, and Assets of Reporting Public Charities by State, 2005

| | Reporting public charities | Revenue $ millions | Expenses $ millions | Assets $ millions | Population | Organizations per 10,000 residents | Expenses per resident ($) | Assets per resident ($) |
|---|---|---|---|---|---|---|---|---|
| United States | 310,683 | 1,144,022 | 1,053,487 | 1,975,792 | 296,410,404 | 10.5 | 3,554 | 6,666 |
| Northeast | 69,812 | 325,571 | 298,464 | 618,796 | 54,641,895 | 12.8 | 5,462 | 11,325 |
| New England | 22,702 | 110,537 | 95,742 | 269,271 | 14,239,724 | 15.9 | 6,724 | 18,910 |
| Connecticut | 4,990 | 23,315 | 19,504 | 62,631 | 3,510,297 | 14.2 | 5,556 | 17,842 |
| Massachusetts | 9,902 | 63,527 | 54,409 | 167,394 | 6,398,743 | 15.5 | 8,503 | 26,160 |
| Maine | 2,312 | 7,533 | 6,932 | 10,070 | 1,321,505 | 17.5 | 5,245 | 7,620 |
| New Hampshire | 1,993 | 6,766 | 6,112 | 14,762 | 1,309,940 | 15.2 | 4,666 | 11,269 |
| Rhode Island | 1,888 | 6,582 | 6,105 | 9,593 | 1,076,189 | 17.5 | 5,673 | 8,914 |
| Vermont | 1,617 | 2,814 | 2,680 | 4,821 | 623,050 | 26.0 | 4,302 | 7,737 |
| Middle Atlantic | 47,110 | 215,034 | 202,722 | 349,525 | 40,402,171 | 11.7 | 5,018 | 8,651 |
| New Jersey | 9,212 | 31,692 | 29,867 | 53,773 | 8,717,925 | 10.6 | 3,426 | 6,168 |
| New York | 23,182 | 115,101 | 109,136 | 176,580 | 19,254,630 | 12.0 | 5,668 | 9,171 |
| Pennsylvania | 14,716 | 68,241 | 63,720 | 119,172 | 12,429,616 | 11.8 | 5,126 | 9,588 |
| Midwest | 72,210 | 268,937 | 250,690 | 470,958 | 65,971,974 | 10.9 | 3,800 | 7,139 |
| East North Central | 47,483 | 187,308 | 174,733 | 321,192 | 46,156,447 | 10.3 | 3,786 | 6,959 |
| Illinois | 12,155 | 53,281 | 49,214 | 100,265 | 12,763,371 | 9.5 | 3,856 | 7,856 |
| Indiana | 6,586 | 23,254 | 21,602 | 42,170 | 6,271,973 | 10.5 | 3,444 | 6,724 |
| Michigan | 8,966 | 34,783 | 32,812 | 52,879 | 10,120,860 | 8.9 | 3,242 | 5,225 |
| Ohio | 12,897 | 52,080 | 48,983 | 89,662 | 11,464,042 | 11.2 | 4,273 | 7,821 |
| Wisconsin | 6,879 | 23,911 | 22,122 | 36,217 | 5,536,201 | 12.4 | 3,996 | 6,542 |
| West North Central | 24,727 | 81,629 | 75,957 | 149,765 | 19,815,527 | 12.5 | 3,833 | 7,558 |
| Iowa | 3,742 | 9,215 | 8,629 | 19,799 | 2,966,334 | 12.6 | 2,909 | 6,675 |
| Kansas | 3,149 | 7,350 | 6,780 | 10,598 | 2,744,687 | 11.5 | 2,470 | 3,861 |

| | | | | | | |
|---|---|---|---|---|---|---|
| Minnesota | 7,339 | 25,894 | 24,178 | 45,622 | 5,132,799 | 14.3 | 8,888 |
| Missouri | 6,053 | 25,435 | 23,530 | 52,285 | 5,800,310 | 10.4 | 9,014 |
| North Dakota | 998 | 2,764 | 2,655 | 3,341 | 636,677 | 15.7 | 5,247 |
| Nebraska | 2,351 | 7,065 | 6,538 | 12,233 | 1,758,787 | 13.4 | 6,955 |
| South Dakota | 1,095 | 3,907 | 3,646 | 5,888 | 775,933 | 14.1 | 7,588 |
| South | 96,785 | 316,040 | 289,197 | 557,503 | 107,505,413 | 9.0 | 5,186 |
| South Atlantic | 55,402 | 194,698 | 176,350 | 350,004 | 56,179,519 | 9.9 | 6,230 |
| District of Columbia | 3,810 | 21,885 | 19,459 | 32,938 | 550,521 | 69.2 | 59,830 |
| Delaware | 1,068 | 2,600 | 2,423 | 12,121 | 843,524 | 12.7 | 14,370 |
| Florida | 13,550 | 46,166 | 42,726 | 71,054 | 17,789,864 | 7.6 | 3,994 |
| Georgia | 7,139 | 27,834 | 24,910 | 48,237 | 9,072,576 | 7.9 | 5,317 |
| Maryland | 6,816 | 25,614 | 22,607 | 51,652 | 5,600,388 | 12.2 | 9,223 |
| North Carolina | 8,830 | 28,103 | 25,525 | 52,589 | 8,683,242 | 10.2 | 6,056 |
| South Carolina | 3,442 | 8,093 | 7,476 | 17,130 | 4,255,083 | 8.1 | 4,026 |
| Virginia | 8,828 | 29,009 | 26,058 | 57,496 | 7,567,465 | 11.7 | 7,598 |
| West Virginia | 1,919 | 5,395 | 5,165 | 6,786 | 1,816,856 | 10.6 | 3,735 |
| East South Central | 14,301 | 44,529 | 41,696 | 76,702 | 17,615,260 | 8.1 | 4,354 |
| Alabama | 3,573 | 7,747 | 7,116 | 12,827 | 4,557,808 | 7.8 | 2,814 |
| Kentucky | 3,601 | 13,077 | 12,378 | 19,426 | 4,173,405 | 8.6 | 4,655 |
| Mississippi | 1,879 | 5,008 | 4,714 | 7,811 | 2,921,088 | 6.4 | 2,674 |
| Tennessee | 5,248 | 18,697 | 17,488 | 36,639 | 5,962,959 | 8.8 | 6,144 |
| West South Central | 27,082 | 76,813 | 71,151 | 130,797 | 33,710,634 | 8.0 | 3,880 |
| Arkansas | 2,381 | 9,365 | 9,036 | 7,708 | 2,779,154 | 8.6 | 2,774 |
| Louisiana | 3,326 | 9,413 | 8,953 | 14,428 | 4,523,628 | 7.4 | 3,189 |
| Oklahoma | 3,288 | 7,747 | 6,844 | 14,897 | 3,547,884 | 9.3 | 4,199 |
| Texas | 18,087 | 50,288 | 46,317 | 93,764 | 22,859,968 | 7.9 | 4,102 |

(continued)

**Table 5.19.** Number, Revenue, Expenses, and Assets of Reporting Public Charities by State, 2005 *(continued)*

| | Reporting public charities | Revenue | Expenses | Assets | Population | Organizations per 10,000 residents | Expenses per resident ($) | Assets per resident ($) |
|---|---|---|---|---|---|---|---|---|
| | | $ millions | | | | | | |
| West | 71,433 | 231,629 | 213,383 | 324,854 | 68,291,122 | 10.5 | 3,125 | 4,757 |
| Mountain | 19,955 | 43,694 | 39,785 | 64,291 | 20,291,305 | 9.8 | 1,961 | 3,168 |
| Arizona | 4,544 | 14,668 | 13,411 | 16,846 | 5,939,292 | 7.7 | 2,258 | 2,836 |
| Colorado | 6,305 | 12,613 | 11,501 | 21,140 | 4,665,177 | 13.5 | 2,465 | 4,531 |
| Idaho | 1,320 | 1,920 | 1,766 | 2,807 | 1,429,096 | 9.2 | 1,236 | 1,964 |
| Montana | 1,734 | 3,244 | 3,025 | 5,429 | 935,670 | 18.5 | 3,233 | 5,802 |
| New Mexico | 2,168 | 3,639 | 3,371 | 5,707 | 1,928,384 | 11.2 | 1,748 | 2,959 |
| Nevada | 1,354 | 2,559 | 2,093 | 4,439 | 2,414,807 | 5.6 | 867 | 1,838 |
| Utah | 1,642 | 4,219 | 3,877 | 6,187 | 2,469,585 | 6.6 | 1,570 | 2,505 |
| Wyoming | 888 | 832 | 741 | 1,736 | 509,294 | 17.4 | 1,455 | 3,409 |
| Pacific | 51,478 | 187,935 | 173,598 | 260,563 | 47,999,817 | 10.7 | 3,617 | 5,428 |
| Alaska | 1,276 | 2,174 | 2,066 | 2,825 | 663,661 | 19.2 | 3,113 | 4,257 |
| California | 35,820 | 141,415 | 130,400 | 197,119 | 36,132,147 | 9.9 | 3,609 | 5,456 |
| Hawaii | 1,555 | 4,988 | 4,279 | 12,694 | 1,275,194 | 12.2 | 3,356 | 9,954 |
| Oregon | 5,213 | 14,986 | 14,210 | 15,428 | 3,641,056 | 14.3 | 3,903 | 4,237 |
| Washington | 7,614 | 24,371 | 22,642 | 32,497 | 6,287,759 | 12.1 | 3,601 | 5,168 |
| U.S. Territories | 443 | 1,846 | 1,754 | 3,681 | 4,306,019 | 1.0 | 407 | 855 |

*Sources:* Urban Institute, National Center for Charitable Statistics, NCCS-GuideStar National Nonprofit Research Database: Special Research Version (2005); U.S. Census Bureau, *Statistical Abstract* (2006).

*Notes:* Reporting public charities include only organizations that both reported (filed IRS Forms 990) and were required to do so. The following were excluded: foreign organizations, government-associated organizations, organizations without state identifiers, and organizations excluded by the authors' discretion. Organizations not required to report include religious congregations and organizations with less than $25,000 in gross receipts.

population). The per capita rankings presented in the following paragraphs exclude the District of Columbia, as many nonprofits in D.C. have a national scope and may not directly benefit D.C. residents.

The density of reporting public charities varied greatly across the states, ranging from 5.6 public charities per 10,000 residents in Nevada to 26.0 public charities per 10,000 residents in Vermont. Ranking states in density gives a much different picture than the 10 states with the most organizations, as discussed above. In density, less-populated states appeared to have more reporting public charities per 10,000 residents. The top 10 states in public charity density are Vermont, Alaska, Montana, Rhode Island, Maine, Wyoming, North Dakota, Massachusetts, New Hampshire, and Oregon. Only one state, Massachusetts, is in the top 10 for both number and density of public charities.

Reported expenses per resident in 2005 ranged from $867 in Nevada to $8,503 in Massachusetts. Three states (Massachusetts, New York, and Pennsylvania) ranked in the top 10 for both total expenses and expenses per resident. Rhode Island, Connecticut, Maine, Minnesota, South Dakota, New Hampshire, and Vermont also ranked among the top 10 in expenses per resident.

For reporting public charities, assets per resident ranged from $1,838 in Nevada to $26,160 in Massachusetts. Four states ranked in the top 10 in both total nonprofit assets and assets per resident—Massachusetts, Pennsylvania, New York, and Connecticut. Hawaii, New Hampshire, Rhode Island, Maryland, Missouri, and Delaware also ranked among the top 10 in assets per resident.

# Trends in Reporting Public Charities by State

The number of reporting public charities in the United States increased from 187,038 in 1995 to 310,683 in 2005, an increase of 66.1 percent over the 10-year period. The percentage increase over this same period varied among the states, ranging from 38.6 percent in North Dakota to 121.6 percent in Nevada. Looking at the growth across census regions reveals the South as having the greatest growth in number of reporting public charities, an increase of 74.1 percent from 1995 to 2005 (table 5.20).

The top 10 states in the growth of reporting public charities are listed in table 5.21. These states also are in the top 15 in population growth during this same time period.

Total revenues for reporting public charities grew by 56.6 percent after adjusting for inflation from 1995 to 2005. The growth in total revenue by state ranged from 40.2 percent (an inflation-adjusted 10.1 percent) in North Dakota to 209.0 percent (an inflation-adjusted 142.6 percent) in Nevada. Among the census regions, the West exhibited the greatest growth with a 129.9 percent increase in revenue over the 10-year period (an inflation-adjusted 80.5 percent) (table 5.22).

Public support for reporting public charities grew from $106.8 billion in 1995 to $243.7 billion in 2005, an increase of 128.3 percent, or an inflation-adjusted 79.2 percent. The growth in public support ranged from an increase of 28.8 percent in Iowa to an increase of 178.1 percent in Nevada (after adjusting for inflation). Among the census

**Table 5.20.** Change in the Number of Reporting Public Charities by State, 1995, 2000, and 2005

| | Number of Organizations | | | Total % Change | Average Annual % Change | | |
|---|---|---|---|---|---|---|---|
| | 1995 | 2000 | 2005 | 1995–2005 | 1995–2005 | 1995–2000 | 2000–2005 |
| United States | 187,038 | 245,749 | 310,683 | 66.1 | 5.2 | 5.6 | 4.8 |
| Northeast | 44,187 | 56,387 | 69,812 | 58.0 | 4.7 | 5.0 | 4.4 |
| New England | 14,399 | 18,413 | 22,702 | 57.7 | 4.7 | 5.0 | 4.3 |
| Connecticut | 3,241 | 4,144 | 4,990 | 54.0 | 4.4 | 5.0 | 3.8 |
| Massachusetts | 6,661 | 8,180 | 9,902 | 48.7 | 4.0 | 4.2 | 3.9 |
| Maine | 1,379 | 1,833 | 2,312 | 67.7 | 5.3 | 5.9 | 4.8 |
| New Hampshire | 1,133 | 1,583 | 1,993 | 75.9 | 5.8 | 6.9 | 4.7 |
| Rhode Island | 1,064 | 1,405 | 1,888 | 77.4 | 5.9 | 5.7 | 6.1 |
| Vermont | 921 | 1,268 | 1,617 | 75.6 | 5.8 | 6.6 | 5.0 |
| Middle Atlantic | 29,788 | 37,974 | 47,110 | 58.2 | 4.7 | 5.0 | 4.4 |
| New Jersey | 5,128 | 6,918 | 9,212 | 79.6 | 6.0 | 6.2 | 5.9 |
| New York | 15,008 | 18,785 | 23,182 | 54.5 | 4.4 | 4.6 | 4.3 |
| Pennsylvania | 9,652 | 12,271 | 14,716 | 52.5 | 4.3 | 4.9 | 3.7 |
| Midwest | 45,932 | 59,199 | 72,210 | 57.2 | 4.6 | 5.2 | 4.1 |
| East North Central | 30,384 | 38,964 | 47,483 | 56.3 | 4.6 | 5.1 | 4.0 |
| Illinois | 7,826 | 9,985 | 12,155 | 55.3 | 4.5 | 5.0 | 4.0 |
| Indiana | 4,111 | 5,369 | 6,586 | 60.2 | 4.8 | 5.5 | 4.2 |
| Michigan | 5,828 | 7,422 | 8,966 | 53.8 | 4.4 | 5.0 | 3.9 |
| Ohio | 8,501 | 10,819 | 12,897 | 51.7 | 4.3 | 4.9 | 3.6 |
| Wisconsin | 4,118 | 5,369 | 6,879 | 67.0 | 5.3 | 5.4 | 5.1 |
| West North Central | 15,548 | 20,235 | 24,727 | 59.0 | 4.7 | 5.4 | 4.1 |
| Iowa | 2,400 | 3,137 | 3,742 | 55.9 | 4.5 | 5.5 | 3.6 |
| Kansas | 2,096 | 2,578 | 3,149 | 50.2 | 4.2 | 4.2 | 4.1 |
| Minnesota | 4,396 | 5,894 | 7,339 | 66.9 | 5.3 | 6.0 | 4.5 |
| Missouri | 3,727 | 4,902 | 6,053 | 62.4 | 5.0 | 5.6 | 4.3 |
| North Dakota | 720 | 902 | 998 | 38.6 | 3.3 | 4.6 | 2.0 |
| Nebraska | 1,511 | 1,926 | 2,351 | 55.6 | 4.5 | 5.0 | 4.1 |
| South Dakota | 698 | 896 | 1,095 | 56.9 | 4.6 | 5.1 | 4.1 |
| South | 55,579 | 74,739 | 96,785 | 74.1 | 5.7 | 6.1 | 5.3 |
| South Atlantic | 31,549 | 42,503 | 55,402 | 75.6 | 5.8 | 6.1 | 5.4 |
| District of Columbia | 2,693 | 3,236 | 3,810 | 41.5 | 3.5 | 3.7 | 3.3 |
| Delaware | 711 | 911 | 1,068 | 50.2 | 4.2 | 5.1 | 3.2 |

*(continued)*

**Table 5.20.** Change in the Number of Reporting Public Charities by State, 1995, 2000, and 2005 *(continued)*

| | Number of Organizations | | | Total % Change | Average Annual % Change | | |
|---|---|---|---|---|---|---|---|
| | 1995 | 2000 | 2005 | 1995–2005 | 1995–2005 | 1995–2000 | 2000–2005 |
| Florida | 7,241 | 10,077 | 13,550 | 87.1 | 6.5 | 6.8 | 6.1 |
| Georgia | 3,668 | 5,244 | 7,139 | 94.6 | 6.9 | 7.4 | 6.4 |
| Maryland | 4,051 | 5,401 | 6,816 | 68.3 | 5.3 | 5.9 | 4.8 |
| North Carolina | 4,977 | 6,741 | 8,830 | 77.4 | 5.9 | 6.3 | 5.5 |
| South Carolina | 1,909 | 2,584 | 3,442 | 80.3 | 6.1 | 6.2 | 5.9 |
| Virginia | 5,109 | 6,719 | 8,828 | 72.8 | 5.6 | 5.6 | 5.6 |
| West Virginia | 1,190 | 1,590 | 1,919 | 61.3 | 4.9 | 6.0 | 3.8 |
| East South Central | 8,517 | 11,251 | 14,301 | 67.9 | 5.3 | 5.7 | 4.9 |
| Alabama | 2,061 | 2,777 | 3,573 | 73.4 | 5.7 | 6.1 | 5.2 |
| Kentucky | 2,310 | 2,875 | 3,601 | 55.9 | 4.5 | 4.5 | 4.6 |
| Mississippi | 1,091 | 1,463 | 1,879 | 72.2 | 5.6 | 6.0 | 5.1 |
| Tennessee | 3,055 | 4,136 | 5,248 | 71.8 | 5.6 | 6.2 | 4.9 |
| West South Central | 15,513 | 20,985 | 27,082 | 74.6 | 5.7 | 6.2 | 5.2 |
| Arkansas | 1,461 | 1,898 | 2,381 | 63.0 | 5.0 | 5.4 | 4.6 |
| Louisiana | 2,034 | 2,668 | 3,326 | 63.5 | 5.0 | 5.6 | 4.5 |
| Oklahoma | 2,083 | 2,672 | 3,288 | 57.8 | 4.7 | 5.1 | 4.2 |
| Texas | 9,935 | 13,747 | 18,087 | 82.1 | 6.2 | 6.7 | 5.6 |
| West | 41,197 | 55,178 | 71,433 | 73.4 | 5.7 | 6.0 | 5.3 |
| Mountain | 10,792 | 15,098 | 19,955 | 84.9 | 6.3 | 6.9 | 5.7 |
| Arizona | 2,352 | 3,364 | 4,544 | 93.2 | 6.8 | 7.4 | 6.2 |
| Colorado | 3,509 | 4,838 | 6,305 | 79.7 | 6.0 | 6.6 | 5.4 |
| Idaho | 682 | 952 | 1,320 | 93.5 | 6.8 | 6.9 | 6.8 |
| Montana | 963 | 1,351 | 1,734 | 80.1 | 6.1 | 7.0 | 5.1 |
| New Mexico | 1,355 | 1,773 | 2,168 | 60.0 | 4.8 | 5.5 | 4.1 |
| Nevada | 611 | 939 | 1,354 | 121.6 | 8.3 | 9.0 | 7.6 |
| Utah | 799 | 1,211 | 1,642 | 105.5 | 7.5 | 8.7 | 6.3 |
| Wyoming | 521 | 670 | 888 | 70.4 | 5.5 | 5.2 | 5.8 |
| Pacific | 30,405 | 40,080 | 51,478 | 69.3 | 5.4 | 5.7 | 5.1 |
| Alaska | 764 | 995 | 1,276 | 67.0 | 5.3 | 5.4 | 5.1 |
| California | 21,709 | 28,087 | 35,820 | 65.0 | 5.1 | 5.3 | 5.0 |

*(continued)*

**Table 5.20.** Change in the Number of Reporting Public Charities by State, 1995, 2000, and 2005 *(continued)*

|  | Number of Organizations | | | Total % Change | Average Annual % Change | | |
|---|---|---|---|---|---|---|---|
|  | 1995 | 2000 | 2005 | 1995–2005 | 1995–2005 | 1995–2000 | 2000–2005 |
| Hawaii | 939 | 1,197 | 1,555 | 65.6 | 5.2 | 5.0 | 5.4 |
| Oregon | 2,767 | 4,041 | 5,213 | 88.4 | 6.5 | 7.9 | 5.2 |
| Washington | 4,226 | 5,760 | 7,614 | 80.2 | 6.1 | 6.4 | 5.7 |
| U.S. Territories | 143 | 246 | 443 | 209.8 | 12.0 | 11.5 | 12.5 |

*Source:* Urban Institute, National Center for Charitable Statistics, Core Files (1995, 2000, 2005).

**Table 5.21.** The 10 States with the Highest Growth in Number of Reporting Public Charities, 1995–2005

| Rank | State | Reporting public charities, 1995 | Reporting public charities, 2005 | % change in public charities, 1995–2005 | % change in population, 1995–2005 |
|---|---|---|---|---|---|
| 1 | Nevada | 611 | 1,354 | 121.6 | 52.7 |
| 2 | Utah | 799 | 1,642 | 105.5 | 22.6 |
| 3 | Georgia | 3,668 | 7,139 | 94.6 | 23.8 |
| 4 | Idaho | 682 | 1,320 | 93.5 | 21.4 |
| 5 | Arizona | 2,352 | 4,544 | 93.2 | 34.0 |
| 6 | Oregon | 2,767 | 5,213 | 88.4 | 14.3 |
| 7 | Florida | 7,241 | 13,550 | 87.1 | 22.4 |
| 8 | Texas | 9,935 | 18,087 | 82.1 | 20.6 |
| 9 | South Carolina | 1,909 | 3,442 | 80.3 | 13.5 |
| 10 | Washington | 4,226 | 7,614 | 80.2 | 14.7 |

*Source:* Urban Institute, National Center for Charitable Statistics, Core Files (1995, 2000, 2005).

**Table 5.22.** Change in Total Revenue for Reporting Public Charities by State, 1995, 2000, and 2005

| | Total Revenue ($ millions) | | | Total % Change | Average Annual % Change | | |
|---|---|---|---|---|---|---|---|
| | 1995 | 2000 | 2005 | 1995–2005 | 1995–2005 | 1995–2000 | 2000–2005 |
| United States | 573,318.6 | 811,362.4 | 1,144,022.2 | 99.5 | 7.2 | 7.2 | 7.1 |
| Northeast | 179,900.0 | 248,039.6 | 325,570.5 | 81.0 | 6.1 | 6.6 | 5.6 |
| New England | 53,149.4 | 87,852.2 | 110,537.0 | 108.0 | 7.6 | 10.6 | 4.7 |
| Connecticut | 11,575.8 | 18,541.3 | 23,314.5 | 101.4 | 7.3 | 9.9 | 4.7 |
| Massachusetts | 30,151.7 | 51,967.3 | 63,526.6 | 110.7 | 7.7 | 11.5 | 4.1 |
| Maine | 2,802.1 | 4,948.4 | 7,533.3 | 168.9 | 10.4 | 12.0 | 8.8 |
| New Hampshire | 3,269.8 | 4,841.0 | 6,766.4 | 106.9 | 7.5 | 8.2 | 6.9 |
| Rhode Island | 3,871.9 | 5,475.0 | 6,582.0 | 70.0 | 5.4 | 7.2 | 3.8 |
| Vermont | 1,478.2 | 2,079.2 | 2,814.1 | 90.4 | 6.6 | 7.1 | 6.2 |
| Middle Atlantic | 126,750.6 | 160,187.4 | 215,033.6 | 69.7 | 5.4 | 4.8 | 6.1 |
| New Jersey | 18,415.7 | 25,567.6 | 31,692.1 | 72.1 | 5.6 | 6.8 | 4.4 |
| New York | 65,929.2 | 84,690.0 | 115,100.6 | 74.6 | 5.7 | 5.1 | 6.3 |
| Pennsylvania | 42,405.6 | 49,929.8 | 68,240.9 | 60.9 | 4.9 | 3.3 | 6.4 |
| Midwest | 140,927.6 | 196,294.8 | 268,936.8 | 90.8 | 6.7 | 6.9 | 6.5 |
| East North Central | 98,452.2 | 135,449.7 | 187,307.7 | 90.3 | 6.6 | 6.6 | 6.7 |
| Illinois | 29,621.6 | 40,391.6 | 53,280.6 | 79.9 | 6.0 | 6.4 | 5.7 |
| Indiana | 12,351.8 | 18,159.2 | 23,254.3 | 88.3 | 6.5 | 8.0 | 5.1 |
| Michigan | 21,190.4 | 27,551.7 | 34,782.5 | 64.1 | 5.1 | 5.4 | 4.8 |
| Ohio | 25,083.7 | 33,576.0 | 52,079.7 | 107.6 | 7.6 | 6.0 | 9.2 |
| Wisconsin | 10,204.6 | 15,771.2 | 23,910.5 | 134.3 | 8.9 | 9.1 | 8.7 |

*(continued)*

**Table 5.22.** Change in Total Revenue for Reporting Public Charities by State, 1995, 2000, and 2005 *(continued)*

| | Total Revenue ($ millions) | | | Total % Change | Average Annual % Change | | |
|---|---|---|---|---|---|---|---|
| | 1995 | 2000 | 2005 | 1995–2005 | 1995–2005 | 1995–2000 | 2000–2005 |
| West North Central | 42,475.4 | 60,845.1 | 81,629.1 | 92.2 | 6.8 | 7.5 | 6.1 |
| Iowa | 5,575.8 | 7,250.4 | 9,215.3 | 65.3 | 5.2 | 5.4 | 4.9 |
| Kansas | 3,843.3 | 5,581.7 | 7,349.9 | 91.2 | 6.7 | 7.7 | 5.7 |
| Minnesota | 11,682.7 | 17,556.2 | 25,893.9 | 121.6 | 8.3 | 8.5 | 8.1 |
| Missouri | 14,511.1 | 19,160.5 | 25,434.8 | 75.3 | 5.8 | 5.7 | 5.8 |
| North Dakota | 1,970.9 | 3,012.7 | 2,763.8 | 40.2 | 3.4 | 8.9 | -1.7 |
| Nebraska | 2,891.0 | 5,221.0 | 7,064.9 | 144.4 | 9.3 | 12.5 | 6.2 |
| South Dakota | 2,000.5 | 3,062.7 | 3,906.5 | 95.3 | 6.9 | 8.9 | 5.0 |
| South | 150,870.3 | 216,183.8 | 316,040.1 | 109.5 | 7.7 | 7.5 | 7.9 |
| South Atlantic | 92,479.7 | 131,290.7 | 194,698.4 | 110.5 | 7.7 | 7.3 | 8.2 |
| District of Columbia | 10,157.8 | 16,532.4 | 21,884.8 | 115.4 | 8.0 | 10.2 | 5.8 |
| Delaware | 1,220.8 | 1,734.4 | 2,599.7 | 113.0 | 7.9 | 7.3 | 8.4 |
| Florida | 21,133.0 | 30,117.2 | 46,166.4 | 118.5 | 8.1 | 7.3 | 8.9 |
| Georgia | 12,494.8 | 18,377.1 | 27,833.6 | 122.8 | 8.3 | 8.0 | 8.7 |
| Maryland | 12,728.9 | 16,698.5 | 25,614.0 | 101.2 | 7.2 | 5.6 | 8.9 |
| North Carolina | 12,982.5 | 19,534.6 | 28,102.9 | 116.5 | 8.0 | 8.5 | 7.5 |
| South Carolina | 4,784.1 | 5,444.0 | 8,093.1 | 69.2 | 5.4 | 2.6 | 8.3 |
| Virginia | 13,709.3 | 18,775.1 | 29,009.0 | 111.6 | 7.8 | 6.5 | 9.1 |
| West Virginia | 3,268.4 | 4,077.4 | 5,394.8 | 65.1 | 5.1 | 4.5 | 5.8 |
| East South Central | 22,017.8 | 30,927.9 | 44,529.1 | 102.2 | 7.3 | 7.0 | 7.6 |
| Alabama | 4,168.7 | 5,768.6 | 7,747.3 | 85.8 | 6.4 | 6.7 | 6.1 |
| Kentucky | 6,298.1 | 8,647.2 | 13,076.7 | 107.6 | 7.6 | 6.5 | 8.6 |
| Mississippi | 2,694.2 | 3,546.6 | 5,008.3 | 85.9 | 6.4 | 5.7 | 7.1 |
| Tennessee | 8,856.8 | 12,965.5 | 18,696.8 | 111.1 | 7.8 | 7.9 | 7.6 |

| | | | | | | |
|---|---|---|---|---|---|---|
| West South Central | 36,372.8 | 53,965.2 | 76,812.7 | 111.2 | 7.8 | 8.2 | 7.3 |
| Arkansas | 3,443.2 | 5,459.1 | 9,364.9 | 172.0 | 10.5 | 9.7 | 11.4 |
| Louisiana | 5,291.6 | 7,160.9 | 9,413.1 | 77.9 | 5.9 | 6.2 | 5.6 |
| Oklahoma | 4,197.3 | 6,305.9 | 7,746.6 | 84.6 | 6.3 | 8.5 | 4.2 |
| Texas | 23,440.7 | 35,039.3 | 50,288.0 | 114.5 | 7.9 | 8.4 | 7.5 |
| West | 100,751.0 | 149,649.8 | 231,629.2 | 129.9 | 8.7 | 8.2 | 9.1 |
| Mountain | 20,140.2 | 28,085.7 | 43,694.3 | 117.0 | 8.1 | 6.9 | 9.2 |
| Arizona | 6,356.8 | 8,272.2 | 14,668.3 | 130.8 | 8.7 | 5.4 | 12.1 |
| Colorado | 6,124.9 | 8,964.3 | 12,613.2 | 105.9 | 7.5 | 7.9 | 7.1 |
| Idaho | 769.8 | 1,035.0 | 1,919.6 | 149.4 | 9.6 | 6.1 | 13.1 |
| Montana | 1,635.5 | 2,161.8 | 3,244.4 | 98.4 | 7.1 | 5.7 | 8.5 |
| New Mexico | 1,962.2 | 2,607.3 | 3,638.8 | 85.4 | 6.4 | 5.8 | 6.9 |
| Nevada | 828.0 | 1,268.5 | 2,558.8 | 209.0 | 11.9 | 8.9 | 15.1 |
| Utah | 2,182.0 | 3,355.4 | 4,219.4 | 93.4 | 6.8 | 9.0 | 4.7 |
| Wyoming | 281.1 | 421.2 | 831.8 | 195.9 | 11.5 | 8.4 | 14.6 |
| Pacific | 80,610.8 | 121,564.0 | 187,935.0 | 133.1 | 8.8 | 8.6 | 9.1 |
| Alaska | 840.4 | 1,574.2 | 2,174.2 | 158.7 | 10.0 | 13.4 | 6.7 |
| California | 61,321.0 | 70,935.0 | 141,415.5 | 130.6 | 8.7 | 3.0 | 14.8 |
| Hawaii | 2,405.3 | 3,928.5 | 4,988.4 | 107.4 | 7.6 | 10.3 | 4.9 |
| Oregon | 4,937.7 | 29,253.3 | 14,986.3 | 203.5 | 11.7 | 42.7 | −12.5 |
| Washington | 11,106.4 | 15,873.0 | 24,370.6 | 119.4 | 8.2 | 7.4 | 9.0 |
| U.S. Territories | 869.6 | 1,194.4 | 1,845.5 | 112.2 | 7.8 | 6.6 | 9.1 |

Source: Urban Institute, National Center for Charitable Statistics, Core Files (1995, 2000, 2005).
Notes: Reporting public charities include only organizations that both reported (filed IRS Forms 990) and were required to do so. The following were excluded: foreign organizations, government-associated organizations, organizations without state identifiers, and organizations excluded by the authors' discretion. Organizations not required to report include religious congregations and organizations with less than $25,000 in gross receipts. The sum of the percentages may not equal due to rounding. The average annual percentage change is a compound rate that assumes a constant growth rate over time.

**Table 5.23.** The 10 States with the Highest Growth in Total Revenue Reported by Public Charities, 1995–2005

| Rank | State | Total revenue for reporting public charities, 1995 ($ millions) | Total revenue for reporting public charities, 2005 ($ millions) | % change (inflation adjusted), 1995–2005 |
|------|-------|------|------|------|
| 1 | Nevada | 828.0 | 2,558.8 | 142.6 |
| 2 | Oregon | 4,937.7 | 14,986.3 | 138.3 |
| 3 | Wyoming | 281.1 | 831.8 | 132.3 |
| 4 | Arkansas | 3,443.2 | 9,364.9 | 113.5 |
| 5 | Maine | 2,802.1 | 7,533.3 | 111.0 |
| 6 | Alaska | 840.4 | 2,174.2 | 103.1 |
| 7 | Idaho | 769.8 | 1,919.6 | 95.8 |
| 8 | Nebraska | 2,891.0 | 7,064.9 | 91.8 |
| 9 | Wisconsin | 10,204.6 | 23,910.5 | 83.9 |
| 10 | Arizona | 6,356.8 | 14,668.3 | 81.1 |

*Source:* Urban Institute, National Center for Charitable Statistics, Core Files (1995, 2000, 2005).

regions, the West reported the greatest growth in public support, increasing from $19.0 billion in 1995 to $49.2 billion in 2005—an inflation-adjusted increase of 103.6 percent (table 5.24).

Expenses for all reporting public charities in the United States grew from $530.3 billion in 1995 to nearly $1.1 trillion in 2005, an increase of 98.7 percent (an inflation-adjusted 56.0 percent). The growth in total expenses across the states ranged from an inflation-adjusted 14.5 percent in North Dakota to an inflation-adjusted 141.5 percent in Oregon. When looking at the growth across census regions, the West reported the largest increase, 125.7 percent (an inflation-adjusted 77.2 percent) (table 5.26).

Total assets for reporting public charities increased from $843.2 billion in 1995 to nearly $2.0 trillion in 2005, a 134.3 percent increase, or an inflation-adjusted 83.9 percent increase. Across the states, the increase ranged from 23.9 percent in North Dakota to 211.8 percent in Delaware (both adjusted for inflation). Looking across the census regions shows the West exhibiting the greatest growth in assets over the 10-year period with a 150.8 percent increase (an inflation-adjusted 96.8 percent) (table 5.28).

Net assets for reporting public charities increased from $515.6 billion in 1995 to $1.2 trillion in 2005, an increase of 136.7 percent, or an inflation-adjusted 85.8 percent. Across the states, the increases ranged from an inflation-adjusted 31.4 percent in North Dakota to an inflation-adjusted 179.1 percent in Wyoming. The West saw the greatest growth in net assets when compared with the other census regions, increasing by an inflation-adjusted 114.3 percent (table 5.30).

**Table 5.24.** Change in Public Support for Reporting Public Charities by State, 1995, 2000, and 2005

| | Public Support ($ millions) | | | Total % Change | Average Annual % Change | | |
|---|---|---|---|---|---|---|---|
| | 1995 | 2000 | 2005 | 1995–2005 | 1995–2005 | 1995–2000 | 2000–2005 |
| United States | 106,761.8 | 173,463.0 | 243,710.8 | 128.3 | 8.6 | 10.2 | 7.0 |
| Northeast | 34,267.0 | 50,413.6 | 68,782.7 | 100.7 | 7.2 | 8.0 | 6.4 |
| New England | 10,935.4 | 17,509.9 | 24,230.2 | 121.6 | 8.3 | 9.9 | 6.7 |
| Connecticut | 2,063.6 | 3,168.9 | 5,552.7 | 169.1 | 10.4 | 9.0 | 11.9 |
| Massachusetts | 6,792.6 | 11,241.3 | 14,616.4 | 115.2 | 8.0 | 10.6 | 5.4 |
| Maine | 509.3 | 850.6 | 1,089.8 | 114.0 | 7.9 | 10.8 | 5.1 |
| New Hampshire | 463.6 | 743.0 | 1,010.0 | 117.9 | 8.1 | 9.9 | 6.3 |
| Rhode Island | 790.9 | 1,020.3 | 1,369.7 | 73.2 | 5.6 | 5.2 | 6.1 |
| Vermont | 315.3 | 485.9 | 591.6 | 87.6 | 6.5 | 9.0 | 4.0 |
| Middle Atlantic | 23,331.5 | 32,903.8 | 44,552.4 | 91.0 | 6.7 | 7.1 | 6.2 |
| New Jersey | 2,632.8 | 4,048.6 | 5,301.0 | 101.3 | 7.2 | 9.0 | 5.5 |
| New York | 15,057.6 | 20,172.4 | 26,894.9 | 78.6 | 6.0 | 6.0 | 5.9 |
| Pennsylvania | 5,641.1 | 8,682.8 | 12,356.6 | 119.0 | 8.2 | 9.0 | 7.3 |
| Midwest | 21,770.0 | 34,286.2 | 44,946.7 | 106.5 | 7.5 | 9.5 | 5.6 |
| East North Central | 14,997.7 | 23,656.9 | 32,024.8 | 113.5 | 7.9 | 9.5 | 6.2 |
| Illinois | 5,030.5 | 7,848.4 | 10,073.8 | 100.3 | 7.2 | 9.3 | 5.1 |
| Indiana | 1,709.0 | 2,962.0 | 3,418.4 | 100.0 | 7.2 | 11.6 | 2.9 |
| Michigan | 2,999.6 | 4,270.1 | 5,251.0 | 75.1 | 5.8 | 7.3 | 4.2 |
| Ohio | 3,923.1 | 6,243.6 | 10,305.3 | 162.7 | 10.1 | 9.7 | 10.5 |
| Wisconsin | 1,335.5 | 2,332.7 | 2,976.3 | 122.9 | 8.3 | 11.8 | 5.0 |

*(continued)*

**Table 5.24.** Change in Public Support for Reporting Public Charities by State, 1995, 2000, and 2005 *(continued)*

| | Public Support ($ millions) | | | Total % Change | Average Annual % Change | | |
|---|---|---|---|---|---|---|---|
| | 1995 | 2000 | 2005 | 1995–2005 | 1995–2005 | 1995–2000 | 2000–2005 |
| West North Central | 6,772.3 | 10,629.3 | 12,921.9 | 90.8 | 6.7 | 9.4 | 4.0 |
| Iowa | 768.0 | 1,172.9 | 1,260.2 | 64.1 | 5.1 | 8.8 | 1.4 |
| Kansas | 640.2 | 1,025.0 | 1,316.0 | 105.6 | 7.5 | 9.9 | 5.1 |
| Minnesota | 2,283.6 | 3,395.0 | 4,071.5 | 78.3 | 6.0 | 8.3 | 3.7 |
| Missouri | 2,135.3 | 3,618.1 | 4,366.5 | 104.5 | 7.4 | 11.1 | 3.8 |
| North Dakota | 141.2 | 198.7 | 266.5 | 88.8 | 6.6 | 7.1 | 6.0 |
| Nebraska | 562.0 | 861.6 | 1,158.4 | 106.1 | 7.5 | 8.9 | 6.1 |
| South Dakota | 242.0 | 358.0 | 482.8 | 99.5 | 7.2 | 8.1 | 6.2 |
| South | 31,449.3 | 53,772.1 | 80,340.5 | 155.5 | 9.8 | 11.3 | 8.4 |
| South Atlantic | 20,654.6 | 35,631.6 | 55,270.2 | 167.6 | 10.3 | 11.5 | 9.2 |
| District of Columbia | 3,850.4 | 7,048.1 | 11,109.9 | 188.5 | 11.2 | 12.9 | 9.5 |
| Delaware | 241.9 | 395.4 | 562.0 | 132.3 | 8.8 | 10.3 | 7.3 |
| Florida | 4,117.9 | 7,054.9 | 11,717.7 | 184.6 | 11.0 | 11.4 | 10.7 |
| Georgia | 3,352.1 | 5,270.9 | 7,504.1 | 123.9 | 8.4 | 9.5 | 7.3 |
| Maryland | 2,166.1 | 3,640.4 | 5,276.7 | 143.6 | 9.3 | 10.9 | 7.7 |
| North Carolina | 2,329.9 | 4,655.1 | 7,123.6 | 205.7 | 11.8 | 14.8 | 8.9 |
| South Carolina | 791.8 | 1,170.3 | 1,730.0 | 118.5 | 8.1 | 8.1 | 8.1 |
| Virginia | 3,444.6 | 5,814.6 | 9,432.6 | 173.8 | 10.6 | 11.0 | 10.2 |
| West Virginia | 359.8 | 581.9 | 813.6 | 126.1 | 8.5 | 10.1 | 6.9 |
| East South Central | 3,911.0 | 6,480.5 | 8,600.7 | 119.9 | 8.2 | 10.6 | 5.8 |
| Alabama | 805.7 | 1,304.8 | 1,681.0 | 108.6 | 7.6 | 10.1 | 5.2 |
| Kentucky | 837.1 | 1,377.2 | 1,841.0 | 119.9 | 8.2 | 10.5 | 6.0 |

| | | | | | | | |
|---|---|---|---|---|---|---|---|
| Mississippi | 498.5 | 843.9 | 1,047.2 | 110.1 | 7.7 | 11.1 | 4.4 |
| Tennessee | 1,769.8 | 2,954.5 | 4,031.4 | 127.8 | 8.6 | 10.8 | 6.4 |
| West South Central | 6,883.6 | 11,660.0 | 16,469.7 | 139.3 | 9.1 | 11.1 | 7.2 |
| Arkansas | 536.2 | 799.6 | 1,152.1 | 114.9 | 7.9 | 8.3 | 7.6 |
| Louisiana | 864.7 | 1,246.8 | 1,741.6 | 101.4 | 7.3 | 7.6 | 6.9 |
| Oklahoma | 954.3 | 1,785.8 | 2,523.4 | 164.4 | 10.2 | 13.4 | 7.2 |
| Texas | 4,528.4 | 7,827.7 | 11,052.6 | 144.1 | 9.3 | 11.6 | 7.1 |
| West | 18,959.6 | 34,656.5 | 49,184.0 | 159.4 | 10.0 | 12.8 | 7.3 |
| Mountain | 4,290.1 | 7,008.8 | 10,309.3 | 140.3 | 9.2 | 10.3 | 8.0 |
| Arizona | 1,300.7 | 1,962.8 | 3,163.1 | 143.2 | 9.3 | 8.6 | 10.0 |
| Colorado | 1,521.4 | 2,428.4 | 3,554.5 | 133.6 | 8.9 | 9.8 | 7.9 |
| Idaho | 153.4 | 255.7 | 375.5 | 144.8 | 9.4 | 10.8 | 8.0 |
| Montana | 246.9 | 387.8 | 541.1 | 119.2 | 8.2 | 9.5 | 6.9 |
| New Mexico | 463.1 | 748.4 | 1,009.4 | 117.9 | 8.1 | 10.1 | 6.2 |
| Nevada | 174.2 | 403.1 | 617.2 | 254.2 | 13.5 | 18.3 | 8.9 |
| Utah | 310.6 | 623.6 | 714.6 | 130.1 | 8.7 | 15.0 | 2.8 |
| Wyoming | 119.8 | 198.9 | 334.2 | 178.9 | 10.8 | 10.7 | 10.9 |
| Pacific | 14,669.5 | 27,647.7 | 38,874.7 | 165.0 | 10.2 | 13.5 | 7.1 |
| Alaska | 500.8 | 969.1 | 1,211.9 | 142.0 | 9.2 | 14.1 | 4.6 |
| California | 10,865.6 | 20,927.1 | 29,207.2 | 168.8 | 10.4 | 14.0 | 6.9 |
| Hawaii | 478.8 | 720.2 | 873.6 | 82.5 | 6.2 | 8.5 | 3.9 |
| Oregon | 868.7 | 1,538.4 | 2,415.6 | 178.1 | 10.8 | 12.1 | 9.4 |
| Washington | 1,955.6 | 3,492.9 | 5,166.4 | 164.2 | 10.2 | 12.3 | 8.1 |
| U.S. Territories | 316.0 | 334.5 | 456.9 | 44.6 | 3.8 | 1.1 | 6.4 |

*Source:* Urban Institute, National Center for Charitable Statistics, Core Files (1995, 2000, 2005).
*Notes:* Reporting public charities include only organizations that both reported (filed IRS Forms 990) and were required to do so. The following were excluded: foreign organizations, government-associated organizations, organizations without state identifiers, and organizations excluded by the authors' discretion. Organizations not required to report include religious congregations and organizations with less than $25,000 in gross receipts. The sum of the percentages may not equal due to rounding. The average annual percentage change is a compound rate that assumes a constant growth rate over time (see chapter 5, appendix A, for details).

**Table 5.25.** The 10 States with the Highest Growth in Public Support Reported by Public Charities, 1995–2005

| Rank | State | Public support for reporting public charities, 1995 ($ millions) | Public support for reporting public charities, 2005 ($ millions) | % change (inflation adjusted), 1995–2005 |
|---|---|---|---|---|
| 1 | Nevada | 174.2 | 617.2 | 178.1 |
| 2 | North Carolina | 2,329.9 | 7,123.6 | 140.0 |
| 3 | District of Columbia | 3,850.4 | 11,109.9 | 126.5 |
| 4 | Florida | · 4,117.9 | 11,717.7 | 123.4 |
| 5 | Wyoming | 119.8 | 334.2 | 119.0 |
| 6 | Oregon | 868.7 | 2,415.6 | 118.3 |
| 7 | Virginia | 3,444.6 | 9,432.6 | 115.0 |
| 8 | Connecticut | 2,063.6 | 5,552.7 | 111.2 |
| 9 | California | 10,865.6 | 29,207.2 | 111.0 |
| 10 | Oklahoma | 954.3 | 2,523.4 | 107.6 |

*Source:* Urban Institute, National Center for Charitable Statistics, Core Files (1995, 2000, 2005).

## Summary

- In 2005, approximately 1.4 million organizations were registered with the IRS. Of these 1.4 million, the vast majority (876,164) were registered as 501(c)(3) public charities.
- Reporting public charities (the 323,530 public charities with over $25,000 in annual gross receipts) spent $1.1 trillion and held nearly $2 trillion in assets in 2005.
- The majority of public charities, however, are relatively small, reporting less than $500,000 in expenses. In 2005, 45.6 percent reported less than $100,000 in expenses and another 28.8 percent reported between $100,000 and $499,999 in expenses.
- Forty-nine percent of reporting public charities report a founding date after 1993.
- Human service public charities, which include organizations that provide job training, legal aid, housing and disaster assistance, youth development, and food distribution programs, account for nearly one-third of public charities. Education organizations account for the second largest proportion of public charities with 18.7 percent.
- Among revenue sources for all public charities, fees for services and goods, which include tuition payments, hospital patient revenues, and ticket sales, accounted for 70.3 percent of total revenue in 2005. Excluding hospitals and higher education organizations shows a different picture, however. The remaining organizations are less dependent on fees for goods and services and more dependent on private contributions and government grants.

**Table 5.26.** Change in Total Expenses for Reporting Public Charities by State, 1995, 2000, and 2005

| | Total Expenses ($ millions) | | | Total % Change | Average Annual % Change | | |
| | 1995 | 2000 | 2005 | 1995–2005 | 1995–2005 | 1995–2000 | 2000–2005 |
|---|---|---|---|---|---|---|---|
| United States | 530,278.5 | 730,761.5 | 1,053,487.3 | 98.7 | 7.1 | 6.6 | 7.6 |
| Northeast | 167,479.9 | 217,523.8 | 298,464.1 | 78.2 | 5.9 | 5.4 | 6.5 |
| New England | 47,318.3 | 70,275.5 | 95,741.7 | 102.3 | 7.3 | 8.2 | 6.4 |
| Connecticut | 10,193.0 | 13,740.3 | 19,504.3 | 91.3 | 6.7 | 6.2 | 7.3 |
| Massachusetts | 26,581.1 | 41,183.8 | 54,408.7 | 104.7 | 7.4 | 9.2 | 5.7 |
| Maine | 2,636.6 | 4,481.3 | 6,931.9 | 162.9 | 10.1 | 11.2 | 9.1 |
| New Hampshire | 2,925.9 | 3,978.0 | 6,111.7 | 108.9 | 7.6 | 6.3 | 9.0 |
| Rhode Island | 3,623.3 | 5,039.7 | 6,104.7 | 68.5 | 5.4 | 6.8 | 3.9 |
| Vermont | 1,358.4 | 1,852.3 | 2,680.4 | 97.3 | 7.0 | 6.4 | 7.7 |
| Middle Atlantic | 120,161.6 | 147,248.3 | 202,722.4 | 68.7 | 5.4 | 4.1 | 6.6 |
| New Jersey | 17,435.8 | 23,078.7 | 29,866.6 | 71.3 | 5.5 | 5.8 | 5.3 |
| New York | 62,466.0 | 77,736.1 | 109,135.5 | 74.7 | 5.7 | 4.5 | 7.0 |
| Pennsylvania | 40,259.8 | 46,433.5 | 63,720.3 | 58.3 | 4.7 | 2.9 | 6.5 |
| Midwest | 129,849.3 | 178,136.2 | 250,689.8 | 93.1 | 6.8 | 6.5 | 7.1 |
| East North Central | 91,202.4 | 122,204.2 | 174,733.0 | 91.6 | 6.7 | 6.0 | 7.4 |
| Illinois | 27,248.2 | 36,096.1 | 49,213.9 | 80.6 | 6.1 | 5.8 | 6.4 |
| Indiana | 11,209.3 | 15,210.6 | 21,602.0 | 92.7 | 6.8 | 6.3 | 7.3 |
| Michigan | 19,990.6 | 26,038.0 | 32,812.2 | 64.1 | 5.1 | 5.4 | 4.7 |
| Ohio | 23,312.0 | 30,411.4 | 48,983.2 | 110.1 | 7.7 | 5.5 | 10.0 |
| Wisconsin | 9,442.4 | 14,448.0 | 22,121.7 | 134.3 | 8.9 | 8.9 | 8.9 |

*(continued)*

**Table 5.26.** Change in Total Expenses for Reporting Public Charities by State, 1995, 2000, and 2005 *(continued)*

| | Total Expenses ($ millions) | | | Total % Change | Average Annual % Change | | |
|---|---|---|---|---|---|---|---|
| | 1995 | 2000 | 2005 | 1995–2005 | 1995–2005 | 1995–2000 | 2000–2005 |
| West North Central | 38,646.9 | 55,932.1 | 75,956.8 | 96.5 | 7.0 | 7.7 | 6.3 |
| Iowa | 5,153.8 | 6,676.7 | 8,628.9 | 67.4 | 5.3 | 5.3 | 5.3 |
| Kansas | 3,534.3 | 5,196.8 | 6,780.2 | 91.8 | 6.7 | 8.0 | 5.5 |
| Minnesota | 10,642.6 | 15,979.1 | 24,177.7 | 127.2 | 8.6 | 8.5 | 8.6 |
| Missouri | 13,073.4 | 17,550.1 | 23,529.9 | 80.0 | 6.1 | 6.1 | 6.0 |
| North Dakota | 1,820.5 | 2,877.8 | 2,655.5 | 45.9 | 3.8 | 9.6 | –1.6 |
| Nebraska | 2,569.3 | 4,809.4 | 6,538.3 | 154.5 | 9.8 | 13.4 | 6.3 |
| South Dakota | 1,852.9 | 2,842.0 | 3,646.4 | 96.8 | 7.0 | 8.9 | 5.1 |
| South | 137,576.2 | 196,550.7 | 289,196.5 | 110.2 | 7.7 | 7.4 | 8.0 |
| South Atlantic | 83,763.1 | 119,021.1 | 176,349.8 | 110.5 | 7.7 | 7.3 | 8.2 |
| District of Columbia | 9,454.4 | 15,237.1 | 19,459.4 | 105.8 | 7.5 | 10.0 | 5.0 |
| Delaware | 1,065.3 | 1,515.7 | 2,423.5 | 127.5 | 8.6 | 7.3 | 9.8 |
| Florida | 19,480.0 | 29,192.5 | 42,726.1 | 119.3 | 8.2 | 8.4 | 7.9 |
| Georgia | 11,505.5 | 16,501.3 | 24,910.1 | 116.5 | 8.0 | 7.5 | 8.6 |
| Maryland | 10,644.4 | 14,448.0 | 22,606.6 | 112.4 | 7.8 | 6.3 | 9.4 |
| North Carolina | 11,801.6 | 16,949.4 | 25,524.7 | 116.3 | 8.0 | 7.5 | 8.5 |
| South Carolina | 4,268.8 | 5,088.5 | 7,476.3 | 75.1 | 5.8 | 3.6 | 8.0 |
| Virginia | 12,414.4 | 16,201.0 | 26,057.9 | 109.9 | 7.7 | 5.5 | 10.0 |
| West Virginia | 3,128.7 | 3,887.5 | 5,165.1 | 65.1 | 5.1 | 4.4 | 5.8 |
| East South Central | 20,146.9 | 28,583.7 | 41,695.6 | 107.0 | 7.5 | 7.2 | 7.8 |
| Alabama | 3,821.2 | 5,399.4 | 7,115.8 | 86.2 | 6.4 | 7.2 | 5.7 |
| Kentucky | 5,790.0 | 8,097.9 | 12,378.3 | 113.8 | 7.9 | 6.9 | 8.9 |

| | | | | | | |
|---|---|---|---|---|---|---|
| Mississippi | 2,486.3 | 3,223.9 | 89.6 | 6.6 | 4,713.5 | 5.3 | 7.9 |
| Tennessee | 8,049.4 | 11,862.5 | 117.3 | 8.1 | 17,487.9 | 8.1 | 8.1 |
| West South Central | 33,666.2 | 48,945.9 | 111.3 | 7.8 | 71,151.2 | 7.8 | 7.8 |
| Arkansas | 3,240.6 | 5,212.4 | 178.8 | 10.8 | 9,036.4 | 10.0 | 11.6 |
| Louisiana | 4,906.8 | 6,657.9 | 82.5 | 6.2 | 8,953.1 | 6.3 | 6.1 |
| Oklahoma | 3,979.8 | 5,711.3 | 72.0 | 5.6 | 6,844.3 | 7.5 | 3.7 |
| Texas | 21,539.0 | 31,364.2 | 115.0 | 8.0 | 46,317.4 | 7.8 | 8.1 |
| West | 94,549.2 | 137,394.4 | 125.7 | 8.5 | 213,382.9 | 7.8 | 9.2 |
| Mountain | 18,587.9 | 25,898.5 | 114.0 | 7.9 | 39,785.2 | 6.9 | 9.0 |
| Arizona | 5,870.8 | 7,826.3 | 128.4 | 8.6 | 13,411.0 | 5.9 | 11.4 |
| Colorado | 5,687.8 | 8,016.0 | 102.2 | 7.3 | 11,501.2 | 7.1 | 7.5 |
| Idaho | 684.2 | 928.2 | 158.2 | 9.9 | 1,766.4 | 6.3 | 13.7 |
| Montana | 1,508.8 | 2,026.3 | 100.5 | 7.2 | 3,024.8 | 6.1 | 8.3 |
| New Mexico | 1,802.4 | 2,454.9 | 87.0 | 6.5 | 3,371.1 | 6.4 | 6.5 |
| Nevada | 749.6 | 1,118.0 | 179.2 | 10.8 | 2,092.9 | 8.3 | 13.4 |
| Utah | 2,041.8 | 3,188.5 | 89.9 | 6.6 | 3,877.0 | 9.3 | 4.0 |
| Wyoming | 242.5 | 340.3 | 205.5 | 11.8 | 740.8 | 7.0 | 16.8 |
| Pacific | 75,961.3 | 111,495.9 | 128.5 | 8.6 | 173,597.8 | 8.0 | 9.3 |
| Alaska | 760.6 | 1,404.9 | 171.6 | 10.5 | 2,066.2 | 13.1 | 8.0 |
| California | 58,039.1 | 63,426.8 | 124.7 | 8.4 | 130,399.7 | 1.8 | 15.5 |
| Hawaii | 2,129.3 | 2,989.0 | 101.0 | 7.2 | 4,279.0 | 7.0 | 7.4 |
| Oregon | 4,618.2 | 29,147.2 | 207.7 | 11.9 | 14,210.4 | 44.6 | −13.4 |
| Washington | 10,414.1 | 14,528.1 | 117.4 | 8.1 | 22,642.5 | 6.9 | 9.3 |
| U.S. Territories | 824.0 | 1,156.4 | 112.9 | 7.8 | 1,754.0 | 7.0 | 8.7 |

*Source:* Urban Institute, National Center for Charitable Statistics, Core Files (1995, 2000, 2005).
*Notes:* Reporting public charities include only organizations that both reported (filed IRS Forms 990) and were required to do so. The following were excluded: foreign organizations, government-associated organizations, organizations without state identifiers, and organizations excluded by the authors' discretion. Organizations not required to report include religious congregations and organizations with less than $25,000 in gross receipts. The sum of the percentages may not equal due to rounding. The average annual percentage change is a compound rate that assumes a constant growth rate over time (see chapter 5, appendix A, for details).

**Table 5.27.** The 10 States with the Highest Growth in Expenses Reported by Public Charities, 1995–2005

| Rank | State | Total expenses for reporting public charities, 1995 ($ millions) | Total expenses for reporting public charities, 2005 ($ millions) | % change (inflation adjusted), 1995–2005 |
|------|-------|-----|-----|-----|
| 1 | Oregon | 4,618.2 | 14,210.4 | 141.5 |
| 2 | Wyoming | 242.5 | 740.8 | 139.8 |
| 3 | Nevada | 749.6 | 2,092.9 | 119.2 |
| 4 | Arkansas | 3,240.6 | 9,036.4 | 118.9 |
| 5 | Alaska | 760.6 | 2,066.2 | 113.2 |
| 6 | Maine | 2,636.6 | 6,931.9 | 106.4 |
| 7 | Idaho | 684.2 | 1,766.4 | 102.7 |
| 8 | Nebraska | 2,569.3 | 6,538.3 | 99.8 |
| 9 | Wisconsin | 9,442.4 | 22,121.7 | 83.9 |
| 10 | Arizona | 5,870.8 | 13,411.0 | 79.3 |

*Source:* Urban Institute, National Center for Charitable Statistics, Core Files (1995, 2000, 2005).

- The number of public charities grew from 187,038 in 1995 to 323,530 in 2005, an increase of 73.0 percent. Over this same 10-year period, revenues grew by 100.0 percent (an inflation-adjusted 57.0 percent), public support grew by 129.5 percent (an inflation-adjusted 80.1 percent), expenses grew by 99.3 percent (an inflation-adjusted 56.4 percent), and assets grew by 134.6 percent (an inflation-adjusted 84.1 percent).
- The number of reporting public charities per state ranged from 914 in Wyoming to 37,559 in California. Not surprisingly, the number of reporting public charities in a state appears to be directly correlated with its population.
- The density of reporting public charities per state ranged from 5.9 public charities per 10,000 residents in Nevada to 26.9 public charities per 10,000 residents in Vermont.
- The top 10 states in growth in number of reporting public charities from 1995 to 2005 were all in the top 15 states in population growth during this same time.

**Table 5.28.** Change in Total Assets for Reporting Public Charities by State, 1995, 2000, and 2005

| | Total Assets ($ millions) | | | Total % Change | Average Annual % Change | | |
|---|---|---|---|---|---|---|---|
| | 1995 | 2000 | 2005 | 1995–2005 | 1995–2005 | 1995–2000 | 2000–2005 |
| United States | 843,173.7 | 1,432,919.2 | 1,975,791.8 | 134.3 | 8.9 | 11.2 | 6.6 |
| Northeast | 273,055.3 | 462,860.6 | 618,795.8 | 126.6 | 8.5 | 11.1 | 6.0 |
| New England | 105,109.3 | 197,758.3 | 269,270.9 | 156.2 | 9.9 | 13.5 | 6.4 |
| Connecticut | 30,784.8 | 59,696.6 | 62,631.2 | 103.4 | 7.4 | 14.2 | 1.0 |
| Massachusetts | 57,109.0 | 107,438.1 | 167,393.6 | 193.1 | 11.4 | 13.5 | 9.3 |
| Maine | 3,997.7 | 7,414.6 | 10,070.5 | 151.9 | 9.7 | 13.2 | 6.3 |
| New Hampshire | 5,704.6 | 10,905.0 | 14,762.2 | 158.8 | 10.0 | 13.8 | 6.2 |
| Rhode Island | 5,438.1 | 8,594.0 | 9,592.7 | 76.4 | 5.8 | 9.6 | 2.2 |
| Vermont | 2,075.2 | 3,710.0 | 4,820.7 | 132.3 | 8.8 | 12.3 | 5.4 |
| Middle Atlantic | 167,946.0 | 265,102.3 | 349,524.8 | 108.1 | 7.6 | 9.6 | 5.7 |
| New Jersey | 23,301.3 | 39,713.7 | 53,772.7 | 130.8 | 8.7 | 11.3 | 6.2 |
| New York | 89,474.5 | 134,956.5 | 176,579.7 | 97.4 | 7.0 | 8.6 | 5.5 |
| Pennsylvania | 55,170.2 | 90,432.2 | 119,172.5 | 116.0 | 8.0 | 10.4 | 5.7 |
| Midwest | 208,433.8 | 344,653.0 | 470,957.9 | 126.0 | 8.5 | 10.6 | 6.4 |
| East North Central | 143,286.6 | 238,877.3 | 321,192.4 | 124.2 | 8.4 | 10.8 | 6.1 |
| Illinois | 45,709.1 | 76,569.6 | 100,264.9 | 119.4 | 8.2 | 10.9 | 5.5 |
| Indiana | 19,352.2 | 34,352.2 | 42,170.0 | 117.9 | 8.1 | 12.2 | 4.2 |
| Michigan | 23,404.9 | 37,001.0 | 52,878.9 | 125.9 | 8.5 | 9.6 | 7.4 |
| Ohio | 41,184.0 | 67,750.4 | 89,661.6 | 117.7 | 8.1 | 10.5 | 5.8 |
| Wisconsin | 13,636.3 | 23,204.2 | 36,217.0 | 165.6 | 10.3 | 11.2 | 9.3 |

*(continued)*

**Table 5.28.** Change in Total Assets for Reporting Public Charities by State, 1995, 2000, and 2005 *(continued)*

| | Total Assets ($ millions) | | | Total % Change | Average Annual % Change | | |
| | 1995 | 2000 | 2005 | 1995–2005 | 1995–2005 | 1995–2000 | 2000–2005 |
|---|---|---|---|---|---|---|---|
| West North Central | 65,147.2 | 105,775.7 | 149,765.5 | 129.9 | 8.7 | 10.2 | 7.2 |
| Iowa | 9,209.4 | 13,665.9 | 19,798.9 | 115.0 | 8.0 | 8.2 | 7.7 |
| Kansas | 4,802.2 | 7,877.5 | 10,597.6 | 120.7 | 8.2 | 10.4 | 6.1 |
| Minnesota | 17,853.2 | 29,746.3 | 45,622.2 | 155.5 | 9.8 | 10.7 | 8.9 |
| Missouri | 21,875.9 | 36,759.6 | 52,285.3 | 139.0 | 9.1 | 10.9 | 7.3 |
| North Dakota | 2,116.2 | 4,438.1 | 3,340.9 | 57.9 | 4.7 | 16.0 | -5.5 |
| Nebraska | 5,886.0 | 9,155.5 | 12,232.7 | 107.8 | 7.6 | 9.2 | 6.0 |
| South Dakota | 3,404.4 | 4,132.9 | 5,887.8 | 72.9 | 5.6 | 4.0 | 7.3 |
| South | 229,794.1 | 396,801.0 | 557,503.3 | 142.6 | 9.3 | 11.5 | 7.0 |
| South Atlantic | 142,154.0 | 245,171.9 | 350,004.1 | 146.2 | 9.4 | 11.5 | 7.4 |
| District of Columbia | 12,843.2 | 24,720.1 | 32,937.8 | 156.5 | 9.9 | 14.0 | 5.9 |
| Delaware | 3,051.8 | 4,881.4 | 12,121.1 | 297.2 | 14.8 | 9.8 | 19.9 |
| Florida | 32,135.8 | 50,323.5 | 71,054.1 | 121.1 | 8.3 | 9.4 | 7.1 |
| Georgia | 18,486.5 | 35,379.1 | 48,237.2 | 160.9 | 10.1 | 13.9 | 6.4 |
| Maryland | 24,580.7 | 40,131.7 | 51,652.4 | 110.1 | 7.7 | 10.3 | 5.2 |
| North Carolina | 19,118.5 | 36,734.4 | 52,589.4 | 175.1 | 10.6 | 14.0 | 7.4 |
| South Carolina | 7,246.1 | 11,897.0 | 17,129.8 | 136.4 | 9.0 | 10.4 | 7.6 |
| Virginia | 21,053.3 | 35,874.0 | 57,496.2 | 173.1 | 10.6 | 11.2 | 9.9 |
| West Virginia | 3,638.0 | 5,230.6 | 6,786.1 | 86.5 | 6.4 | 7.5 | 5.3 |
| East South Central | 31,358.6 | 54,018.2 | 76,702.1 | 144.6 | 9.4 | 11.5 | 7.3 |
| Alabama | 6,040.8 | 10,299.3 | 12,826.7 | 112.3 | 7.8 | 11.3 | 4.5 |
| Kentucky | 8,151.9 | 14,007.6 | 19,425.8 | 138.3 | 9.1 | 11.4 | 6.8 |

| | | | | | | |
|---|---|---|---|---|---|---|
| Mississippi | 3,545.3 | 5,862.9 | 7,810.7 | 120.3 | 8.2 | 10.6 | 5.9 |
| Tennessee | 13,620.6 | 23,848.4 | 36,639.0 | 169.0 | 10.4 | 11.9 | 9.0 |
| West South Central | 56,281.6 | 97,610.9 | 130,797.1 | 132.4 | 8.8 | 11.6 | 6.0 |
| Arkansas | 3,442.8 | 5,828.1 | 7,708.3 | 123.9 | 8.4 | 11.1 | 5.8 |
| Louisiana | 8,151.8 | 11,982.0 | 14,428.0 | 77.0 | 5.9 | 8.0 | 3.8 |
| Oklahoma | 6,660.6 | 11,079.5 | 14,897.2 | 123.7 | 8.4 | 10.7 | 6.1 |
| Texas | 38,026.4 | 68,721.3 | 93,763.6 | 146.6 | 9.4 | 12.6 | 6.4 |
| West | 129,547.4 | 225,532.1 | 324,853.8 | 150.8 | 9.6 | 11.7 | 7.6 |
| Mountain | 25,743.8 | 44,031.7 | 64,290.9 | 149.7 | 9.6 | 11.3 | 7.9 |
| Arizona | 6,816.6 | 10,779.5 | 16,846.4 | 147.1 | 9.5 | 9.6 | 9.3 |
| Colorado | 8,213.1 | 15,854.5 | 21,139.8 | 157.4 | 9.9 | 14.1 | 5.9 |
| Idaho | 1,212.3 | 2,098.2 | 2,806.8 | 131.5 | 8.8 | 11.6 | 6.0 |
| Montana | 2,264.6 | 3,341.3 | 5,429.1 | 139.7 | 9.1 | 8.1 | 10.2 |
| New Mexico | 2,876.5 | 4,361.9 | 5,706.8 | 98.4 | 7.1 | 8.7 | 5.5 |
| Nevada | 1,718.6 | 2,625.5 | 4,438.6 | 158.3 | 10.0 | 8.8 | 11.1 |
| Utah | 2,148.0 | 3,987.3 | 6,187.3 | 188.1 | 11.2 | 13.2 | 9.2 |
| Wyoming | 494.1 | 983.5 | 1,736.0 | 251.4 | 13.4 | 14.8 | 12.0 |
| Pacific | 103,803.5 | 181,500.4 | 260,562.9 | 151.0 | 9.6 | 11.8 | 7.5 |
| Alaska | 974.1 | 1,698.1 | 2,825.4 | 190.1 | 11.2 | 11.8 | 10.7 |
| California | 78,003.4 | 121,016.4 | 197,119.1 | 152.7 | 9.7 | 9.2 | 10.2 |
| Hawaii | 5,223.4 | 10,549.6 | 12,693.5 | 143.0 | 9.3 | 15.1 | 3.8 |
| Oregon | 5,492.7 | 25,875.7 | 15,428.1 | 180.9 | 10.9 | 36.3 | −9.8 |
| Washington | 14,109.9 | 22,360.5 | 32,496.8 | 130.3 | 8.7 | 9.6 | 7.8 |
| U.S. Territories | 2,343.1 | 3,072.5 | 3,681.0 | 57.1 | 4.6 | 5.6 | 3.7 |

*Source:* Urban Institute, National Center for Charitable Statistics, Core Files (1995, 2000, 2005).
*Notes:* Reporting public charities include only organizations that both reported (filed IRS Forms 990) and were required to do so. The following were excluded: foreign organizations, government-associated organizations, organizations without state identifiers, and organizations excluded by the authors' discretion. Organizations not required to report include religious congregations and organizations with less than $25,000 in gross receipts. The sum of the percentages may not equal due to rounding. The average annual percentage change is a compound rate that assumes a constant growth rate over time.

**Table 5.29.** The 10 States with the Highest Growth in Assets Reported by Public Charities, 1995–2005

| Rank | State | Total assets for reporting public charities, 1995 ($ millions) | Total assets for reporting public charities, 2005 ($ millions) | % change (inflation adjusted), 1995–2005 |
|------|-------|------|------|------|
| 1 | Delaware | 3,051.8 | 12,121.1 | 211.8 |
| 2 | Wyoming | 494.1 | 1,736.0 | 175.8 |
| 3 | Massachusetts | 57,109.0 | 167,393.6 | 130.1 |
| 4 | Alaska | 974.1 | 2,825.4 | 127.7 |
| 5 | Utah | 2,148.0 | 6,187.3 | 126.1 |
| 6 | Oregon | 5,492.7 | 15,428.1 | 120.5 |
| 7 | North Carolina | 19,118.5 | 52,589.4 | 115.9 |
| 8 | Virginia | 21,053.3 | 57,496.2 | 114.4 |
| 9 | Tennessee | 13,620.6 | 36,639.0 | 111.2 |
| 10 | Wisconsin | 13,636.3 | 36,217.0 | 108.5 |

*Source:* Urban Institute, National Center for Charitable Statistics, Core Files (1995, 2000, 2005).

**Table 5.30.** Change in Net Assets for Reporting Public Charities by State, 1995, 2000, and 2005

| | Net Assets ($ millions) | | | Total % Change | Average Annual % Change | | |
|---|---|---|---|---|---|---|---|
| | 1995 | 2000 | 2005 | 1995–2005 | 1995–2005 | 1995–2000 | 2000–2005 |
| United States | 515,646.6 | 946,222.3 | 1,220,434.9 | 136.7 | 9.0 | 12.9 | 5.2 |
| Northeast | 169,003.2 | 320,619.8 | 393,706.9 | 133.0 | 8.8 | 13.7 | 4.2 |
| New England | 72,332.3 | 153,219.3 | 184,337.2 | 154.8 | 9.8 | 16.2 | 3.8 |
| Connecticut | 22,988.5 | 49,671.6 | 49,696.8 | 116.2 | 8.0 | 16.7 | 0.0 |
| Massachusetts | 37,991.6 | 82,277.7 | 108,494.6 | 185.6 | 11.1 | 16.7 | 5.7 |
| Maine | 2,364.5 | 4,817.2 | 6,894.7 | 191.6 | 11.3 | 15.3 | 7.4 |
| New Hampshire | 3,883.8 | 7,682.9 | 9,331.4 | 140.3 | 9.2 | 14.6 | 4.0 |
| Rhode Island | 3,751.9 | 6,173.5 | 6,611.8 | 76.2 | 5.8 | 10.5 | 1.4 |
| Vermont | 1,352.1 | 2,596.3 | 3,308.0 | 144.6 | 9.4 | 13.9 | 5.0 |
| Middle Atlantic | 96,670.8 | 167,400.5 | 209,369.7 | 116.6 | 8.0 | 11.6 | 4.6 |
| New Jersey | 13,521.7 | 25,282.0 | 32,474.1 | 140.2 | 9.2 | 13.3 | 5.1 |
| New York | 51,258.1 | 84,410.3 | 104,188.1 | 103.3 | 7.4 | 10.5 | 4.3 |
| Pennsylvania | 31,891.0 | 57,708.1 | 72,707.5 | 128.0 | 8.6 | 12.6 | 4.7 |
| Midwest | 124,673.4 | 224,973.5 | 283,528.5 | 127.4 | 8.6 | 12.5 | 4.7 |
| East North Central | 85,639.1 | 158,259.5 | 196,746.9 | 129.7 | 8.7 | 13.1 | 4.4 |
| Illinois | 27,651.0 | 50,994.9 | 61,468.8 | 122.3 | 8.3 | 13.0 | 3.8 |
| Indiana | 12,329.0 | 24,614.9 | 28,112.2 | 128.0 | 8.6 | 14.8 | 2.7 |
| Michigan | 12,892.9 | 22,190.9 | 29,458.1 | 128.5 | 8.6 | 11.5 | 5.8 |
| Ohio | 24,487.3 | 46,098.1 | 55,712.0 | 127.5 | 8.6 | 13.5 | 3.9 |
| Wisconsin | 8,278.8 | 14,360.8 | 21,995.8 | 165.7 | 10.3 | 11.6 | 8.9 |

*(continued)*

**Table 5.30.** Change in Net Assets for Reporting Public Charities by State, 1995, 2000, and 2005 (*continued*)

| | Net Assets ($ millions) | | | Total % Change | Average Annual % Change | | |
|---|---|---|---|---|---|---|---|
| | 1995 | 2000 | 2005 | 1995–2005 | 1995–2005 | 1995–2000 | 2000–2005 |
| West North Central | 39,034.4 | 66,714.0 | 86,781.6 | 122.3 | 8.3 | 11.3 | 5.4 |
| Iowa | 4,573.9 | 7,668.2 | 10,884.1 | 138.0 | 9.1 | 10.9 | 7.3 |
| Kansas | 2,886.8 | 4,727.2 | 6,339.8 | 119.6 | 8.2 | 10.4 | 6.0 |
| Minnesota | 10,625.4 | 18,272.1 | 23,246.1 | 118.8 | 8.1 | 11.5 | 4.9 |
| Missouri | 14,799.8 | 24,185.2 | 32,037.4 | 116.5 | 8.0 | 10.3 | 5.8 |
| North Dakota | 1,165.7 | 2,508.6 | 1,950.7 | 67.3 | 5.3 | 16.6 | -4.9 |
| Nebraska | 3,466.1 | 6,776.3 | 8,823.1 | 154.5 | 9.8 | 14.3 | 5.4 |
| South Dakota | 1,516.7 | 2,576.2 | 3,500.3 | 130.8 | 8.7 | 11.2 | 6.3 |
| South | 148,508.1 | 265,964.6 | 342,743.0 | 130.8 | 8.7 | 12.4 | 5.2 |
| South Atlantic | 91,579.3 | 166,174.9 | 216,815.1 | 136.8 | 9.0 | 12.7 | 5.5 |
| District of Columbia | 8,018.4 | 17,255.4 | 23,085.9 | 187.9 | 11.2 | 16.6 | 6.0 |
| Delaware | 1,853.8 | 3,163.1 | 3,993.2 | 115.4 | 8.0 | 11.3 | 4.8 |
| Florida | 19,345.0 | 31,747.8 | 42,083.7 | 117.5 | 8.1 | 10.4 | 5.8 |
| Georgia | 12,198.0 | 24,926.4 | 30,244.9 | 147.9 | 9.5 | 15.4 | 3.9 |
| Maryland | 16,895.1 | 27,497.0 | 33,630.5 | 99.1 | 7.1 | 10.2 | 4.1 |
| North Carolina | 12,724.8 | 25,156.7 | 34,954.0 | 174.7 | 10.6 | 14.6 | 6.8 |
| South Carolina | 4,542.3 | 7,362.4 | 8,945.3 | 96.9 | 7.0 | 10.1 | 4.0 |
| Virginia | 13,641.5 | 25,684.5 | 35,687.7 | 161.6 | 10.1 | 13.5 | 6.8 |
| West Virginia | 2,360.4 | 3,381.5 | 4,189.8 | 77.5 | 5.9 | 7.5 | 4.4 |
| East South Central | 19,702.5 | 33,990.5 | 42,936.1 | 117.9 | 8.1 | 11.5 | 4.8 |
| Alabama | 3,711.4 | 6,179.2 | 7,473.3 | 101.4 | 7.3 | 10.7 | 3.9 |
| Kentucky | 5,188.1 | 9,071.8 | 10,246.7 | 97.5 | 7.0 | 11.8 | 2.5 |

| | | | | | | | |
|---|---|---|---|---|---|---|---|
| Mississippi | 1,930.1 | 3,467.6 | 4,538.1 | 135.1 | 8.9 | 12.4 | 5.5 |
| Tennessee | 8,873.0 | 15,271.9 | 20,677.9 | 133.0 | 8.8 | 11.5 | 6.2 |
| West South Central | 37,226.3 | 65,799.3 | 82,991.8 | 122.9 | 8.3 | 12.1 | 4.8 |
| Arkansas | 2,248.9 | 4,099.9 | 5,512.6 | 145.1 | 9.4 | 12.8 | 6.1 |
| Louisiana | 5,223.2 | 7,646.6 | 8,903.9 | 70.5 | 5.5 | 7.9 | 3.1 |
| Oklahoma | 4,713.4 | 8,166.4 | 11,014.4 | 133.7 | 8.9 | 11.6 | 6.2 |
| Texas | 25,040.9 | 45,886.3 | 57,561.0 | 129.9 | 8.7 | 12.9 | 4.6 |
| West | 72,882.6 | 133,670.2 | 199,000.8 | 173.0 | 10.6 | 12.9 | 8.3 |
| Mountain | 13,962.4 | 25,455.5 | 40,077.5 | 187.0 | 11.1 | 12.8 | 9.5 |
| Arizona | 2,945.3 | 5,522.7 | 9,675.5 | 228.5 | 12.6 | 13.4 | 11.9 |
| Colorado | 4,946.6 | 9,215.9 | 14,357.6 | 190.3 | 11.2 | 13.3 | 9.3 |
| Idaho | 741.6 | 1,319.6 | 1,785.6 | 140.8 | 9.2 | 12.2 | 6.2 |
| Montana | 1,132.8 | 1,898.5 | 2,755.7 | 143.3 | 9.3 | 10.9 | 7.7 |
| New Mexico | 1,424.8 | 2,593.4 | 3,474.3 | 143.8 | 9.3 | 12.7 | 6.0 |
| Nevada | 1,185.8 | 1,831.4 | 3,021.7 | 154.8 | 9.8 | 9.1 | 10.5 |
| Utah | 1,270.3 | 2,476.2 | 3,886.8 | 206.0 | 11.8 | 14.3 | 9.4 |
| Wyoming | 315.1 | 597.8 | 1,120.3 | 255.5 | 13.5 | 13.7 | 13.4 |
| Pacific | 58,920.2 | 108,214.7 | 158,923.3 | 169.7 | 10.4 | 12.9 | 8.0 |
| Alaska | 597.5 | 1,102.5 | 1,909.8 | 219.6 | 12.3 | 13.0 | 11.6 |
| California | 42,579.5 | 72,446.9 | 117,286.6 | 175.5 | 10.7 | 11.2 | 10.1 |
| Hawaii | 3,874.1 | 8,638.5 | 9,682.1 | 149.9 | 9.6 | 17.4 | 2.3 |
| Oregon | 3,362.3 | 12,071.9 | 9,923.0 | 195.1 | 11.4 | 29.1 | −3.8 |
| Washington | 8,506.7 | 13,955.0 | 20,121.7 | 136.5 | 9.0 | 10.4 | 7.6 |
| U.S. Territories | 579.3 | 994.3 | 1,455.8 | 151.3 | 9.7 | 11.4 | 7.9 |

*Source*: Urban Institute, National Center for Charitable Statistics, Core Files (1995, 2000, 2005).
*Notes*: Reporting public charities include only organizations that both reported (filed IRS Forms 990) and were required to do so. The following were excluded: foreign organizations, government-associated organizations, organizations without state identifiers, and organizations excluded by the authors' discretion. Organizations not required to report include religious congregations and organizations with less than $25,000 in gross receipts. The sum of the percentages may not equal due to rounding. The average annual percentage change is a compound rate that assumes a constant growth rate over time.

**Table 5.31.** The 10 States with the Highest Growth in Net Assets Reported by Public Charities, 1995–2005

| Rank | State | Total net assets for reporting public charities, 1995 ($ millions) | Total net assets for reporting public charities, 2005 ($ millions) | % change (inflation adjusted), 1995–2005 |
|---|---|---|---|---|
| 1 | Wyoming | 315.1 | 1,120.3 | 179.1 |
| 2 | Arizona | 2,945.3 | 9,675.5 | 157.9 |
| 3 | Alaska | 597.5 | 1,909.8 | 150.9 |
| 4 | Utah | 1,270.3 | 3,886.8 | 140.2 |
| 5 | Oregon | 3,362.3 | 9,923.0 | 131.7 |
| 6 | Maine | 2,364.5 | 6,894.7 | 128.9 |
| 7 | Colorado | 4,946.6 | 14,357.6 | 127.8 |
| 8 | District of Columbia | 8,018.4 | 23,085.9 | 126.0 |
| 9 | Massachusetts | 37,991.6 | 108,494.6 | 124.4 |
| 10 | California | 42,579.5 | 117,286.6 | 116.2 |

*Source:* Urban Institute, National Center for Charitable Statistics, Core Files (1995, 2000, 2005).

# Technical Notes

For this chapter we used three primary datasets: (1) the IRS Business Master Files of Tax-Exempt Organizations, (2) a special research version of the NCCS Core Files that excludes organizations marked as "out of scope" by the authors, and (3) the NCCS-GuideStar National Nonprofit Research Database. Below are the descriptions of the three datasets as well as a description of the organizational classification system used throughout the chapter.

## IRS Business Master Files of Tax-Exempt Organizations, 1996–2006

The IRS Business Master Files (BMFs) are cumulative files containing descriptive information on all active tax-exempt organizations. Data contained on the BMFs are mostly derived from the IRS Forms 1023 and 1024 (the applications for IRS recognition of tax-exempt status). Organizations must apply for recognition, except religious congregations or those having less than $5,000 in annual gross receipts.

NCCS downloads BMFs semiannually; here, we used them for information on the number of nonprofits and filers contained in table 5.1. For each year reported—1995, 2000, and 2005—we used the BMF for the next year. For example, for the 1995 total nonprofit number, we used the 1996 BMF.

## NCCS Core Files

The NCCS Core Files dataset is based on the IRS's annual RTFs, which contain data on all organizations that were required to file a Form 990 or Form 990-EZ and complied. The IRS does not record financial data for approximately 80,000 organizations that filed a Form 990 but were not required to do so, either because they are religious congregations or because they received less than $25,000 in annual gross receipts. In addition, NCCS also excludes a few other organizations, such as foreign organizations or those generally considered part of government.

The NCCS Core Files (1995, 2000, and 2005) contain several key financial variables from the Form 990, including contributions, program revenue, total revenue, total expenses, and assets.

To create the datasets used for chapter 5, we excluded organizations we consider out of scope. These include mutual benefit organizations, foreign organizations, private foundations filing the wrong forms, organizations with missing geographical information, government-related organizations, and fundraising foundations controlled by public universities.

This special research version of the NCCS Core Files for 1995, 2000, and 2005 was used for all total financial figures; these files were used in conjunction with the NCCS-GuideStar National Nonprofit Research Database to estimate variables not included in the NCCS Core Files.

## NCCS-GuideStar National Nonprofit Research Database

The NCCS-GuideStar National Nonprofit Research Database includes all Forms 990 and Forms 990-EZ filed by 501(c)(3) organizations that are required to file with the IRS. GuideStar and its contractors manually entered most variables from the IRS forms, schedules, and attachments into the database. NCCS then checked the financial variables for accuracy and added organization-level descriptive variables, such as National Taxonomy of Exempt Entities–Core Codes classification, and geographic identifiers, such as county and metropolitan statistical area codes.

The NCCS-GuideStar national database contains more than 500 variables and allows more detailed financial analysis than the NCCS Core Files. The additional variables in this database include government-grant figures as well as functional expense variables. The latest data available in the NCCS-GuideStar national database are from 2003.

Data from the NCCS-GuideStar national database were used for the detailed subsector tables. While the NCCS Core Files served as the basis for these tables, the NCCS-GuideStar data for fiscal year 2003 were used to estimate 2005 figures for variables not available in the NCCS Core Files. For these tables, we assumed that the distribution of sources of revenue and types of expenses was similar in 2003 and 2005, and used revenue and expense ratios from the NCCS-GuideStar national database to estimate certain 2005 figures. (For a complete listing of variables available in the NCCS Core Files, go to http://nccsdataweb.urban.org/PubApps/showDD.php?section=Core%20Data. For the NCCS-GuideStar National database, go to http://nccsdataweb.urban.org/PubApps/showDD.php?section=Digitized%20Data.)

# Classification of Organizations

Tables in chapter 5 that group organizations into subsectors based on their primary activities use the National Taxonomy of Exempt Entities–Core Codes. Both summary and detailed information on this classification system is available at http://www.nccs.urban.org/classification/index.cfm. Also, a complete listing of the NTEE Core Codes used for each subsector breakout is available in appendix B.

While the vast majority of organizations are assigned a specific NTEE-CC code, a few are coded as unknown. This classification is normally temporary but may be permanent if no detailed information on the organization—a Form 990 with its program descriptions or a web site—is available.

# Classification of Organizations Based on the National Taxonomy of Exempt Entities–Core Codes

## Arts, Culture, and Humanities

### Performing Arts Organizations
A60—Performing Arts
A61—Performing Arts Centers
A62—Dance
A63—Ballet
A65—Theater
A68—Music
A69—Symphony Orchestra
A6A—Opera
A6B—Singing and Choral Groups
A6C—Bands and Ensembles
A6E—Performing Arts Schools

### Historical Societies and Related Organizations
A80—Historical Societies and Related Historical Activities
A84—Commemorative Events

### Museums and Museum Activities
A50—Museums and Museum Activities
A51—Art Museums
A52—Children's Museums
A54—History Museums
A56—Natural History and Natural Science Museums
A57—Science and Technology Museums

### Other Arts, Culture, and Humanities
A01—Alliances and Advocacy
A02—Management and Technical Assistance
A03—Professional Societies and Associations
A05—Research Institutes and Public Policy Analysis
A11—Single-Organization Support
A12—Fundraising and Fund Distribution
A19—Support n.e.c.
A20—Arts and Culture
A23—Cultural and Ethnic Awareness
A25—Arts Education
A26—Arts Councils and Agencies
A30—Media and Communications
A31—Film and Video
A32—Television
A33—Printing and Publishing
A34—Radio
A40—Visual Arts
A70—Humanities
A90—Arts Services
A99—Arts, Culture, and Humanities n.e.c.

## Education

### Higher Education
B40—Higher Education
B41—Two-Year Colleges
B42—Undergraduate Colleges
B43—Universities
B50—Graduate and Professional Schools

### Student Services
B80—Student Services
B82—Scholarships and Student Financial Aid
B83—Student Sororities and Fraternities
B84—Alumni Associations

**Elementary and Secondary Education**

B20—Elementary and Secondary Schools
B21—Preschools
B24—Primary and Elementary Schools
B25—Secondary and High Schools
B28—Special Education
B29—Charter Schools

**Other Education**

B01—Alliances and Advocacy
B02—Management and Technical Assistance
B03—Professional Societies and Associations
B05—Research Institutes and Public Policy Analysis
B11—Single-Organization Support
B12—Fundraising and Fund Distribution
B19—Support n.e.c.
B30—Vocational and Technical Schools
B60—Adult Education
B70—Libraries
B90—Educational Support
B92—Remedial Reading and Encouragement
B94—Parent and Teacher Groups
B99—Education n.e.c.

## Environment and Animals

**Environment**

C01—Alliances and Advocacy
C02—Management and Technical Assistance
C03—Professional Societies and Associations

C05—Research Institutes and Public Policy Analysis
C11—Single-Organization Support
C12—Fundraising and Fund Distribution
C19—Support n.e.c.
C20—Pollution Abatement and Control
C27—Recycling
C30—Natural Resources Conservation and Protection
C32—Water Resources, Wetlands Conservation and Management
C34—Land Resources and Conservation
C35—Energy Resources, Conservation and Development
C36—Forest Conservation
C40—Botanical, Horticultural, and Landscape Services
C41—Botanical Gardens and Arboreta
C42—Garden Clubs
C50—Environmental Beautification
C60—Environmental Education
C99—Environment n.e.c.

**Animals**

D01—Alliances and Advocacy
D02—Management and Technical Assistance
D03—Professional Societies and Associations
D05—Research Institutes and Public Policy Analysis
D11—Single-Organization Support
D12—Fundraising and Fund Distribution

D19—Support n.e.c.
D20—Animal Protection and Welfare
D30—Wildlife Preservation and Protection
D31—Protection of Endangered Species
D32—Bird Sanctuaries
D33—Fisheries Resources
D34—Wildlife Sanctuaries
D40—Veterinary Services
D50—Zoos and Aquariums
D60—Animal Services n.e.c.
D61—Animal Training
D99—Animal Related n.e.c.

## Health

**Nursing Services**

E90—Nursing
E91—Nursing Facilities
E92—Home Health Care

**Hospitals and Primary Treatment Facilities**

E20—Hospitals
E21—Community Health Systems
E22—General Hospitals
E24—Specialty Hospitals

**Outpatient Facilities**

E30—Ambulatory and Primary Health Care
E31—Group Health Practices
E32—Community Clinics

**Mental Health**

F01—Alliances and Advocacy
F02—Management and Technical Assistance
F03—Professional Societies and Associations
F05—Research Institutes and Public Policy Analysis

F11—Single-Organization Support

F12—Fundraising and Fund Distribution

F19—Support n.e.c.

F20—Substance Abuse Dependency, Prevention, and Treatment

F21—Substance Abuse Prevention

F22—Substance Abuse Treatment

F30—Mental Health Treatment

F31—Psychiatric Hospitals

F32—Community Mental Health Centers

F33—Residential Mental Health Treatment

F40—Hotlines and Crisis Intervention

F42—Sexual Assault Services

F50—Addictive Disorders

F52—Smoking Addiction

F53—Eating Disorders

F54—Gambling Addiction

F60—Counseling

F70—Mental Health Disorders

F80—Mental Health Associations

F99—Mental Health n.e.c.

## Disease Specific

G01—Alliances and Advocacy

G02—Management and Technical Assistance

G03—Professional Societies and Associations

G05—Research Institutes and Public Policy Analysis

G11—Single-Organization Support

G12—Fundraising and Fund Distribution

G19—Support n.e.c.

G20—Birth Defects and Genetic Diseases

G25—Down Syndrome

G30—Cancer

G32—Breast Cancer

G40—Diseases of Specific Organs

G41—Eye Diseases, Blindness, and Vision Impairments

G42—Ear and Throat Diseases

G43—Heart and Circulatory System Diseases and Disorders

G44—Kidney Diseases

G45—Lung Diseases

G48—Brain Disorders

G50—Nerve, Muscle, and Bone Diseases

G51—Arthritis

G54—Epilepsy

G60—Allergy-Related Diseases

G61—Asthma

G70—Digestive Diseases and Disorders

G80—Specifically Named Diseases

G81—AIDS

G82—Alzheimer's Disease

G84—Autism

G90—Medical Disciplines

G92—Biomedicine and Bioengineering

G94—Geriatrics

G96—Neurology and Neuroscience

G98—Pediatrics

G9B—Surgical Specialties

G99—Diseases, Disorders, and Medical Disciplines n.e.c.

## Medical Research

H01—Alliances and Advocacy

H02—Management and Technical Assistance

H03—Professional Societies and Associations

H05—Research Institutes and Public Policy Analysis

H11—Single-Organization Support

H12—Fundraising and Fund Distribution

H19—Support n.e.c.

H20—Birth Defects and Genetic Diseases Research

H25—Down Syndrome Research

H30—Cancer Research

H32—Breast Cancer Research

H40—Disease-Specific Research

H41—Eye Diseases, Blindness, and Vision Impairments Research

H42—Ear and Throat Diseases Research

H43—Heart and Circulatory System Diseases and Disorders Research

H44—Kidney Diseases Research

H45—Lung Diseases Research

H48—Brain Disorders Research

H50—Nerve, Muscle, and Bone Diseases Research

H51—Arthritis Research

H54—Epilepsy Research

H60—Allergy-Related Diseases Research

H61—Asthma Research

H70—Digestive Diseases and Disorders Research
H80—Specifically Named Diseases Research
H81—AIDS Research
H83—Alzheimer's Disease Research
H84—Autism Research
H90—Medical Discipline Research
H92—Biomedicine and Bioengineering Research
H94—Geriatrics Research
H96—Neurology and Neuroscience Research
H98—Pediatrics Research
H9B—Surgical Specialties Research
H99—Medical Research n.e.c.

## Other Health

E01—Alliances and Advocacy
E02—Management and Technical Assistance
E03—Professional Societies and Associations
E05—Research Institutes and Public Policy Analysis
E11—Single-Organization Support
E12—Fundraising and Fund Distribution
E19—Support n.e.c.
E40—Reproductive Health Care
E42—Family Planning
E50—Rehabilitative Care
E60—Health Support
E61—Blood Banks
E62—Emergency Medical Transport
E65—Organ and Tissue Banks

E70—Public Health
E80—Health (General and Financing)
E86—Patient and Family Support
E99—Health Care n.e.c.

# Human Service

## Crime and Legal Related

I01—Alliances and Advocacy
I02—Management and Technical Assistance
I03—Professional Societies and Associations
I05—Research Institutes and Public Policy Analysis
I11—Single-Organization Support
I12—Fundraising and Fund Distribution
I19—Support n.e.c.
I20—Crime Prevention
I21—Youth Violence Prevention
I23—Drunk Driving–Related
I30—Correctional Facilities
I31—Halfway Houses for Offenders and Ex-Offenders
I40—Rehabilitation Services for Offenders
I43—Inmate Support
I44—Prison Alternatives
I50—Administration of Justice
I51—Dispute Resolution and Mediation
I60—Law Enforcement
I70—Protection against Abuse
I71—Spouse Abuse Prevention
I72—Child Abuse Prevention
I73—Sexual Abuse Prevention
I80—Legal Services

I83—Public Interest Law
I99—Crime and Legal Related n.e.c.

## Employment and Job Related

J01—Alliances and Advocacy
J02—Management and Technical Assistance
J03—Professional Societies and Associations
J05—Research Institutes and Public Policy Analysis
J11—Single-Organization Support
J12—Fundraising and Fund Distribution
J19—Support n.e.c.
J20—Employment Preparation and Procurement
J21—Vocational Counseling
J22—Job Training
J30—Vocational Rehabilitation
J32—Goodwill Industries
J33—Sheltered Employment
J40—Labor Unions
J99—Employment n.e.c.

## Food, Agriculture, and Nutrition

K01—Alliances and Advocacy
K02—Management and Technical Assistance
K03—Professional Societies and Associations
K05—Research Institutes and Public Policy Analysis
K11—Single-Organization Support
K12—Fundraising and Fund Distribution
K19—Support n.e.c.
K20—Agricultural Programs
K25—Farmland Preservation

K26—Animal Husbandry
K28—Farm Bureaus
and Granges
K30—Food Programs
K31—Food Banks and Pantries
K34—Congregate Meals
K35—Soup Kitchens
K36—Meals on Wheels
K40—Nutrition
K50—Home Economics
K99—Food, Agriculture,
and Nutrition n.e.c.

## Housing and Shelter
L01—Alliances and Advocacy
L02—Management and
Technical Assistance
L03—Professional Societies
and Associations
L05—Research Institutes
and Public Policy Analysis
L11—Single-Organization
Support
L12—Fundraising and
Fund Distribution
L19—Support n.e.c.
L20—Housing Development,
Construction, and
Management
L21—Public Housing
L22—Senior Citizens' Housing
and Retirement Communities
L25—Housing Rehabilitation
L30—Housing Search
Assistance
L40—Temporary Housing
L41—Homeless Shelters
L50—Homeowners' and
Tenants' Associations
L80—Housing Support
L81—Home Improvement
and Repairs
L82—Housing Expense
Reduction

L99—Housing and
Shelter n.e.c.

## Public Safety and Disaster Preparedness
M01—Alliances and Advocacy
M02—Management and
Technical Assistance
M03—Professional Societies
and Associations
M05—Research Institutes
and Public Policy Analysis
M11—Single-Organization
Support
M12—Fundraising and
Fund Distribution
M19—Support n.e.c.
M20—Disaster Preparedness
and Relief Services
M23—Search and
Rescue Squads
M24—Fire Prevention
M40—Safety Education
M41—First Aid
M42—Automotive Safety
M99—Public Safety, Disaster
Preparedness and Relief n.e.c.

## Recreation and Sports
N01—Alliances and Advocacy
N02—Management and
Technical Assistance
N03—Professional Societies
and Associations
N05—Research Institutes
and Public Policy Analysis
N11—Single-Organization
Support
N12—Fundraising and
Fund Distribution
N19—Support n.e.c.
N20—Camps
N30—Physical Fitness and
Community Recreational
Facilities

N31—Community
Recreational Centers
N32—Parks and Playgrounds
N40—Sports-Training
Facilities
N50—Recreational Clubs
N52—Fairs
N60—Amateur Sports
N61—Fishing and Hunting
N62—Basketball
N63—Baseball and Softball
N64—Soccer
N65—Football
N66—Racket Sports
N67—Swimming and
Other Water Recreation
N68—Winter Sports
N69—Equestrian
N6A—Golf
N70—Amateur Sports
Competitions
N71—Olympics
N72—Special Olympics
N80—Professional Athletic
Leagues
N99—Recreation and
Sports n.e.c.

## Youth Development
O01—Alliances and Advocacy
O02—Management and
Technical Assistance
O03—Professional Societies
and Associations
O05—Research Institutes
and Public Policy Analysis
O11—Single-Organization
Support
O12—Fundraising and
Fund Distribution
O19—Support n.e.c.
O20—Youth Centers
and Clubs
O21—Boys Clubs

O22—Girls Clubs
O23—Boys and Girls Clubs
O30—Adult and Child
Matching Programs
O31—Big Brothers
and Big Sisters
O40—Scouting
O41—Boy Scouts of America
O42—Girls Scouts of the U.S.A
O43—Camp Fire
O50—Youth Development
Programs
O51—Youth Community
Service Clubs
O52—Youth Development,
Agriculture
O53—Youth Development,
Business
O54—Youth Development,
Citizenship
O55—Youth Development,
Religious Leadership
O99—Youth Development
n.e.c.

### Children and Youth Services
P30—Children and
Youth Services
P31—Adoption
P32—Foster Care
P33—Child Day Care

### Family Services
P40—Family Services
P42—Single-Parent Agencies
P43—Family Violence Agencies
P44—In-Home Assistance
P45—Family Services for
Adolescent Parents
P46—Family Counseling

### Residential and
### Custodial Care
P70—Residential Care
P73—Group Homes

P74—Hospice
P75—Senior Continuing
Care Communities

### Services Promoting
### Independence
P80—Centers to Support
the Independence of
Specific Populations
P81—Senior Centers
P82—Developmentally
Disabled Centers
P84—Ethnic and
Immigrant Centers
P85—Homeless Centers
P86—Blind and Visually
Impaired Centers
P87—Deaf and Hearing-
Impaired Centers

### Other Human Services
P01—Alliances and Advocacy
P02—Management and
Technical Assistance
P03—Professional Societies
and Associations
P05—Research Institutes
and Public Policy Analysis
P11—Single-Organization
Support
P12—Fundraising and
Fund Distribution
P19—Support n.e.c.
P20—Human Services
P21—American Red Cross
P22—Urban League
P24—Salvation Army
P26—Volunteers of America
P27—Young Men's or
Women's Associations
P28—Neighborhood Centers
P29—Thrift Shops
P50—Personal Social Services
P51—Financial Counseling

P52—Transportation
Assistance
P58—Gift Distribution
P60—Emergency Assistance
P61—Travelers' Aid
P62—Victims' Services
P99—Human Service n.e.c.

### International and
### Foreign Affairs
Q01—Alliances and Advocacy
Q02—Management and
Technical Assistance
Q03—Professional Societies
and Associations
Q05—Research Institutes
and Public Policy Analysis
Q11—Single-Organization
Support
Q12—Fundraising and
Fund Distribution
Q19—Support n.e.c.
Q20—Promotion of
International Understanding
Q21—International
Cultural Exchanges
Q22—International
Student Exchanges
Q23—International Exchanges
Q30—International
Development
Q31—International
Agricultural Development
Q32—International Economic
Development
Q33—International Relief
Q40—International Peace
and Security
Q41—Arms Control
and Peace
Q42—United Nations
Associations
Q43—National Security

Q70—International Human Rights
Q71—International Migration and Refugee Issues
Q99—International, Foreign Affairs and National Security n.e.c.

## Other

### Civil Rights and Advocacy

R01—Alliances and Advocacy
R02—Management and Technical Assistance
R03—Professional Societies and Associations
R05—Research Institutes and Public Policy Analysis
R11—Single-Organization Support
R12—Fundraising and Fund Distribution
R19—Support n.e.c.
R20—Civil Rights
R22—Minority Rights
R23—Disabled Persons' Rights
R24—Women's Rights
R25—Seniors' Rights
R26—Lesbian and Gay Rights
R30—Intergroup and Race Relations
R40—Voter Education and Registration
R60—Civil Liberties
R61—Reproductive Rights
R62—Right to Life
R63—Censorship, Freedom of Speech and Press
R67—Right to Die and Euthanasia
R99—Civil Rights, Social Action, and Advocacy n.e.c.

### Community Improvement

S01—Alliances and Advocacy
S02—Management and Technical Assistance
S03—Professional Societies and Associations
S05—Research Institutes and Public Policy Analysis
S11—Single-Organization Support
S12—Fundraising and Fund Distribution
S19—Support n.e.c.
S20—Community and Neighborhood Development
S21—Community Coalitions
S22—Neighborhood and Block Associations
S30—Economic Development
S31—Urban and Community Economic Development
S32—Rural Economic Development
S40—Business and Industry
S41—Chambers of Commerce and Business Leagues
S43—Small Business Development
S46—Boards of Trade
S47—Real Estate Associations
S50—Nonprofit Management
S80—Community Service Clubs
S81—Women's Service Clubs
S82—Men's Service Clubs
S99—Community Improvement and Capacity Building n.e.c.

### Philanthropy and Voluntarism

T01—Alliances and Advocacy
T02—Management and Technical Assistance
T03—Professional Societies and Associations
T05—Research Institutes and Public Policy Analysis
T11—Single-Organization Support
T12—Fundraising and Fund Distribution
T19—Support n.e.c.
T20—Private Grantmaking Foundation
T21—Corporate Foundations
T22—Private Independent Foundations
T23—Private Operating Foundations
T30—Public Foundations
T31—Community Foundations
T40—Voluntarism Promotion
T50—Philanthropy, Charity, and Voluntarism Promotion
T70—Federated Giving Program
T90—Named Trusts and Foundations n.e.c.
T99—Philanthropy, Voluntarism, and Grantmaking n.e.c.

### Science and Technology

U01—Alliances and Advocacy
U02—Management and Technical Assistance
U03—Professional Societies and Associations
U05—Research Institutes and Public Policy Analysis
U11—Single-Organization Support
U12—Fundraising and Fund Distribution
U19—Support n.e.c.

U20—General Science
U21—Marine Science
and Oceanography
U30—Physical and
Earth Sciences
U31—Astronomy
U33—Chemistry and
Chemical Engineering
U34—Mathematics
U36—Geology
U40—Engineering and
Technology Research
U41—Computer Science
U42—Engineering
U50—Biological and
Life Sciences
U99—Science and Technology

**Social Science**
V01—Alliances and Advocacy
V02—Management and
Technical Assistance
V03—Professional Societies
and Associations
V05—Research Institutes
and Public Policy Analysis
V11—Single-Organization
Support
V12—Fundraising and
Fund Distribution
V19—Support n.e.c.
V20—Social Science
V21—Anthropology
and Sociology
V22—Economics
V23—Behavioral Science
V24—Political Science
V25—Population Studies

V26—Law and Jurisprudence
V30—Interdisciplinary
Research
V31—Black Studies
V32—Women's Studies
V33—Ethnic Studies
V34—Urban Studies
V35—International Studies
V36—Gerontology
V37—Labor Studies
V99—Social Science n.e.c.

**Other Public and
Societal Benefit**
W01—Alliances and Advocacy
W02—Management and
Technical Assistance
W03—Professional Societies
and Associations
W05—Research Institutes and
Public Policy Analysis
W11—Single-Organization
Support
W12—Fundraising and
Fund Distribution
W19—Support n.e.c.
W20—Government and
Public Administration
W22—Public Finance,
Taxation, and Monetary Policy
W24—Citizen Participation
W30—Military and Veterans
Organizations
W40—Public Transportation
Systems
W50—Telecommunications
W60—Financial Institutions
W61—Credit Unions

W70—Leadership
Development
W80—Public Utilities
W90—Consumer Protection
W99—Public and Societal
Benefit n.e.c.

**Religion Related**
X01—Alliances and Advocacy
X02—Management and
Technical Assistance
X03—Professional Societies
and Associations
X05—Research Institutes and
Public Policy Analysis
X11—Single-Organization
Support
X12—Fundraising and
Fund Distribution
X19—Support n.e.c.
X20—Christian
X21—Protestant
X22—Roman Catholic
X30—Jewish
X40—Buddhist
X70—Hindu
X80—Religious Media
and Communications
X81—Religious Film and Video
X82—Religious Television
X83—Religious Printing and
Publishing
X84—Religious Radio
X90—Interfaith Coalitions
X99—Religion Related n.e.c.

**Unknown, Unclassified**
Z99—Unknown

---

n.e.c. = not elsewhere classified

# Glossary

Some of these definitions have been taken from other publications, including the "Glossary of Philanthropic Terms" in Council on Foundations, *Corporate Philanthropy: Philosophy, Management, Trends, Future, Background* (Washington, D.C.: Council on Foundations, 1982); U.S. Census Bureau, *Statistical Abstract of the United States* (Washington, D.C.: U.S. Government Printing Office, 1985); and U.S. Census Bureau, *Social Indicators III* (Washington, D.C.: U.S. Government Printing Office, various years). We have revised many of the definitions from these publications to reflect their specific relationship to the independent sector. Other definitions of specific terms used to describe the functions of activities of this sector, such as *assigned value for volunteer time,* have been written by the authors.

**Adjusted gross income (AGI).** This is total income as defined by the tax code, less statutory adjustments (primarily business, investment, or certain other deductions, such as payments to a Keogh retirement plan or an individual retirement account).

**Assets.** An organization's financial holdings, such as property or resources, cash, accounts receivable, equipment, and so on, and balances against liabilities.

**Assigned value for volunteer time.** The monetary value of volunteer time is calculated as the total number of hours formally volunteered to organizations in a year, multiplied by the hourly wage for nonagricultural workers for that year.

**Average.** A single number of values often used to represent the typical value of a group of numbers. It is regarded as a measure of the "location" or "central tendency" of a group of numbers. The *arithmetic mean* is the type of average used most frequently. It is derived by totaling the values of individual items in a particular group and dividing that total by the number of items. The arithmetic mean is often referred to as simply the "mean" or "average." The *median* of a group of numbers is the number or value that falls in the middle of a group when each item in the group is ranked according to size (from lowest to highest or vice versa); the median generally has the same number of items above it as below it. If there is an even number of items in the group, the median is taken to be the average of the two middle items.

**Average annual percentage change.** A figure computed by using a compound interest formula. This formula assumes that the rate of change is constant throughout a specified compounding period (one year for average annual rates of change). The formula is similar to the one used to compute the balance of a savings account that earns compound interest. According to this formula, at the end of a compounding period, the amount of accrued change (for example, employment or bank interest) is added to the amount that existed at the beginning of one period. As a result, over time (for example, with each year or quarter), the same rate of change is applied to an even larger figure.

**Charitable contribution.** A gift to a charitable cause that is allowed by the IRS as a deduction from taxable income. Both individual taxpayers and corporations can deduct contributions for charitable causes from their taxable incomes.

**Community foundation.** A public charity supported by combined funds contributed by individuals, foundations, nonprofit institutions, and corporations. A community foundation's giving is limited almost exclusively to a specific locale, such as a city, a county or counties, or a state.

**Constant-dollar estimate.** A computation that removes the effects of price changes from a statistical series reported in dollar terms. Constant-dollar series are derived by dividing current-dollar estimates by appropriate price indexes, such as the consumer price index, or by the various implicit price deflators for gross national product. The result is a series as it would presumably exist if prices remained the same throughout the period as they were in the base year—in other words, if the dollar had constant purchasing power. Changes in such a series would reflect only changes in the real (physical) volume of output. *See also* **Current dollars** *and* **Gross national product (GNP)**.

**Consumption expenditure.** Expenditures for goods and services purchased by individuals; operating expenses of nonprofit institutions; the value of food, fuel, clothing, and rental of dwellings; financial services received in kind by individuals; and net purchases of used goods. All private purchases of dwellings are classified as gross private domestic investment. Per capita personal consumption expenditures are total personal consumption expenditures divided by the appropriate population base. Per capita components of personal consumption expenditures are derived in the same way. *See also* **Per capita.**

**Contributions deduction.** Taxpayers can deduct from their taxable income contributions made to certain religious, charitable, educational, scientific, or literary 501(c)(3) organizations. These could be in the form of cash, property, or out-of-pocket expenses incurred while performing volunteer work.

**Corporate contribution.** A general term referring to charitable contributions by a corporation. The term usually describes cash contributions only but may also include other items, such as the value of loaned executives, products, and services.

**Corporate foundation.** A private philanthropic organization set up and funded by a corporation. A corporate foundation is governed by a board that may include members of the corporation board and contributions committee, other staff members, and representatives of the community.

**Corporate social responsibility program.** A philanthropic program operated within a corporation. The program may be managed through a department of its own or through a community affairs (or similar) department.

**Current dollars.** The dollar amount that reflects the value of the dollar at the time of its use. *See also* **Constant-dollar estimate.**

**Current operating expenditures.** All expenses included in the Statement of Revenue, Expenses, and Changes in Net Assets on Form 990, except for grants and allocations, specific assistance to individuals, and benefits paid to or for members. Among current operating expenditures are such components as wages and salaries, fringe benefits, supplies, communication charges, professional fees, and depreciation and depletion charges. *See also* **Form 990** *and* **Total expenses.**

**Earnings.** All cash income of $1 or more from wages and salaries and net cash income of $1 or more from farm and nonfarm self-employment.

**Employment.** *See* **Labor force.**

**Endowment.** Stocks, bonds, property, and funds given permanently to nonprofit entities, primarily to foundations, hospitals, or schools, so that the nonprofit entities may produce their own income for grantmaking or operating purposes.

**Form 990.** The annual tax return that tax-exempt organizations with gross revenue of more than $25,000 must file with the IRS. The Form 990 is also required by many state charity offices. This tax return includes information about the organization's assets, income, operating expenses, contributions, paid staff and salaries, names and addresses of persons to contact, and program areas. *See also* **Form 990-PF.**

**Form 990-PF.** The annual information return that must be filed with the IRS by private foundations and nonexempt charitable trusts that are treated as private foundations by the IRS. This form replaced Form 990-AR circa 1981.

**Foundation.** A nongovernmental nonprofit organization with funds and a program managed by its own trustees and directors, established to further social, educational, religious, or charitable activities by making grants. A private foundation receives its funds from, and is subject to control by, an individual, family, corporation, or other group consisting of a limited number of members. In contrast, a community foundation receives its funds from multiple public sources and is classified by the IRS as a public charity. *See also* **Community foundation** *and* **Public charity.**

**Full-time employment.** Full-time workers are those who usually work 35 hours or more in a given week, regardless of the number of hours worked in the reference week.

**Full-time-equivalent volunteer.** A figure derived from an estimation procedure used to transform total hours formally volunteered to an organization into a figure equivalent to the value of full-time paid employment. The total annual volunteer hours are divided by 1,700 (which is a reasonable approximation of actual hours worked by a full-time worker during a year).

**Gross national product (GNP).** GNP is the total national output of final goods and services valued at market prices. *See also* **National income.**

**In-kind contribution.** *See* **Noncash (in-kind) contribution.**

**Independent sector.** The portion of the economy that includes all 501(c)(3) and 501(c)(4) tax-exempt organizations as defined by the IRS, including all religious institutions (such as churches and synagogues) and all persons who give time and money to serve charitable purposes. The independent sector is also referred to as the voluntary sector, the nonprofit sector, and the third sector. *See also* **Section 501(c)(3)** *and* **Section 501(c)(4).**

**Labor force.** The civilian labor force is the sum of employed and unemployed civilian workers. The total labor force is the sum of the civilian labor force and the armed forces. "Employed" persons are all persons 16 years of age and older in the civilian noninstitutional population who, during the reference week, worked at all (as paid employees, in their own business or profession, or on their own farm) or who worked 15 hours or more as unpaid workers in an enterprise operated by a family member.

For purposes of this profile, the full-time-equivalent employment of volunteers has been added to the traditional definition of the labor force. Also included are workers who were not working but who had jobs or businesses from which they were temporarily absent because of illness, vacation, bad weather, labor-management dispute, or personal reasons, whether or not they were paid for the time off or were seeking other jobs. Each employed person is counted only once. Workers holding more than one job are counted in the job at which they worked the most hours during the reference week. *See also* **Full-time-equivalent volunteer.**

**National income.** The earnings of the private sector plus compensation (wages, salaries, and fringe benefits) earned by government employees during a specified period of time. Earnings are recorded in the forms in which they are received, and they include taxes on those earnings. Earnings in the private sector consist of compensation of employees, profits of corporate and incorporated enterprises, net interest, and rental income of persons. National income is a component of gross national product and is less than gross national product, mainly because it does not include capital consumption (depreciation) allowances and indirect business taxes. *See also* **Gross national product (GNP).**

**National Taxonomy of Exempt Entities–Core Codes (NTEE-CC).** A classification system for tax-exempt nonprofit organizations, consisting of 26 major groups under 10 broad categories. (See the NCCS web site, http://nccs.urban.org/, for further details.)

**Noncash (in-kind) contribution.** An individual or corporate contribution of goods or commodities as distinguished from cash. Noncash contributions from individuals can include such items as clothing, works of art, food, furniture, and appliances. Noncash contributions from corporations may also take a variety of forms, such as donation of used office furniture or equipment, office space, or the professional services of employees. Although noncash contributions from individuals are tax deductible, noncash contributions from corporations generally are not. *See also* **Corporate contribution.**

**Nonprofit.** A term describing the IRS designation of an organization whose income is not used for the benefit or private gain of stockholders, directors, or any other persons with an interest in the company. A nonprofit organization's income is used to support its operations. Such organizations are defined under section 501(c) of the Internal Revenue Code. Nonprofit organizations that are included in the definition of the independent sector are nonprofit, tax-exempt organizations that are included in sections 501(c)(3) and 501(c)(4) of the code. *See also* **Section 501(c)(3)** *and* **Section 501(c)(4).**

**Nonprofit Institutions Serving Households (NPISH).** The nonprofit sector as defined by the Bureau of Economic Analysis. Includes tax-exempt organizations providing services in religion and welfare, medical care, education and research, recreation, and personal business, such as labor unions, legal aid, and professional associations. The category excludes nonprofits—such as chambers of commerce, trade associations, and homeowners' associations—that serve businesses rather than households, and excludes nonprofits that sell goods and services in the same way as for-profit businesses, such as tax-exempt cooperatives, credit unions, mutual financial institutions, and tax-exempt manufacturers, such as university presses.

**North American Industry Classification System (NAICS).** NAICS was the basis used by the 1997 Economic Census. Earlier censuses had used the SIC system. Although many of the individual NAICS industries correspond directly to industries in the SIC system, most of the higher-level groupings do not. As such, data comparison between the two systems should be done carefully. *See also* **Standard Industrial Classification (SIC).**

**Operating foundation.** A private foundation that devotes most of its earnings and assets directly to the conduct of its tax-exempt purposes (for example, operating a museum or home for the aged) rather than making grants to other organizations for these purposes.

**Operating organization.** An operating organization engages in a variety of activities, such as producing information or delivering services and products to its members and the public, in contrast to other entities that function as sources of financial support by raising funds and delivering them. Examples of operating organizations are museums, colleges, universities, and social services agencies.

**Out-of-scope organization.** An organization identified as being either foreign in origin or as a governmental or supporting government entity (such as a public or state college), which has been excluded from the IRS file of tax-exempt organizations for purposes of this book.

**Part-time employment.** Part-time workers are those who usually work less than 35 hours per week (at all jobs), regardless of the number of hours worked in the reference week.

**Per capita.** A per capita figure represents an average computed for every person in a specific group (or "population"). It is derived by taking the total of an item (such as income, taxes, or retail sales) and dividing it by the number of persons in the specified population.

**Personal income.** Income received by persons from all sources. Personal income is the sum (less personal contributions for social insurance) of wage and salary disbursements, other labor income, proprietors' income, rental income of persons, dividends, personal interest income, and transfer payments. Per capita personal income is total personal income divided by the appropriate population base. *See also* **Per capita.**

**Pretax income.** A corporation's annual income before it has paid taxes. The IRS allows corporations to deduct up to 10 percent of the corporation's taxable income as contributions to charitable organizations and to carry forward such contributions in excess of 10 percent over a five-year period. Corporations do not usually release information on their taxable income, however, and data collected by groups such as the Conference Board are based on income before calculation of income taxes. Taxable income and income before taxes may be similar or very different, pending on the industry and the corporation's tax structure.

**Public charity.** The largest category of 501(c)(3) organizations, which serve broad purposes, including assisting the poor and the underprivileged; advancing religion, education, health, science, art, and culture; and protecting the environment, among others. A public charity that is identified by the IRS as "not a private foundation" (as defined in section 509(a) of the Internal Revenue Code) normally receives a substantial part of its income, directly or indirectly, from the general public or from government sources, which a private foundation does not. The public support must be fairly broad and not limited to a few individuals or families. Only public charities and religious organizations can receive tax-deductible contributions.

**Reporting public charity.** Public charities that report to the IRS on Form 990. Charities that do not have to file Form 990 are religious organizations and congregations and charities with less than $25,000 in annual gross receipts.

**Section 501(c)(3).** The Internal Revenue Code section that defines tax-exempt organizations organized and operated exclusively for religious, charitable, scientific, literary, educational, or similar purposes. Contributions to 501(c)(3) organizations are deductible as charitable donations for federal income tax purposes.

**Section 501(c)(4).** The Internal Revenue Code section that defines tax-exempt organizations organized to operate as civic leagues, social welfare organizations, and local associations of employees. They are included in the independent sector.

**Standard Industrial Classification (SIC).** The classification system and definition of industries in accordance with the composition of the economy. Although this classification is designed to cover all economic activity in the United States, government statistical collections emanating from this classification system do not distinguish between private nonprofit organizations and private for-profit organizations. This system was replaced by the NAICS starting in 1999.

**Support organization.** Support organizations collect funds and distribute them primarily to operating organizations. Support organizations usually do not operate service delivery programs. Examples include federated fundraising organizations such as United Ways or Catholic Charities. *See also* **Operating organization.**

**Tax exempt.** A classification granted by the IRS to qualified nonprofit organizations that frees them from the requirement to pay taxes on their income. Private foundations, including endowed company foundations, are tax exempt; however, they must pay a 1 or 2 percent excise tax on net investment income. All 501(c)(3) and 501(c)(4) organizations are tax exempt.

**Total expenses.** All current operating expenditures plus grants and allocations, specific assistance to individuals, benefits paid to or for members, and payments to affiliates. *See also* **Current operating expenditures.**

**Volunteer.** A person who gives time to help others for no monetary pay. *Formal volunteering* is defined as giving a specified amount of time to organizations such as hospitals, churches, or schools. *Informal volunteering* is ad hoc and involves helping organizations as well as individuals, including neighbors, family, and friends.

**Volunteer hours.** The average number of hours per week volunteered and the total number of hours volunteered by the population in a particular year. To calculate the average hours volunteered per week, volunteer hours are estimated by using information on volunteering reported for the most recent time period (such as three months or one week) in a particular survey by activity area (such as health or religion). These hours are then totaled and multiplied by the percentage of people in the population in that period who reported volunteering in that area. Total volunteer hours are calculated by multiplying the percentage of the population volunteering in each of the activity areas specified in Gallup surveys (health, education, and so on) by the average volunteer hours worked in each of the areas. Then all the figures for these areas are summed to get the total number of hours per time period. If the particular time period is three months, these totals would then be multiplied by four to arrive at the total hours volunteered in a particular year. *See also* **Volunteer.**

# Sources

Center on Philanthropy at Indiana University. 2006. "Center on Philanthropy Panel Study." http://www.philanthropy.iupui.edu/Research/COPPS/COPPS.aspx. (Accessed January 3, 2008.)

Centre for Time Use Research. 2006. "American Heritage Time Use Study (AHTUS)." http://www.timeuse.org/ahtus/. (Accessed January 3, 2008.)

Chairman of the Council of Economic Advisers. 2007. *Economic Report of the President.* Washington, DC: U.S. Government Printing Office. http://www.gpoaccess.gov/eop/. (Accessed January 3, 2008.)

Foundation Center. 2006, 2007. "Research Studies: National Trends." http://foundationcenter.org/gainknowledge/research/nationaltrends.html. (Accessed January 3, 2008.)

Giving USA Foundation. 2007. *Giving USA,* 51st ed. Bloomington, IN: Giving USA Foundation.

Golladay, Kendall, and Thomas Pollak. 2003. "The Reporting of 'Other Expenses' in Part II of the Form 990." Washington, DC: The Urban Institute. National Center for Charitable Statistics FAQ+ Item: Technical Note. http://nccsdataweb.urban.org/faq/detail.php?linkID=226&category=121. (Accessed January 3, 2008.)

Muirhead, Sophia A. 2004. "The 2004 Corporate Contributions Report." Report R-1355-04-RR. New York: The Conference Board Inc. http://www.conference-board.org/publications/describe.cfm?id=873. (Accessed January 3, 2008.)

———. 2005. "The 2005 Corporate Contributions Report." Report R-1381-05-RR. New York: The Conference Board Inc. http://www.conference-board.org/publications/describe.cfm?id=1080. (Accessed January 3, 2008.)

———. 2007. "The 2006 Corporate Contributions Report." Report R-1399-06-RR. New York: The Conference Board Inc. http://www.conference-board.org/publications/describe.cfm?id=1261. (Accessed January 3, 2008.)

Salamon, Lester M., and S. Wojciech Sokolowski. 2006. "Employment in America's Charities: A Profile." Nonprofit Employment Bulletin 26. Baltimore: Johns Hopkins University, Center for Civil Society Studies, December.

U.S. Census Bureau. 1991–2007. "County Business Patterns." http://www.census.gov/epcd/cbp/view/cbpview.html. (Accessed January 3, 2008.)

———. 1997. "1997 Economic Census." http://www.census.gov/epcd/www/econ97.html#1997. (Accessed January 3, 2008.)

———. 2002. "2002 Economic Census." http://www.census.gov/econ/census02/. (Accessed January 3, 2008.)

———. 2006. *Statistical Abstract of the United States 2006: The National Data Book.* Washington, DC: U.S. Census Bureau.

U.S. Department of Commerce, Bureau of Economic Analysis. 2006–2007. "National Income and Product Accounts." http://www.bea.gov/national/nipaweb/. (Accessed January 3, 2008.)

———. 2007. "Gross Domestic Product: Percent Change from Preceding Period." http://www.bea.gov/national/xls/gdpchg.xls. (Accessed January 3, 2008.)

U.S. Department of Education, National Center for Education Statistics. 2006. "Integrated Postsecondary Education Data System (IPEDS)." http://nces.ed.gov/ipeds/. (Accessed January 3, 2008.)

U.S. Department of Labor, Bureau of Labor Statistics. 1990–2007. "Quarterly Census of Employment and Wages." http://www.bls.gov/cew/home.htm. (Accessed January 3, 2008.)

———. 1998–2004, 2006, 2007. "Employment, Hours, and Earnings from the Current Employment Statistics Survey (National)." http://www.bls.gov/ces/home.htm. (Accessed January 3, 2008.)

———. 2002–2007. "Current Population Survey." http://www.bls.gov/cps/home.htm. (Accessed January 3, 2008.)

———. 2002–2006. "American Time Use Survey." http://www.bls.gov/tus/home.htm. (Accessed January 3, 2008.)

———. 2007. "Consumer Price Indexes." http://www.bls.gov/cpi/home.htm. (Accessed January 3, 2008.)

U.S. Department of the Treasury, Internal Revenue Service. 1985–2005. "SOI Tax Stats—Individual Income Tax Returns Publication 1304 (Complete Report)." http://www.irs.gov/taxstats/indtaxstats/article/0,,id=134951,00.html. (Accessed January 3, 2008.)

———. 1987, 1990, 1992–2005. "SOI Tax Stats—Estate Tax Statistics." http://www.irs.gov/taxstats/indtaxstats/article/0,,id=96442,00.html. (Accessed January 3, 2008.)

———. 2004. "Title 26—Internal Revenue Code." http://www.access.gpo.gov/uscode/title26/title26.html. (Accessed January 3, 2008.)

Urban Institute, National Center for Charitable Statistics. 1998. "National Taxonomy of Exempt Entities: NTEE Core Codes (NTEE-CC)." http://nccs.urban.org/classification/NTEE.cfm. (Accessed January 3, 2008.)

———. 1998–2006. "Core Files." http://nccs2.urban.org/product.htm#CORE. (Accessed January 3, 2008.)

———. 1998–2006. "IRS Statistics of Income Form 990 Sample Files." http://nccs2.urban.org/product.htm#SOI. (Accessed January 3, 2008.)

———. 1995, 1998–2006. "IRS Statistics of Income Form 990-EZ Sample Files." http://nccs2.urban.org/product.htm#SOI _EZ. (Accessed January 3, 2008.)

———. 2000. "NCCS NTEE/NAICS/SIC Crosswalk." http://nccs.urban.org/classification/NAICS.cfm. (Accessed January 3, 2008.)

———. 2005. "NCCS-GuideStar National Nonprofit Research Database: Special Research Version." http://nccsdataweb.urban.org/FAQ/index.php?category=93. (Accessed January 3, 2008.)

———. 2006. "IRS Business Master Files, Exempt Organizations (1996, 2001, 2006)." http://nccs2.urban.org/product.htm#BMF. (Accessed January 3, 2008.)

Weitzman, Murray S., Nadine T. Jalandaloni, Linda M. Lampkin, and Thomas H. Pollak. 2002. *The New Nonprofit Almanac and Desk Reference,* 6th ed. San Francisco: Jossey-Bass.

# About the Authors

**Kennard T. Wing** is a senior consultant and researcher with 30 years of experience. For the last 10 years he has worked exclusively in the nonprofit sector, focusing on consulting for improved operational effectiveness and applied research. He was a senior researcher on the Nonprofit Overhead Cost Project and has won an Excel Award from the Society of National Association Publications. Mr. Wing has taught management at the graduate level at the University of Pennsylvania and Immaculata College. He holds a master's degree from the Wharton School and a bachelor's degree from Brown University and is a certified management accountant.

**Thomas H. Pollak** is program director of the National Center for Charitable Statistics, a program of the Center on Nonprofits and Philanthropy at the Urban Institute. His recent research projects include a study of overhead costs in the nonprofit sector and an analysis of private contributions to U.S.-based international development organizations. In addition to these and other research projects, Mr. Pollak manages NCCS's web site, data development, and online data services. He holds a law degree from Georgetown University and is a member of the Maryland and District of Columbia bars.

**Amy Blackwood** is a consultant with the Urban Institute's National Center for Charitable Statistics, working on a variety of nonprofit research projects. Prior to that, she was a research associate at NCCS and also worked as a policy analyst at the Corporation for National and Community Service. Amy's work with NCCS has focused on examining public charities in the health and education subsectors. She holds a master's degree in public service and administration from Texas A&M University.

# Index

*Tables and figures are referred to by "t" and "fig" after the page number.*

## A

Adjusted gross income, giving as percent of, 79, 81, 90–92*t*, 96*t*

Agricultural associations, 22–23, 140

American Heritage Time Use Study (AHTUS), 98, 102, 102*t*, 113–14

American Time Use Survey (ATUS), 83, 88, 94, 98, 102*t*, 112–14

Animal-related organizations. *See* Environment and animal organizations

Arts, culture, and humanities organizations: asset growth, 162*t*, 164*t*; as BEA and NAICS categories, 129–30; contributions to, 74–75*t*, 76*fig*, 82*t*, 83*fig*; expense trends, 159*t*; grants from foundations, 109–10*t*; growth in number of, 149*t*; net margin, 169; public support for, 152, 156*t*, 169*fig*; reporting revenues, by subsector, 144*t*; reporting revenues and expenses, 166, 167–68*t*, 169–70, 169*fig*; revenue growth, 153*t*; revenues, by year and source, 133–37*t*; types of (NTEE-CC), 228; volunteers and, 89, 98*fig*

Assets: growth in, 158, 162–65*t*, 166; as source of revenue, 116–18*figs*, 117–18, 120*fig*, 121; state reporting, 208, 217–20*t*

## B

Benevolent life insurance associations, 24

Bequests, 72, 76, 77–78*t*, 78, 88*t*, 89*fig*

Black lung benefits trusts, 25

Bureau of Economic Analysis (BEA): criticism of estimates of, 18; employment data from, 64; estimates of nonprofit size and contribution to economy, 5, 9; estimates of NPISH revenues, 14–18; NAICS industries and, 129–30*t*; National Income and Product Accounts data, 63, 115; outlay/expenditure trends data, 121–26*figs*, 123, 125, 128*t*; revenue trends data from, 115, 116–20*figs*, 117–18, 125, 127*t*, 131–32*t*; role of, 5; wage data from, 27, 63, 64, 66

Bureau of Labor Statistics' Quarterly Census of Employment and Wages (QCEW), 64–68

Business leagues, 23, 140

Business (for-profit) sector, 5, 9–11*figs*, 10, 12–14*t*

## C

Cemetery companies, 24

Census Bureau. *See* U.S. Census Bureau

Center on Philanthropy, 70

Charitable contributions. *See* Private giving

Charitable deductions, 81, 95*t*, 96*t*

Charitable organizations. *See* 501(c)(3) charitable organizations; 501(c)(4) social welfare organizations

Church organizations. *See* Religion-related organizations

Civil rights and advocacy public charities, 188, 197*fig*

Community foundations. *See* Foundations

Community improvement public charities: finances of, 188, 197*fig*; household giving to, 82*t*, 83*fig*

The Conference Board's Corporate Contributions Report (Muirhead), 70, 111

Contributions to charities. *See* Private giving

Cooperative hospital service organizations, 25

Cooperative utility companies, 24

Corporate foundations: giving by, 70, 77–78*t*, 111; number of, 104, 105–6*t*, 106*fig*

Credit unions, state chartered, 24

Cultural organizations. *See* Arts, culture, and humanities organizations

Current Population Survey (CPS), 83, 89, 113–14

## D

Demographics: of private giving, 76, 84–87*t*; of volunteers, 94, 99*t*

## E

Earnings. *See* Employment (nonprofit); Wages (nonprofit)

Economic Census (U.S. Census Bureau), 63–64, 65–66, 131

Education organizations: asset growth, 158, 162*t*, 164*t*, 166; as BEA and NAICS categories, 129–30; contributions to, 72, 74–75*t*, 76*fig*, 82*t*, 83*fig*; expense growth, 158, 159*t*; 501(c)(3) status, 22; 501(f) status, 26; grants from foundations, 107, 109–10*t*; growth in number of, 149*t*; public support for, 156*t*; reporting revenues, by subsector, 144*t*; reporting revenues and expenses, 170, 171–72*t*, 173–74, 173*fig*; revenue growth, 153*t*; revenues, by year and source, 131, 133–37*t*; size and scope of, 143; types of (NTEE-CC), 228–29; volunteers and, 89, 98*fig*; wage estimates, 27, 32

Employment (nonprofit): annual growth rate, by industry, 32, 34*fig*; estimated number of, by industry (2004), 39, 59*t*; growth in nonprofit sector (1998–2005), 18–20, 20*t*, 21*fig*; industries covered by unemployment insurance, 35–36, 39, 39*t*, 40*t*, 50–58*t*; industries not covered by unemployment insurance, 35, 41*t*; by NAICS industry codes, 27, 30*t*, 32, 34–35, 39, 59*t*; sources of, 63–64, 66–68; total number of (1998–2005), 19, 21*fig*; trends in, 27–68; wages per employee, by industry, 27, 31*t*, 32, 33*fig*, 35*fig*. *See also* Volunteers; Wages (nonprofit)

Environment and animal organizations: asset growth, 158, 162*t*, 164*t*, 166; as BEA and NAICS categories, 129–30; contributions to, 72, 74–75*t*, 76*fig*, 82*t*, 83*fig*; expense growth, 158, 159*t*; grants from foundations, 109–10*t*; growth in number of, 148, 149–51*t*; public support for, 152, 156*t*; reporting revenues and expenses, 174, 175–76*t*, 177–78, 177*fig*; revenue growth, 152, 153*t*; revenues, by year and source, 133–37*t*; types of (NTEE-CC), 229; volunteers and, 89, 98*fig*

Estate tax returns, 78–83, 88*t*. *See also* Bequests

Ethnic differences. *See* Demographics

Expenses. *See* Outlays

## F

Fees for services as source of revenues, 115, 116–18*figs*, 143, 145*fig*

Financial trends, 115–37. *See also* Outlays; Revenues

501(c)(3) charitable organizations: annual revenue change, by subsector, 132*t*; described, 1, 3; growth in number of reporting charities (1995–2005), 148, 149–51*t*, 152; number and expenses of, 142, 142*fig*; registration and filing requirements for, 141, 141*t*; reporting, by size and age, 141–42, 142*fig*; reporting,

by subsector, 142–43, 144*t*; scope of, 22; size, scope, and finances of, 139–41, 140*t*; by subsector, 142–43, 228–35; types of, 2–3*t*. *See also* Outlays; Revenues; *specific subsectors*

501(c)(4) social welfare organizations: described, 1, 3; scope of, 22, 140; types of, 2–3*t*. *See also* Human service organizations

Forms. *See* IRS Forms

For-profit sector. *See* Business (for-profit) sector

Foundation Center, 102, 111

Foundations: assets of and gifts received, 72, 74–75*t*, 76*fig*, 102, 103*t*, 104, 105–6*t*, 106*fig*; giving by, 70, 76, 77–78*t*, 79*fig*, 102–11, 106*fig*; grants made, by assets, 104, 107*t*; grants made, by major categories, 107, 109–10*t*; grants made, by year, 102, 103*t*, 104*fig*, 105–6*t*; number of, 102, 103*t*, 105–6*t*; private contributions to, 72, 76*fig*; as public charities, 139–40, 141*t*; types of, 104, 105–6*t*, 106*fig*, 108*t*

Fraternal organizations, 23, 140

## G

Gender differences. *See* Demographics

*Giving USA* (Giving USA Foundation), 70

Giving USA Foundation, 70, 111

Golladay, Kendall, 148

Government grants, 131*t*, 132, 132*t*, 145*fig*, 152, 156–57*t*, 158

Government sector, 9–11*figs*, 12–14*t*

Grants. *See* Foundations; Government grants

Gross domestic product (GDP): nonprofit growth compared with (1995–2005), 140–41; NPISH contribution to, compared with other sectors, 9, 9*fig*, 12–14*t*, 14

GuideStar-NCCS National Nonprofit Research Database, 225, 226

## H

Health organizations: asset growth, 158, 162*t*, 164*t*; as BEA and NAICS categories, 129–30; contributions to, 72, 74–75*t*, 76*fig*, 82*t*, 83*fig*; cooperative hospital service organizations, 25; expense growth, 158, 159*t*; grants from foundations, 109–10*t*; growth in number of, 148, 149–51*t*, 152; insurance coverage for high-risk individuals, 25; as major category of nonprofits, 5, 22; NPISH expenditures for, 123–24*figs*; private contributions to, 72, 76*fig*; public support for, 156*t*; reporting revenues and expenses, 178, 179–80*t*, 181, 181*fig*; revenue growth, 152, 153*t*; revenues, by year and source, 133–37*t*; types of (NTEE-CC), 229–31; volunteers and, 89, 98*fig*; wage estimates, 27

Humanities organizations. *See* Arts, culture, and humanities organizations

Human service organizations: asset growth, 163*t*, 165*t*; as BEA and NAICS categories, 129–30; contributions to, 72, 74–75*t*, 76*fig*; expense growth, 160*t*;

growth in number of, 148, 149–51*t*; NPISH expenditures for, 123–24*figs*; private contributions to, 72, 76*fig*; public support for, 157*t*, 158; reporting, by subsector, 144*t*; reporting revenues and expenses, 182–88, 183–85*t*, 186*fig*; revenues, 133–37*t*, 150–51*t*, 152, 154*t*; size and scope of, 142–43; types of (NTEE-CC), 231–33

**I**

Independent foundations, 104, 105–6*t*, 106*fig*, 107
Individual giving, 69, 70–78; average charitable deduction by, 81, 95–96*t*; demographics of, 84*t*, 85–87*t*; IRS data from estate tax returns, 88*t*, 89*fig*; IRS data on bequests, 89*fig*; IRS data on charitable deductions returns, 95*t*, 96*t*; IRS records and, 78–79, 81; by itemizers vs. nonitemizers, 76, 79, 81, 90–93*t*, 95*t*. *See also* Private giving
Integrated Postsecondary Education Data System (NCES), 65
Internal Revenue Code provisions for tax exemption: section 501(c)(1), 22; section 501(c)(2), 22; section 501(c)(3), 1, 22, 139–41; section 501(c)(4), 1, 22, 140; section 501(c)(5), 22–23, 140; section 501(c)(6), 23, 140; section 501(c)(7), 23; section 501(c)(8), 23, 140; section 501(c)(9), 23; section 501(c)(10), 23; section 501(c)(11), 23; section 501(c)(12), 24; section 501(c)(13), 24; section 501(c)(14), 24; section 501(c)(15), 24; section 501(c)(16), 24; section 501(c)(17), 24; section 501(c)(18), 24; section 501(c)(19), 24; section 501(c)(20), 24; section 501(c)(21), 25; section 501(c)(22), 25; section 501(c)(23), 25; section 501(c)(24), 25; section 501(c)(25), 25; section 501(c)(26), 25; section 501(c)(27), 25; section 501(d), 25; section 501(e), 25; section 501(f), 26; types of tax-exempt organizations by code section, 1, 2–3*t*, 3, 22–26
Internal Revenue Service. *See* IRS
International and foreign affairs organizations: asset growth, 158, 163*t*, 165*t*, 166; contributions to, 72, 76*fig*, 82*t*, 83*fig*; expense growth, 158, 161*t*; growth in number of, 148, 149–51*t*; private contributions to, 76*fig*; public support for, 152, 157*t*; reporting revenues and expenses, 188, 189–91, 192*fig*; revenue growth, 152, 155*t*, 157*t*; revenues, by year and source, 133–37*t*; types of (NTEE-CC), 233–34
Internet resources. *See* Web sites
Investment income as source of revenues, 131*t*, 132, 132*t*, 144, 145*fig*
IRS Business Master Files (BMFs) of Tax-Exempt Organizations, 225
IRS Forms: 990 and 990-EZ, 64, 66, 67, 115, 140, 141, 148, 225–27
IRS Return Transaction File (RTF), 64, 66, 225
IRS Statistics of Income (SOI) file, 64, 67, 78–79, 81; bequests and estate tax returns data, 77–78*t*, 78, 88*t*, 89*fig*; charitable deductions returns, data from, 95*t*,

96*t*; charitable giving data, by itemizers, 76, 90–93*t*; estimates of individual giving data, 78–83
Itemizers vs. nonitemizers as charity givers, 76, 79, 81, 90–93*t*, 95*t*

**J**

Johns Hopkins Center for Civil Society Studies, 67–68

**L**

Labor unions, 22–23, 140
Legal services organizations, 24
Livestock credit associations, 24
Living individuals, giving by. *See* Private giving
Lodge system, 23

**M**

Muirhead, Sophia A., 70, 111
Museums. *See* Arts, culture, and humanities organizations
Mutual insurance companies or associations, 24

**N**

National Center for Charitable Statistics (NCCS): Core Files, 66, 225–26; employment data shortcomings, 67; GuideStar National Nonprofit Research Database, 225, 226
National Center for Education Statistics (NCES), 65
National economy and nonprofit sector, 1–21. *See also* Gross domestic product (GDP)
Net assets to expense ratio: arts, culture, and humanities organizations, 170; defined, 166; education organizations, 174; environment and animal organizations, 177, 178; health organizations, 181; human service organizations, 188; international and foreign affairs organizations, 188; other organizations, 196
Net margin: arts, culture, and humanities organizations, 169; defined, 166; education organizations, 173–74; health organizations, 178; human service organizations, 188; international and foreign affairs organizations, 188; other organizations, 196
Nonprofit institutions serving business, 5, 9, 17, 18, 19*t*
Nonprofit institutions serving households (NPISHs): BEA area subsectors and, 123, 129–30*t*; BEA data and, 67, 115; estimates of size and contribution to economy of, 5, 9–19; outlays/expenditures, 121, 123, 125, 128*t*; revenues and outlays of, 14–18, 15–16*t*, 17*fig*; revenues (types and sources) for, 115–18, 119–20*figs*, 125, 127*t*; sources of wages for, 63–64; subsector outlays/expenditures for, 123, 128*fig*; uses of funds by, 121–22*figs*; wage estimates for, 27. *See also* Outlays; Revenues
Nonprofit organizations: classification of (NTEE-CC), 227, 228–35; compared to other sectors, 5–14, 12–14*t*; employment in, 18–20, 20*t*; expenses and assets of, by category, 4–5*t*; expenses and assets of, by

Nonprofit organizations: classification of *(continued)*
IRC provision, 2–3*t*; GDP of, 9, 9*fig*, 12–14*t*; organizations, expenses, and assets by category, 4–5*t*;
revenues, by source and type of public charity,
133–37*t*; scope of, by NAICS codes, 6–8*t*, 27; size,
scope and finances of, 139–41, 140*t*. *See also specific
types*

North American Industry Classification System
(NAICS): BEA consumption categories and, 129–30*t*;
codes (NTEE-CC) for NAICS industries, 39, 60–62*t*,
67–68; nonprofits by NAICS codes, 5, 6–8*t*, 9, 34–35,
66; wages by industry codes, 27, 28–29*t*

National Taxonomy of Exempt Entities (NTEE): core
codes (NTEE-CC), 39, 60–62*t*, 67–68, 226, 227;
nonprofit organizations, expenses, and assets by
NTEE category, 3, 4–5*t*, 5; types of organizations
and subsectors (NTEE-CC), 228–35

### O

Operating public charities: compared with supporting
organizations, 144, 146–47*t*, 148; reporting, by subsectors, 143, 144*t*; size and scope of, 143

Other nonprofit organizations: included groups, 143,
169, 173, 235; public charities and, 144*t*; reporting
revenues and expenses, 188, 192, 193–95*t*,
196–97*figs*; revenues, by year and source, 133–37*t*.
*See also specific subsectors*

Outlays: consumption expenditures, 121–24*figs*, 123,
129–30*t*; operating vs. supporting organizations,
144, 146–47*t*, 148; "other" expenses on Form 990,
148; source data, 125, 128*t*, 225–27; state reporting,
208, 213–16*t*; by subsectors, 158, 159–61*t*; transfer
payments, 121–22*figs*, 123, 125–26*figs*; trends in,
121–25, 144, 148, 158. *See also specific types of
nonprofits*

### P

Philanthropy and voluntarism public charities, 188,
197*fig*. *See also* Volunteers

Pollack, Thomas, 148

Private giving: average charitable deduction, 81,
95–96*t*; bequests and estate tax returns, 78, 88*t*,
89*fig*; cash and noncash by year, 79, 93*t*, 94*fig*; compared with national income and nonprofit outlays,
70, 71–72*t*, 73*fig*; demographics of, 84*t*, 85–87*t*; distribution of, 74–75*t*, 76*fig*; estimates from IRS
records, 78–83; by household, 82*t*, 83*fig*; per capita,
76, 80–81*t*, 82*fig*; reporting as revenue, 143–44; as
revenue source, 131*t*, 132, 132*t*, 145*fig*, 152, 156–57*t*,
158; by source, 76, 77–78*t*, 79*fig*; trends in, 69,
70–83, 131, 131*t*, 132, 132*t*; by type of nonprofit, 72,
74–75*t*, 76*fig*; by year and subsector, 133–37*t*

Private payments as source of revenues, 131*t*, 132,
132*t*

Public-society benefit organizations: contributions to,
72, 76*fig*

Public support: growth in, 152, 156–57*t*, 158; state
growth in, 201, 209–12*t*. *See also* Government
grants; Private giving

### Q

Quarterly Census of Employment and Wages (QCEW;
U.S. Bureau of Labor Statistics), 64–68

### R

Racial differences. *See* Demographics

Religion-related organizations: asset growth, 163*t*,
165*t*; as BEA and NAICS categories, 129–30; demographics of contributions to, 85–87*t*; exemption
from registering with IRS, 1, 139; expense growth,
161*t*; 501(c)(3) status, 22; 501(d) status, 25; grants
from foundations, 109–10*t*; growth in number of,
148, 149–51*t*; NPISH expenditures for (percent of),
123–24*figs*; private contributions to, 72, 76*fig*; as
public charities, 139, 141*t*, 151*t*, 155*t*, 157*t*,
197*fig*; as recipients of contributions, 72, 82*t*, 83*fig*,
85–87*t*; reporting revenues and expenses, 188;
types of (NTEE-CC), 235; volunteers and, 89,
98*fig*

Revenues: asset income as source of, 116–18*figs*,
117–18, 120*fig*, 121, 158, 162–65*t*, 166, 208, 217–20*t*;
fees for services as source of, 115, 116–18*figs*, 143,
145*fig*; 501(c)(3) charities, revenue trends, 131–32,
131*t*, 132*t*, 143–48; government grants as source of
(501(c)(3) charities), 131*t*, 132, 132*t*, 145*fig*, 152,
156–57*t*, 158; investment income as source of
(501(c)(3) charities), 131*t*, 132, 132*t*, 144, 145*fig*;
private contributions as source of (501(c)(3) charities), 131*t*, 132, 132*t*, 143–44, 145*fig*, 152, 156–57*t*,
158; private payments as source of (501(c)(3) charities), 131*t*, 132, 132*t*; sales receipts as source of, 115,
116–18*figs*, 117, 118; by source and type of charity
(1992–2005), 133–37, 152, 153–55*t*; source data,
125, 127*t*, 225–27; by state reporting, 201, 205–8*t*;
transfer receipts as source of, 115, 116–19*figs*, 117,
118; trends in, 115–21, 143–44, 152. *See also specific
types of nonprofits*

### S

Salaries. *See* Wages (nonprofit)

Sales receipts as source of revenues, 115, 116–18*figs*,
117, 118

Science and technology public charities, 188, 197*fig*

Sectors and subsectors: as BEA and NAICS categories,
129–30; revenue trends for, 131–32, 131*t*, 132*t*; sectors compared, 5–14, 12–14*t*; types of organizations
within subsectors (NTEE-CC), 228–35; wage accruals compared, 10–11*figs*, 15–16*t*

Small nonprofits exempt from registering with IRS, 1

Social and recreational clubs, 23

Social science public charities, 188, 197*fig*

Social welfare organizations: as BEA and NAICS categories, 129–30; described, 1, 3. *See also* 501(c)(4) social welfare organizations
Standard Industrial Classification, 65
State reporting: expenses, 208, 213–16*t*; growth in number, 201, 202–4*t*; number, revenue, expenses, and assets, 196–97, 198–200*t*, 201; public support, 201, 209–12*t*; revenues, 201, 205–8*t*
Supplemental unemployment benefit trusts, 24
Supporting public charities: compared with operating organizations, 144, 146–47*t*, 148; reporting by subsectors, 143, 144*t*; size and scope of, 143

### T

Tax-exempt organizations. *See* Internal Revenue Code provisions for tax exemption
Teachers' retirement fund associations, 23
Title-holding corporations or trusts, 25
Transfer receipts as source of revenues, 115, 116–19*figs*, 117, 118

### U

U.S. Bureau of Economic Analysis (BEA). *See* Bureau of Economic Analysis
U.S. Census Bureau: Current Population Survey (CPS) publication, 83, 89, 113–14; Economic Census nonprofit wage and employment estimates, 63–64, 65–66

### V

Veterans associations, 24, 25
Voluntary employee-beneficiary associations, 23
Volunteers: BEA failure to include in estimates, 18; demographics of, 94, 99*t*; public charities and, 192, 196, 197*fig*; trends in volunteering, 69–70, 83, 97*t*, 98, 111; types of activities, 94, 98, 100–101*t*, 100*fig*, 100*t*, 112–14; types of organizations, 88–89, 97*t*, 98*fig*; wage value of work, 18, 20*t*, 21, 97*t*, 102*t*, 114

### W

Wages (nonprofit): accrual by sectors compared, 10–11*figs*, 15–16*t*; annual growth rate, by industry, 32, 33, 34–35*figs*; average annual per employee, by industry, 32, 33*fig*; comparison of NPISHs with other sectors, 10–11*figs*; as expenses for public charities, 144, 146–47*t*; gross value of sectors compared, 12–14*t*; industries covered by unemployment insurance, 33, 35–36, 36*t*, 37*t*, 39*t*, 42–49*t*, 65–66; industries not covered by unemployment insurance, 35, 38*t*; by NAICS-coded industries, 5, 6–8*t*, 27, 28–29*t*, 31*t*, 32–33*figs*, 34–35, 66; at nonprofits serving business, 18, 19*t*; sources of, 63–64; trends in, 27–68; volunteer work, value of, 18, 20*t*, 21, 97*t*, 102*t*, 114
War veterans organizations, 24
Web sites: classification system (NTEE) information, 226, 227